# THE POWER ELITE AND THE STATE

## How Policy is Made in America

# SOCIAL INSTITUTIONS AND SOCIAL CHANGE

*An Aldine de Gruyter Series of Texts and Monographs*

EDITED BY

Michael Useem • James D. Wright

# THE POWER ELITE AND THE STATE
## How Policy is Made in America

G. WILLIAM DOMHOFF

**ALDINE DE GRUYTER**
New York

# ABOUT THE AUTHOR

*G. William Domhoff* is Professor of Sociology at the University of California, Santa Cruz. His books on the American power structure include *The Higher Circles* (1970), *The Bohemian Grove and Other Retreats* (1974), *The Powers That Be* (1979), *Jews in the Protestant Establishment* (1982, with Richard L. Zweigenhaft), and *Who Rules America Now?* (1983).

ALDINE DE GRUYTER
A Division of Walter de Gruyter, Inc.
200 Saw Mill River Road
Hawthorne, New York 10532

**Library of Congress Cataloging-in-Publication Data**

Domhoff, G. William.
   The power elite and the state:how policy is made in America / G. William Domhoff,
      p. cm.—(Social institutions and social change)
   Includes bibliographical references.
   ISBN 0-202-30372-1      —ISBN 0-202-30373-X (pbk.):
   1. Elite (Social sciences)—United States.  2. Power (Social sciences)  3. United States—Politics and government—20th century.
   I. Title.    II. Series.
   HN90.E4D648  1990
   305.5′2′0973—dc20

                                  90-393
                                  CIP

Manufactured in the United States of America

10 9 8 7 6 5 4 3 2

To the friends who have meant so much to me personally and intellectually over the past twenty years

The pedant and the priest have always been the most expert of logicians—and the most diligent disseminators of nonsense and worse. The liberation of the human mind has never been furthered by such learned dunderheads; it has been furthered by gay fellows who heaved dead cats into sanctuaries and then went roistering down the highways of the world, proving to all men that doubt, after all, was safe.

H. L. Mencken, *Prejudices: Fourth Series*, 1924

Yet it must be remembered that what appears to us as an extensive, complicated, and yet well ordered institution is the outcome of ever so many doings and pursuits, carried on by savages, who have no laws or aims or charters definitely laid down. They have no knowledge of the *total outline* of any of their social structure. They know their own motives, know the purpose of individual actions and rules which apply to them; but how, out of these, the whole collective institution shapes, this is beyond their mental range. Not even the most intelligent native has any clear idea of the Kula as a big, organized social construction, still less of its sociological function and implications. If you were to ask him what the Kula is, he would answer by giving a few details, most likely by giving his personal experiences and subjective views on the Kula, but nothing approaching the definition just given here. Not even a partial coherent account could be obtained. For the integral picture does not exist in his mind; he is in it, and cannot see the whole from the outside.

Bronislaw Malinowski, *Argonauts of the Western Pacific*, 1922 (his italics)

# CONTENTS

# PREFACE

I have benefited greatly from the suggestions of several social scientists and historians in writing this book. In particular, I would like to thank Michael Goldfield, Clarence Stone, and James Wright for their useful and detailed comments on the book. They have saved me from many specific mistakes and my worst rhetorical excesses. I am also grateful to Joe Feagin, Harvey Feigenbaum, Mark Mizruchi, Harvey Molotch, Joe Peschek, and Laurence Shoup for their helpful suggestions on one or more of the chapters.

The interest in this project expressed by Trev Leger of Aldine de Gruyter and the series editors, Michael Useem and James Wright, when it was only a prospectus gave me the energy and enthusiasm that made it possible to complete the writing. I am deeply appreciative of their support.

I have been aided by the research assistance given to me on parts of this project by Michael Webber while he was a graduate student in sociology at the University of California, Santa Cruz. His dissertation research on campaign finance and the Democratic party has been especially helpful to me (Webber, 1990). I am also grateful to my son Joel Domhoff and a close family friend Steve Glass for their research assistance. In addition, I want to thank Robert Bulman, a recent graduate in sociology from the University of California, Santa Cruz, for his research and editorial help in the final stages of the project. Finally, I am grateful to the Research Committee of the Academic Senate at the University of California, Santa Cruz, for the financial support that made it possible to hire Michael Webber.

Chapter 3 is a greatly expanded and updated version of a paper published in *Politics and Society* (Domhoff, 1986–87). Parts of the argument in Chapter 4 were published in a very different version in *Political Power and Social Theory* (Domhoff, 1987a). Chapter 7 is an expanded version of a paper published in the *Journal of Political and Military Sociology* (Domhoff, 1986b). A small portion of the empirical information in Chapter 9 was published in a brief review essay in *Theory and Society* (Domhoff, 1988).

I cannot pretend to be fully expert in each of the many specialist areas I have drawn on to construct my general framework in this book: organizational theory, welfare policy, labor relations, foreign policy, monetary policy, congressional voting patterns, and party politics. I am extremely appreciative of the fact that my work has been made possible by the many detailed studies in each of these areas. However, I have not been able to read everything, and I apologize to those I may have overlooked, and to those who feel that I did not study their work closely enough.

# INTRODUCTION

The general question that animates this book is the nature and distribution of power in the United States. It is in one sense a highly abstract and theoretical question, made all the more difficult by disagreements over what is meant by the concept of power, but the issues immediately become very clear when we think of power as manifesting itself in terms of who benefits, who shapes the political agenda, who holds key positions, and who has a say-so on the big decisions. Nor is the question abstract when it comes to hopes for greater freedom and equality, for such hopes soon bump up against the power of social classes, economic institutions, political groups, and state agencies.

For all its seeming relevance, however, few social scientists want to talk about how power operates in the United States, let alone try to study it. Maybe the concept becomes too vague when we try to define it, as many mainstream (pluralist) social scientists claim when they reduce power to mere "influence" or narrow it to "decision-making," and then limit their studies to specific issues or organizations at best.

Whatever the reasons for avoiding the study of the power structure in America, it has no disciplinary home in the social sciences. Research on power therefore crops up at the edges of disciplines, or in the interstices between disciplines, especially between political science and sociology. The pariah status of power in the social sciences can be seen most glaringly in economics. There, in the most celebrated of the social sciences, widely admired because of its seemingly hard-nosed assumptions about rationality, efficiency, and competition, not to mention its heavily quantitative orientation, there is virtually no concern with power. In a perusal of over 2000 entries in a comprehensive and highly regarded four-volume encyclopedia of economics that covered every topic imaginable, Robert Heilbroner (1988:23) could not find a single one focused on power. He concludes that by ignoring power the field of economics misses the heart of its subject matter, and what he says about economics applies almost equally as well to the other social sciences. Instead, the emphasis is on social "exchanges" that take place in a political vacuum. The social structure is a given. People merely try to "maximize utilities" rationally, which Heilbroner (1988:3) translates into plain

English as "bettering our condition" or "making money." The capitalist system is seen as "a regime without rulers and ruled" (1988:25).

To the degree that there is any discussion of power among conventional social science practitioners, it is mostly theoretical in nature, and it usually concerns the power of one hypothetical individual or group over another, or focuses on a single issue or policy. When all is said and done, the mainstream literature on power never has gone beyond the excellent old book on the topic by the great philosopher Bertrand Russell, who defined power as "the production of intended effects" (1938:35). This is demonstrated by the fact that Dennis Wrong ends up with a slightly modified version of Russell's definition after surveying the entire social science literature until 1979: he tells us that power "is the capacity of some persons to produce intended and foreseen effects on others" (1979:2).

Russell's definition of power also has been my starting point because it does not reduce power to underlying economic arrangements, as in Marxian theory, or to organized violence, as in Weberian theory. As Russell emphasizes:

> The fundamental concept in social science is Power, in the same sense in which Energy is the fundamental concept in physics. Like energy, power has many forms, such as wealth, armaments, civil authority, influence on opinion. No one of these can be regarded as subordinate to any other, and there is no form from which the others are derivable (1938:10–11).

The only exceptions within the academic community to the avoidance of any sustained focus on the actual operations of power in the United States have been the studies inspired by the seminal work of Floyd Hunter (1953) on Atlanta and of C. Wright Mills (1956) on the national level. Both held to theories that rooted power in organizations and institutions, putting them at odds, on the one hand, with the classical liberal emphasis on individuals and groups and, on the other, with the Marxian emphasis on classes. For Hunter, there was a "power structure," defined as the associational, clique, or institutional patterns that maintain the general social structure and generate new policy initiatives (1953:1–6); in Atlanta this meant the major developers, retailers, and associated bankers in the downtown business community. For Mills, there was a "power elite", who share a common experience, interest, and outlook as the top leaders of the three major institutional hierarchies of the society—giant corporations, the executive branch of the federal government, and the Pentagon. Both concepts have become part of the everyday language of social scientists and political commentators. They an be seen as two sides of the same coin if we note that a "power elite" is the set of people who are the individual actors within the associational and institutional roles that comprise the "power structure."

Hunter's work inspired dozens of studies because he had developed a new approach called the "reputational method," which involves systematically interviewing people about the who and how and why of power in a given city, issue area, or country. Most of the findings from these further studies at the local level were similar to Hunter's, and a later study by Hunter (1959) at the national level identified the same individuals and institutions that Mills did through his historical and archival investigations. Later work on Atlanta by Clarence Stone (1976, 1989) has supported Hunter's claims while adding many original insights and theoretical understandings.

But mainstream social scientists, and especially political scientists, did not like Hunter's method or conclusions. One of the leading political theorists of the past 35 years, Robert Dahl (1961), even decided to undertake the only major empirical study of his academic career, an analysis of "notables" and decision-making in his hometown, New Haven, where he found that different groups had influence on different political issues. More importantly, he found that government officials were the most important power figures. Dahl's book became one of the most widely cited books in all the social sciences. Not only was it seen as a refutation of Hunter at the local level, but of Mills at the national level as well. Raymond Bauer, Ithiel de Sola Pool, and Lewis Dexter, for example, wrote that Dahl "answered" Mills "most effectively" (1972:vii). America was merely New Haven writ large.

Dahl's study was in fact seriously flawed, as I subsequently showed with memos, minutes, letters, and interview material from New Haven unavailable to Dahl at the time of his inquiry, and even with material in his own protocols that contradicted his thesis (Domhoff, 1978; 1983a: Chapter 6). It was clear that the downtown business community and Yale University were the moving forces behind the all-important urban renewal program, not the new Democratic mayor, as Dahl believed from interviews with the mayor and his aides. But none of these new findings has stopped theorists as varied as Eric Nordlinger (1981:100–101) and Theda Skocpol (1985:4) from quoting his conclusions as support for their view that government is free of undue private influence. There is not the slightest hint to readers that these conclusions have been challenged empirically.

The theory and findings presented by Mills for the national level met with an even greater hue and cry, although there were no attempts at mere empirical refutation. Whereas Mills had studied the social backgrounds, educational training, and occupational careers of thousands of American leaders down through the ages before concluding that since World War II the United States has been dominated by an institutionally based power elite, his critics simply asserted he was wrong or else attacked his methodology. Dahl, speaking for a great many others on this score, said it was "a remarkable and indeed astonishing fact" that Mills could make his claims without studying "an array of specific cases to test his major hypothesis" (1958:466).

Even a political scientist who later concluded that much of the American government had been captured by specific business interests, Grant McConnell joined the hunt by writing a pluralist pamphlet for the Advertising Council, an organization created by large corporations to sell themselves to America (Hirsch, 1975). The pamphlet was meant for the use of media employees and discussion groups as background material for dealing with the kind of claims being made by Mills and Hunter. On the first page it said:

> Frequently, individuals have drawn the conclusion that policy-making lies in the hands of a small and powerful class. This conclusion is a gross misunderstanding of the political processes by which political and economic power is diffused and which extend the wide sharing of economic benefits in a people's capitalism (1958:1).

The 54-page pamphlet went on to say that "interest groups" are a "vital and indispensable form of political representation," and that they "stand as barriers against the conquest of power by any pathological mass movement" (1958:1). It included a summary of the arguments for the usefulness of interest groups by representatives of the American Farm Bureau Federation and the AFL-CIO, government officials, business leaders, and University of Chicago professors. The pamphlet received a friendly send-off in the *New York Times* (July 12, 1958:48) under the headline "Pressure Groups Called Integral: Chicago Study Says Most Perform Governmental Functions in the Open." The participants in the discussion leading to the pamphlet were listed, including executives from *Time*, Marsh and McLennan Insurance Company, Union Tank Car Company, and the Farm Foundation.

As negative as mainstream social scientists were toward the theories proposed by Hunter and Mills, I believe the issue of methodology upset critics almost as much. There was always the whisper in the halls that research on power structures is just so much "muckraking," little better than what a good investigative journalist might do. But the real problem was that this research did not fit into the conventional categories that are taught in courses on methodology—experimental, survey, interview, case study, field observation, historical, and comparative. Since it is their unique methods that mark social scientists off as specialists deserving of some respect, power structure researchers must be something else because they did not have a sanctioned methodology. Only slowly did social scientists realize that the tracing of individuals, money flows, and ideas through institutions and social classes is a form of sociometry (Kadushin, 1968), an approach described by Granovetter as "curiously peripheral—invisible, really" (1973:1360) within the main traditions of sociology. Finally, in the 1970s, advances in graph theory and computer science combined with respectable new work in social anthropology to rechristen the field as "network analysis." The work of Phillip Bonacich (1972, 1982, 1987) and Richard Alba (1973) then provided the essential quantitative techniques for studying large corporate and social data bases (e.g., Sonquist and Koenig, 1975; Domhoff, 1975; Mariolis, 1975; Bonacich and Domhoff, 1981; Mizruchi, 1982; Salzman and Domhoff, 1983; Mintz and Schwartz, 1981a,b, 1983, 1985). Thus, many social scientists came to understand that power structure research was a form of "membership network analysis" (Breiger, 1974).

However, the real breakthrough to respectability began when the new network analysts emphasized that social networks can include institutions as well as individuals. It became clear that the network of people and institutions that is the foundation of all power structure research, whether it is done by pluralists, Marxists, or anyone else, is not reductionistic to the individual level, but instead incorporates individuals into organizations, institutions, or classes. Both an individual clique network and an institutional interlock network are imbedded in the matrix of people and institutions that is the mathematical representation of a social network (Breiger, 1974; Domhoff, 1978: Chapter 4; 1983a:23–26, 187–89). As Breiger (1974:70–71) succinctly put it, such matrices incorporate the two social relations of concern to all social theorists, personal relationships and memberships in collectivities.

Despite the general rejection of the theory, methods, and findings provided by Mills and Hunter, there were a few social scientists and activists of the 1960s generation who produced empirically based studies of social power. Many of them turned to American Marxists like Paul Sweezy, Paul Baran, and Harry Magdoff as well as to Mills and Hunter for their inspiration, infusing a class dimension into power structure research. By and large, people like Sweezy, Baran, and Magdoff were what Mills approvingly called "plain Marxists" (1962:98–99), meaning Marxists who worked within the spirit and method of Marxism, but were not dogmatic about every one of its historical and political claims. He even decided to include himself in the category, to the horror of many Marxists. This easy mingling of Mills, Hunter, and the plain Marxists found expression in my work (Domhoff, 1967, 1970c; Domhoff and Ballard, 1968) and in many of the analyses done by members of the Student Non-Violent Coordinating Committee (SNCC), Students for a Democratic Society (SDS), and the North American Committee on Latin America (NACLA). Much of this work proved to be useful in civil rights, campus, and antiwar organizing. Several of the most enduring of these studies were on major universities and how they fit into the larger power structure: "Who Rules Columbia?", "How Harvard Rules," and "Go To School, Learn to Rule", a study of Yale University and its role in New Haven.

Just as this work seemed to be taking off, it was slowed down and put on the defensive by the decline of the New Left and attacks on it by those Mills would have called the sophisticated Marxists (1962:96–97), who manage to find a way to rescue every Marxian formulation from refutation through exegesis, reinterpretation, or contrived reformulation. The substance of these critiques by the new "structural Marxists" will be presented in detail in the following chapters, but for now the point is that their criticisms had an impact in some quarters.

The structural Marxists were soon joined in the attack on power structure studies by those who called themselves "state-centric" or state autonomy theorists. While the state autonomy theorists certainly had their major differences with all varieties of Marxists, they did share with the structural Marxists the belief that plain Marxists had a crude view of the state as the simple tool or "instrument" of capitalists. This "instrumentalist" view of the state was said to rest on personal linkages between capitalists and government officials, and to require the direct participation of capitalists in the state. Instrumentalism was then contrasted with "structuralism," which was said to be more sophisticated because it saw the state as an organizational entity within an overall system with underlying rules and imperatives. For the structural Marxists, the state has "relative autonomy" from any specific capitalists or the capitalist class, but is in the general service of capitalism. For state autonomy theorists such as Theda Skocpol (1979), states are administrative, policing, and military organizations with a logic and interests of their own. These interests are not necessarily equivalent to or related to the interests of a dominant class or the members of society as a whole. The state is concerned with maintaining order and competing with other states. In the process of carrying out these tasks, the state may compete with the dominant class in the society for resources or subordinate that class to its own interests.

Structural Marxists and state autonomy theorists also shared a common lack of interest in the work of Mills and Hunter. Mills was sometimes footnoted by them for his work on union leaders (1948) or his ringing critique of conventional sociology (1959), but rarely for his work on power. As for Hunter, he never made it into a single footnote in any of the major works in either of the new approaches, despite the fact that a thoughtful theorist sympathetic to the efforts of all structural thinkers, John Walton (1976), argued that Hunter's work was far more sophisticated than most social scientists were willing to grant, and potentially useful to new work in political economy as well.

Structural Marxists and state autonomy theorists shared one final point beside their common disdains. They abandoned the study of social power in general for more narrow concerns such as "class structure" or "state power." Just as the pluralists tend to reduce power to mere influence or decision-making, so these theorists cut it down to a topic in political economy (structural Marxists) or politics (state autonomy theorists). When this narrowing is combined with their emphasis on very traditional historical and comparative methods acceptable to everyone, it comes as no surprise that they have been welcomed into the mainstream academic community. The work of state autonomy theorists will be critiqued along with that of structural Marxists in subsequent chapters.

I might have concluded it was futile to argue with these new critics if the study of social power in all its manifestations had not been revived in 1986 with the publication of Michael Mann's *The Sources of Social Power: From the Beginnings of Civilization to 1760 A.D.* The new theory in this book, which roots power in four interacting social networks, makes it possible to deal with both structural Marxists and state autonomy theorists in a way that is completely compatible with the aims, findings, and middle-range theorizing that characterizes the Mills–Hunter tradition. I must admit that it is invigorating to have such a congenial theoretical home after all those years spent wandering in the empirical wilderness, surrounded on every side by pluralists, structural Marxists, and utility maximizers.

The purpose of this book now can be stated more specifically. I intend to show that Mann's theory provides the general framework and rationale for the more limited interpretation of the American power structure that I have developed over the past 25 years. I aim to demonstrate this through bringing new data and arguments to bear on several major policy initiatives at the national level that were analyzed previously by structural Marxists, state autonomy theorists, or other prominent theorists with whom I disagree. That is, each of the case studies directly challenges a previous analysis by one or more of my opponents with empirical information that I think to be contradictory to their most important claims.

The book has two organizing principles. First, it descends from the general–theoretical–historical in Chapters 1 and 2 to the specific–empirical–contemporary in Chapters 3–10. Second, once at the specific–empirical–contemporary level, the book marches in chronological fashion from the early 1930s to the early 1980s, dealing with important New Deal legislation such as the Social Security Act and the National Labor Relations Act, significant postwar legislation such as the Employment Act and Trade Expansion Act, and more recent issues, such as the decline of the Democrats and the revival of conservatism.

# SOCIAL NETWORKS, POWER, AND THE STATE

## Introduction

By the early 1980s, contrary to the pious hopes I had expressed at the turn of the decade for continuing dialogue and innovation (1980:15), the debate on power in America triggered by Hunter and Mills had become depressingly predictable. There were said to be three general theories—pluralist, institutional elitist, and Marxist—and three basic methods—decisional, positional, and reputation. There were also three main indicators of power—who decides, who sits, and who benefits. Attempts were made to show that the three theories could be in part synthesized if they were understood as different levels of analysis (e.g., Alford and Friedland, 1985), and I argued that the three methods were not as different or as tied to any one theory as sometimes claimed (Domhoff, 1978: Chapter 4), but the holy trinities were in place, and it was proving difficult to dislodge them.

From the very outset, it had been my aim to combine an institutional analysis with a class analysis. I tried to do so by seeing if Mills's institutionally based power elite could be grounded in the upper (capitalist-based) class. I redefined the power elite in such a way that it included active, working members of the upper class and high-level employees in private institutions controlled by members of the upper class, and then explored the extent to which the members of this power elite overlapped with those encompassed by Mills's concept. I found that the overlap was nearly perfect, and then showed how these people dominated policy-making in the executive branch of the federal government through a variety of direct and indirect means.

Despite this explicit attempt at transcending the usual categories, the taxonomists of the 1980s insisted that everyone had to be put in one category or another. One textbook in political sociology had me listed as a Marxist (Marger, 1981), another decided that I was an institutional elitist (Sherman and Kolker, 1987). Alford and Friedland had me down as an elitist in an early version of their manuscript, then decided that I was a class theorist who worked at the individual level of analysis (1985:301). For me, the research tradition started by Mills and Hunter, and invigorated by the activists and plain Marxists of the 1960s, had become as sterile and polemical as the old mainstream literature on power. The orthodoxies of the structural Marxists and state autonomy theorists only added to the problem.

It was in this context that I encountered Mann's new theory of social power. As a British sociologist who had immersed himself in the study of history over the previous ten years, he was one step removed from many of the controversies that were polarizing studies of power in America. He certainly was alive to the key general issues at stake, but he was not caught up in the details and personal politics of the American debate. His work, then, offered an opportunity for a new look, a fresh start.

Mann begins by doing away with the usual notion of a "bounded society" or a "social system." Since there is no "totality," there can be no "subsystems," "levels," or "dimensions." Instead, social organization must be understood in terms of four "overlapping and intersecting sociospatial networks of power" (1986:1) that run off in different directions and have varying extensions in physical space. This is music to the ears of those who analyze American power structures as networks of people and institutions. Network analysis is no longer a mere "methodological strategy" for studying power structures defined as "a network of people and institutions who differentially benefit from the functioning of the social system," as I claimed in the 1970s (Domhoff, 1978:133), but a theoretical stance as well.

These four interacting networks—ideological, economic, military, and political—are conceptualized as organized means of attaining human goals. Mann's concern is with the "logistics" of power (1986:9–10, 518). No one of the networks is more fundamental than the others. Each one presupposes the existence of the others, which fits nicely with Russell's (1938:10–11) point that power cannot be reduced to one basic form. Thus, there can be no "ultimate primacy" in the "mode of production" or "the normative system" or "the state." Since the emphasis is on people acting through social networks, the distinction between "social action" and "social structure," which also happens to underlie the debate over "instrumental" and "structural" theories of the state, is simply abolished. There no longer needs to be a periodic revival of the "agency vs. structure" debate. Since the four networks have different and constantly changing boundaries that vary with the invention of new technologies and the emergence of new organizational forms, the old division between "endogenous" and "exogenous" factors in the understanding of social conflict is discarded as "not helpful" (Mann, 1986:1). It is a freeing set of conceptualizations, the best thing since Mills (1962: Chapter 6) briefly stated his alternative to Marxism as a prolegomenon to the worldwide historical comparison of social structures that he was working on at his death in 1962 (Horowitz, 1963), only better. Mann's summary statement on his overall framework is as follows:

> A general account of societies, their structure, and their history can best be given in terms of the interrelations of what I call the four sources of social power: ideological, economic, military, and political (IEMP) relationships. These are (1) overlapping networks of social interaction, not dimensions, levels, or factors of a single social totality. This follows from my first statement. (2) They are also organizations, institutional means of attaining human goals. Their primacy comes not from the strength of human desires for ideological, economic, military, or political satisfaction but from the particular organizational means each possesses to attain human goals, whatever they may be (1986:2).

Mann defines the ideology network in terms of those organizations concerned with meaning, norms, and ritual practice (1986:22). It generates "sacred" authority and intensifies social cohesion. Its usual manifestations are in organized religion, and its most prominent historical power actor was the Catholic Church.

The economic network is that set of institutions concerned with satisfying material needs through the "extraction, transformation, distribution and consumption of the objects of nature" (1986:24). The economic network gives rise to classes, defined in terms of their power over the different parts of the economic process from extraction to consumption. But there is not always class struggle, which has been important only in certain periods of history, such as ancient Greece, early Rome, and the capitalist era. The term "ruling class" is defined as "an economic class that has successfully monopolized other power sources to dominate a state-centered society at large" (1986:25). Geographically extensive classes arose only slowly in Western history, for they were dependent upon advances in infrastructure made possible by developments in the other power networks. For the first 2500 years of Western civilization, economic networks were extremely localized, especially in comparison to political and military networks.

The military network is defined in terms of organized physical violence. It is the power of direct and immediate coercion. Military power had a greater range throughout most of history than either political or economic power. Even so, we often forget that until very recently an army could only carry enough food for a 50–60 mile march, which forced it to rely on the local countryside in extensive campaigns. Military power was central to the theorizing of many nineteenth-century thinkers, but "has been neglected of late in social theory" (1986:26).

The state is defined as a political network whose primary function is territorial regulation (1986:26–27). Its usefulness in laying down rules and adjudicating disputes in specific territories is the source of its uniqueness (Mann, 1984). This unique function is the basis for its potential autonomy, but it gains further autonomy due to the fact that it interacts with other states, especially through warfare (Mann, 1986:511). The state can take on other functions besides territorial regulation and has had varying degrees of influence at different phases of Western history (1977, 1986:514). There is a tendency for present-day social scientists to project the state's great importance in the contemporary world back to earlier times when its powers were weak.

Most theorists regard military power as one aspect of state power, but Mann provides four pieces of evidence for distinguishing the two. First, the original states did not have any military capability. Second, most historical states have not controlled all the military forces within the territory they claim to regulate. Third, there are historical instances where conquest was undertaken by armies that were not controlled by the states where they reside. Fourth, the military is usually separate from other state institutions even when it is officially controlled by the state, making possible the overthrow of the political elite by military leaders (Mann, 1986:11).

Looking at the growth and development of the four networks in Western history, Mann concludes that our theoretical goals as social scientists must be tempered by a respect for the complex realities of history. The historical record does not bear out the claims of any one "grand theory." There are too many exceptions. Lower-level, contingent generalizations are the best we can do. There seems to be a pattern in Western history, but only barely, and this pattern is conditioned by a number of historical accidents, not by some inevitable and immanent societal principles (1986:531–532). The "European miracle," meaning the tremendous growth in power resources over the past several hundred years, is seen as "a series of giant coincidences" (1986:505).

Even the rise of independent civilizations in only four or five separate places was in good part due to a concatenation of relatively rare geographical coincidences, not evolutionary inevitability. Mann shows that in many times and places prehistorical social groups reached a level of social development that seemed to suggest that civilization—defined in terms of cities, ceremonial centers, and writing—was about to appear, only to fall back or remain at the same level. Significantly, one factor in this "failure" to develop civilizations may have been the ability of ordinary people to control the actions of their leaders: they seemed to fear the development of full-fledged power structures (1986:38–39, 67–68). Only where river flooding allowed the possibility of alluvial agriculture, in conjunction with close proximity to geographical areas that encouraged different but complementary networks, did the "caging" of populations make possible the development of the fixed power structures of domination and exploitation that have characterized all civilizations (1986: Chapter 3).

Furthermore, comparative studies are far more limited in their usefulness than most social scientists believe because there really aren't enough separate social systems to make meaningful comparisons, and comparisons back and forth in historical time can be downright silly due to the vastly different levels of power development at different historical epochs (1986:173, 501–503, 525). For the most burning questions, historical studies of specific countries or systems of nation-states are the best we can do. This historical emphasis recalls Mills's (1962:119–126) similar admonitions, and it justifies the kind of detailed studies that have characterized research on contemporary power structures.

Mann underscores his general point about the interacting and intersecting nature of the four power networks by noting "the promiscuity of organizations and functions" (1986:17). That is, the four networks can fuse and borrow from each other in complex ways. Once again, we are on wonderfully empirical ground, for everything varies from time to time and place to place. For example, medieval European states were "overwhelmingly, narrowly political" (1986:17) and they were autonomous, but states in modern capitalist societies are both political and economic, and they usually are not autonomous.

In all, then, Mann's innovative and flexible theory is an ideal framework for the findings on the American power structure over the past 40 years. It is network based, historically focused, and empirical. The only reservation I have about the theory, one that is tangential to the concerns of this book, relates to Mann's claim that human nature expresses an unchanging "rational restlessness" (1986:4). In this, Mann is following Max Weber, whom he calls "the greatest sociologist" (1986:4), but in my view Sigmund Freud is far and away the greatest social theorist of the past 200 years. Shorn of such unnecessary metatheoretical concepts as the life and death instincts, id–ego–superego, and oral–anal–phallic, and placed on an interpersonal basis (e.g., Chodorow, 1978; Stern, 1985), Freud's clinical insights about repression and unconscious processes provide the starting point for a theory of culture as a group defense mechanism against infantile fears and anxieties. The key to understanding human nature and society is not in instincts, desires, or rationality, but in the repressions, ambivalences, and projections that are an inevitable product of a long infancy within the family structure that evolved in the context of primate group living. It is in long infancy and the repressions that result in order to make family living possible that we find the "material" basis for Mann's ideology network, as well as the basis for understanding such strange phenomena as human sacrifice, initiation ceremonies, and the origins of priestly city-states, as I have argued elsewhere (Domhoff, 1969a, 1970a,b). But all this is a separate story from the one I want to focus on in this book, and it must be saved for another time and place. For now I only want to register my dissent from all those social scientists and historians who start their theorizing with a rational utilitarian ego psychology, whether derived from Adam Smith, John Locke, Emile Durkheim, Karl Marx, or Max Weber, and place my bets on Freud (1913, 1921, 1927, 1930) and those who brilliantly developed his basic insights on social structure and culture (Roheim, 1943, 1945, 1950; LaBarre, 1954, 1970). Human beings are best characterized by a restless discontent that is irrational, not rational, and "human nature" is not fixed and unchanging, but variable in terms of the changing relationship between the repressed and consciousness. There is thus a dimension of irrationality involved in power and subjugation that is untapped in our most honored theories (cf. Gregor, 1985; Benjamin, 1988).

## Liberalism, Marxism, and State Theory

Mann's four-network theory of social power rather obviously challenges many orthodoxies of the past and present, including the Weberian one from which he draws his insights about the organizational basis of power. However, his main targets are what he calls liberalism (and Americans call pluralism), rooted in good part in neoclassical economic theory, and Marxism—the same two theories that were contested by Hunter and Mills from their own organizational perspectives. In this section I will draw together his main criticisms of these two theories and of state autonomy theory as well, leaving aside his comments on theories that have not been part of the American debate. In addition, I will add a few critical points of my own on Marxian state theory. Then, in the following section, I will show how Mann applies his theory to the rise of capitalism and the state in Western history.

Liberalism is found wanting because the historical record does not sustain its view that all of history is essentially "capitalism writ large" (Mann, 1986:534). Individuals did not scratch out private property and then decide to create the state as umpire and regulator, as in the myth of the social contract. Markets have not been the only avenue to new economic developments, and military empires of the past are not merely parasitic hindrances to economic growth, but sometimes stimulative of such growth. Moreover, liberal theory fails to understand that a framework of normative regulation is required before markets can develop:

> Regulated competition is not "natural." If competition is not to degenerate into mutual suspicion and aggression and so result in anarchy, it requires elaborate, delicate social arrangements that respect the essential humanity, the powers, and the property rights of the various decentralized power actors (1986:534).

Given its great limitations, Mann renders a very harsh judgment on liberalism–pluralism: "In the light of world history, neoclassical theory should be seen as bourgeois ideology, a false claim that the present power structure of our own society is legitimate because it is natural" (1986:534).

Mann finds Marxism in all its varieties equally wanting. The idea that all power is rooted ultimately in the ownership and control of the means of production, with the ensuing class struggle providing the motor of history, does not fit the origins of civilization in the years 3000 to 2300 B.C., when most property was held by the state and there was no class conflict; nor the 2500 years of empires of domination, when military networks were in the ascendancy; nor the 900 years after the fall of the Roman Empire, when the ideology network called "Christendom" combined with the independent armies of the nobility to create the framework within which a class-ridden capitalism and a closely intertwined system of nation-states began to rise to the fore. In short, there have been great stretches of history when economic forces, no matter how broadly conceived to rescue the Marxian claim about the primacy of the "mode of production," were not primary in either the first or last instance, and other epochs where the activities of the ruling class were far more important in understanding new developments than any "class struggle" with direct producers, who were far too localized and lacking in organizational infrastructure to challenge the dominant class, let alone to be considered a class themselves.

But it is on the relationship between states and social classes, the crucial issue of this book, that Mann is most critical of all previous theories, not just liberalism and Marxism. At one extreme, all the non-Marxian theories have a tendency to see states and social classes as inherently in opposition. This includes state autonomy theory. In Mann's words, "in modern thought classes and nations are usually regarded as antithetical" (1986:529). This can be seen very clearly in the usual liberal theory:

> Liberalism views property rights as originating in the struggles of individuals to exploit nature, to acquire its surplus, and to transmit it to family and descendants. In this view public power is essentially external to private property rights. The state may be brought in to institutionalize property rights, or it may be viewed as a dangerous threat to them; but the state is not a part of the *creation* of private property. Yet we have seen repeatedly that this is not historical fact. Private property emerged in the first place, and has usually been subsequently enhanced, through the struggles and fragmenting tendencies of public power organizations (1986:536, his italics).

Marxists go to the other extreme: the state is always a structure of domination that protects property, even though they argue mightily among themselves about the way in which this state domination takes place (e.g., Gold, Lo, and Wright, 1975:31). Some Marxists have tried to justify these disagreements by claiming that Marx did not have a fully developed theory of the state, but a detailed exposition of all Marx's writing between 1842 and 1847 by Gary Teeple (1984) has shown otherwise. Marx's theory of the state followed logically from the "the first historic act" of human productivity. The surplus created by this productivity led to inevitable conflict between the forces and relations of production, an increasing division of labor, inevitable class conflict, and then the creation of the political state as the defender of property. Teeple summarizes Marx's conclusions as follows:

> The state, as an estranged power, as the "community" outside of its members, arises because of the advance of the division of labor, because of the decline of the real community, of real common interest. The development of the division of labor is consonant with the development of private property which in turn is expressed as class relations. The state arises, therefore, as the expression of already existing and evolving class relations. The fact that the state is an

instrument of the powers that be is a fact which derives from the nature of its genesis, not from the design or will of the ruling class (1984:185).

As early as 1843 Marx called the legislature "the sanctioned, legal lie of constitutional states" because it claimed to represent the national interest when it really represented various types of private property (Teeple, 1984: 71). Similarly, he saw the "form" of the state bureaucracy as universalistic, but said that its "content" was the protection of private property in general (1984:65).

There are several problems with this theory of the state. Archaeological and historical evidence do not support the claim that the state has its origins in class struggle and the rise of private property. Nor are changes in the nature of the state usually a product of changes in civil society caused by conflict between social classes. Much of this evidence is summarized by Mann (1986:49–63, 84–87), but others have come to the same conclusions (e.g., Cohen and Service, 1978; Claessen and Skalnik, 1978).

Then, too, states as most theorists conceive of them are not always involved in subjugating the producing classes. Sometimes dominant classes do the subjugating directly, as during the Middle Ages. Both Mann (1986:391–392, 411) and the Marxists agree that the demesnes of the nobility were the basis for dominating the peasantry during this epoch, but they draw different conclusions from this fact because the Marxists define the state as "a concept for the concentrated and organized means of legitimate class domination" (Zeitlin, 1980:15). Given the historical evidence that the means of class domination and the territorial state can be separate, it is my view that this terminological disagreement should be eliminated by using the term "power structure" to describe "the concentrated and organized means of legitimate class domination," thereby allowing for historical variability on whether or not the territorial state is involved in enforcing class domination.

Finally, I believe that the Marxian analysis of the state in democratic capitalist societies is wrong because it incorporates a false homology between the economy and the state that distorts its view of the state and creates a tendency to downplay the importance of representative democracy. For many Marxists, representative democracy is an illusion that grows out of the same type of mystification that is created by the marketplace. Just as the capitalists appropriate surplus value "behind the backs" of the workers through the seemingly fair mechanism of the market, when the real story is in ownership and control of the forces of production, so too does representative democracy appropriate the political power of the workers through the seemingly fair mechanism of elections, when the major action is over in a state bureaucracy that responds to the interests of the owners of private property. This view is best summarized in Stanley Moore's *A Critique of Capitalist Democracy,* a book based on an extremely close reading and synthesis of everything that Marx, Engels, and Lenin wrote on the subject:

These distinctive features of the bourgeois democratic state correspond to distinctive features of the capitalist economy. The capitalist economy appears to be controlled through a series of competitive exchanges, in which all members of the society participate voluntarily under conditions of universal freedom and equality. Similarly, the bourgeois democratic state appears to be controlled through a series of competitive elections, in which all members of the society participate voluntarily under conditions of universal freedom and equality. But beneath the formal freedom and equality of capitalist exchange lie the material bondage and exploitation of capitalist production, resulting from the monopoly over the means of production exercised by members of the capitalist class. And beneath the formal freedom and equality of bourgeois democratic elections lie the material bondage and oppression of bureaucratic administration, resulting from the monopoly over the means of coercion exercised by agents of the capitalist class. The democratic republic is the optimum political shell for capitalism because the relation between bureaucratic administration and universal suffrage is the optimum political counterpart for the relation between capitalist exploitation and commodity exchange (1957:87–88).

The staying power of this analysis can be seen in the work of James O'Connor, who has combined European theorizing on the state by Claus Offe (1974) and Nicos Poulantzas (1973) with his own ideas:

In Marxist theory, the "liberal democratic state" is still another capitalist weapon in the class struggle. This is so because the democratic form of the state conceals undemocratic contents. Democracy in the parliamentary shell hides its absence in the state bureaucratic kernel; parliamentary freedom is regarded as the political counterpart of the freedom in the marketplace, and the hierarchical bureaucracy as the counterpart of the capitalist division of labor in the factory (1984:188).

Rather than downplaying the legislature, I will argue in the next chapter that its existence is essential if a state is not to become autonomous and autocratic, even over capitalists. The existence of a legislature breaks down the unity of the state and thereby greatly limits its autonomy. In other words, representative democracy is one of the few counterpoints to the great potential power of an autocratic state, and it should not be dismissed as a mystification of class rule, even if legislatures tend to be dominated by capitalists.

To this point my argument has been at a fairly abstract level in order to establish a general framework. It is now necessary to turn to an historical account of the rise of capitalism and the state to provide a more concrete basis for understanding the power structure in the United States.

## States and Social Classes

The modern era of state and class relations had its origins in the first few centuries after the collapse of the Roman Empire. The institution of private property developed in the context of the system of numerous small, weak states that struggled along in the territory previously dominated by the militarized

Roman state. This economic development was made possible by the "normative pacification" provided by the Catholic Church and by the predominance of military techniques that rendered armored knights on horseback ascendant over serfs and peasants (Mann, 1986:376–378, 390–391). In this situation, as noted earlier, feudal lords did not need "states," defined primarily as territorial regulators, to protect their private property and increase the exploitation of producing classes. If anything, the weakness of the states was one factor that allowed the system of private property to take deeper root without the danger of state appropriation, and for an independent merchant class to develop. The result was a growing independence for the economic network in general: "By the time trade was really buoyant (1150 to 1250 A.D.)," claims Mann (1986:397), "it was accompanied by merchant and artisan institutions with an autonomy unparalleled in other civilizations."

Meanwhile, the state had very few functions. It tried to guard its borders and control armies in its territory, and it had a role in settling some types of disputes within its confines. The state consisted primarily of the king and his retainers, and the bulk of its revenues came from the king's own lands and judicial fees. Strikingly, any increases in its budget were directly tied to warfare and war debts, a situation that was to continue even after the state began to gain in importance as a regulator of economic activity within its boundaries (Mann, 1980, 1986:486, 511) and to supplant the Church as the primary means of normative pacification. As late as 1505, according to Mann (1986:452), the powers of the state were few:

> Paying the expenses of his household, buying the political advice of a few counselors, administering supreme justice, regulating trade across territorial boundaries, issuing a coinage, and waging occasional war with the help of loyal barons—that was the sum of state functions, which almost certainly involved less than one percent of national wealth and were marginal to the lives of most of the state's subjects.

Although private property and the first stages of capitalism developed without strong states, the situation began to change in the twelfth and thirteenth centuries for a number of reasons. As markets grew within state boundaries, there was more and more need for state regulation, and as merchants increased the scope of their trade into larger and larger territories, they needed more protection against bandits and the petty rulers of small territories (Mann, 1986:423–424, 431–32). Merchants also developed an interest in aggressive wars that would widen the territory in which they could operate: "From now on commercial motivations, the conquest of markets as well as land, were to play a part in wars" (1986:432). Merchants thus quietly encouraged the growth of the state, lending it the money necessary to raise a larger army (1986:426–27).

Dramatic developments in the military network also triggered changes in the relationship between private property and the state. The sudden emergence of the disciplined military phalanx, that is, spear-armed infantry in close formation, quickly unhorsed the nobility in a series of dramatic battles between 1302 and 1315 (1986:18–19, 428). The nobility had to turn increasingly to the state to raise a standing army of full-time foot soldiers to protect its lands. There soon followed a series of technological innovations that added up to a "military revolution" (1986:453–454). In particular, large artillery guns made it possible to destroy castles. The arms race was on, with few peaceful interludes between that time and the present. Only states with large armies could survive, and only states that could gain the loyalty of lords and merchants could afford large armies.

From that point forward capitalism and the nation-state grew powerful together because they needed and aided each other, and in the process subordinated the previously independent ideological and military networks. States now began to fit the Weberian definition: the organizations that control the military and police within given geographical areas. As a state extended its regulatory powers over a new territory, so too did capitalism diffuse more fully in that territory (1986:454). Rather than being antithetical, then, classes and states are closely intertwined in Western history. The class system generated by capitalism was segmented into a small number of "class-nations" of roughly equal power that together formed a multistate system. But from the start there was also tension within each state between these two dominant networks of modern Western civilization. Feudal lords wanted protection for their lands, and merchants wanted protection and regulation for their goods and markets, but both feared the taxing power of the state (1986:433). Conversely, state elites tried to gain as much autonomy as they could.

As the power of the market system developed, merchants, lords, and rich peasants gradually merged into a capitalist class in many of these countries (1986:479). However, there were some differences from country to country. Constitutional regimes fostered the unity of a property-owning class. Absolutist regimes tended to preserve the social structure of feudalism (1986:481). Either way, Mann concludes that these European states were not very powerful in relation to the dominant class or classes:

> Thus constitutional and absolutist regimes were subtypes of a single form of state: a weak state in relation to the powerful groups of civil society, but a state that increasingly coordinated those groups' activities to the point where we may begin to talk of an organic class-nation whose central point was either the court or the court/parliament of the state (1986:481).

Gradually, the relationship between dominant classes and the state became even closer and their interests began to merge. "In the seventeenth and eighteenth centuries," concludes Mann (1986:516), "it begins to make sense to describe the state—paraphrasing Marx—as an executive committee for managing the common affairs of the capitalist class." This is because the state had no distributive power over the classes of "civil society" and because power flowed "primarily from economic power relations to the state" (1986:516). However, this does not mean that Marx's analyses of key historical events in Europe in the eighteenth and nineteenth centuries are necessarily correct. In fact, they are usually fundamentally wrong, as Richard Hamilton (1990) has shown convincingly in a detailed synthesis of American and European historiography on the issues Marx wrote about. Generally speaking, Marx overstated the importance of industrial capitalists as compared to landed elites within the ruling circles, and of urban workers as compared to other urban dwellers and peasants. Moreover, there is very little basis for his claims about the autonomous "Bonapartist" state in France in the 1850s, claims that were accepted uncritically by structural Marxists and made a central feature of their arguments about state autonomy (e.g., Poulantzas, 1973).

Questions about the relative power of states and social classes cannot be answered in the abstract for the recent period either. States may become relatively autonomous by playing nobles off against merchants, or one set of capitalists against another. They can be dominated by a coalition of social classes, or a single dominant class. They can become so powerful militarily that they can extract resources from civil society. None of these possibilities should be precluded beforehand.

Which brings us to a first take on the specific case of the United States. How does power operate in this particular capitalist country? Does power belong to the people through their elected representatives or through their organized interest groups, with the state serving as an impartial umpire that tries to reach compromises among the differing factions? Is power lodged in the institutional elites who run the corporate, political, and military institutions of the society, or in a dominant (hence ruling) capitalist class? Or do state elites dominate both capitalists and noncapitalists, either in their own interests or in the interests of the capitalist system? These, rather obviously, are the specific questions that inform the investigations that will be reported in the following chapters.

When the United States is viewed in historical-comparative perspective as a fragment of the European system of capitalist nation-states, there is a prima facie case that leaders from the capitalist class are more powerful than in European nations and in comparison to any other group or the state in the United States. America did not have a feudal past, so its capitalists were not hindered by a rival dominant class that had to be battled, assimilated, or deferred to in attempting to dominate the state. Conversely, the absence of such a class meant that the state could not play off one dominant class against another in an attempt to gain autonomy. This basic historical insight was taken for granted in the 1960s; even I used it as context for my argument (Domhoff, 1967:12).

The lack of any dangerous rival states on its borders, along with the protection from European states provided by the British navy throughout most of the nineteenth century, meant that the United States never had to have a "permanent military establishment" until World War II (see Mills, 1956: Chapter 8, for an excellent account of these matters). Thus, there was no strong military network within the state to challenge the capitalists.

Nor did the United States have an institutionalized church, meaning that there was no ideology network that could rival capitalists for power. Fragmented as it is into hundreds of rival churches and self-help groups, the ideology network has been subordinated to the economic and political (i.e., state) networks. Calvin Coolidge said that the business of America is business, but he just as well could have said that the religion of America is business, for in America the sacred assumptions of capitalism are as much an ideology as is religion. Marxists and state autonomy theorists have made little of the absence of an institutionalized church in understanding American power, but it is rightly stressed by Seymour M. Lipset (1963) in his account of the founding of the "first new nation."

Finally, the United States has not had a strong, independent, centralized state for a variety of historical reasons that are very familiar. First, the prerevolutionary history of the United States as a set of separate colonial territories outside the context of a multistate system led to a federal form of government with many government functions located at the state as compared to the national level. The state level in turn ceded some of its power to the city level, where landed elites— place entrepreneurs—have been able to form powerful governments that protect and enhance their interest in intensifying land use by whatever means necessary (Molotch, 1976, 1979; Logan/Molotch, 1987).

Second, the rivalries among the economic elites of the new states were a big factor in the creation of a system of checks and balances at the national level that has made the powerful legislative branch of the American government very accessible to private groups. If I had to make one major criticism of my work in the 1960s, it is that it did not give enough weight to Congress in the American power equation. I began to correct this mistake in the 1970s, and will do so even more in this book. Third, the "country" party of Jefferson that won out politically over the "court" party of Hamilton until the Civil War, worked very hard to keep the federal government small (Murrin, 1980; reprinted in Banning, 1989:427). In particular, as will be argued throughout this book, the southern rich played an enormous role in restraining the growth of a strong centralized state that might challenge its domination of its African-American workforce.

The small size of the nineteenth-century American state meant there were powerful corporations before there was a large national government, another contrast of major importance with Europe (Mills, 1956:272). Corporate elites thus had a big hand in how the national government grew, contrary to the account by Stephen Skowronek (1982) that is drawn upon by state autonomy theorists. With the coming of World War II, of course, there was no choice but to expand the state dramatically.

Because the national state and the military were relatively unimportant in American history until the past 50 or 60 years, most analysts of power in the

United States have started with the premise that the private groups or social classes of "civil society" dominate the state. Thus, their main focus has been on the relative power of various interest groups, private institutions, or social classes. Most of these "society-centric" analysts have been pluralists. That is, they have concluded that power is lodged in a variety of interest groups and in the people as a whole through party politics and elections. They do not claim that power is equally distributed, but only that no one group, power elite, or social class holds preeminent power. Within this society-centric context, pluralists see the elected representatives who run the government as having an independence or autonomy that allows them to create compromises among the competing private interests and look out for the general interests of the society.

The few dissident analysts within the academic community—Hunter, Mills, myself, the plain Marxists of the 1960s—contested the general pluralist vision only in the sense of saying that power was in the hands of the few—an institutional elite for Mills, the rich capitalists for the plain Marxists, a combination of the two for Hunter and me. That is, the dissidents were as society-centric as the pluralists and put no special emphasis on the state.

The new combatants, structural Marxists and state autonomists, want to give far more independent power to the state than the previous rivals. They admit that the American state is relatively "weak" on a scale of state autonomy, often repeating the historical arguments I just have summarized as if they were not accepted by everyone, but they nonetheless chide pluralists, Millsians, and plain Marxists alike for being society-centric rather than "state-centric" about the United States. They have created a new battle line concerning power in America, and much of this book is cast as a direct challenge to them.

Still, the general view I have adopted puts me in the same camp as the state autonomy theorists in one sense, for I too believe—and always have believed, following Mills (1956:170, 277; 1962:119)—that the state is "potentially autonomous," to borrow the useful phrase that Skocpol (1979:29) employs in an attempt to distance her theorizing from that of any other American. Indeed, I thought one main reason for doing power structure research was to see if and how the state was autonomous in the United States. At the same time, following Mann, I believe that the most important social actors in advanced capitalists countries in at least the past 150 years have been social classes and states. The military and ideological networks have been subordinated gradually to these other two networks throughout Europe, and even more so in the United States.

When I have completed my case studies, it will be clear that my conclusions concerning the United States are closer to those of plain Marxists than to those of structural Marxists or state autonomy theorists. This is not, I repeat, because I started with the assumption that capitalists inevitably dominate the state as long as there is capitalism, but because the kind of research to be presented in the following chapters leads me to that conclusion. I hope the eclecticism of my view, sharing some aspects with state autonomy theorists, and other aspects with plain Marxists, does not continue to create confusion for the pigeonholers, tax-onomists, and single-cause theorists who now dominate discussions of power in America. But on the chance that it will, I include the following chart, which provides the answers various theorists give to three key questions: Is the state potentially autonomous? Is civil society more powerful than the state in most capitalist countries? Does a ruling class dominate the state in the United States? As can be seen, I am the only one who answers "yes" to all three questions.

|  | Pluralist | State autonomy | Structural Marxist | Mills | Plain Marxist | Me |
|---|---|---|---|---|---|---|
| Potential state autonomy? | yes/no* | yes | no | yes | no | yes |
| Civil society dominant? | yes | no | yes | yes | yes | yes |
| Ruling class dominates U.S.? | no | no | no | no | yes | yes |

*"Yes," in that government officials make their own decisions in the general interest; "no," in that government was created at the behest of civil society.

Before turning to the case studies, there is one final general issue that must be tackled. It concerns the relevance of studying the social, educational, and oc-cupational backgrounds of those who run the state, whether as elected politi-cians, appointed officials, or career bureaucrats. State autonomy theorists of all varieties say that such studies are usually misleading and at best worthless. They don't think it much matters who governs, but in the next chapter I provide a series of arguments as to why it does matter. This does not mean that I am going to rely heavily on that kind of information in this book. To the contrary, my greatest emphasis is on the decisional approach called for by pluralists. However, I do want to make the general point so that such claims will not go uncontested, and I do want to be able to include such information when it seems relevant.

# 2

## DOES IT MATTER WHO GOVERNS?

In the summer of 1965 I wrote a manuscript with the working title "Is the American Upper Class a Governing Class?" It was a title that implied my full thesis: that there is an upper class and, yes, it is a governing class, by which I meant a dominant class or ruling class, terms I avoided back then because they were identified with Marxism.

By the time the manuscript was revised in 1966 and published in 1967, it had a jazzier title because the publisher thought that the working title was too long and cumbersome. I resisted the change, but the new title that popped into the mind of a friend (a political scientist, no less) one evening was too good to pass up. That title, *Who Rules America?*, still asked a question, and it admitted of a clear answer: the upper class, rooted in the ownership and control of large corporations, rules or governs through a leadership group called the power elite at the national level (Domhoff, 1967:156). I saw the answer as a rather obvious synthesis of the work of C. Wright Mills, Paul Sweezy, and the Tocquevillian sociologist E. Digby Baltzell (1958, 1964), and I am still proud of the fact that I try to draw together as many good ideas as I can find rather than practice the narrow exclusionary purism of the theorists I will be challenging in this book (Domhoff, 1967:1).

*Who Rules America?* was an appealing title in the context of the social movements of the 1960s, and the use of many names in the book itself helped to popularize and make concrete a framework that combined a class and institutional analysis. But when radical strategies seemed to be failing and the search for theoretical scapegoats began, structural Marxists came to see the title and the use of names as symbols of an allegedly flawed analysis that supposedly personalized the problem of power by putting too much emphasis on which individuals were in power. It came to be believed that "who rules" or "who governs" does not matter because the structure of the economic and political systems produces a set of roles and imperatives that minimize personal discretion even for state managers.

The charge was misguided from the outset in that it misunderstood the nature of my argument, but it gained a following because it had the apparent imprimatur of the European structural Marxist Nicos Poulantzas (1969), who seemed far more theoretically astute to discouraged radicals than any of the Americans they had been reading. By 1975 the critics had an epithet or stigma as well—instrumentalism—for what were alleged to be my views, and by the mid-1970s the structural Marxist Scott McNall (1977) and his student Sally Margolin (1976) could be writing papers with titles like "Does Anybody Rule America?" and "Who Rules? Who Governs? Who Cares?"

Still, the arguments for one or another version of state autonomy theory were not without merit or plausibility. Some argued that the state is able to be autonomous because the capitalists are too divided and unsophisticated to dominate it, but that this does not lead state managers to anticapitalist policies because they have to maintain some reasonable level of economic activity to ensure adequate state revenues and avoid disruption by angry workers. Others suggested that the state's involvement in relations with other states can give it a degree of autonomy from the strictly economic interests of the capitalists. Some pointed to policies that were implemented against the apparent wishes of capitalists, and to the fact that there have been social democratic governments in Western Europe that have no businesspeople in them but continue to follow procapitalist policies nonetheless.

Although the structural Marxist framework that generated most of these arguments has been fading fast of late, some of its specific indictments still linger. Even 20 years later, when admitting that the specific arguments used against views such as mine were wrong, Fred Block (1987:6–8) can barely control his disdain for the alleged emphasis on individuals in what he now calls the "business dominance" perspective. Lack of "sophistication" seems to be his key criticism. The theory "was simply not theoretically sophisticated enough; it seemed pedestrian and unmistakably American" (Block, p. 6). Then Poulantzas is praised for taking the discussion to a "more sophisticated level" even though he was wrong in the particulars (p. 7). "The rush to embrace Poulantzas' more sophisticated formulations" (p. 8) was "unfortunate" because it led to the neglect of some useful research findings.

Given the kind of analysis that Block and others continue to put forth, it seems worthwhile to answer the question, Does it matter who governs? in a very direct way. This is especially the case because new work has appeared that makes it possible to deepen such an answer (DiTomaso, 1980; Zeitlin, 1980, 1984; Feigenbaum, 1985; Mann, 1984, 1986). The chapter is divided into five separate and distinct arguments that operate at very different levels.

I am not so sanguine as to believe that any of these arguments will carry the day on its own, although the final argument seems conclusive to me. All I hope to do is inflict some damage on the current presumption that the arguments of the state autonomy theorists are probably right because they seem so plausible, especially to those who secretly believe that "business-dominance" theorists are merely simple-minded Americans. If this presumption can be shaken, the empirical evidence in later chapters that massively contradicts state autonomy theory for the United States might be taken more seriously.

## Indicators of Power

In "Who Rules America? I never asserted that it was "necessary" for members of the upper class or corporate community to be part of the state in order to rule. Instead, I made the assumption that "overrepresentation" in the "key institutions and decision-making groups" is "evidence" that an upper class is powerful (Domhoff, 1967:5–10). Trained in the tradition of "intervening variables" and "underlying traits" (Lazarsfeld, 1966), I saw "overrepresentation" as one of several "indicators" of power. Such a conception in no way implies a causal statement concerning the "necessity" of members of the power elite being present in government.

There is irony in the fact that this argument was completely misunderstood by the structural Marxists of the 1970s. This is because my argument is at bottom the same one that Poulantzas ended up with after criticizing the idea that capitalists had to be part of the state in order to dominate it:

> The *direct* participation of members of the capitalist class in the state apparatus and in the government, even where it exists, is not the important side of the matter. The relation between the bourgeois class and the State is an *objective relation*. This means that if the *function* of the State in a determinate social formation and the *interests* of the dominant class in this formation *coincide*, it is by reason of the system itself: the direct participation of members of a ruling class in the State apparatus is not the *cause*, but the *effect*, and moreover a chance and contingent one, of this objective coincidence (Poulantzas, 1969:73, his italics).

Capitalists in government as the "effect" of power. That is precisely how Paul Lazarsfeld used indicators to study underlying traits. There is evidence for the usefulness of this approach. Everyone seems to agree that women and minorities are "underrepresented" in American government and that they have very little power. The decline of the aristocracy in England is mirrored by its declining representation in Parliament (Guttsman, 1963), and the proportion of working-class representatives in modern West European parliaments correlates with greater equality in income and greater social welfare benefits (Hewitt, 1977; Stephens, 1980). Many people seem to forget that Dahl (1961), for all his emphasis on decision-making in his theoretical statements, used the social backgrounds of mayors as his major evidence that power in New Haven fell from the aristocracy to the industrialists to the "ex-plebes" from 1784 to 1953.

I recognize it is not a hard and fast rule that people must occupy official positions in order to be powerful. We are talking about a "contingent" relationship, as both Lazarsfeld and Poulantzas agree. Indicators are only the beginning of wisdom, and they are not perfect. Nevertheless, the many, many studies showing the vast overrepresentation of the upper class and corporate community in government should be given their due in contemplating the power structure in America (e.g., Matthews, 1954; Mills, 1956; Stanley, Mann, and Doig, 1967; Mintz, 1975; Freitag, 1975; Zweigenhaft, 1975; Dye, 1976; Burch, 1980/81; Useem, 1984).

I agree that all this has little to do with the how and why of power. It does not tell us if who governs "really" matters in terms of the actual power struggles among organizations, classes, and the state. For that type of question we need to turn to other arguments.

## Uncertainty in Organizations

Disagreements in American social science about the importance of "who governs" did not begin in the late 1960s and early 1970s with the sudden arrival of European structural Marxism on the scene. Instead, they had existed for some time between those who study the sociology of organizations in terms of "the relative explanatory power of 'leadership' versus the 'structure' of the organization" (DiTomaso, 1980:260).

Organizational theory portrays action as constrained by roles that have been institutionalized and routinized. Organizations try to structure each position to decrease the importance of discretion in decision-making and thus restrict the influence of social background. While this is indeed a major goal of organizations, it does not follow that they are always successful. Therefore, rather than opting for a completely structural explanation, organizational theorists have "sought to specify the conditions under which differences in people are important and, alternatively, the conditions under which structure constrains the personal motivations, actions, or characteristics of people" (1980:261).

Summarizing a wide range of literature, Nancy DiTomaso (1980:261) argues that people are less constrained by organizational structures in positions involving (1) the allocation of resources, (2) uncertainty about the choices that will be faced, and (3) contacts outside the organization. Since the work done by people in such positions cannot be accomplished effectively if they are hedged in by rules and other constraints, it is necessary for the owners or chief officers of the organization to predict and control discretionary behavior in some other way. Organizational researchers find that this is usually done by selecting persons for such positions who are thought to have internalized the same values as the owners. Importantly, and here we arrive at the first implication of this work for the "does it matter" question, the owners and top officers infer common values from social and educational background along with familiar external evidence of common values such as style of dress, mannerisms, and personal interests. It is for this reason that everyone in the corporation tends to dress alike, affect a button-down manner, and play golf: employees are concerned to show exterior evidence of more profound underlying similarities to the top leaders so they can advance to positions of discretion.

Rosabeth Kanter, in a study of managers in a large eastern corporation, also argues that the need for trust in key decision-making positions in an organization creates a pressure toward a stress on social backgrounds and conformity:

> It is the uncertainty quotient in managerial work, as it has come to be defined in the large modern corporations, that causes management to become so socially restricting; to develop tight inner circles excluding social strangers; to keep control in the hands of socially homogeneous peers; to stress conformity and insist upon a diffuse, unbounded loyalty; and to prefer ease of communication and thus social certainty over the strains of dealing with people who are "different" (1977:49).

I would like to generalize this analysis from organizational theory and call the whole package "the argument from uncertainty." It can be brought to bear on the state through another finding of organizational theory, namely, that organizations attempt to control any conditions in the "organizational environment" that breed uncertainty within the organization. More specifically, American corporations probably would claim that one of the major "uncertainties" in their environment is governmental policy. Thus, organizational theory would expect that corporations are going to attempt to reduce this uncertainty as much as possible by trying to place people they can trust, that is, "people of their own kind," in governmental positions. From an organizational point of view, then, it most decidedly matters who governs the state.

But there is another way corporations can reduce their uncertainty about government. They can hire former government officials to predict and interpret governmental policies, and to be the corporate liaisons with the government. If this argument is correct, we should expect to find a "revolving door" between corporations and government, that is, a "two-way street," and of course that is exactly what has been found for the "military–industrial complex" in particular (e.g., Adams, 1981) and the government in general (e.g., Salzman and Domhoff, 1980).

We can go one step further with this argument. The American state itself can be conceptualized as a network of organizations existing in a very uncertain environment. Much of that uncertainty is created by the constant attacks on these government organizations by corporate leaders and antigovernment ideologues (McConnell, 1966:294). Thus, as Clarence Stone (1989) argues, we can expect to find government entities, including newly elected administrations, seeking out coalition partners to stabilize their environment. For a variety of reasons, the local elected administrations studied by Stone usually conclude that their best possible coalition partner is the downtown business community. The result is the integration of government and business leaders into a stable power structure that is not easily displaced because no other organizations or groups in the city can put together a viable alternative coalition that would be as attractive to state elites as the one they have with business. Stone emphasizes that his argument is not one of domination of the state and underclasses by business, but of a dominant coalition between business and state elites. Thus, it is not quite the same as the argument to be presented in this book. It is very similar in its structure to the viewpoint I will argue, but for me it does not go far enough empirically in terms of the great power that business owners have in this class–state coalition and in their direct relations with workers. What I want to stress here, however, is that I believe Stone's argument is a sound one from the point of view of organizational theory.

While the concern with uncertainty explains why who governs can matter for corporations, this does not prove that it "really" matters who governs. That is, this argument does not refute the claim by the structural Marxists that the relationship between the state and social classes is an objective one that leads to certain outcomes due to the underlying imperatives that determine everything. But it is a start toward explaining why states find it hard to be autonomous. The next section adds to that explanation.

## The Cohesion of Class Segments

Those who say it does not matter who governs sometimes claim that a degree of state autonomy is possible and useful in a capitalist society because the capitalists are shortsighted and highly divided among themselves. Capitalists therefore cannot develop the class consciousness that would be necessary if they were going to challenge for state power and rule in a way that would be beneficial to capitalism as a system.

However, this assumption about extreme disorganization may not be correct in all cases. If it overstates to talk about a completely unified capitalist class with fully common interests, as I always have believed it does (Domhoff, 1967:28–31), then it also may overstate to go to the other extreme. Much of the material in later chapters can be seen as an empirical elaboration of this point for the twentieth-century United States, but here I want to demonstrate it with a quick look at rival class segments. By "class segments" I mean groupings within either the ownership class or the working class that have somewhat different interests due to their particular position within the overall social structure. In the case of the ownership class, these rival segments have different bases of wealth and partially conflicting interests on at least some issues even though they share a common concern with the defense of the system of private property. In the case of the working class, there are divisions based on skills and race that will be discussed in later chapters. More precisely, I am working within the framework developed by Zeitlin, who defines segments within the ownership class as follows:

These segments of the class are differentiated by their relatively distinct locations in the process of production and appropriation of surplus value. As a consequence, they may have specific political economic requirements and concrete interests in contradiction to those of other segments of the class, although they share a common relationship to the means of production (1980:6).

Although Zeitlin derives his specific definition of class segments from Marx, the general idea behind this conception is not original to Marx. The following passage written in 1787 expresses a very sophisticated understanding of both interclass and intraclass conflict. It was written as part of a conscious attempt to create a state that could deal with both types of conflict simultaneously in a peaceful way while assuring that the rights of property would not be challenged. The author, of course, is James Madison:

But the most common and durable sources of factions has been the various and unequal distribution of property. Those who hold and those who are without property have ever formed distinct interests in society. Those who are creditors, and those who are debtors, fall under a like discrimination. A landed interest, a manufacturing interest, a mercantile interest, a moneyed interest, with many lesser interests, grow up of necessity in civilized nations, and divide them into different classes, actuated by different sentiments and views. The regulation of these various and interfering interests forms the principal task of modern legislation, and involves the spirit of party and faction in the necessary and ordinary operations of the government (Madison, *Federalist* #10, 1787, as reprinted in Chambers, 1964:10–11).

The reason why class segments are relevant to the question of state autonomy is that there is every reason to believe that some class segments are organized enough to challenge independent state managers for domination of the state. They have overcome the extreme disorganization alleged to exist among most capitalists even if they have not attained the overall level of class consciousness that would meet the high definitional standards of structural Marxists. Moreover, they often feel so strongly about their interests that they can find no way to compromise with their intraclass rivals. The result is sometimes an all-out battle—civil war—to dominate the state if it possibly can be dominated.

This general analysis, demonstrated in detail for Chile by Zeitlin (1984; Zeitlin and Ratcliff, 1988), is directly relevant to the United States. It is widely agreed that the American upper class originally had at least two rival segments, with northern manufacturing interests and southern slaveholding interests opposing each other on fundamental issues relating to economic development and territorial expansion almost from the day they temporarily settled even more fundamental issues of power and governance in an "elite pact" known as the Constitution (Higley and Burton, 1989). Their differences were buffered a bit by northern bankers and merchants who had business ties with both segments, especially by those in New York City (Albion, 1939; Foner, 1941), but the "extremists" on both sides saw their differences on slavery, tariffs, and state subsidies as major problems in the long run.

But why couldn't the state elites work these matters out free from the interference of the class segments? In the case of the powerful southerners, at least, the answer is clear: they couldn't entrust matters to state elites. They understood that the slave system that lasted until 1860, and the Jim Crow system of the next 100 years, were not supported "naturally" by the underlying laws of capitalism, and that state power was essential to control their labor force. Further, the southerners must have known at some level that their system was completely at odds with their own great obsession with freedom and liberty, now officially enshrined as the ideology of all (white) Americans (see Patterson, 1987, for a brilliant discussion of the fact that the concern with freedom has been greatest in slave-based societies like ancient Greece, Rome, and the early United States). In short, southern slaveholders believed that they had to labor mightily to make sure that northern liberals and the federal government did not tamper with the "peculiar institution" of their region. They saw themselves as a beleaguered, misunderstood, and even persecuted minority that had to be vigilant every minute to make sure that their way of life was not destroyed. In fact, the fear that northerners might turn against slavery in the South was a key factor in the creation of the first American political party in 1792:

> The insistence that slavery was uniquely a Southern concern, not to be touched by outsiders, had been from the outset a *sine qua non* for Southern participation in national politics. It underlay the Constitution and its creation of a government of limited powers, without which Southern participation would have been unthinkable. And when in the 1790s Jefferson and Madison perceived that a constitution was only the first step in guaranteeing Southern security, because a constitution meant what those who governed under it said it meant, it led to the creation of the first national political party to protect that constitution against change by interpretation (Brown, 1966, as reprinted in Banning, 1989:436).

Thus, southerners did everything they could to control the state, and out of necessity the northerners had to become involved in trying to shape the state to their own ends even if they hadn't intended to originally. Nonetheless, the southerners were the dominant segment from 1801 to 1860. After the northern victory in the Civil War, which led to a federal government highly supportive of industrial development, the southerners redoubled their efforts to control at least parts of the federal state (namely, Congress) because they did not want their new methods of oppressing African-Americans to be challenged and they needed federal money to repair and build infrastructure in their war-torn area.

It is not my purpose in this chapter to describe the segments of the American ruling class in detail or to explain their relationship to the party system. An elaboration of the segments within the ruling class will be the task of the next two chapters, and the nature of their involvement in party politics will be explored in Chapter 9. For now I only want to stress that the existence of a class segment rooted in slavery set in motion a chain of events that makes the idea of state autonomy highly questionable for the United States.

## States and Social Democrats

It has become commonplace among those who say it does not matter who governs to point to countries in Western Europe where Social Democratic parties have been in power. These parties are fairly critical of capitalism and have few or no capitalist members, but they go right on supporting capitalist policies when they are in office.

There are two answers to this point. First, as noted earlier in the chapter, their presence does matter to some extent. These countries have more income equality and better social welfare programs than those with no social democrats anywhere in sight (Hewitt, 1977; Stephens, 1980). In that sense, they show quite the opposite of what the critics claim.

But there is a larger point. In a certain very real sense these countries do not have a full-fledged state at all. They are in my view subsidiary states within a world capitalist system whose "state" in terms of defending territory and enforcing capitalist rules is in Washington, D.C. It is the United States that joined with the Soviet Union to defeat the Nazis in a world war just 45 years ago and thereby kept these countries from becoming colonial appendages of Imperial Germany. Since that time, it is the United States that has kept its troops all over Europe and provided military aid to the armies of these countries, even the proud and allegedly independent French. Further, the United States did direct political battle with the major opponents of capitalism within these countries, the Communists, by means of the CIA and surreptitious campaign donations to acceptable political candidates. The United States also served as the state for Western Europe in an economic way, providing it with a stable monetary system and other economic aid that made possible a restoration of capitalism. In fact, this aid is one factor that has allowed these states to have a "relative autonomy" from their capitalist classes, for they have been until recently as dependent upon the United States as on their capitalist classes.

This does not mean that these countries operate exactly as the United States would wish them to. The social democrats are a distant second choice for the United States as the dominant party in any country. However, given the strength of working-class movements in many countries in Western Europe, and the imminent danger of communism after World War II, social democrats have been the best the United States has been able to do in some cases. But this hardly makes these states comparable to the United States. From the thirteenth century until 1945 there was a multistate system in Europe. However, it is a myth to think the postwar system in Western Europe has been "multistate" in the full sense of the term.

There is one country, Sweden, that may not seem to fit this analysis because its social democrats came to power in the 1930s and the country was "neutral" during World War II. But Sweden is too small to prove anything. Most of its 8.5 million people live in an area about the size of Illinois, which has a population of

11.2 million. Its economy is 2.7 percent the size of the American economy. Sweden could not have defended itself in World War II if Germany had decided to occupy it, and its economy is so tied to Western Europe and the United States that it is completely vulnerable to the kind of sanctions the United States imposed on Cuba, Chile, and Nicaragua when successful insurgents dared to challenge their capitalists.

But the capitalists of Sweden have never felt threatened enough to cry for help. The social democrats very early struck a deal: no attack on capitalism if the capitalists would agree to extensions of the welfare state that had been developed over the early decades of the century. Moreover, even though the social democrats control the government, much of the political negotiating of concern to capitalists takes place between the "peak associations" that speak for the highly organized employers and the equally unionized working class. The result is that 90 percent of the economy is private, the wealth distribution is almost as skewed as in other capitalist countries, and class differences in education and other important areas of everyday life remain very great.

In short, to use a country like Sweden as a major piece of "evidence" about the relationship between the state and social classes in modern capitalist nation-states is the structural Marxist equivalent to the pluralist claim that who governs in New Haven can be generalized to the United States as a whole.

## The Need for State Unity

I do not consider any of the preceding arguments to be definitive answers to the structuralists and state autonomists. Strong states might be autonomous even though organizations and class segments don't want them to be, and the argument concerning social democrats in Western Europe is not relevant to the United States. Those arguments merely nudge open-minded people toward empirical studies of specific situations.

We reach higher ground when we consider Harvey Feigenbaum's (1985: 172ff.) insight that only a very unique kind of state, a completely unified one, could withstand the attempts to control it by organizations, class segments, and classes. Theories of state autonomy make an implicit assumption, Feigenbaum argues, that does not seem to hold for a democratic capitalist society: a unified state pursuing a unified interest. A state has to be unified to be autonomous, he points out, because the various branches and bureaucracies of a fragmented state are "vulnerable to the demands of the already privileged" (1985:172). If private elites are able to penetrate parts of a fragmented state, then the ball game is all over for state autonomy because state elites can no longer act together to implement policies. And the most obvious avenue into a modern democratic state, the legislature, is also the avenue that makes it most difficult for other parts of the state to maintain any autonomy (Harvey Feigenbaum, personal communication,

August 15, 1989). In the United States, for example, the White House can go very far in pursuing its own goals, as Ronald Reagan proved once again by continuing to support the contras in Nicaragua despite a congressional prohibition on any aid, but in the end the investigative powers of the legislative branch finally forced him to curtail his secret operations.

Mann makes a related argument in a more general discussion of two dimensions of state power and four general types of states. He begins by distinguishing between "despotic power," meaning "the range of actions which the elite is empowered to undertake without routine institutionalized negotiations with civil society groups," and "infrastructural power," defined as "the capacity of the state to actually penetrate civil society, and to implement logistically political decisions throughout the realm" (1984:188–89). This distinction leads to four "ideal types" that approximate to the feudal, imperial, bureaucratic, and authoritarian states that can be found in various times and places.

The feudal states of medieval Europe were low in both despotic and infrastructural power, as argued in the previous chapter. Imperial states like the Roman Empire were high on despotic power but had little ability to "co-ordinate civil society without the assistance of other power groups" (1984:191). Modern-day authoritarian states like Nazi Germany and the Soviet Union have despotic power over civil society and the ability to reach into the lives of all their citizens. They are unitary and autonomous. But contemporary capitalist democracies are low on despotic power because their elected officials "are largely controlled by outside civil society groups (either by their financiers or by the electorate) as well as by law" (1984:190). In Feigenbaum's terms, Mann is saying that democratic capitalist states are fragmented states in the sense that at least parts of them include elected officials. Put differently, once there is anything less than a military dictator, or a disciplined Communist party that closes ranks when the Politburo concludes its deliberations, then the strongest groups in civil society are likely to gain a toehold in parts of the state. Thus, once there is an elected legislature open to even a narrow slice of civil society, it becomes very difficult to maintain the unity that is necessary for autonomy. There will be a tug of war between private interests and state elites, which is the story of Western history over the past 600 years as outlined in the previous chapter.

When it comes to a large modern state with many functions, there are of course other agencies of the state besides the legislature that are open to capture. This is true of seemingly insulated planning bureaucracies as well as agencies with resources to distribute. Only the military bureaucracy is usually immune to such penetration, and it is precisely the military that often takes over in many countries when other state elites can no longer coordinate or control civil society.

There are very few theories of state autonomy that stand up very well against this argument. The structural Marxists find it difficult to claim the state is looking after the general capitalist interest when so many different capitalists are able to capture different pieces of the state and demand so many different things. State autonomists like Skocpol end up with every part of the state maximizing its own narrow self-interest, usually in terms of mere bureaucratic expansion. More ambitious state autonomy theorists like Stephen Krasner, whose work will be analyzed in Chapter 5, have to shrink the American state to the White House and the State Department to be able to endow it with autonomy and its own goals.

## Conclusion

The overall effect of these five arguments is to raise serious questions about the plausibility of a theory of state autonomy for any advanced capitalist country, and especially the United States. It seems unlikely that any democratic capitalist state can achieve the kind of unity that is necessary to sustain a large degree of autonomy. The historical importance of the cohesive southern segment of the dominant economic class in the United States makes it doubtful that the American state ever was autonomous, and the emphasis on uncertainty within organizational theory suggests that the most powerful of American organizations, the large corporations, also have involved themselves in the state. The fact that social democrats have formed governments in some postwar Western European states appears irrelevant to an argument about the United States.

However, an argument against state autonomy is not an argument for domination by a ruling class. It only suggests that there is likely to be a complex interaction between states and social classes in democratic capitalist societies. Clearly, then, it is time to compare and contrast rival viewpoints on some specific cases in recent American history. It is time to see capitalists, experts, workers, and state managers in action.

# 3

## BUSINESS LEADERS, EXPERTS, AND THE SOCIAL SECURITY ACT

### Introduction

Shortly after *Who Rules America?* appeared, I was challenged by several friendly critics to analyze a series of important policy decisions at the national level as the only proper way to support a class-dominance thesis. In particular, they thought that some pieces of New Deal legislation might contradict my theory, especially the Social Security Act and National Labor Relations Act.

As a result of this challenge I decided to see if the organizations discussed in the chapter in *Who Rules America?* entitled "The Shaping of the American Polity" could be used to provide a new angle on a variety of policy issues. One of the most satisfying of these analyses concerned the Social Security Act. I had read the standard accounts pitting "business," as symbolized by the National Association of Manufacturers (NAM) and state chambers of commerce, against the experts, middle-class reformers, and Democratic politicians who make up the liberal opposition. I thought Arthur Schlesinger, Jr., quite typical on this score in his history of the New Deal:

> While the friends of social security were arguing out the details of the program, other Americans were regarding the whole idea with horror. Organized business had long warned against such pernicious notions (1959:311).

I felt this quote gave me my opening because I knew that some parts of organized business had been for the Social Security Act. Indeed, I was able to show that one organization in particular, the Business Advisory Council, had a role in formulating it. At the same time, I argued that the "archconservatives and Southerners" in Congress made the bill even less liberal than it had been in the first place, especially in eliminating minimum state-level standards for old-age assistance (Domhoff, 1970c:216).

I did not think all this occurred in a social vacuum caused by "need." In fact, I argued that none of this would have happened if there had not been general unrest and a social movement for old-age pensions among the elderly in particular. My full analysis is contained in the following paragraph:

> The development of the Social Security Act can be summarized as follows: There was considerable distress and discontent bubbling up from the lower levels within the depression-ridden society. This was producing expensive solutions such as the Townsend Plan to give every oldster $200 a month, and the economic system in general was being criticized. The moderate members of the power elite, with the help of academic experts, decided to accommodate these demands on the basis of plans developed by such elite-backed organizations as the American Association for Labor Legislation. These moderates carried their plans to a Congress that was more in sympathy with the less moderate NAM members of the power elite. Within Congress these moderate and conservative views reached a compromise that became the Social Security Act. The act was a far cry from what had been hoped for or demanded by the extremists, but it was probably their pressure that activated the moderate members of the power elite and enabled them to effect an improvement in the situation. While it is certainly true that many people benefited from the measure, which is what pluralists would quickly point out, it is also true that the result from the point of view of the power elite was a restabilization of the system. It put a floor under consumer demand, raised people's expectations for the future and directed political energies back into conventional channels. The difference between what could be and what is remained very, very large for the poor, the sick and the aged. The wealth distribution did not change, decision-making power remained in the hands of upper-class leaders, and the basic principles that encased the conflict were set forth by moderate members of the power elite (1970c:217–18).

There were no critical reactions to my analysis in the 1970s. Pluralists probably were not persuaded, if they were interested at all, and structural Marxists and state autonomy theorists were not involved in empirical studies of the New Deal at the time. Then, starting in 1980, structural Marxists and state autonomy theorists suddenly realized that the Social Security Act was an ideal issue on which to compare rival theories of the state. A lively debate ensued in which the participants had only one main agreement, that my analysis was either inaccurate or theoretically irrelevant (Skocpol, 1980, 1986/87; Skocpol and Ikenberry, 1983; Skocpol and Amenta, 1985; Quadagno, 1984, 1988; Domhoff, 1986c, 1986/87).

According to Skocpol, my overall framework underestimates the role of class struggle and overestimates the farseeing rationality of corporate leaders. It forgets that this is a democracy, and it does not give proper attention to political parties and state structures. Designating me as a member of the "corporate-liberal" school of recent American historiography that will be discussed in the next section, she writes as follows about my analysis of the New Deal:

> The corporate-liberal explanation of the New Deal is highly misleading. It can only be substantiated through a purely illustrative and selective citing of the facts. When the theory is subjected to a rigorous, skeptical examination, corporate liberalism fails to explain even those aspects of the New Deal that seem most consonant with it (1980:162–63).

As for the Social Security Act, the many experts involved in its formulation are not part of a capitalist-based policy-planning network, as I claimed, but are independent "third-force" mediators that stand between capital and labor. Moreover, the few business people who favored social security legislation were "mavericks" who were marginal to the policy process and often overruled by the state officials who formulated the act (Skocpol, 1986/87:331–32).

For Quadagno, the problems with my general view are not quite so serious. She believes that what it says about the role of sophisticated conservatives from the large corporations has much to recommend it, but she also sees flaws: "Corporate liberal arguments cannot explain why those interventions sometimes fail, however, because corporate liberalism underestimates the weight other power blocs carry" (1984:646). Ironically, Quadagno did not even know when she wrote this comment that I had written a detailed account of the Social Security Act that is very similar to hers. Nor did she realize that I understood the power of the conservative coalition in Congress (Domhoff, 1970c:349–53). I think this is clear testimony to the success that the structural Marxists of the 1970s had in making my work irrelevant for most Marxist researchers on power in the United States. It is a commentary on how the invention of a negative label such as "instrumentalist" can ensure that books are not read.

It will be the main purpose of this chapter, then, to compare my analysis with those by Skocpol and Quadagno. The first section prepares the ground for this comparison by setting the record straight on the origins and claims of corporate-liberal theory in order to correct misunderstandings by both structural Marxists and state autonomy theorists. It shows I was drawing as much on the work of Mills as I was on the Marxist historians who founded the corporate-liberal school. In the second section I argue that more recent theorists misinterpret the framework I was working in because they do not understand its basic assumptions or pose the same questions that concerned its creators. This section also explains how my view was distorted because it was drawn into a political dog-fight among Marxists concerning who was the purest or truest Marxist and whose interpretation of Marxism was the most useful politically.

But the problem is not merely one of general perspectives. There are also issues of evidence involved, and they will be discussed at length in the final section of the chapter. There I will combine my past research with that of Quadagno, and with new research by Barbara Brents (1984, 1989; Jenkins and Brents, 1989), to show that business leaders were central to framing the Social Security Act and that the third-force experts emphasized by Skocpol in fact worked very closely with corporate leaders on this particular issue.

When all is said and done, I think the chapter will show that my relatively brief analysis of the Social Security Act in 1970 has stood the test of time fairly well. New research by Quadagno and Jenkins and Brents has added many things I did not know or fully understand, but this research is far more in keeping with my analysis than these structural Marxist will concede. Lest readers think this conclusion might arise from an inability to see the error of my ways, let me say right here that in Chapter 4 I will admit that new and better information forced me to change my analysis of the National Labor Relations Act.


## Corporate Liberalism and Mills

Critics of my work on domestic legislation insist on calling it "corporate liberalism," a theory that came on stream in the 1960s and had a strong impact for a brief time. While I draw on corporate-liberal theory, this label is more a half-truth, as I will now show as a lead-in to the origins of the civil war that developed among Marxists in the 1970s, where I was caught in the crossfire.

The corporate-liberal view of big-business involvement in reformist social legislation can be traced to the work of history graduate students influenced by William A. Williams at the University of Wisconsin in the late 1950s and early 1960s. Although Williams (1961:343–488) didn't use the term "corporate liberal," his work emphasized the reformist tendencies of the new "corporation capitalists," and he referred to several of the corporate policy discussion organizations later studied by those he influenced. Most important for the issues of this chapter, several of the fledgling historians influenced by Williams had been members of the Communist party or its youth group in the 1940s and 1950s. They left the party out of discouragement, not because they became anticommunists, and they remained socialists or even revolutionaries in some cases (Weinstein and Eakins, 1970:v, 6). They turned to graduate work in history to learn where their theory of class struggle had gone wrong and how it could be improved. To this end, they founded *Studies on the Left* in 1959, a journal that was to last until 1967 and play a part in influencing New Left thinking.

Given this agenda, one of the most important findings of these historians was the way in which both the Communist and Socialist parties in the United States had distorted the pre–World War I history of the Socialist Party in order to justify their bitter rivalry after the war. Although the original Socialist Party had been antiwar and probolshevik, the Communists claimed just the opposite on both issues in order to justify their decision to split from the Socialists and form a new party. Meanwhile, the Socialist party did not work very hard to resist the antibolshevik charge because it had become thoroughly anticommunist (Weinstein, 1963, 1965).

As part of their study of left history, the corporate-liberal historians became interested in understanding how the capitalists had reacted to the growing Socialist party of the first 14 years of the century. This interest brought them into contact with the archival materials of the policy groups discussed by Williams. Their most important conclusion was that attempts to create a Socialist movement in the United States had failed partly because some corporate leaders came to support reform on many important social issues. These businessmen were labeled "corporate liberals" for two reasons. First, they wanted to solidify a social order rooted in corporations as the most important institution for the accumulation of capital. For this reason they saw their main problems as the socialists to their left and the free-market, antistatist competitive capitalists on their right. Second, these corporate capitalists were "liberal" in the sense that they accepted and wanted to work with the "liberal democratic state" that was the historic legacy of the United States. That is, they were not for a "corporatist" or an antidemocratic solution to their problems with labor, farmers, socialists, and small business.

In short, the corporate liberals were defined as business leaders who opted for progressive social change as a way to defuse class struggle and halt Socialist gains. At the very time that the growing Socialist party of 1900–12 was taking aim at an industrial capitalism that was driving workers to political alienation, the corporate liberals began creating welfare programs in their factories, backing workmen's compensation legislation, meeting with leaders of the American Federation of Labor (AFL), and supporting legislation for such extensions of the state as the Federal Reserve Board, Bureau of the Budget, and Federal Trade Commission:

> Ironically, these struggles [of the 1890s] finally led to the emergence of a unified socialist movement just as the more sophisticated corporations were beginning to organize to reduce overt class antagonism and the threat of class-conscious politics that a frustrated trade union movement was producing. . . . But precisely because the development of corporate liberalism was in large part a response to the long-term struggles in which the Socialists participated, it was difficult for them to understand the changes in the political economy then taking place (Weinstein, 1975:3–4).

Corporate-liberal theory was first articulated in a statement by the editors in *Studies on the Left* in 1962. The editorial challenged the concern expressed by many leftists with "the threat to democracy posed by the activities of the ultra-right" (Editors, 1962:3). The statement argued that the real threat came from modern-day corporate liberals who were prosecuting the cold war and creating a consensus based on "a program of gains for all major classes or interest groups, in the context of more or less continuous economic expansion" (1962:6). Since the standard communist line for most of the years from 1935 to the present has been the imminent danger of fascism, thus leading communists to help liberals whenever possible, this was a major political and theoretical break by these excommunists with their old comrades.

The corporate liberals were said to differ from other businessmen in several ways. They believed in creating new relations among groups, including farmers and workers, with corporate capitalism at the center. They emphasized "responsibility" over "individualism." They were willing to allow government "to regulate 'destructive' competition and provide other standards that would increase prosperity and stability" (Eakins, 1972:191). They tended to be representatives of the biggest and most international corporations, which had a broader view than the smaller, regional corporations who opposed them from an ultraconservative view:

> In general, as we will see, the smaller businessmen were tied much more immediately to the market than were many of the larger corporations. Their attitudes toward trade unions, working conditions, and wages were more rigid and uncompromising. This was so because their financial positions and profit margins were generally poorer and because their relative provincialism kept many of them from an awareness of the larger problems of interclass harmony and social (as opposed to purely individual) efficiency posed by the growth of the unions, the radical insurgents in both major parties, and by the Socialist Party of America (Weinstein, 1968:4).

However, corporate liberalism was not the product of a mere market situation or cosmopolitanism or even farsightedness, as critics wrongly claim. Instead, as David Eakins emphasizes: "Corporate liberalism was also, and most importantly, a product of unremitting class struggle and of pressure from labor and other groups who demanded more change than reformers were ever willing to give" (Eakins 1972:191). In short, this is a theory that emphasizes both intra- and interclass conflicts, precisely the combination of elements seen to be essential for a more sophisticated understanding of states and revolutions by analysts such as Maurice Zeitlin, who is a critic of the critics of corporate liberalism without claiming any allegiance to corporate-liberal theory (Zeitlin, 1980:1–37). The amazing thing is that the new Marxists of the 1970s could think for a minute that the corporate-liberal view minimized classes or class conflict.

The corporate-liberal theorists were partially anticipated by Gabriel Kolko in *The Triumph of Conservatism* (1964) and *Railroads and Regulations* (1965). Kolko's study of railroad regulation in the late nineteenth century claimed that the larger railroads actually welcomed the agency established to regulate them by the Interstate Commerce Act of 1887. This thesis was a controversial one, contradicting as it did the conventional pluralist wisdom that the Interstate Commerce Commission was created by the government at the behest of aroused pressure groups and against the wishes of the railroad magnates.

Kolko carried this theory one step forward in *The Triumph of Conservatism* (1964) by arguing that several of the regulatory agencies of the Progressive Era were set up at the request of reformist big businessmen who wanted to regulate competition, quell the protests of one group or another, or improve their ability to sell their products overseas. However, Kolko shared little with the corporate-liberal school and never referred to or cited Williams or the corporate-liberal historians until he expressed his scorn, wrongly arguing that they imputed too much rationality to capitalists and experts alike (Kolko, 1980).

Most of the work of the corporate-liberal historians focused on the Progressive Era. Little or none of it dealt with New Deal legislation. Eakins's (1966) dissertation showed how the corporate liberals created a wide variety of research organizations and policy-discussion groups between 1900 and 1960, but he made only passing mention of New Deal innovations. Ronald Radosh's work (1966, 1967) demonstrated the way in which the corporate-liberal view meshed with the corporatist views of labor leaders such as Samuel Gompers and Sidney Hillman, with some discussion of Hillman's role during the New Deal.* Stephen Scheinberg's (1966) dissertation looked at the attitudes and policies of leading corporate-liberal businessmen between 1900 and 1939; once again, there is little mention of social legislation. Weinstein's *The Corporate Ideal in the Liberal State* (1968), perhaps the most influential and widely available application of the theory to American history, dealt primarily with the ideas of the National Civic Federation, a big-business policy group that was influential in the Progressive Era, but it also anticipated later theorizing on the role of businessmen in reshaping city governments in that same era.

My work comes into the picture in this context. I first encountered the ideas of Weinstein, Eakins, and Radosh in 1967 and 1968, well after I had written *Who Rules America?* Weinstein in particular had a strong influence on my thinking on power and social change in America from that time forward, through his writings and our lengthy discussions. I was immediately receptive to the empirical claims of Weinstein and the others because they fit so well with concepts that I had learned from reading C. Wright Mills. Even though the corporate-liberal view came into historical research in the way I have described, similar ideas had been introduced into sociology by Mills as early as 1948 in his first book, *The New Men of Power,* an analysis of labor leaders. There he distinguishes between the "sophisticated conservatives" and the "practical conservatives" in the business community on the basis of his reading of what corporate leaders said and wrote about major policy issues in *Business Week* and *Fortune* in 1946 and 1947. His characterizations of the two groups are savage and astute, and they still apply:

> The practical conservatives can duel noisily with the liberals because they have the same short-run, shifting attention and the same agitated indignation. The practical conservatives always enter politics with an economic gleam in their eyes. . . . Ideologically, the practical conservatives are wild-eyed Utopian capitalists; strategically, they are practical men. They have much will and a continuity that comes from much backward vision. "Remembering" imaginary situations, they long for the golden age of Harding, Coolidge, and Hoover. Their ideas are a hodge podge of anything they can use to throw at the enemy. . . .
>
> The sophisticated conservatives, represented by magazines like *Fortune* and *Business Week,* are similar to the far left in that their political demands are continuous and specifically focused. They leave the noise to the practical right; they do not attempt to arouse the people at large; they work in and among other elite groups, primarily the high military, the chieftains of

---

*Radosh (1972) later wrote a very distorted account of the New Deal that was based in part on my work. Called "The Myth of the New Deal," it contains most of the mistakes that are challenged by structural Marxists, and is widely cited by them. I did not like the article at the time, but did not realize it would be used against me. I also want to add that I never have met Radosh or discussed ideas with him in writing. I only find useful his early work on labor leaders.

large corporations, and certain politicians. Knowing what they want, wanting it all the time, and believing the main drift is in their favor, these sophisticated conservatives try to realize their master aim quietly (Mills, 1948:23–24, 25).

Mills also wrote briefly about these two tendencies within the business community in his better known *The Power Elite:*

> In the higher circles of business and its associations, there has long been a tension, for example, between the "old guard" of practical conservatives and the "business liberals," or sophisticated conservatives. What the old guard represents is the outlook, if not always the intelligent interests, of the more narrow economic concerns. What the business liberals represent is the outlook and the interests of the new propertied class as a whole. They are "sophisticated" because they are more flexible in adjusting to such political facts of life as the New Deal and big labor, because they have taken over and used the dominant liberal rhetoric for their own purposes, and because they have, in general, attempted to get on top of, or even slightly ahead of, the trend of these developments, rather than to fight it as practical conservatives are wont to do (Mills, 1956:122).

It was this line of thinking that influenced my views about "antagonisms within the upper class" in *Who Rules America?* There I emphasized the institutional networks and political party factions through which the two tendencies operated:

> Most important of all, there is a split between what Mills called the "business liberals" and the "old guard." The business liberals, who usually come from the biggest, most internationally minded companies, speak through such organizations as the Council on Foreign Relations, the Business Advisory Council, the Committee for Economic Development, the Democratic Party, and the moderate wing of the Republican Party, while the "old guard" of practical conservatives, who tend to be nationally oriented businessmen, speak through the National Association of Manufacturers and the conservative wing of the Republican Party (Domhoff, 1967:28).

As can be seen from this quote, I had taken the step of tying the two segments of the corporate community to different types of businesses, bigger and more international firms on the one hand, more nationally oriented companies on the other hand. Although I was hesitant about calling the ultraconservatives merely smaller businessmen since there are so many glaring exceptions, such as the du Ponts and Pews (Domhoff, 1972:163–64), my later research has convinced me that the basis of the ultraconservatives *now* lies primarily in smaller firms in the *Fortune* 500 (Domhoff, 1975).

Moreover, I felt an affinity for the corporate-liberal view because the institutional framework of policy shaping on domestic issues suggested by Eakins and Weinstein was parallel to what I had proposed in *Who Rules America?* and dealt with in much detail shortly afterwards in a study of foreign policy-making (Domhoff, 1969b). Eakins (1969, 1972) published only two articles from his excellent dissertation that carried this network into the post-World War II era.

However, the substance of his work is presented in detail in my chapter on domestic legislation in *The Higher Circles* (1970c). I extended his analysis of the social backgrounds and corporate connections of the policy experts and corporate leaders he discusses and then used his general framework to trace the history of four policy issues: workmen's compensation and the creation of the Federal Trade Commission in the Progressive Era, and the Social Security Act and National Labor Relations act in the New Deal. The first two case studies were drawn from Kolko and Weinstein, but the other two were put together by me after a great deal of reading in newspapers, congressional reports, and secondary sources.

Although I incorporated the findings of corporate-liberal historians, I did not accept their terminology. Except for one use of the phrase "business liberals" in *Who Rules America?*, I always have talked of moderates or moderate conservatives, who are often in opposition to conservatives or ultraconservatives. Corporate-liberal theorists are sophisticated in their understanding of both "corporate" and "liberal," but I knew from the start that the term would be misunderstood and that it was politically loaded. I think that the term suggested by Mills— "sophisticated conservatives"—should be adopted for this viewpoint, a term that is equally accurate conceptually and much more accurate in terms of the U.S. political spectrum. "Moderate conservatives" and "corporate moderates" are equivalent terms I have utilized in the past, and all three phrases will be used interchangeably in this book to provide continuity with my past work and a little editorial variety.

Even though I never considered myself a Marxist for several reasons, including a rejection of historical materialism, the labor theory of value, and the class-struggle origins of the state, I did retain the intra- and interclass conflict perspective stressed by corporate-liberal theorists. Anticipating later Marxist formulations on rival class fractions and power blocs, and their power bases in different parts of the state apparatus, I stressed from 1970 on that the moderates had great access to the executive branch of the federal government and that the ultraconservatives had great strength in Congress due to the conservative coalition and the seniority system (Domhoff, 1970c:351–53). I also noted that there is a liberal–labor coalition that can have influence on some issues, especially in times of crisis and disruption. The liberal–labor coalition, of course, is the functional equivalent of the more reductionistic emphasis of many Marxists on blue-collar workers in generating class conflict. The viewpoint is best summarized in this quote from a formulation in the late 1970s:

> The leanings of the moderate conservatives usually determine the outcome of any policy struggle. If the CFR-CED [Council on Foreign Relations-Committee for Economic Development] wing of the power elite decides to go in the direction of change, it develops a plan or modifies a plan already developed by the liberals and labor, and then enlists the support of liberals, organized labor, and minority group organizations. If the CFR-CED wing decides there is no need for any policy changes, which means it is in agreement with the ultraconser-

vative wing and the power elite is united, then it sits by silently while the ultraconservatives destroy within Congress any suggestions put forth by liberals or labor. In short, the liberal-labor coalition is rarely successful without at least the tacit support of the moderate conservatives within the power elite. The ultraconservatives, on the other hand, are not helpless without the moderates. Due to their strength in Congress, they are often able to delay or alter the proposals put forth by the moderates (Domhoff, 1979:118).

In terms of Zeitlin's class-segment theory, which I have since adopted and will use throughout this book, I am now arguing that there are four segments in the American ruling class. There is first of all an internationalist segment that includes all those banks, corporations, service businesses, and law firms that have a strong interest in overseas sales, investments, or raw materials extraction. These firms tend to be the largest of American corporations. Historically they tended to be located on the two coasts, but that has not been the case for at least forty years. The views of this segment are expressed by such organizations as the Council on Foreign Relations and the Committee for Economic Development.

There is secondly a nationalist manufacturing segment of the ruling class that is rooted in domestic markets that traditionally may have been more competitive than the markets dominated by the internationalists. This segment is symbolized by the NAM and similar employer organizations. There is at least some reason to believe that the firms in this segment have been smaller than those in the internationalist segment, but they are hardly small businesses or mom and pop stores. Most of the leading firms in this segment have been worth many tens of millions of dollars, and traditionally they probably constituted the great majority of the firms in the *Fortune* 1000, if not the *Fortune* 500 as well. The members of this segment are far more conservative than the members of the internationalist segment, if their testimony before Congress (McLellan and Woodhouse, 1960) and their replies to attitude surveys are any guide (McLellan and Woodhouse, 1966).

Third, as noted in the previous chapter, there is a southern segment of the ruling class. This segment was first rooted in slave ownership and then from 1865 to the post-World War II era in land ownership and low-wage labor (Wright, 1986). Its unique situation and needs lead it to policy positions on some issues that are independent of either the international or nationalist segments in the North. However, until the 1950s it sided with the internationalists on foreign policy issues because of its concern with the export of cotton and other commodities. Since the 1940s it has sided with the nationalists on labor and social welfare issues. It is the southern and nationalist segments that are the backbone of the conservative coalition in Congress. In the new Marxian language, they form a "power bloc" within the legislative branch of the state, but that is something we have been saying for a long time in plain English.

Finally, there is a historically more localized segment of the ruling class that is rooted in real estate and development. Its members are organized into citywide growth coalitions that seek to advance their fortunes by increasing the value of their land (Mollenkopf, 1975b; Molotch, 1976; Stone, 1976). They are in the business of selling "locations." Rival growth coalitions from different cities are in competition with each other to provide the sites needed by other capitalists, universities, and governments. There also can be tensions between growth coalitions and corporations, for the corporations often have the flexibility to move to another location, even outside the country, if local conditions are not made favorable for them. Growth coalitions have an eager junior partner in many cities in the form of the building trades unions, the traditional mainstays of the labor movement. The common interest of growth coalitions and construction unions in generating growth often overrides their class differences. They have worked closely in the Democratic Party in some cities in the North.

However, it is not enough to think in terms of leaders from these four class segments in characterizing the power structure in the United States. We also have to recognize that there are many upper-class families rooted in wealth that has been diversified over the generations into a combination of stocks, bonds, and real estate. I believe that members of such families develop a general class interest. Many members of these families become corporate lawyers, investment bankers, policy experts, university professors, or even politicians in some cases. Put another way, the power elite as I understand it cannot be reduced to "business leaders" or "corporate executives," as Skocpol and others do in caricaturing my work. The power elite is the leadership group of a segmented capitalist class that is also a social upper class, and the interests of that social class are both more general and more narrow than mere "business" interests. That is, the social class has a general interest in class and nation-state power, and there are specific "business" interests for each class segment.

The tendency toward at least some general leaders is reinforced by common schooling and social experiences for families from all segments of the class. Drawing on studies in social psychology, it is my conclusion that social cohesion facilitates policy cohesion (Domhoff, 1974b: Chapter 3). Policy-discussion groups also tend to produce some general leaders. Useem (1984) presents interview evidence that the business leaders themselves recognize that those who lead major policy groups often take a more classwide perspective on many issues.

The power elite at the national level in America, then, is made up of leaders and high-level employees from the three major class segments *and* from the class as a whole. At the local level the real estate segment is represented by city growth coalitions, or what I will sometimes call "growth machines." There are thus forces leading toward both intraclass conflict and class solidarity, and there can be tensions between the power elite and the growth machines. There is the possibility for shifting alliances within the overall power structure on different issues. Perhaps we could call it "pluralism at the top." And of course the tensions within the power elite are conditioned by interclass conflict as well, as will be seen in this and later chapters.

The way in which this theory of class segments and power blocs applies to the

Social Security Act will be shown after I explain why the corporate-liberal view and my closely related work were attacked in the 1970s.

## The Distortion of Corporate-Liberal Theory

Right around the turn of the 1970s, I thought power structure researchers in the Mills tradition and plain Marxists, corporate liberal and otherwise, were on a roll. Our historical and sociological investigations were gaining academic attention, if not exactly acceptance. We had soundly based explanations for regulatory agencies and reformist social legislation that our common opponent, the pluralists, had claimed we could not handle. Although the pluralists were (and are) by far the dominant group in academia, at least they were on the defensive. But the harmony among the challengers did not last long. Conflicts among Marxists created a schism that drew in people like me as the "instrumentalist" and "elitist" scapegoats.

Most social scientists apparently believe that the criticism of corporate-liberal theory began with the publication of Nicos Poulantzas's (1969) review of Ralph Miliband's *The State in Capitalist Society* (1969). After all, the review did say there was a tendency to view the state as a mere "tool" or "instrument" that could be easily and directly manipulated by leading capitalists through pressure on politicians and direct appointments in the government itself. But the review did not propose the structuralist–instrumentalist distinction that became a key ingredient in the attacks and it had nothing to do with work going on in the United States. Nor did the review have anything to do with what Miliband actually said, for Poulantzas—and those who uncritically accepted his claims—completely distorted Miliband's theory of the state, as I will show in great detail in Chapter 7.

The argument against views such as mine actually began in 1971 in a review of Miliband in the American Marxist journal *Monthly Review* by Isaac Balbus. According to Balbus, Miliband was not really a Marxist, even though he claimed to be one. Instead, he was actually an "elitist" like his friend Mills, to whose memory the book was dedicated. Balbus charged that Mills had a theory that leads to a "profound pessimism" and an inability to account for social change (Balbus, 1971:40). The key sentences in this indirect attack on Miliband read as follows:

> Although ostensibly a class analysis of advanced capitalist systems, on close examination it becomes clear that what is being offered is not class analysis at all but rather yet another, if highly sophisticated, version of elite-stratification theory. The result is a static analysis of capitalist societies which shares many of the difficulties in explaining, interpreting, and anticipating social and political change which we have attributed to early elite theorists like Mills (1971:40–41).

Drawing on the work of Poulantzas and Balbus, the theme of elitist pessimism is merged with the idea of "instrumentalism" in a critique made of Miliband and me by David Gold, Clarence Lo, and Erik Wright (1975) as a result of discussions within the Bay Area *Kapitalistate* Group founded by James O'Connor. Saying that instrumentalists are those who merely trace personal and social connections and have a rather crude view of the state as a tool of the capitalists, these authors criticize instrumentalists for not being true Marxists. After saying that instrumentalists have been successful in challenging pluralists, they assert that instrumentalists are in effect just like pluralists because they have

> failed to transcend the framework that the pluralists use. The emphasis, especially in American power-structure research, has been on social and political groups rather than classes [here they cite Balbus]. Furthermore, like most pluralists, instrumentalist writers tend to see social causes simply in terms of the strategies and actions of individuals and groups (1975:34–35).*

Gold, Lo, and Wright also offer an empirical objection to the instrumentalist–corporate-liberal view. It supposedly cannot explain certain reforms, especially those of the New Deal. Even this critique is not entirely empirical, however. It is also a political attack on the pessimism that Balbus decried. My kind of view, they say, denies that political struggles can make a difference:

> On a number of occasions, reforms undertaken by the state were opposed by large segments of the business community, as, for example, during the New Deal. Even when such reforms are ultimately co-optive, to treat all reforms as the result of an instrumentalist use of the state by capitalists is to deny the possibility of struggle over reform (1975:35).

Similar comments are presented in a critique of my work by John Mollenkopf, another member of the Bay Area *Kapitalistate* Group. After stating that "power structure research underestimates the extent to which specific policies are the product of social conflict or are designed to maintain a mass political consensus in order to prevent such conflict," Mollenkopf adds that "the implicit notion that business can easily manipulate the populace at large can have unfortunate and erroneous political implications as well" (1975a:252–53).

Here, in these seeming political asides by Gold–Lo–Wright and Mollenkopf, I think we find the real differences that shaped the conflict between corporate-liberal theorists and the then-young Marxist academicians in the *Kapitalistate* groups. Whereas the original corporate-liberal Marxists were concerned to understand why their many years of grass-roots efforts in factories and communities to create socialism and revolution had led only to liberal reforms, *Kapitalistate* Marxists were interested in cheering on the activists of the 1970s by emphasizing that reforms were possible, significant, and the products of working-class de-

---

*Clarence Lo (1982:434) later graciously wrote that he no longer believed that the label "instrumentalist" applied to me. I have no ax to grind with Lo, whose empirical work I admire.

mands. Not sharing the questions of the corporate-liberal Marxists, the *Kapitalis-tate* Marxists saw the theory as somehow too elitist, manipulative, and pessi-mistic. They thought it was saying reforms were impossible, but it hardly denies the possibility of reforms even if some reforms are "cooptive." Perhaps it is not surprising, then, that Mills, who came to the conclusion that Marxism was a "labor metaphysic," had a strong reaction to those earlier Marxists of this type who alleged there was "pessimism" in his work because he did not see class struggle everywhere he turned:

> Many people tend, often without knowing it, to judge a position in terms of optimism-pessimism, the pessimistic being not nearly so good as the optimistic. Personally, as you know, I'm a very cheerful type, but I must say that I've never been able to make my mind whether something is so or not in terms of whether or not it leads to good cheer. First you try to get it straight, to make an adequate statement. If it's gloomy, too bad; if it's cheerful, well fine (1968:249).

Gold, Lo, and Wright contrast the abstraction called "instrumentalism" with something called "structuralism." The dichotomy was an exegesis of a cryptic comment in an otherwise interesting and provocative book by O'Connor (1973), who had been part of the *Studies on the Left* group for a year or two in the mid-1960s and a friend of several corporate-liberal historians around the turn of the 1970s. After summarizing the corporate-liberal view of how big business dominates the executive branch, O'Connor wrote:

> But the President and his key aides must remain independent; they must interpret class (as opposed to particular economic) corporate interests and translate these interests into action, not only in terms of immediate economic and political needs, but also in terms of the relations between monopoly capital and competitive sector labor and capital. Monopoly capitalist class interests (as a social force rather than as an abstraction) are not the aggregate of the particular interest of this class but rather emerge within the state administration "unintentionally." In this important sense, the capitalist state is not an "instrument" but a "structure" (1973:68–69).

With that brief and abstruse construction, which lends itself to many possible interpretations, the text moves on in the next paragraph to consider ways in which "production relations are expressed politically." In other words, nothing further is said about the distinction between the state as "instrument" and "struc-ture." However, the dichotomy implied by O'Connor's phrasing became a major discussion point in his collectives, as evidenced by a review of his book written by the Bay Area *Kapitalistate* collective (1975) on the basis of discussions with him. The new dichotomy then was incorporated into the article by Gold–Lo–Wright, which was introduced with the comment that "the present paper, while written by three of the members, is part of the work of the group as a whole" (1975:29).

The stage was now set for the views of the various Kapitalistate members to become the new Marxian orthodoxy. The Gold–Lo–Wright article became the basis for a dialectical progression to a higher level of theorizing. For starters there was the "instrumental" view. It had done valuable work in showing the pluralists were wrong, but it really wasn't very sophisticated, at least as I allegedly preached it:

> There are, of course, examples, of instrumental work done at various levels of sophistication. Much of the work of G. William Domhoff, for example, rests almost entirely at the very personal level of showing the social connections between individuals who occupy positions of economic power (1975:33).

It was not hard for people to catch the drift of these slightly coded remarks. I wrote a reply that *Kapitalistate* finally deigned to publish after making me cut its length considerably, but that did little good (Domhoff, 1976). The stigma had been applied. Erik Wright wrote me a letter after my article appeared saying that my use of phrases like "discontent bubbling up from the lower level" and "reacting to pressure from below" in my discussion of the Social Security Act suggested that I had "a less systematic theory of contradictions in the society than accompanies expressions like class struggle, working class, etc." He also appended a PS saying that "you are justifiably pissed at us for the statement that your work 'rests almost entirely at the very personal level of showing the social connections . . . etc.,' " but he never got around to saying that in print.

The crude instrumental view then was contrasted with the structuralist view of Poulantzas, but it too was found wanting. The necessary higher synthesis was found in the work of O'Connor, Offe, and Alan Wolfe, all coincidentally members of *Kapitalistate* collectives. It was a brilliant stroke of self-promotion. Meanwhile, the *Kapitalistate* journal published an article by a German Marxist, Ingrid Lehmann, that chastised Weinstein for "the lack of a Marxist framework" (1975:161). Marxism had been purged of its corporate liberals and the new orthodoxy was in place.

The argument that corporate-liberal theory underestimates the role of class struggle, as well as the independent nature of the state, was repeated in a pair of articles in 1977 by Fred Block, a fellow graduate student at Berkeley with Gold, Lo, and Wright, but a member of the "Socialist Revolution" collective rather than the *Kapitalistate* one. Block described the relationship of the theory to Marxism as "complex," and then argued that incorporation of the theory into "contemporary neo-Marxist discourse" is "harmful to the attempt to construct a neo-Marxist theory of capitalism" (1977a:354). Edward Silva (1978) trenchantly pointed out the many mistakes in Block's claims about corporate-liberal theory, but no one paid any attention. Block's own theory will be dealt with in Chapters 6 and 7.

It was at this point that Skocpol and Quadagno entered the argument, with Skocpol footnoting Gold–Lo–Wright and Block for her criticisms of corporate-

liberal theory, and Quadagno relying on Block and Skocpol. Thus, a theory that
began as an effort to understand why socialism had failed to make any headway
in the United States had become a theory that allegedly does not put enough
emphasis on class conflict and pressure from below. A theory that saw both intra-
and interclass conflicts operating at the same time, but did not chant that fact at
the start of every paragraph, became a theory that supposedly sees the state as a
simple instrument of the ruling class and cannot explain why corporate-liberal
initiatives sometimes fail. In the process, I had been labeled a crude neo-Marxist,
and the longtime Marxists with views somewhat akin to mine had been cast aside
as being tainted by elitist theory and its alleged pessimism.

Completely unnoticed, Mills's work also had disappeared. Whereas his views
had been central to those starting out in the early 1960s, he was rarely taken
seriously by the structural Marxists and state autonomy theorists. Balbus and
like-minded Marxists had done a job on him. He doesn't even appear in the
bibliographies of Gold–Lo–Wright or Block. When Skocpol refers to him in her
book on *States and Social Revolution* (1979), it is for his comments on methods
in *The Sociological Imagination* (1959). Nor does his work on power appear in
her paper on the New Deal even though she comes to the same conclusion he did
about corporate adaptation to and utilization of New Deal reforms. Indeed, her
comment that "capitalists learned to live with and use many aspects of the New
Deal reforms" (1980:199) sounds similar to Mill's claim that "in due course,
they did come to control and to use for their own purposes the New Deal
institutions whose creations they had so bitterly denounced" (1956:272–73).
Only when I decided it was impossible to reconcile differences with these new
theorists did I realize that I too had tried to back as far away from Mills as
possible as the attack continued. I had to reread my earliest work to get my
bearings again.

It is now time to demonstrate the ways in which the misinterpretations of
corporate-liberal theory led to distortions of what I said about the Social Security
Act, and to add the new evidence to the picture.

## The Social Security Act of 1935

My analysis of the origins of the Social Security Act occurred in the context of
my historical account of corporate involvement in twentieth-century reform, with
a special emphasis on the policy-discussion groups and research organizations
that helped to create the new policies and a consensus around those policies. My
starting point was an organization called the American Association for Labor
Legislation (AALL), whose history, financing, leadership, and policy successes I
had discussed in an earlier chapter (Domhoff, 1970c:170–79). To show the
importance of the AALL for social security, I quoted the conclusion from detailed research by the mainstream historian Roy Lubove (1968:207) that this

organization led the effort for social insurance in this country. I then criticized his claim that the AALL was an association of middle-class reformers, which was typical of the pluralist interpretations of social legislation in the 1950s and 1960s.

Skocpol starts more generally than I did. She first places the movement toward social security in the context of the patronage-oriented political parties of the nineteenth century, and she also stresses that there was a "hidden" social security system of pensions to Civil War veterans that took up 34 percent of the federal budget in 1890 and 27 percent in 1900. These factors may help to explain why the welfare state was "late" in the United States compared with other industrialized capitalist countries.

Nevertheless, when she gets down to the origins of social security legislation, she begins where Eakins and I did, with what American experts and business leaders learned from new programs in Europe, particularly in Bismarck's Germany (Skocpol and Ikenberry, 1983:98, 100; Eakins, 1966: Chapter 1; Domhoff, 1970c:158–62). She notes that at the turn of the century there was an "emerging network" of "educated and intellectually cosmopolitan" people from the "upper-middle and upper social classes" who were interested in various kinds of reform, and that many of these people were women (Skocpol and Ikenberry, 1983:99, 104). The emphasis on this network and the importance of upper-class women within it is also a theme in my work (Domhoff, 1970c:44–54, 163–82).

Skocpol and Ikenberry then focus on the AALL as the "chief vehicle" for the social insurance movement (1983:99). They note that the money for the organization came from wealthy individuals, but their stress is on "reform-minded scientific experts" as the people "whose activities sustained the Association" (1983:100). They thus echo Lubove's claim that "the AALL testified to the emergence of the social scientist as an influence in social legislation and reform" (1968:29). What corporate-liberal theory sees as a classic corporate reform group, Skocpol and Lubove see as an organization of experts.

Quadagno starts with attempts to create pension plans at the state level. She establishes that southern plantation owners vehemently opposed old-age pensions because they might help to undermine the low-wage bondage in which African-Americans were trapped. She also shows that pension plans were strongly opposed by most small manufacturers, who feared that higher taxes would hurt them in highly competitive markets. Finally, she notes the handful of welfare programs initiated by very large corporations, thereby setting the stage for her later demonstration of conflicts in the 1930s between large and small corporations over the need for social insurance.

Quadagno does not attach much importance to the AALL. She thinks that emphasis on an organization of experts overlooks the power of corporations inside and outside the state. She describes this corporate power as a "matrix of social power within the state, both in terms of the access to power held by various class factions and in terms of the ability of these factions to shape the environment of decision-making" (1988:100).

Given these differing views on the nature and role of the AALL, it becomes essential to spell out its origins, financing, leadership, and policy orientation so that readers can decide for themselves whether it should be seen as part of a policy network related to the upper-class and corporate community, as I claim, a "third-force" mediator, as Skocpol believes, or a relatively unimportant collection of experts, as Quadagno argues.

The AALL was conceived at the meetings of the American Economic Association in 1905 as an affiliate of an international association for labor legislation. After preliminary discussions among members of a founding executive committee consisting of four economists and a lawyer, it came into being the following year. The original purpose of the AALL was merely to do research on working conditions, write model legislation, and disseminate educational material. Only in 1910 when its headquarters were moved from Madison, Wisconsin, to New York City did it begin its efforts as an active lobbying organization for labor legislation relating to industrial disease and accident, workmen's compensation, health insurance, unemployment insurance, and, later, old-age pensions. Its early motto was "Conservation of Human Resources," but it later added "Social Justice Is the Best Insurance Against Labor Unrest" (Eakins, 1966:97).

The founding members and directors of the AALL were economists, lawyers, and reformers who had been active in a variety of organizations that were housed together in the so-called Charities Building at Twenty-second Street and Fourth Avenue in New York. They included leaders from the National Consumers League, the National Child Labor Committee, and the Charity Organization Service. One author tells the story of a friendly journalist who looked in on a meeting at the Charities Building one day and asked, "Ah, what's this bunch calling itself today" (Goldmark, 1953:69). "In point of fact," writes Josephine Goldmark, herself a part of one of the groups, "this was a meeting of the new American Association for Labor Legislation which John R. Commons had come from Wisconsin to introduce in New York, and which, under John B. Andrews, was soon to make the first American investigation into industrial poisoning, the dreaded 'phossy-jaw' among phosphorus match workers" (1953:69).

The reform network of which the AALL was a part had a distinct upper-class flavor. The AALL itself had such well-known upper-class women reformers as Alice Hamilton, Mary Dreier, Florence Kelley, and Anne Morgan, daughter of the most powerful banker of the era, on its advisory board. All of these organizations, as Irwin Yellowitz makes clear, were financed by wealthy leaders from the upper class:

> Although increasing public support provided the impetus for social Progressive legislation, most of the reform organizations depended upon a small group of wealthy patricians, professional men, and social workers for their financial support and leadership. Wealthy women, including some from New York City society, were indispensable to the financing and staffing of the Consumer League. There was only one labor member on the governing board of the National Child Labor Committee in 1905, and by 1907 his name had disappeared. The

Committee's leading members included many wealthy men from business and banking, as well as professional men and social workers. The New York Women's Trade Union League had substantial support from wealthy contributors. Mary Dreier, who led the League until 1913, and made vital contributions to it thereafter, came from a wealthy, socially established family; many of the other "allies" were also women of leisure (1965:71).

In addition to becoming part of this network, the AALL leaders were careful to position the organization so that it appealed to active employers as well. In particular, the founders were concerned with the National Civic Federation (NCF), the organization with a wide cross section of the leading employers of the day that I mentioned earlier in the chapter as being of special interest to corporate-liberal historians (Weinstein, 1968). The first secretary of the AALL, Adna Weber, the chief statistician for the New York Department of Labor, wrote as follows to a colleague when the organization was being formed:

It seems clear to my mind that the work of an Association for Labor Legislation would appeal not only to economists and to members of the American Political Science Association, but also to the men of affairs who belong to the Civic Federation. To attain the largest measure of success, indeed, I think we ought to make a particular point of inducing manufacturers to join, that is, the class of manufacturers who appreciate the value and need of enlightened labor laws (Lyon, 1952:41).

Not surprisingly then, the AALL drew many of its most visible business supporters from the NCF, whose efforts on behalf of collective bargaining and welfare capitalism will be discussed in Chapter 4. Then too, its first and only major success, the passage of workmen's compensation legislation in most states between 1910 and 1920, was registered in a tandem effort with the NCF (Domhoff, 1970c:196–201). Among the prominent business leaders of the day who lent their names to the organization at one point or another were Louis Brandeis, then a corporate lawyer; V. Everit Macy, an heir to the Macy Department Store fortune and a director of four banks; banker Felix Warburg; and Elbert Gray of U.S. Steel. Its business supporters in later years included Gerard Swope, president of General Electric; Wall Street lawyer and financier Thomas Chadbourne, who was president from 1920 to 1926 and gave $10,000 a year over a three-year period; textile executive Robert Amory of Boston; copper magnate Samuel Lewisohn, who served as president from 1927 to 1928; and Morris Leeds of Leeds and Northrup in Philadelphia.

The AALL also did fund-raising in business circles. Its modest budgets of $20,000 to $70,000 per year, which paid for meetings, travel, publications, and the salary of secretary Andrews, were raised primarily from a few donors of anywhere from $500 to $5,000 (Yellowitz, 1965:72–73). John D. Rockefeller, Jr., Charles M. Cabot of the Boston Cabot family, and Bernard Baruch were among these donors. Foundation gifts came from Carnegie, Milbank, and Russell Sage at one point or another (Pierce, 1953:36–37). Early fund-raising was made easier by the fact that the first treasurer was Isaac N. Seligman, scion of one of the most successful investment banking families in America and the head of J. and W. Seligman & Co.

The business leaders and donors were not mere figureheads, and the relationship between some of them and the organization was not always smooth. For example, Rockefeller backed off from his small donations because he thought the AALL's stance toward labor was too positive (Brents, 1989:31–32). In January 1914, P. Tecumseh Sherman, a leading corporation lawyer of the day, resigned from the sickness insurance committee because of disagreements over whether such insurance should be compulsory (Arluck, 1974:48). Sometimes business leaders put direct pressure on the organization to lobby for particular legislation (1974:52). At the least, then, business leaders played an active role in encouraging some programs and discouraging others (cf. Brents, 1989).

Still, the organization included many middle-class liberals and even a few socialists, and I said so in the first paragraph of my first analysis of the AALL (Domhoff, 1970c:170). There were also several labor leaders in the years between 1907 and 1915, but they were not very active and finally dropped out because of their antistatist, voluntarist orientation. AALL leaders were not very successful in urging them to support labor legislation (Yellowitz, 1965:55). Later, some of the liberal members dropped out because of the AALL's narrow emphasis on business-oriented unemployment insurance and old-age pensions (Brents, 1989:41–43).

The bulk of the bill writing and lobbying by the AALL was done by the handful of economist members, most of whom taught at Yale, Columbia, or the University of Wisconsin. However, this does not necessarily mean, as Skocpol implies, that there was a gap between the upper-class members and the experts, for some of these experts were from the upper class. Edwin R. A. Seligman of Columbia University, for example, was the brother of Isaac Seligman. Henry W. Farnam, an economist at Yale who served as president of the AALL from 1907 to 1909, was from a wealthy New Haven family and provided major financial support as well as advice to the organization. Frank Taussig, an economist at Harvard, was from an upper-class family in St. Louis. Richard Ely, the founding president, who taught first at Johns Hopkins and then at Wisconsin, came from a large and successful extended family with about 100 graduates of Yale at the time (Ely, 1938:19), although his own parents were of modest means and he had to rely on relatives and friends for support and loans (1938:24, 36).

But the most important economist in the organization, and the one who provides an ideal example of the "expert" in the Progressive Era, John R. Commons, was far from being upper-class. He prided himself on his humble Hoosier origins. After completing undergraduate work at Oberlin in 1888 at the age of 26, he trained as an economist at Johns Hopkins under Ely, but did not earn a degree. During the 1890s he worked as a professor in a series of short-term jobs as well as doing investigatory work and reform advocacy. Commons was a freethinker who was radical of mind but cautious and practical of spirit. He told the chancellor at Syracuse University in 1895 that he was a "socialist, a single-taxer, a free-silverite, a greenbacker, a municipal-ownerist, a member of the Congregational Church" (Commons, 1934:53). He abandoned most of these views a few years later, but not the willingness to take new and independent positions that often annoyed or alienated old friends.

After his sociology position was abolished by the trustees at Syracuse in 1899, Commons moved to New York to do studies for a small research bureau, and then in 1902 he became an employee of the NCF. His investigations and work as a labor mediator for the NCF brought him into close contact with business leaders, who admired his empirical bent. He was so popular with at least some of the capitalists at the Federation that they paid half of his salary when his former teacher Ely brought him to Wisconsin. As Commons explained:

> I came to the University in 1904 at the same salary, $3,000, which I had been getting from the Civic Federation. That was all I was worth, and even more than I was worth to the University. The University paid only one-half of it; Professor Ely raised the other half from donations by private capitalists. The latter thought, perhaps, that I might be worth what the Civic Federation, another association of capitalists, was paying me (1934:133).

A few years later, upon returning to the University of Wisconsin after two years with the Wisconsin Industrial Commission, a wealthy friend from NCF days, Charles R. Crane of the Crane Company plumbing fixtures fortune, provided him with an extra $1,000 a year in salary and $1,500 for a secretary and miscellaneous expenses (1934:164). Commons does not mention the other capitalists who helped pay his salary, but he does list the names of the men who gave him $30,000 to support his multivolumed study of labor history. They are worth a quick rundown to give a flavor of the kind of men who were part of the NCF at the time (1934:135–37):

- State Senator William H. Hatton of Wisconsin is described by Commons as a wealthy lumberman.
- V. Everit Macy was a member of the executive committee of the NCF and later its president. He served as the treasurer of the AALL from 1910 to 1913. In 1912 he was a director of City Club Realty Company, Mechanics and Metals National Bank, Union Trust Company, Seamans Savings Bank, Federal Light and Power Company, Albany and Southern Railroad, and Provident Loan Society.
- Charles R. Crane of Chicago became president of the family pipe company in 1912 at the age of 54 after serving as a vice president for many years. He was a director of the National Bank of the Republic and a member of the American Economic Association.
- R. Fulton Cutting was a financier in New York as well as president of Tropical Land Company and chairman of City and Suburban Homes Com-

pany. He also was president of the Association for Improving the Condition of the Poor and a member of the American Economic Association.

- P. Henry Dugro was a judge in New York who earlier built the Hotel Savoy and the Hotel Seville, and organized the Union Square Bank. He served in Congress from 1881 to 1883.
- Ellison Adger Smythe was president of Pelzer Manufacturing Company, the largest cotton mill in the South. He was a director of two banks and several corporations. He was a former president of the American Cotton Manufacturers' Association. He lived in Greenville, South Carolina.
- Stanley McCormick of Chicago was a member of the family that owned International Harvester. He served as the company's controller for a number of years and managed his real estate holdings.

A person such as Commons, who was arguably the best-known and most respected economist of the first 30 years of the century, is the perfect entry point into an argument about the role of experts. From one point of view he would seem to be a bundle of contradictions because he was an independent thinker, but worked for capitalists. This may seem contradictory if one assumes that capitalists only associate with "bourgeois intellectuals," as David Plotke (1989:132) does in trying to win the argument against me by innuendo. But it is not at all a problem if we focus on the fact that some experts are of possible use to people of power, as demonstrated by the fact that they have been invited to be in business-supported policy groups, rather than on their independence or the radicalness of their overall stance. From my point of view, it is wrong to think of a person like Commons as a toadie or lackey, but equally wrong to think of him as part of a "third force." The point was expressed very well by Farnam of Yale, who once remarked to Commons, "Curious, isn't it, that you, a radical, and I, a conservative, find ourselves working together." Commons then adds: "It was curious, but good for me during all the remaining years of Farnam's life" (Commons, 1934:139).

It is noteworthy that Commons himself explicitly denied that any "intellectual" could be powerful. He thought intellectuals were incapable of being leaders, and he thought they were particularly detrimental for working people and their unions if they got into positions of power (1934:86–87). The only role for experts was to align themselves with leaders, and then let the leaders make the decisions:

> I learned . . . that the place of the economist was that of adviser to the leaders if they wanted him, and not that of propagandist to the masses. The leaders alone had the long experience of success and defeat (1934:88).

Nor is Commons atypical, as Edward Silva and Sheila Slaughter (1984) show in their detailed study of experts and business leaders in the Progressive Era. Then too, the same type of relationship between a "radical" economist and conservative business leaders will be seen in Chapter 5, which describes how the most liberal Keynesian economist of the late 1930s was hired by a policy group to help with planning for the postwar era. Similarly, the work of Charles O'Connell (1988, 1989) on the Russian Research Center at Harvard University in the postwar era reveals the way in which liberal anthropologists and sociologists worked secretly with the Carnegie Corporation, CIA, and State Department to aid in the Cold War against the Soviets while acquiescing in the firing of a left-liberal colleague who resisted the Cold War.

Brents (1989) puts the relationship between AALL experts and business leaders in a useful perspective by comparing the situation of AALL experts to that of experts whose ideas had little or no appeal to business leaders. She shows that the more liberal experts received little financial support or attention, and that they were not brought into the process of creating the Social Security Act even when some of their ideas had to be adopted because of the enormity of the depression (1989:44–45). Instead, it was the large number of students trained by Commons who were asked to help with the formulation of that act. They were economists who had gotten to know the new generation of upper-class leaders and reformers through the AALL.

In short, the "functions" of the AALL were two. First, it developed a set of ideas for social insurance that were compatible with basic business principles. This did not lead most business leaders to adopt the ideas right away, as the many failures of the AALL show, but it did mean that such ideas were available when the disruption generated by the depression made them useful. Second, the AALL provided a meeting ground where upper-class leaders could sort through experts to find ones they could work with in government. More than this I have never claimed for such organizations when it comes to the place of their experts. However, to claim less is to endow experts with a power base they do not have.

The role of experts will be a recurring theme in the following chapters, and will be discussed more fully at the end of Chapter 6. As a first look at experts as a "third force," however, the AALL does not make an impressive case for Skocpol. It started out to appeal to business leaders, and it was successful in doing so with at least some of them. It became part of a general reform thrust that was not merely middle class. But Quadagno's dismissive attitude toward these experts goes too far the other way. They were a necessary part of the process: for ideas, for legitimation of claims, for day-to-day work in government. Looked at in the larger scheme of things, as Quadagno tends to do, the AALL was not a very big deal, but it is a microcosm of the relationship between the power elite and experts in the United States.

From this point on in this chapter, the AALL will disappear as an organizational force. Skocpol, Quadagno, and I agree that it did not play a further role as an organization, and that none of its plans or members had much impact until the devastation of the depression forced unemployment insurance and then pensions onto the political agenda. Moreover, we agree that the AALL members who played a part in formulating the act did so as individuals. In other words, larger forces now come into play. From my point of view, the AALL had done its job.

After describing the political situation that finally led Roosevelt to act on social security, I followed several standard sources in showing the role played by corporate leaders in shaping the act's general framework (e.g., Witte, 1963; Lubove, 1968). In particular, I noted the important role played by Gerard Swope as a member of the AALL and head of the Business Advisory Council (BAC), an organization of top business leaders from firms such as General Electric and Standard Oil of New Jersey formed in 1933 to advise the government through the Department of Commerce.* However, I also emphasized that Roosevelt may not have needed much persuading by Swope because Roosevelt and his wife had been close to the Charities Building groups for many years and had people from these groups around them when Roosevelt was governor of New York (Domhoff, 1970c:211–12).

In my earlier account, it was a matter of following the standard histories on the details of how the act was formulated in the executive branch. I thought that these standard histories made it clear that big-business leaders and their experts in policy groups were very important in shaping key aspects of the legislation. Most of this influence happened through the AALL and the BAC, but experts from the Rockefellers' Industrial Relations Counselors, Inc., as will be shown shortly, joined with experts from the AALL to play leading roles. Quadagno tells the story in much the same way as I did. She adds information on the BAC's role that I did not have, as do Jenkins and Brents (1989) in more recent work. Quadagno (1984) also shows how the big businessmen lost to smaller businessmen on the nature of unemployment insurance, with big business advocating a national-level insurance plan and small business and the South favoring a plan that allowed payment variations from state to state.

Contrary to Quadagno and me, Skocpol denies that business leaders played a major role in shaping the legislation. She believes that government officials were the central figures and that they frequently overrode the preferences of business advisers:

> The Social Security Act was launched in 1934 and guided to enactment in 1935, by Roosevelt himself and by Labor Secretary Frances Perkins, who had been his Industrial Commissioner when he was Governor of New York. Perkins, in turn, gave the key post for coordinating policy planning and legislative drafting of the Act to Edwin Witte, who had served as Secretary of the Wisconsin Industrial Commission (1917–22) and then as Chief of the Legislative Reference Library for Wisconsin state government (1923–33) (Skocpol and Ikenberry, 1983:124).

---

*The origins of the BAC and information on its membership will be presented in Chapter 4. Suffice it to say here that the directorships of this forty-one-person group extended to a cross section of the corporate community in the 1930s.

The dispute over national-level versus state-level unemployment insurance, which is seen by Quadagno as a battle between larger companies on the one hand and smaller companies and southern plantation owners on the other hand, is treated very differently by Skocpol. She sees it as a conflict between, on the one side, many Cabinet officials, national-level capitalists, labor leaders, and social insurance experts, and, on the other side, local and state-oriented politicians and economic interests. Thus, for her the cabinet-level Committee on Economic Security in charge of creating the program decided against a national system "when interviews with members of Congress suggested that nothing but a federal system would stand a chance of legislative enactment" (Skocpol and Ikenberry, 1983:129). This battle inside government was one of the factors in influencing staff director Witte to argue for a federal system despite his sympathy with welfare capitalist plans:

> Welfare capitalists had always thought of government involvement in social insurance as primarily a way to keep "progressive" employers from being undercut by low-cost competitors—something the Wisconsin plan (for example) was designed to do. Thus, it is supremely ironic that Edwin Witte's desire to protect the state of Wisconsin's autonomy in unemployment insurance helped to bring into being a federal unemployment system in which, once Congress gave the states discretion to unevenly adjust effective business taxes through "merit ranking" provisions, very great possibilities for inter-state balkanization were opened up (1983:128).

But, contrary to Skocpol's implication, these members of Congress were almost surely southern Democrats, and a brief consideration of the power structure of the Democratic party provides evidence for Quadagno's rebuttal that southerners were far more important in Roosevelt's calculations than experts with ties to the Wisconsin legislature. Although the southern Democrats were outnumbered in Congress for the first time since 1915, they completely controlled the machinery of both houses through a variety of devices that had the force of tradition going back at least to the 1840s, and in the Senate they had the filibuster as well (Potter, 1972:18, 53–58). Roosevelt had close ties to all southern leaders going back to his seven years as assistant secretary of the navy in the Wilson administration, and southern delegates had been essential to his nomination in 1932 (Potter, 1972:66). "Certainly more than any other northern Democratic leader" says Frank Freidel (1984:23), "he understood and empathized with Southerners and their problems." A more complete account of the Democrats as the party of the southern segment of the ruling class will be presented in Chapter 9, but these few comments should be enough for now to make clear how unimportant northern states like Wisconsin were in Roosevelt's strategic calculations.

The importance of the southerners in Congress also contradicts one of Skocpol's more general claims about the New Deal. She argues that Roosevelt relied on state and local government to administer many New Deal programs because the national state lacked "bureaucratic capacity" (e.g., Finegold and Skocpol,

1984). But this argument has the causal problem backwards because it does not take the material basis of the Democratic party seriously. The national state lacked bureaucratic capacity in good part because the South did not want it to have bureaucratic capacity (Murrin, 1980). Roosevelt knew that he dare not challenge the southern leaders of the party. Indeed, he failed when he did try to "purge" some of its leaders in the 1938 elections (Brinkley, 1984:101). Any attempt to increase state "capacity" would have been axed by the southerners, just as they had done in the past.

As part of her state-oriented argument, Skocpol also claims that the prior existence of state-level proposals and bills led congressional leaders to favor a federal–state system. However, only Wisconsin had passed unemployment legislation before the federal–state issue was debated (Nelson, 1969:173, 179), and there is no evidence that those states permitting counties to set up pension plans were opposed to a national plan (Quadagno, 1988:122).

Skocpol does not discuss business involvement at any length in her original article on social security. She stresses her view concerning the minor and oppositional role of business more directly and strongly in a reply she coauthored to Quadagno's critique of her work. There she claims (Skocpol and Amenta, 1985:572) that "by 1934–35 virtually all politically active business leaders and organizations strongly opposed national and state-level pensions and social insurance, along with other legislation perceived as 'pro-labor' and/or likely to raise taxes" (Berkowitz and McQuaid, 1980:90–92; Burch, 1973; Hawley, 1975:65–66; McQuaid, 1979; Nelson, 1969:202–203, 217)."

My reading of the evidence on business involvement is quite different, including that in the references cited in the above quote. First, Berkowitz and McQuaid (pp. 90–92) are primarily concerned with the disintegration of the National Recovery Administration. Labor relations are mentioned but not social security. Moreover, just a few pages later Berkowitz and McQuaid document what they see as the great influence of business on social security, particularly on old-age pensions: "The old-age insurance program, despite its unprecedented grant of federal power, represented the acceptance of approaches to social welfare that private businessmen, not government bureaucrats, had created" (Berkowitz and McQuaid, 1980:103).

Second, the article by Burch focuses solely on the NAM and the nature of its leadership in the twentieth century. The only comment it makes concerning New Deal legislation does not suggest blanket business opposition: "Indeed, this [leadership change in the NAM] represented an almost complete transformation of the upper echelons of the organization, and may well have stemmed from the vehement opposition in certain major business circles to the reforms and innovative efforts of the New Deal" (Burch, 1973:102). Moreover, Burch (1980/81:42) later wrote on the basis of his own analysis of the BAC that "there would appear to be a great deal of truth" to my claim that the BAC supported social security, but Skocpol does not entertain that judgment.

Nor do the references in the Skocpol and Amenta commentary to McQuaid (1979) and Hawley (1975) sustain her claim. The McQuaid citation says that liberal members of the BAC "could not restrain their more conservative peers from opposing legislation (such as the Social Security Act's provisions for old-age pensions and unemployment insurance) which they themselves favored" (1979:701), but McQuaid also reports that the BAC as a whole supported the act. As for the Hawley reference, it only says that "such fears and beliefs also led most businessmen to approve the deficit financing, work relief projects, and social insurance programs that might have solved most of their problems" (1975:65). His only supporting footnote for the paragraph in which this sentence appears is to four speeches by business leaders that appeared in *Vital Speeches* (1934–35). One of the speechmakers, Winthrop Aldrich of Chase Manhattan Bank, ended up a supporter of the act.

Nelson, in the most detailed history to date of the unemployment compensation component of social security, does indeed say that there was "growing opposition among businessmen to unemployment insurance" in 1934 and 1935, but he does so in the context of a book that shows strong business involvement in the shaping of the program. For example, even a committee of the Chamber of Commerce of the United States supported the unemployment portion of the legislation in a report issued in March 1935. When Nelson discusses the all-out attack on the Roosevelt program by delegates to a national chamber meeting in early May of that year, he also points out that "the Business Advisory and Planning Council, including many leading New Emphasis employers, called on Roosevelt to reject the stand of the chamber" (1969:202, 214, 217).

Arthur Altmeyer, whose history of the Social Security Act carries some weight because he was the overseer of the legislative struggle as an assistant secretary of labor at the time, did not see the business community as overwhelmingly opposed to the act. Instead, he saw the business community as "divided" along the following lines:

> Employers's groups were divided in their attitude toward the proposed legislation. The employers who were members of the advisory council to the Committee on Economic Security, most of whom were also members of the Business Advisory Council of the Department of Commerce, favored the program. The United States Chamber of Commerce and the National Retail Dry Goods Association also supported the program. However, the National Association of Manufacturers, the National Metal Trades Association, the National Publishers Association, the Connecticut Manufacturers Association, the Illinois Manufacturers Association, and the Ohio Chamber of Commerce were opposed (1966:33).

Jenkins and Brents (1989) present new evidence on the views of business leaders. It turns out that the NAM actually supported the program at its convention in December 1934, just before the proposed legislation was sent to Congress. Jenkins and Brents argue that the NAM debate over the issue probably was based on a good understanding of the proposals because three NAM leaders were

BAC members. Only in 1935 did NAM change its mind as part of its general disenchantment with the Roosevelt administration.

I believe that Skocpol mistakenly confuses discontent over New Deal labor and business regulation policies with alleged discontent over social security. As Robert M. Collins later wrote in an independent assessment of the issue that I see as consonant with my view: "Yet, even amid the squabbling and criticism there existed some significant areas of agreement between the BAC and the New Deal. The council was the staunchest advocate within the business community of a social security system" (Collins, 1981:61). Skocpol also misunderstands the timing of defections from the BAC in relation to social security legislation. According to Skocpol:

> Of course, at this stage of the New Deal, most capitalists were feuding with the Roosevelt Administration. The BAC had only liberal welfare-capitalists left in its diminished ranks. But these are the "farsighted vanguard" capitalists often cited by neo-Marxists as the shapers of Social Security (Skocpol and Ikenberry, 1983:143).

As a matter of fact, "most capitalists" did not begin to feud with the Roosevelt administration until late in the spring of 1935, when the Social Security Act had been formulated and acted on favorably in the House. Up until that point, the main big-business defections had been the du Ponts and their business associates, who formed the American Liberty League in the fall of 1934. Most of them were Democrats who had favored their friend Al Smith for the presidential nomination in 1932. As for the six or seven defections from the BAC to which Skocpol's quote alludes, they began in late June 1935 and did not involve the Social Security Act. Instead, BAC anger was directed toward the National Labor Relations Act, which it did heartily oppose, and toward proposed legislation on public utility holding companies (*New York Times,* 1935c:5; 1935d:2; 1935e:29; 1935g:11).

The actual relation between the BAC and the Roosevelt administration in the spring of 1935 concerning the Social Security Act can be seen in the aforementioned action that BAC leaders took following the bitter attack launched by chamber delegates at their annual meeting in May. In the face of a rejection of all New Deal legislation by these delegates, including the previous chamber endorsement of the Social Security Act, BAC leaders quickly assembled for a meeting with Roosevelt at which they gave their support to the extension of the National Recovery Administration and to social security legislation. According to the front-page story in *The New York Times,* which appeared under the heading "Business Advisors Uphold the President," the 22 corporate executives in the delegation included such figures as Henry I. Harriman, outgoing president of the Chamber of Commerce; Robert L. Lund, president of Lambert Pharmaceuticals and the NAM; and Winthrop W. Aldrich, president of the Chase

Manhattan Bank and a prominent member of the Rockefeller clan by marriage (*New York Times,* 1935b:1).

I believe the evidence presented in the preceding paragraphs demonstrates considerable corporate support for the Social Security Act. But it does not demonstrate that corporate leaders actually played a role in shaping the act. To accomplish this task, it is necessary to look more closely at historical accounts concerning the two key features of the act, old-age pensions and unemployment compensation, in the context of an advisory organization on labor issues called Industrial Relations Counselors, Inc. (IRC). A discussion of IRC arises more naturally in the context of the next chapter, for it was a product of capital–labor conflict in mines and factories, and expended much of its energy attempting (without success) to create a new harmony between management and workers. Suffice it to say here that the organization was the creation of John D. Rockefeller, Jr., and was financed by him. Its board of directors included the chairmen of U.S. Steel and Standard Oil of New Jersey. For now, it is my claim that any paid employee of such a closely controlled private organization who also worked on the Social Security Act is evidence for direct business involvement. Employees at the IRC were not exactly equivalent to postwar tenured professors at Harvard or Yale in their independence.

The issue of old-age pensions is the most clear-cut as far as an influential role for business. All studies agree that the key actors were part of business-led organizations and institutes, starting with the AALL, and then moving on to the IRC and the BAC. This point is made most directly by beginning with the staff that wrote the old-age pension provisions. Two of the four, Murray W. Latimer and J. Douglas Brown, were part of the policy network that John D. Rockefeller, Jr., had put together over the course of the previous fifteen years to deal with labor relations issues (Bernstein, 1960:159–69; Scheinberg, 1966:152–69; Mulherin, 1979: Chapter 3; Gitelman, 1988:331–35). Latimer was a direct employee of IRC from 1926 to 1933, when he went to work for the New Deal on railroad pensions. He was a member of the AALL advisory council and a Democrat. J. Douglas Brown was a professor of economics who had been the director of the Rockefeller-created Industrial Relations Section at Princeton University since 1926. He was very close to the IRC group.

The third staff member, Otto Richter, was an actuary for the Metropolitan Life Insurance Company, which gave its public support to the program in early 1935 (*New York Times,* 1935f:29). The fourth, Barbara Armstrong, was a professor of law at the University of California, Berkeley, who had earlier earned a B.A. (1913), J.D. (1915), and Ph.D. (1921) from that campus. She taught in several capacities in the law school from 1919 to 1929 and then as professor of law from 1929 until her retirement in 1957. She wrote a book on social security in 1932 entitled *Ensuring the Essentials.*

Witte, the AALL member from Wisconsin, to whom so much emphasis is given by Skocpol, demonstrates the large role of the IRC in a book written in 1936, when his experience as executive director of the Committee on Economic Security "was still fresh in his mind" (1963:xi). It is based on a daily diary that he kept for his own guidance during the drafting of the legislation:

> It was agreed by everyone consulted that the best person in the field was Murray W. Latimer, who was unavailable because he was chairman of the Railroad Retirement Board. Latimer, however, served the committee as chairman of the Committee on Old Age Security of the Technical Board, and throughout was in closest touch with the development of the program for old age security. On his recommendation, Professor J. Douglas Brown of the Industrial Relations Section of Princeton University was first offered the position (Witte, 1963:29–30).

When Brown said he could serve only as a consultant due to time pressures, Armstrong was put in charge of the old-age drafting group. The group strongly urged a national-level system on the hesitant Committee on Economic Security, arguing that separate state plans would be an administrative and actuarial nightmare.

According to Brown's account, the cabinet committee was more interested in unemployment insurance than in old-age pensions. He recalled that he and others on the staff were not at all sure that their proposals would be included in the final package. He then claimed that the corporate leaders on the Advisory Council, appointed by Roosevelt to advise the Committee on Economic Security, played a key role in ensuring that the old-age sections were included in the bill. All of these business leaders were members of either the AALL or the BAC:

> The likelihood of gaining the support of the Cabinet Committee for our proposals was still in doubt. At this critical time, December 1934, help came from an unexpected source, the industrial executives on the Committee's Advisory Council. Fortunately included in the Council were Walter C. Teagle of the Standard Oil Company of New Jersey, Gerard Swope of General Electric, and Marion Folsom of Eastman Kodak, and others well acquainted with industrial pension plans. Their practical understanding of the need for contributory old age annuities on a broad, national basis carried great weight with those in authority. They enthusiastically approved our program (Brown, 1972:21–22).

Further support for the importance of business influence on old-age pensions comes from the work of William Graebner (1980, 1982), who argues on a variety of evidentiary grounds that old-age pensions were designed by business leaders and business-oriented reformers to create more openings in the labor force for younger and more efficient workers. One part of his argument involves the labor relations backgrounds of several of the experts who formulated the old-age program. He quotes an oral history from Wilbur Cohen, an assistant to Witte throughout the drafting process:

> The roots of the social insurance movement came out of the work and consideration of the people in the field of labor legislation. Social insurance was to them a form of remedial

legislation to deal with the problems of labor unrest in industrial society which grew out of labor-management problems (Graebner, 1982:25).

Cohen's statement is classic support for the corporate-liberal view. He sees social reform as a way of dealing with "labor unrest," but of course there has to be "labor unrest" before anything happens.

So much for the pension plan. I do not see how business involvement could be more complete and direct unless dozens of CEOs quit their lucrative positions and moved to Washington. The experts involved are also rather clearly business employees in the case of Latimer and Richter and closely tied to the policy network in the case of Brown. Armstrong is the only independent expert of the kind Skocpol talks about.

Turning to the formulation of the provision for unemployment compensation, the relationship between the corporate community and the government was if anything even more intimate than it was on old-age pensions. Once again, the key link was IRC, this time through Bryce Stewart, an employee of IRC since 1926 and its director of research since 1930. Witte described the situation as follows:

> To head the study on unemployment insurance, Dr. Bryce Stewart of the Industrial Relations Counselors, Inc., New York, was under consideration before I became executive director. I felt that he was well qualified for this task, and at once began negotiations to procure his services. It developed that he did not feel that he could leave his position and would consider only an arrangement under which his work for the committee could largely be done in New York, and under which he could use his own staff to assist him. Such an arrangement was objected to by some members of the technical board, but was finally made. Almost the entire research staff of the Industrial Relations Counselors, Inc. was placed on the payroll of the Committee on Economic Security, so that the arrangement in effect amounted to employing the Industrial Relations Counselors, Inc. to make this study (1963:29).

As if hiring the IRC to be part of the state were not enough, the organization was at the same time serving as the adviser to the BAC. It is hard to imagine how experts could be any more tied to business than this.

But despite these cozy arrangements, the IRC and BAC people did not get their way entirely. The national-level unemployment program recommended by Stewart and his staff was rejected by the Committee on Economic Security. This led to considerable infighting between BAC leaders and the government committee. At one point in the process, the committee actually went back to the national-level plan, but then decided against it again. The question is why it switched back.

Skocpol thinks the decision reflects the influence of people such as Altmeyer and Witte of the AALL and Wisconsin who wanted to protect state plans such as had been passed in Wisconsin (Skocpol and Ikenberry, 1983:129). Altmeyer (1966:24) says this claim was made at the time of the argument, and he denies its validity; he points out that he suggested a compromise that would have satisfied both sides. Quadagno believes the switch shows the power of the southerners in

Congress, who said that they would never accept a national-level plan. Jenkins and Brents (1989) argue that the committee feared the Supreme Court would overturn a national plan, as it recently had done in the case of the Railway Pension Fund.

Since later events showed it was southern Democrats who opposed the program, and forced further alterations in it on the floor of Congress, they appear to me to be the major factor in altering the plan. Roosevelt, highly sensitive to the importance of the South to the Democratic Party, also favored the federal–state plan. It seems likely that the Supreme Court decision stressed by Jenkins and Brents would reinforce the disposition toward a federal–state plan. Only the power of Witte and Wisconsin seems unimportant to me on this issue. What we have, in short, is a conflict between two slightly different business plans, with the more conservative one winning out because of the nature of the Democratic coalition and the power of the southern segment of the ruling class in Congress through a variety of mechanisms to be discussed in Chapter 9.

However, even if Skocpol were right, not very much can be made of this "defeat" for the corporate moderates as far as state autonomy theory is concerned. This is because a key business activist on the issue, Marion Folsom of Eastman Kodak, pointed out in congressional testimony that corporate moderates "preferred" the national system, but found the federal–state system acceptable (Nelson, 1969:213).

Skocpol and Amenta (1985:572–73) emphasize the fact that other aspects of the corporate-moderate plan were ignored by the cabinet committee. However, they do not mention that several of these aspects were incorporated in the final legislation by giving individual states the right to deal with them. According to Nelson (1969:213, 218) and Witte (1963:89), this change was due in part to impressive congressional testimony by Folsom and other sophisticated conservatives.

In the end, then, the only real "defeat" on a specific proposal for the sophisticated conservatives came at the hands of organized labor on the question of having employees as well as employers contribute to unemployment reserves. Labor deeply opposed such contributions. Ironically, it seems likely that the business plan that lost was more "liberal" than the labor plan. As Altmeyer (1966:258) knew at the time, it would have been easier to raise benefit levels if it could be argued that employees had a "right" to this money because they were contributing some of it. This was the strategy on old-age pensions, and it worked. In other words, labor was shortsighted on this one and business was farsighted. This mild progressiveness on the part of the sophisticated conservatives is once again support for one aspect of the corporate-liberal thesis, but it is overlooked by those for whom business can do no right and labor can do no wrong. But, to repeat, I admit that the sophisticated conservatives "lost" on this issue in terms of a scorecard on who "initiates" and who "vetoes" (Dahl, 1958, 1961).

Finally, Skocpol, Quadagno, and I agree that there was little outside pressure at any stage from organized labor at the national level. Workers had their "input" as part of the general disruption in the social structure. We also agree that most of the specific pressure was generated by the Townsend movement, which was sweeping the country with its plan for pensions for everyone over 60 years old on the proviso that the money be spent each month. More recently, Jenkins and Brents (1989) have criticized Skocpol and Quadagno for not putting emphasis on the importance of working-class actions through illegal strikes and mass protests, but even they agree that organized workers did not play much of a direct role in shaping the overall Social Security Act.

Skocpol summarizes her analysis as follows. The emphasis is on the role of government officials in responding to the "democratic ferment" created by the depression:

> During the New Deal, Franklin Roosevelt and Frances Perkins, themselves progressive politi-
> cians from New York state, called upon the successfully established reformers of Wisconsin
> to help them fashion politically viable new American welfare institutions within the federal
> system and amidst the tugs and pulls of cabinet officers, outside experts, Congressional
> representatives, and judicial overseers. The new welfare regime was a response to the demo-
> cratic ferment and the popular spending unleashed by the Great Depression. But it was a
> cautious response, determined to be fiscally "sound" in the face of what were perceived to be
> "irrational" radical schemes for social welfare provision (Skocpol and Ikenberry, 1983:140).

My main criticism of this analysis is that it does not go far enough. It does not take seriously the role of business leaders through the AALL and the BAC, nor the role of IRC employees in providing specific provisions of the act. Skocpol, in turn, finds the type of analysis and information presented in this chapter "unten-able" for three reasons:

> (1) treating maverick individual liberal businessmen, such as those who remained on the
> Business Advisory Council in 1935, as 'representatives' of the capitalist class or of entire
> sectors of business; (2) highlighting only the occasions on which such businessmen's prefer-
> ences coincided with policy outcomes and ignoring the more frequent occasions when their
> preferences were ignored, overridden, or simply did not matter; and (3) treating all middle-
> class professionals as if they were witting or unwitting tools of business interests (Skocpol,
> 1986/87:331).

Quadagno sees the battle as an intraclass one when it comes to the legislative process, but she is very much alive to the sense of crisis and urgency created by the depression, the Townsend movement, labor strife, and extremist political organizations. She also sees a mediating role for the state. The following sentences capture most of her analysis:

> National state managers operating within the broad constraints of the economic crisis of the
> Depression were more immediately responsive to the goals of monopoly capitalists, but the
> implementation of those goals was confined within the parameters of a federal system in

which nonmonopoly corporations could exert pressure on local state managers. Since no legislation could pass without congressional support, a "states-rights" agenda served to maintain the confidence of the rest of the business community (1984:64–65).

In her first analysis Quadagno approvingly quotes Poulantzas on how fractions of capital and the power blocs they form sometimes use sections of the state as their power bases. By 1988 she had decided that there was a "tautological element" in Poulantzas's argument, so she switched her allegiance to the German structural Marxist Claus Offe because he "provides a more historically grounded analysis that involves no predetermined vision of the relationship between labor, capital, and the state" (Quadagno, 1988:9). She adopts his view that there are three "tiers" in the political process: (1) political decision-making by politicians and parties within government, (2) agenda setting within a "matrix of social power that shapes the environment of decision-making," and (3) class struggles over resources which shape access to agenda-setting power (1988:9). Within this context, she doesn't find much of a state in the United States. In fact, she no longer thinks the state exists as an "entity":

> Even ignoring the salient fact that different elements within the state structure are influenced by factions in civil society, it is apparent that no such entity as "the state" exists. Such different components of government as the executive, Congress, the courts, political parties, and the state bureaucracy all, either directly or indirectly, influenced the formation of social benefit programs, not infrequently in conflicting directions. While at times the state took direct action to mediate conflicts between capital and labor, the evidence indicates that just as often events in the private sector galvanized the state into action. To the extent that the state set an agenda, it reflected pressures from civil society—often, but not always, those of monopoly businessmen. More typically events in the private sector set limits upon or even determined the course of state action (1988:190).

Either way, Poulantzas or Offe, there is not much difference between Quadagno's views and those of mere American theorists. For example, I do not think any pluralist would object to the concluding sentence of her first analysis: "The state mediates between various interest groups with unequal access to power, negotiating compromises between class fractions and incorporating working class demands into legislation on capitalist terms" (1984:646). The only phrase in that sentence that might be missing from a pluralist summary is "on capitalist terms." Even there, this would be largely a matter of taking capitalism for granted as the social system within which the American state operates. In the United States, policies that are anticapitalist, that is, not on "capitalist terms," are unthinkable except by a few utopians and Marxist academicians. Short of a revolutionary challenge, Quadagno and pluralists are talking about roughly the same thing.

Nor would anybody be bowled over by her enthusiastic references to Offe's three tiers of power, which correspond to the systemic, organizational, and situational levels in American terms (Alford, 1975; Alford and Friedland, 1975). Moreover, Offe's agenda-setting level is the same thing that I wrote about in my

1967 chapter "The Shaping of the American Polity," and what by 1970 I came to call the policy-planning network. Thomas Dye (1976) and I (Domhoff, 1979:63) have labeled the policy-planning network the "decision-making" phase and shown how it feeds into the "law-making" phase. These two phases correspond exactly to Offe's agenda-setting and political-decision levels.

In the most recent analysis of the Social Security Act, Jenkins and Brents (1989) draw on their own original research and the theorizing of Poulantzas to criticize both Quadagno and Skocpol. They think that both fellow structural Marxist Quadagno as well as Skocpol overemphasize the autonomy of the state and that both underestimate the importance of illegal strikes, mass marches, and other forms of disruption. They stress that "These protests were multiclass based, drawing on the unemployed, industrial workers, small farmers, and the middle class" (1989:906). Their general conclusion is that

> The formulation and passage of the Social Security Act was critically shaped by two political processes: a sustained wave of social protest, interacting with electoral instability, that created an elite sense of political crisis; and the hegemonic competition of rival capitalist blocs that responded to this crisis with opposing policy-planning and electoral efforts (1989:905).

Jenkins and Brents would not agree, but this sounds to me like what I thought I said in 1970, although their theory is more detailed and nuanced. But maybe I have lost all perspective. Readers can decide for themselves by comparing their conclusion with the summary of my earlier analysis that I quoted in the introduction to this chapter.

More generally, it seems that there are far more similarities than there are differences among all these rival interpretations. Although my differences with Skocpol loom the largest due to her emphasis on the independent role of the state system, there are points of similarity in our common emphasis on the AALL and its experts, the conservative role of Congress, and the lack of national-level pressure of major consequence from labor unions. I do not want to push my claim about theoretical similarities too far, but I do want to make the point that the theoretical differences are too small to account for the extreme nature of the attack on my analysis. It is hardly "misleading." Nor is it unable to explain why the sophisticated conservatives sometimes lose. It hardly rests on personal connections among individuals. In other words, I believe something more was going on to exaggerate minor differences and create the proverbial straw man. The alleged theoretical differences on the "nature of the state" are far less important in understanding the distortions of my work by Skocpol and Quadagno than the kinds of factors I used to explain the mangling of corporate-liberal theory by the *Kapitalistate* Marxists and those who followed after them. When these non-theoretical considerations are added to the obvious but unmentionable fact that each new generation of scholars, even a radical generation, is out above all else to make a name for itself by stressing its originality, then I think I am safe in concluding that the fate of corporate-liberal theory and my application of a version of it to the Social Security Act will be comprehended someday as yet another chapter in the sociology of knowledge and in internecine battles among Marxists.

We are back, then, to where we always were, attempting to understand the relative importance of classes and class segments that pressure the American state, try to capture parts of it, and vie with each other to dominate it through policy groups, lobbying, political parties, elections, and influence on public opinion. When it comes to the Social Security Act, there doesn't seem to me to be much question about what was going on. It was a conflict within the state between rival segments of the ruling class that were feeling the pressure from the tens of millions of people from all walks of life whose everyday routines had been severely disrupted by the Great Depression.

# 4

## THE WAGNER ACT AND CLASS CONFLICT, 1897–1948

The National Labor Relations Act of 1935, commonly known as the Wagner Act after its major sponsor, Senator Robert F. Wagner of New York, put the legitimacy and force of the American state behind the right of workers to organize unions and bargain collectively with employers. The bill passed easily over the united and vigorous opposition of virtually every employer in the internationalist and nationalist segments of the ruling class despite the fact that it intrudes into the relationship between capital and labor. It was the first and only serious defeat these employers were to suffer on a labor relations issue in the first 90 years of the twentieth century, and historian Ellis Hawley (1975:82) has written that its primary effect was merely to increase the size of corporate labor relations departments, but no amount of after-the-fact rationalization can turn attention from the bitter and sustained opposition to the act by employers before and after its passage. Indeed, it was probably the most disliked piece of New Deal legislation that any elite group had to swallow, and employers did not rest until they reigned in the National Labor Relations Board (NLRB) created by the act through congressional hearings in 1939 and major amendments in 1947 called the Taft-Hartley Act.

The Wagner Act thus provides a challenge for anyone who thinks that power in the United States is concentrated in a power elite and ruling class. However, it is not only class theorists who have a problem explaining the act. As the mainstream historian William Leuchtenberg wrote in his classic work *Franklin D. Roosevelt and the New Deal,* "no one, then or later, fully understood why Congress passed so radical a law with so little opposition and by such overwhelming margins" (1963:151). The mystery is heightened by the fact that the same session of Congress that passed the Wagner Act toned down the Social Security Act, the Federal Reserve Act, the Public Utility Holding Company Act, and the wealth tax proposed by Roosevelt.

Structural Marxists and state autonomy theorists had a field day with the Wagner Act in the 1980s. They immediately took the defeat of the employers to mean that independent state managers, or politicians and their middle-class expert advisers, have greater power over the capitalist class than people like me realize. They gleefully pointed out that I was wrong to claim in 1970 in *The Higher Circles* that the Wagner Act's history was similar to that of the Social Security Act in the sense that some sophisticated conservatives among employers either supported the act or did not oppose it. Thanks to the detailed history of the act by James Gross (1974) and the then-unpublished work of Kim McQuaid (1979, 1982), I had known about my mistake since the mid-1970s, and had commented on it briefly in 1979 and 1983. I also did new research on the subject in the late 1970s and wrote a long chapter for *Who Rules America Now?* (1983a) that I finally cut out of the book, partly because its historical focus did not fit with the format of the book, but also because the analysis still did not seem quite right to me. Finally, after several more false starts, I published a brief amended analysis in 1987 that was a step in the right direction.

The purpose of this chapter, then, is to do the Wagner Act once again, this time with gusto, conviction, and historical depth. I will take on the best of the many new critics and extend my 1987 analysis. Along the way I will explain how and why I went astray the first time, in good part because my method failed me, but for theoretical reasons as well. In saying that I was wrong, I do not mean that I was all wrong. In fact, I think I was in part correct, so I did not abandon my basic theory. The result is that the theory has become more nuanced, particularly in its utilization of class-segment theory.

This final attempt to get the Wagner Act right will be divided into five sections. In the first one I will present my analysis of how the concept of collective bargaining was developed and legitimated between 1897 and the New Deal. I tell this story to contradict those who claim that corporate elites had little or no role in creating the general principles on which the act is based. The conclusion will be that the use of collective bargaining in some industries and the advocacy of it by many business leaders made collective bargaining legitimate in the eyes of Congress by 1935. The great majority in Congress simply could not take seriously the hysterical outcries about the unconstitutional and un-American nature of collective bargaining from manufacturers whose profits had skyrocketed between 1933 and 1935 after several very bad years (Levine, 1988:104–6).

In the second section I explain in detail how business leaders dominated government policy on labor relations between February 1933 and March 1934, that is, right up to the moment when the first version of the Wagner Act was introduced in Congress. I think this account is a necessary corrective because structural Marxists and state autonomy theorists, in their celebration of experts and liberal Democrats, tend to ignore or skip over the direct involvement of businesspeople in the creation of many of the specific procedures that went into the Wagner Act. It is in this section that I explain how I went wrong, for I missed the fact that virtually all employers abandoned New Deal labor policy in the spring of 1934.

The third section looks closely at the actual authors of the act within the labor boards that were the precursors to the NLRB created by the Wagner Act. This is necessary because these people have been characterized as merely bureaucrats, state managers, independent experts, or middle-class liberals by the theorists with whom I disagree.

The fourth section, after disposing of or incorporating rival explanations, presents my new analysis of why the act passed. This explanation involves both an unusual coalition within the power elite and a temporary unity between the craft and industrial segments of the working class. The plausibility of this analysis is strengthened because it also explains the unraveling of the act within a few years after its passage. That is, the alliances within the power elite and the working class that made the act possible fell apart in 1937 and 1938. Finally, in the fifth section I present my general conclusions about class power, class conflict, and labor relations in the United States in the first 50 years of the twentieth century.

Before turning to these tasks, however, it is necessary to introduce the opposing lineup. There have been so many interpretations of the Wagner Act from various Marxian and state autonomy perspectives in recent years that it will be necessary to focus on the three that are the most thorough, most cited, and most representative. Thus, David Plotke (1989) will carry the banner for those who emphasize the role of experts and liberals, Christopher Tomlins (1985) will hold forth for the structural Marxists, and of course Skocpol (1980; Finegold and Skocpol, 1984) will take the field for the state autonomists.

In making these choices, I am leaving aside well-known articles, dissertations, and books by Karl Klare (1978), Daniel Sipe (1981), Stanley Vittoz (1987), and Rhonda Levine (1988) for a variety of reasons. Klare's law journal article, a favorite among structural Marxists, deals with the judicial interpretation of the Wagner Act, which I find peripheral to my concerns with its origins. Moreover, for my money Richard Cortner's *The Wagner Act Cases* (1964) remains the best account of the judicial aspects of the National Labor Relations Act, including its anticipation of Tomlin's emphasis on the act's continuity with previous regulatory legislation such as the Federal Trade Commission (Domhoff, 1970c:221–222, 246; 1987a:169, 173).

The dissertation by Daniel Sipe, completed with the advice of Fred Block, is mentioned only in passing for two reasons. First, it is unpublished. More importantly, its emphasis on the weakness of business in 1935 can be found in Skocpol and its encomium to temporary government lawyers as a "small group of bureaucrats" who "boldly established the common laws of labor relations and defined their own role" (Sipe, 1981:143) is adopted by Plotke in his published article. The Vittoz book fully establishes that no business leaders supported the Wagner Act, and it contains information that I will be using on how a right to collective bargaining was endorsed in the National Industrial Recovery Act of 1933, but it is more concerned "with the economic implementation of New Deal labor policy than with its political or legislative origins" (1987:11).

As for Rhonda Levine's integration of a class-struggle analysis with a Poulantzian view of the state for a new look at the New Deal, it gives over only seven paragraphs to the Wagner Act (1988:134–136). While she predictably puts great stress on "rising labor militancy" in creating the conditions for this "victory for workers" (1988:135), she draws her account from standard sources and adds no new arguments on why the act passed.

In addition to the many reanalyses that disagree with my past analysis, there is one new study which has a considerable amount of sympathy for it, that by Michael Goldfield (1989) from a class-struggle Marxian perspective. Goldfield emphasizes capitalist domination of the state in the United States and the importance of both working-class militancy and radical political organizations in understanding the Wagner Act. He presents a detailed critique of Skocpol's claims as well. Although Goldfield and I differ slightly on how much emphasis we put on liberal fears of organized leftists in explaining liberal support for the act, he is my kind of Marxist, and it is comforting to have at least one good ally going into this particular battle.

I turn now to a brief overview of the three designated opponents in their order of appearance on the scene. Skocpol's first account of the origins of the Wagner Act appeared in her initial overview article on the New Deal. As is her wont, she emphasized the state as the key actor. State bureaucrats inside the predecessors to the NLRB of 1935 teamed up with liberal legislators to create a bigger and better board. Indeed, serving the labor movement in order to expand their board became their meaning in life: "NLRB administrators achieved their entire raison d'être through the spread of unions; they had a natural institutional bias (as well as legal mandate) in favor of protecting all legitimate unions and union drives" (1980:192). Skocpol deepens her analysis in 1984 in an article with Kenneth Finegold. There she explains the growing importance of urban liberals in Congress and the way in which business lost power due to the failures of the National Recovery Administration. She downplays any direct role for labor militancy because unions were not very strong in the early 1930s and the militancy of 1934 had subsided long before the act passed in summer, 1935.

The analysis by Tomlins is classic structural Marxism in every way. Reaching new heights of abstraction, Tomlins divines constraining structures rooted in a "historical homology of legal form and commodity form" as the key to why the capitalist state must sooner or later meet "the needs of the greater capitalist system:"

> Historically, state institutions have escaped political and ideological constraints arising from private capital's strategic influence over investment, output, and employment only in rather exceptional circumstances. Even then, the very form and structure of the state, and of the law which is the state's language, has continued to exhibit an "essential identity" with the essence of capitalism—the securing of profit through the production and exchange of commodities— sufficient to ensure that even those courses of action consciously chosen and pursued by state managers out of institutional self-interest, or out of idealistic concern for the public interest,

courses of action demonstrably damaging to the interests of particular capitalists, will in the long run exhibit an overall bias toward reproduction of the political-economic status quo. Indeed, it is precisely this historic homology of legal form and commodity form underpinning the capitalist state that gives it the capacity to take action which does not necessarily accord with the interests of particular capitalists and yet meets the needs of the greater capitalist system (1985:xiv).

In dismissing my analysis, Tomlins goes so far as to call it "conspiratorial," citing work by Poulantzas (1973), Block (1977a), and Skocpol (1980) as support for this unfair claim, which is about the meanest thing you can say about academics other than calling them plagiarists. It is an old tactic borrowed from the pluralists, and it is especially inappropriate in this instance because it does not acknowledge my chapter-long contrast of my views with self-professed conspiracy theories in the same book he is quoting from (Domhoff, 1970c: Chapter 8). To add insult to injury, his claim about "conspiratorial," a word that should be reserved for the secret planning and execution of illegal actions by a small handful of people, appears in the context of his agreement with Block that the independent state managers at the labor board were out to enhance their position by expanding their bureaucracy:

> My analysis, unlike that of some earlier revisionists, is not founded on a conspiratorial model of political and legal decision making, in which all outcomes consciously serve the interests of identifiable business elites. Nicos Poulantzas, Fred Block, and others [the only "others" mentioned in the footnote is Skocpol] have in recent years convincingly demonstrated the theoretical inadequacies of such an instrumentalist approach, and the material I present here amply confirms, I think, Block's contention that the actions of "state managers"—whether nineteenth-century judges or twentieth-century labor relations bureaucrats—owe quite as much to their concern for their own institutional power and prestige as to the lobbying initiatives of businessmen (Tomlins 1985:xiii).

The most recent entrant into the oppositional lists, David Plotke (1989), is a reconstructed Marxist who has turned away from his previous economistic ways with an equal overemphasis on the political. His article abounds with phrases like "prediscursive," "discursive," "binary choices," and strangest of all, "capitalist auto-reform," none of which is defined. Although he has spent time in the Roosevelt Library in Hyde Park, and read through the records of congressional hearings, his effort is primarily one of adjudication, even to the point that he has mild criticisms for his friends Block and Skocpol, for he knows that they have overemphasized the independence of the state bureaucracy far too much for the New Deal:

> The Wagner Act did not result from an effort to take greater power by a preformed state; it was not mainly the self-serving initiative of state managers seeking to expand their power. Rather, it was a *political* initiative by forces within and outside the state, which had the *effect* of reshaping and extending the state (1989:122, his italics).

Plotke also finds fault with Tomlins because he supposedly loses sight of the overall ideological and political context. In my work he sees a different problem. I allegedly don't distinguish between independent experts and "bourgeois intellectuals" (Plotke, 1989:132), a phrase I never utilize; besides, most intellectuals are antibourgeoisie (Mann, 1975). Ignoring the fact that what I call "content analysis" is the same thing as studying "discourse," Plotke says that I only focus on the personal and social connections among intellectuals, a familiar enough refrain, and then claims that their connections prove little "without a textured account of political discourses and the ways they were shaped and articulated by intellectuals" (Plotke, 1989:132). His specific example involves my comment about the sponsor of the Wagner Act himself:

> Domhoff asserts that Robert Wagner should be treated as an agent of capitalist auto-reform on the basis of a definition of "reformers, politicians, and experts who started by accepting the existence of the emerging framework of corporate capitalism and then attempted to incorporate other groups into that framework." Given the structure of American political discourse, this definition includes just about everyone, and with only slight work on the notion of "accepting," Popular Front Communist intellectuals could be added (1989:132, footnote 79).

Plotke's own view is that "The Wagner Act was passed by Progressive liberals inside and outside the government, in alliance with a mass labor movement" (1989:105). They were able to pull this off because both business and the voluntarist elements in the AFL had been weakened, and the Republican Party had lost its "grip on the national state" (1989:116). "Grip on the national state?" Perhaps this crude instrumentalist phrasing is a mere slip of the tongue that will be overlooked by Skocpol, Block, and Erik Wright. Otherwise, Plotke has risked banishment.

Plotke is deeply impressed with the middle-class character of the people inside and outside the state who pushed for the New Deal. He stresses that they are lawyers, planners, and social workers, and he notes that they have many social identities, and were busy forming these identities even while working on the Wagner Act (1989:118, 120, 127). There is a certain heroic cast about them:

> There were real struggles, among socioeconomic groups linked to class positions, but they were not prediscursive, and were always intertwined with political efforts to make sense out of "objective" structures of class positions. The debates over the Wagner Act were partially constitutive of the economic and political identities and the actions of the labor movement, not a distraction (1989:127–128).

With the contestants now properly situated on the field of combat, I conclude this lengthy introduction with some very specific questions that can be kept in mind in reading through the following sections. Is the account that follows "conspiratorial" about business involvement in the legitimation of collective bargaining and in creating several aspects of the Wagner Act itself, or do Tomlin and Plotke downplay the role of business leaders and their policy groups in establishing collective bargaining as a viable possibility? Are the "experts" involved in this issue "independent" of the corporate community and power elite? Are the New Deal lawyers who played central roles in formulating the Wagner Act in 1934 and 1935 really middle-class reformers or independent state managers out to expand the state? Is Senator Robert Wagner of New York nothing more than an "urban liberal" responsive to his working-class constituency, or is it fair to say that his wealth and his reliance on the AALL and the Brookings Institution for advice link him to the corporate moderates as well? Finally, did the urban liberal Democrats have the crucial power role, or must we give that honor to the same southern Democrats who shaped the Social Security Act to fit their needs?

## The Origins and Tribulations of Collective Bargaining

To hear Plotke tell it, the idea of collective bargaining developed in a diffuse kind of way over the first part of the century. It just sort of happened without any business involvement in an issue of great moment to all employers:

> The Wagner Act's substantive origins were in several decades of Progressive reform experience, and in emergent policy networks, most of which were formally nonstate at the national level. These networks intersected governmental institutions, universities, and professional associations (1989:124).

This is simply too vague to be acceptable, and it borders on the disingenuous to leave out the fact that these networks "intersected" with business as well as with universities, professional associations, and government, especially when Plotke later will claim business to be nonimportant in shaping the Wagner Act.

Tomlins (1985:120) lists out a specific set of precedents, most of which will be discussed in this section, without any hint that corporate leaders were centrally involved in each case. Tomlins also assigns a role to labor relations experts like John R. Commons without acknowledging that they were intimately involved in business networks. As for Skocpol, she makes no judgments on these matters. Her historical concerns are with "the lack of state capacity in industry" (Finegold and Skocpol, 1984:184), not with precedents.

To understand the origins of the collective bargaining concept, the violence and volatility of American labor relations in the last part of the nineteenth century must be emphasized. That era was characterized by constant strikes and work stoppages by workers, fierce resistance to unions by employers, and repressive action against labor militancy by the state. Mostly the workers lost in these battles, but strikes continued throughout the 1890s even though there was a depression from 1892 to 1896 and labor suffered major defeats at the hands of large corporations.

Somewhere around 1897, despite growing strike actions, there began an Era of Good Feelings that was coincident with a round of corporate mergers and the return of prosperity. Some of the new corporations seemed to welcome unions as a possible way to stabilize their relations with labor. Some smaller businesses, especially in bituminous coal mining, now thought that unions that could insist on a minimum wage might be one way to limit the vicious wage competition that plagued their industries (Ramierz, 1978:19–27). Moreover, companies were urged by some of the expert advisers of the day to organize themselves into employer associations so they could bargain collectively with organized labor. Some trade union leaders were among the voices encouraging employers to form their own organizations—on the grounds that such organizations would make cooperation between corporations and labor all the easier (Bonnett, 1921:100–103, 554–557; Brody, 1980:23–24).

The most conspicuous organization to develop in this changed atmosphere was the NCF—the National Civic Federation. Formed in 1900 and composed of leaders from both big corporations and major trade unions, as well as leading citizens from the worlds of finance, academia, and government, it was in effect the first policy-discussion group created by the newly emerging corporate community (Green, 1956; Jensen, 1956; Weinstein, 1968). The explicit goal of the federation was to develop means to harmonize capital–labor relations, and its chosen instrument for this task was the trade union agreement, or what we now call collective bargaining. The hope for the NCF rested on the fact that some of its corporate leaders, and in particular the mining magnate and Republican king-maker from Ohio, Mark Hanna, stated publicly that conservative trade unions could play a constructive role in reducing labor strife and in helping American business sell its products overseas. Hanna, who became the first president of the NCF, claimed that the improved productivity and efficiency that would follow from good labor relations would make it possible for American products to compete more effectively in overseas markets because they would be of both a higher quality and a lower price. In exchange, labor would be able to benefit through employment security and the higher wages that would come with in-creased productivity and sales (Weinstein, 1968: Chapter 1).

Conversely, some labor leaders led by AFL president Samuel Gompers had come to the conclusion that cooperation with the big corporations was both necessary and possible. It was necessary because the experience of the 1890s had convinced Gompers that major strikes could not be won against these new behemoths of the capitalist world, and it was possible because the kind of men who created the NCF had shown themselves willing on occasion to cooperate with trade unions. As far as Gompers was concerned, this was particularly the case with Hanna, who had dealt fairly with striking workers in his mines a few years earlier (Radosh, 1967:6–9). Gompers and his colleagues happily joined the NCF.

The NCF did not hesitate to make use of experts. As noted in Chapter 3, it hired John R. Commons to manage its New York office in 1902, and Commons later claimed that his two years with the NCF were among the "five big years" of his life (Commons, 1934: Chapter 4). He adopted the NCF emphasis on collective bargaining and championed the concept ever afterwards. He also did fact-finding studies and served on commissions concerning labor disputes during his NCF years. Common's tenure with NCF, his close connection to it for many years thereafter, and his direct support from capitalists during his early years at the University of Wisconsin are not mentioned by Tomlins.

The NCF focus on collective bargaining may seem to reflect an equal relation between capital and labor, but in reality it reflects the underlying balance of power in favor of capital. From the corporate point of view, a focus on collective bargaining involved a narrowing of worker demands to a manageable level. It contained the potential for satisfying most workers at the expense of the socialists among them, meaning that it removed the possibility of a challenge to the capitalist system itself, and that point was articulated by the business leaders of the time. Structural Marxists and state autonomy theorists love to deride my view for allegedly making capitalists too farsighted and clever, but they were not so stupid as to miss the conservative potential of trade unions. They fully understood that they preferred unions to socialism or full-time disruption, and they also knew that they preferred craft unions to industrial unions that might encompass all of their work force.

From the labor standpoint, collective bargaining over wages, hours, and working conditions seemed to be the best that it could do. Most workers did not think it was possible to organize a political challenge to capitalism, and they could not force capital to bargain over the production process itself, that is, the organization of work, so they decided to fight for what their power to disrupt had forced the capitalists to concede in principle. In other words, the process and content of collective bargaining is actually a complicated power relationship that embodies the strengths and weaknesses of both sides. Its narrowness shows the power of capital, its existence reveals the power of labor. The point is made extremely well in Bruno Ramirez's study of labor relations in the Progressive Era:

> Only by viewing labor relations as part of the continuing dynamics of capital-labor confrontation is it possible to lay bare the essential historical significance of collective bargaining in the Progressive Era; it was both a result of labor's power as well as a vehicle to control workers' struggles and channel them in a path compatible with capitalist development (1978:215).

Still, it must be stressed that the unionism the NCF leaders were willing to support was a limited one, focused almost exclusively on skilled or craft workers, with little or no provision for unskilled industrial workers in mass-production industries. Furthermore, the corporation leaders in the NCF objected to any "coercion" of nonunion workers by union members, and to any laws that might "force" employers to negotiate. Everything was to be strictly voluntary, although government could be called in to mediate when that seemed necessary. In my allegedly crude and conspiratorial analysis in 1970, I summarized the bargain as follows. It still doesn't sound too bad to my ear, but perhaps I have a tin ear:

> Within the NCF, then, the moderates of the corporate and labor communities got to know each other, and reached a sort of ideological bargain. From the side of capital, the concessions were collective bargaining (but no employer was to be forced by law to bargain), the right to organize unions (but no closed shops), protection against wage cuts, the possibility of gradual wage increases commensurate with increases in productivity and efficiency, and a real voice in the setting of working conditions. The concessions concerning collective bargaining and organizing were important ones for labor, but they were never much more than hopes until they were put into law in 1935, forcing all employers to comply with them. . . . [W]hile it is important to note how early this general arrangement was visualized, it is certainly the case that it was realized in practice only haltingly and unevenly until after World War II (Domhoff, 1970c:224–225).

Within this limited perspective, the NCF seemed to be having some success in its first two years of existence. Leaders in some of the new employers' associations not only signed agreements with their workers, but spoke favorably of the NCF and its work. None was in a major mass-production industry, however, and the new era did not last very long. As unions grew in membership and began making more and more demands, the employers' dislike of unions returned accordingly. In an unusual twist of the dialectic, this hostility soon led to organized antiunionism within the very employer associations that had been created to encourage trade agreements.

Symptomatic of this change, the agreement between the National Metal Trades Association and the International Association of Machinists, signed in May 1900 was abrogated by the employers only 13 months later. This turnabout occurred when the machinists tried to place limits on the number of apprentices in a shop and resisted piece rates and doubling up on machines. It was then that angry employers adopted what David Brody (1980:25) calls a "bristling" Declaration of Principles asserting that "we will not admit of any interference with the management of our business." In this small episode we see rather clearly what the Marxists mean by the inherent class struggle that is built into the capitalist system.

The individual employer associations were heartened in their struggle in late 1902 by the addition of the NAM to the antiunion ranks. Formed in 1896 to encourage the marketing of American products overseas, its president from 1896 to 1902, who was also a founding member of the NCF, had kept the NAM clear of the union question. However, when the association was "captured" by antiunion employers in a three-way race for the presidency, it quickly turned into the largest and most visible opponent of trade unions in the United States, a role it has played ever since for the nationalist segment of the ruling class. In the eyes of the new leaders of the NAM, the battle was between "unionism" and "Americanism," and their successors never have seen it as anything less.

The rise of the antiunion movement caused the NCF to draw back somewhat from its collective-bargaining program, but the policy division between it and the NAM was nonetheless clear, reflecting differences between the internationalist and nationalist segments. The NCF continued to endorse collective bargaining as a principle even if it did not work as vigorously for it. As if to emphasize this ideological difference in a symbolic way, several NCF members supported Gompers in a court case brought against him by leaders of the NAM in a suit involving a nationwide boycott (Weinstein, 1968:49). However, at the same time the NCF began to put greater emphasis on urging employers to install welfare programs in their factories. "After 1905," writes Weinstein (1968:18), "welfare work increasingly was seen as a substitute for the recognition of unions." These widespread efforts were successful in many large corporations and were an important forerunner of the "welfare capitalism" strategy to combat unions that was emphasized during the 1920s.

Despite the counterattack on unions, collective bargaining seemed to work quite well as a moderating influence in the few cases where workers were strong enough to force its adoption. This usually occurred in industries where the capitalists were small and competitive. According to John Laslett (1970), who studied five unions with significant socialist wings in the period from 1890 to 1920, the signing of collective-bargaining agreements was an important factor in bringing even the socialists within the unions into a more conventional frame of mind, just as the farseeing capitalists at the NCF had expected:

> The adoption of collective bargaining techniques had profound and far-reaching implications for the relation between labor and management, especially where such cooperation (as in the garment and shoemaking industries) made a great difference to the worker's security of employment. . . . The notion of contract implies a recognition by the union of its responsibilities for the enforcement of the agreement, which sometimes placed even radical union leadership in the seemingly anomalous position of having to act against its own constituency when the contract was violated by members of the rank and file. . . . The most dramatic effects of this development may be seen in the case of the Boot and Shoe Workers Union. But similar consequences occurred in the coal industry, the garment industry, and the western metal mines (1970:301).

Collective bargaining received further legitimation from the Commission on Industrial Relations, which was appointed by President Woodrow Wilson in 1913 to examine the causes of the industrial unrest and labor sabotage that had resurfaced after 1910. Once again, the effort had a considerable NCF imprint. The nine-member commission consisted of three corporate leaders, all members of the NCF; three labor leaders, also members of the NCF; and three public members, two of whom, Commons and socialite Mrs. Borden Harriman, were members of the NCF. Still, the chairman of the commission and only non-NCF member, a populist-leaning attorney named Frank P. Walsh, led the commission into battles and pronouncements that angered the nonlabor members (Adams, 1966; Weinstein, 1968: Chapter 7).

Although the commissioners could not come to general agreement after hearing hundreds of hours of testimony and debating numerous legislative proposals, the weight of their separate reports favored greater use of the collective-bargaining mechanism. As Commons noted in a report that also was signed by Mrs. Harriman and the business members, but not the labor members, the important issue was "whether the labor movement should be directed towards politics or toward collective bargaining" (Weinstein, 1968:202). Commons went so far as to recommend government advisory boards to mediate capital–labor relations and channel protest into collective bargaining, clearly foreshadowing the kinds of solutions that eventually were tried during the early New Deal.

Employers may have been ambivalent about unions during normal times, but collective bargaining made gains during World War I because employers and government officials wanted to secure the loyalty of workers and guarantee the smooth flow of war production. Dissenters from radical unions and the Socialist Party were promptly clamped in jail. A War Labor Board composed of corporate and trade union leaders, not unlike that proposed by Commons in his report for the Commission on Industrial Relations, was put in charge of ensuring that management and unions reached agreements. The arrangement worked reasonably well for both sides; the craft unions grew during the war period and the corporations made handsome profits. Leaders within the AFL therefore were hopeful that this renewed harmony would continue after the war.

But such was not to be the case except for some railroad unions, which will be discussed shortly. The defeat of a massive strike at U.S. Steel in 1919 sealed the fate of collective bargaining in the ensuing decade. Unions lost strike after strike as employers used their usual mixture of heavy-handed repression, appeals to Americanism, and employee-benefit plans to defeat unionism. Union strength dropped from about 20 percent of the nonagricultural labor force in 1920 to less than 10 percent at the beginning of the New Deal (Bernstein, 1960:84).

Two specific plans of action, the American Plan and the Rockefeller Plan, were used by corporate leaders to combat unions in the 1920s. The American Plan was the same old set of violent antiunion tactics that had been utilized in the past. The Rockefeller Plan called for the election of local employees to talk with management; Rockefeller called the idea "employee representation," critics called it "company unionism." In some cases the American and Rockefeller plans were supplemented by the kinds of benefit programs and paternalistic practices called "welfare capitalism." Although the American Plan was favored by most employers, especially those below the highest peaks of corporate power, the Rockefeller Plan is of greater theoretical relevance because it was a new alternative to collective bargaining with independent trade unions. Moreover, the creators and defenders of his plan are important because they played a role in shaping labor policy in the first years of the New Deal.

The Rockefeller Plan had its origins in the disastrous public pilloring John D. Rockefeller, Jr., received in 1914 for the complicity of a Rockefeller-dominated coal company in the Ludlow Massacre in Colorado, which took the lives of 2 women and 11 children when members of the state militia set fire to tents where striking workers were living. Rockefeller's immediate response was to hire publicist Ivy Lee to guide his public statements and improve his image, but he also acquired the services of labor relations expert McKenzie King, a Canadian who had worked for 12 years in that country's Ministry of Labor. King suggested that Rockefeller create a program whereby workers could elect their own representatives to talk with management periodically on company time about their grievances. King's "Rockefeller Plan" was soon installed in several Rockefeller-controlled companies, including Standard Oil of New Jersey and Standard Oil of Indiana. The plan was based on the theory that there was a potential "harmony of interests" between the social classes if employers and workers began to think of each other as human beings. The stress was on human relations in industry.

In addition to utilizing employee representation plans in his own corporations, Rockefeller and the numerous aides hired by his family took three other steps to further their approach to class conflict. These steps created the beginnings of a policy-planning network for labor relations. First, ten of the largest corporations of the era, including U.S. Steel, General Motors, General Electric, and the Rockefeller oil companies, were brought together in the secret Special Conference Committee made up of chief executive officers and the industrial relations executives. Its purpose was to share information and to coordinate labor policy, although it never was fully successful on the second score. The industrial relations executives of the individual companies met several times a year with each other and once a year with the CEOs. They were kept informed of ongoing developments in the field of labor relations by an executive secretary. The Special Conference Committee, as we will see in the next section, had an essential role in early New Deal labor relations, but I did not know that fact in 1970.

As a second method of furthering his program, Rockefeller and his aides created a public organization called IRC—Industrial Relations Counselors, Inc.,—which figured in Chapter 3 as part of the story on the Social Security Act. This organization employed a staff of experts to conduct surveys and convince other companies of the value of a more moderate approach to labor conflict. According to Irving Bernstein, the firm also was "the pioneer consulting group in the field of industrial relations research and application" (1960:168–69).

Finally, in order to provide the expertise needed to bring about harmonious labor relations, the Rockefeller group started institutes at major universities. The first grant was in 1922 to Princeton University to create an Industrial Relations Section within the Department of Economics. Later, separate institutes were created at several universities, including MIT, Stanford, the University of Michigan, and Cal Tech (Gitelman, 1984a:24). Still, for all these efforts, most employers did not adopt employee representation plans in the 1920s. Less than 4 percent of companies with 10 to 250 employees had plans in 1929, and only 8.7 percent of the companies with over 250 employees had plans (1984a:38). As the 1930s showed, employers only were willing to adopt the Rockefeller Plan as a possible stopgap when unionization seemed imminent.

What makes the story of the Rockefeller Plan relevant here is that it actually represented a step backward from the views of the NCF because it undercut the legitimacy of unions and collective bargaining among sophisticated conservatives. Few members of the NCF had gone so far as to think that government should enforce the right of collective bargaining, but at least some of its members understood that conflict between capital and labor was inevitable, and that collective bargaining was a way of regulating that conflict. The Rockefeller Plan, on the other hand, denied that conflict was endemic, and therefore did not focus on ways of regulating it. Indeed, most adherents of the Rockefeller Plan found any emphasis on regulation to be objectionable, and they were strong critics of Commons and his proregulation students at the University of Wisconsin. Thus, the conflict over labor policy during the New Deal at the expert level involved a dispute between Rockefeller experts and those who agreed with Commons.

However, the one other new development in labor relations during the 1920s legitimated collective bargaining and showed that it was not a dangerous idea. I refer to the creation of a government mediation board in 1926 that dealt successfully with labor disputes in the railroad industry. The law establishing the new board was the result of private negotiations between leaders of the Association of Railway Executives on the employer side and representatives of four craft unions on the labor side. The law was developed in the wake of debilitating conflict that led to victory for neither side. Once agreed upon by the two warring camps, the new law was accepted readily by Republican leaders in Congress who just a few years earlier had roundly denounced the railroad unions. Indeed, they accepted it in spite of protests from the NAM and its close ally, the American Farm Bureau Federation. The law contained "the first explicit congressional endorsement of the right of collective bargaining, thus at least theoretically protecting the railroad employees against employer coercion in their choice of representatives for collective bargaining (Zeiger, 1968:34). At the same time, the law in effect permitted the continuation of attacks by the railroad corporations on the fast-failing, noncraft unions in the railroad industry. Put differently, the AFL unions showed little interest in unskilled workers. As Robert Zeiger notes, "the Brotherhood chieftains were satisfied and showed little inclination to risk their interests for the sake of their fellow rail unionists" (1968:34).

This brief account of the origins of collective bargaining and employer attitudes toward it in the first three decades of the century has several implications for arguments over the Wagner Act. First, it is rather clear, contrary to Plotke's characterization of precedents, that some major business figures were intimately involved in the creation and legitimation of the idea of collective bargaining. Second, employers in general obviously were of two minds about collective bargaining, and that includes some of those who advocated it (cf. Gitelman, 1984b). Third, business leaders knew that they could live with collective bargaining when they had to, as the experience of World War I or the situation of the railroad industry showed. Fourth, they figured that they had company unionism Rockefeller style to fall back on before they acquiesced in independent unions. Fifth, the business leaders believed on the basis of negotiations such as those in the railroad industry that if they had to they could make a deal with the craft unions that would not include industrial workers.

Finally, as Brody (1980: Chapter 2) has argued convincingly, employers had won the day against unionism by the end of the 1920s. They didn't think they would have to use any of their fallback positions. There was no underlying trend toward unionism, no old moles that were slowly working their way to the surface. Collective bargaining was a respectable idea, but not one that seemed very likely to be implemented.

## Labor Policy in the Early New Deal

Even if it is granted that business played a far greater role in legitimating collective bargaining than Plotke and Tomlins recognize, there remains the fact that many aspects of the Wagner Act were developed in the two and one-half years before it passed. As my critics emphasize, key provisions of the act emerged out of the actual practice of labor mediation and negotiation by the government officials who tried to manage labor strife in the early New Deal.

There is much to be said for this view, but the question is how these practices were created and implemented. Who proposed them? How did they get on the government agenda? How did they become legitimate in the eyes of the White House and legislators? On these questions my critics are extremely vague, as always. They usually discuss the origins of the National Industrial Recovery Act (NIRA) of 1933 because it included a nonbinding statement of labor's right to form unions and engage in collective bargaining, but they do not discuss the origins of the first labor board or its procedures.

There is a general consensus on the origins of the NIRA that was designed to bring the corporations of various business sectors into formal discussions with each other and government officials in order to negotiate agreements on prices, wages, and output. The specific mechanism for this activity was the National Recovery Administration (NRA). The only controversial feature of the plan was

Section 7a, which stated the right of employees "to organize and bargain collectively through representatives of their own choosing" (Bernstein, 1970:30).

The plan for the NRA was a compromise worked out by corporate leaders, academic advisers, labor leaders, and government officials from among several proposals that had been suggested by prominent corporate spokespersons and experts from well-known policy-discussion organizations. Labor leaders, and in particular John L. Lewis of the United Mine Workers and Sidney Hillman of the Amalgamated Clothing Workers, had put forth plans similar to those suggested by corporate officials, but there was one major difference. The unions' plan called for the recognition of unions and the guarantee of the right to collective bargaining. Both Lewis and Hillman later took credit for the inclusion of a statement about collective bargaining in Section 7a. Whichever, and it was probably both of them who insisted on it, the exact contact point was economist W. Jett Lauck, an independent consultant who had worked for the War Labor Board in 1917 and 1918, and provided advice during the 1920s to both Congressman Clyde Kelly of Pennsylvania, a friend of the coal industry, and Lewis (Vittoz, 1987:88–90, 195). Lauck could play this role because he was on the small committee that drafted the final compromise from among the rival plans (Huthmacher, 1968:146).

Despite vigorous protests by leaders of the NAM, Section 7a was included in the final bill because it had the backing of a loose network of "proto-Keynesians" who believed that a lack of mass purchasing power had been a key factor in bringing about the depression. This network, led by Felix Frankfurter and Justice Louis Brandeis, the latter a former member of the NCF, included businesspeople in retailing and light industry, labor relations experts from the Taylor Society, labor leaders like Hillman, and, not least, Senator Robert Wagner of New York, who was chair of the informal committee drafting the NIRA. People in this network believed that collective bargaining through unions would help to raise wages and thereby restore purchasing power (Friedlander, 1987; Fraser, 1984, 1989).

In addition to his involvement with the proto-Keynesians, Wagner had very close ties to the AFL. He had argued and won legal cases for it even while serving in the Senate (Huthmacher, 1968:64–65), and his longtime friend and law partner, Jeremiah Mahoney, served on the board of the AFL's little bank in New York, the Federation Bank and Trust, and as general counsel to its insurance company in Washington, Union Labor Life.

The NAM carried its fight against Section 7a to the floor of the Senate, where its amendments were defeated soundly by an overwhelmingly Democratic body. However, its usual ally, the Chamber of Commerce, remained neutral because it had made a private agreement with the AFL that it would accept the collective bargaining provision in exchange for labor's support for the price-setting provisions (Bernstein, 1950:35). Still, the final form of the NRA was far more to the liking of the sophisticated conservatives among its authors, like Gerard Swope of

General Electric, than it was to Hillman or Lauck because Section 7a was merely a statement of good intentions, not an enforceable mandate. The NAM and other trade associations decided to stonewall the prounion provisions by claiming that the law did not outlaw company unions nor designate trade unions as the sole bargaining agents within a plant.

To the surprise of many business leaders, the effect of the new legislation on workers was electric. "Those provisions," concluded Frances Piven and Richard Cloward (1977:110), "were to have an unprecedented impact on the unorganized working people of the country, not so much for what they gave, as for what they promised." The idea of collective bargaining had arrived due to its legitimation and support by the state.

However, only the United Mine Workers, the Amalgamated Clothing Workers, and the International Ladies Garment Workers unions were able to make significant gains under the new law, partly because they were industrial unions that brought all workers in the industry into a single union, partly because the capitalists in their industries were small and competitive. Then, too, some of these small employers thought that unions might be able to eliminate cutthroat competition within their industries by insisting upon a uniform minimum wage (Piven and Cloward, 1977:110; Dubofsky and Van Tine, 1977:173–74, 186). The workers who were defeated in the first surge of unionizing efforts were in a very different situation. They faced large industrial corporations that were well organized into the Special Conference Committee, NAM, and numerous trade associations, and they did so through fragmented craft unions that had little interest in organizing the large number of industrial workers, a problem that will be explained in a later section.

My concern at this point is the immediate effect of the passage of the NIRA. There was so much labor strife and unrest six weeks later that major business figures began to contemplate a compromise with organized labor. The corporate leaders who sought this compromise were members of a unique governmental advisory agency that had been developed in the spring of 1933 by the Secretary of Commerce, Daniel Roper, a former lobbyist for corporations who had extensive contacts throughout the corporate world. It is here that the plot begins to thicken again, for this part of the story is not emphasized by any of the people I am criticizing.

The new advisory committee originally was called the Business Advisory and Planning Council of the Department of Commerce, but its name was soon shortened to the Business Advisory Council (BAC). It had 41 members at the outset, representing a cross section of business and financial executives from all four segments of the ruling class. Most sat on several corporate and bank boards; 18 of the 60 largest banks, railroads, utilities, and manufacturing corporations of the day were linked to the BAC through the multiple directorships of BAC members. At the same time there were numerous regional and local businessmen from around the country.

Although the BAC was a government advisory group, its members were selected by the corporate community itself. Through consultation with the leading policy groups and trade associations, a deliberate attempt was made to enlist "statesmen of business." Among them were several members of the Special Conference Committee, including the chairmen of Standard Oil of New Jersey, General Electric, du Pont, and General Motors, as well as officers of the largest banks, retail firms, policy groups, and trade associations. McQuaid, whose original work on this group is a major contribution to an understanding of the corporate community during the New Deal era, concludes his characterization of the council with the following comment:

> Here, plainly, was a corporate council to reckon with—a council, moreover, whose membership was self-selected; whose advisory mandate was informally and broadly conceived; whose meetings were kept strictly secret from the press; and whose deliberations quite often took place independently of any federal administrative oversight whatever. If a corporate "power elite" existed during the formative stage of the New Deal, the BAC was its headquarters (1979:685).

Gerald Swope, president of General Electric and an intimate advisor to President Roosevelt, was named chairman of the council. Walter Teagle, president of Standard Oil of New Jersey, was selected as chairman of the council's Industrial Relations Committee. Both were members of the Special Conference Committee. One of Teagle's first decisions was to appoint all the members of the Special Conference Committee to the BAC's Industrial Relations Committee, thereby making the secret private group into a governmental body in a way that would be expected by my theory. The secretary employed by the Special Conference Committee was made secretary of the new BAC committee as well. This secretary then wrote as follows to an AT&T executive, documenting the total overlap of the two groups:

> Each member is invited as an individual, not as a representative of his company, and the name of the Special Conference Committee will not be used. The work of the new committee will supplement and broaden—not supplant—that of the Special Conference Committee. Probably special meetings will not be needed since the necessary guidelines for the Industrial Relations Committee's work can be given at our regular sessions (U.S. Senate, 1939:16800).

The first task of the new committee, not surprisingly, was to prepare a report on employee representation and collective bargaining. To say the least, the report was not friendly to the idea of independent unions.

The BAC as a whole held its first meeting in Washington on June 26, 1933, ten days after the NRA was created. Among those in attendance was Hugh S. Johnson, a former employee and associate of Democratic financier Bernard Baruch. Newly appointed to head the NRA, Johnson was attending the BAC meeting to ask its members to form an Industrial Advisory Board to function as a formal advisory group to the NRA. The members of the Industrial Advisory Board would be appointed by the Secretary of Commerce. BAC members accepted the idea, and Secretary of Commerce Roper proceeded to appoint an Industrial Advisory Board that included a majority of members from the BAC (McQuaid, 1979:685–686). The overlap between the corporate community and the NRA was nearly complete, especially when it is added that other top businesspeople came to Washington to serve NRA as "residential industrial advisers" on temporary loan from their corporations.

However, it was not business alone that had an advisory board overseeing the functioning of the NRA. Johnson also appointed a Labor Advisory Board of six members, including Lewis of the United Mine Workers, Hillman of the Amalgamated Clothing Workers, and William Green, president of the AFL. (He appointed a Consumer Advisory Board as well, but its role was peripheral within the NRA, especially on problems of union organizing, so it will not be mentioned further in this account.)

The BAC members on the Industrial Advisory Board hosted a private meeting with the Labor Advisory Board on August 3, 1933, in the first attempt to deal with the increasing labor militancy following enactment of Section 7a. BAC minutes reveal that Teagle opened the meeting by suggesting a "truce" until the NRA could establish the numerous codes that would set price, hours, and wages in a wide variety of industries. He emphasized that he had no complaint with labor's efforts. "It was only natural," he said, "for labor to try to use this opportunity to organize and for employers to resist" (McQuaid, 1979:688). But some degree of harmony was needed so that the recovery process could begin. Teagle therefore proposed that the two boards create an agency to arbitrate the problems that were being caused by differing interpretations of Section 7a.

The labor leaders were skeptical about Teagle's proposed truce, for he also was asking that organizing drives and strikes be halted. One union official countered that he might agree to forego the strikes if the right to continue organizing was stated clearly by the Industrial Advisory Board. Teagle did not like this suggestion. Swope, searching for compromise, then suggested that a small subcommittee of four people, including himself, meet for a short time to see if it could work out a common declaration on labor policy.

The suggestion was accepted, and the subcommittee came back to the full meeting a few minutes later with a proposal for "a bipartisan arbitration board composed equally of IAB and LAB members and headed by an impartial 'public' chairman" (1979:680). The similarity of the proposed board to the earlier War Labor Board was not lost on any of the participants, many of whom had been involved in management–labor cooperation during World War I. The problem of union organizing was left unmentioned, but to reassure the labor leaders, Swope suggested Wagner as the public member and chairman. While there was general acceptance of Wagner, Hillman of the Amalgamated Clothing Workers remained doubtful about the overall plan:

He reiterated his earlier opinion that the "right to organize on the part of labor" should be unambiguously announced as an overall board policy. William Green [AFL] thereupon responded that Hillman's view was as "extreme" as Teagle's proposal to halt all organizing drives for the duration. Where Hillman preferred definition, Green, like Swope, hoped to preserve a "cooperative spirit" by leaving the issue of organizing rights suspended securely in mid-air (1979:689–690).

After more discussion, general agreement was reached on the subcommittee proposal, and the following day it was approved by both the Industrial Advisory Board and the Labor Advisory Board. President Roosevelt accepted the agreement immediately, and announced on the next day the formation of a National Labor Board (NLB) to arbitrate strikes and seek voluntary consent to Section 7a. The process by which this governmental decision was reached is very much like what I have found for many other issues. It reads like a hypothetical example from a textbook on the ruling class and the state in America. Theoretically speaking, sophisticated conservatives, in a compromise with labor leaders, had generated a new state structure and asked that it be put in place, thereby giving collective bargaining and government mediation of labor disputes even more legitimacy.

The three business members of the NLB were Teagle, Swope, and Louis Kirstein. Kirstein was a vice-president of a large Boston department store, William Filene & Sons. The Filene family, one of whose members was on the BAC, had been proponents of liberal business policies for several decades. Like Teagle and Swope, Kirstein was a member of the NRA's Industrial Advisory Board and had been present at the August 3 meeting with the labor leaders. The labor representatives on the new board were Lewis, Green, and Leo Wolman, an economist at Columbia University and an adviser to Hillman.

But why would Swope suggest Wagner as the swing vote? This question is particularly intriguing given Wagner's ties to the AFL and Plotke's derisive rejection of the idea that Wagner might have leanings toward corporate liberalism. The biography of Wagner is silent on the reason for his appointment. All we know is that Wagner was on one of his long summer vacations in Europe when the deal was made and that he had to cut his trip short to come home to his new duties (Huthmacher, 1968:152–153). So we need to take a brief look at Wagner's life and career to see if we can place him sociologically.

Wagner, born in Germany, came to this country at the age of nine with his parents. His father worked as a janitor in tenement buildings. An older brother who worked as a cook at the New York Athletic Club helped pay his way through college at CCNY. The younger Wagner also made useful connections when his brother found him part-time work at the club. He then took the two-year law degree at New York Law School and in 1900 began his law practice with the aforementioned Jeremiah Mahoney. He joined the Democratic political machine at Tammany Hall to augment his law practice (1968:15) and he was elected to the state assembly in 1904 and the state senate in 1908. By 1910, at the age of 33, he could afford a second home on the shore of Long Island due to the great success of his law practice, but doing what and defending whom is not something his biography tells us (1968:22).

In 1918 Wagner was elected to the New York Supreme Court. In 1920 his wife was killed in a car accident and he never remarried. He is described as fairly well off financially in the 1920s by his biographer and he sent his only child, Robert Wagner, Jr., later to be a New York socialite, three-term mayor, and appointed city official, to prep school (1968:44). After being elected to the Senate in 1928, he "quickly resumed in Washington the familiar role as spokesman for advanced social thinkers and reformers that he had filled at Albany" (1968:63), meaning that he was very close to the AALL, League of Women Voters, and Russell Sage Foundation (for his ties to the AALL, see Huthmacher, 1968:31, 39, 62, 72, 73, 79, 81, 110, 174, 263). "No member of Congress makes more frequent use of the research facilities of the Brookings Institution," according to one observer at the time (1968:110). Huthmacher notes that Wagner was so dependent upon these outside experts for his ideas that some people wondered what he brought to the process. Huthmacher finds the answer in a statement by Columbia law professor Milton Handler, who was general counsel to the labor board headed by Wagner:

> First, his ingrained, humanitarian, progressive philosophy; second, his uncanny capacity to recruit good men to do the detail work for him; third, his masterful ability to maneuver bills through the legislative mill; and fourth, and most important of all, his willingness and determination to stick to his basic convictions (1968:115).

In all, it seems to me that Wagner's wealth and policy connections make him something more than a mere "urban liberal," although he is that, too. Moreover, he was part of a political organization, Tammany Hall, funded by the ethnic real estate owners and developers of New York City, and he was close to progressive business leaders like Swope as well as AFL leaders. He was for corporations *and* unions. I therefore stick to my claim that he is a "corporate liberal" in addition to all the other roles that he played extremely well, the heavy sarcasm from Plotke notwithstanding.

From the tenor of the August 3 meeting of corporate and labor leaders, and the composition of the new labor board, it appeared that sophisticated conservatives within the corporate community were prepared to adopt a cooperative stance toward organized labor. It seemed that they might be willing to accept the collective-bargaining solution that had been urged by the National Civic Federation and the Industrial Relations Commission in the Progressive Era, implemented for the duration of World War I, accepted by railroad executives in 1926, and legislated by Congress as a suggested part of the NRA. The presence of Teagle, from a Rockefeller-dominated company, and Swope, from one of the major companies created by the famous J. P. Morgan financial interests, seemed to signal that two of the richest and most powerful business groups in America were now in favor of a more "enlightened" approach to labor strife in the context of a serious depression.

The new board did have considerable success in its first few weeks in establishing procedures and settling several strikes. On August 11, just six days after it was created, it announced a five-step procedure that was successful in ending a strike at 45 hosiery mills in Reading, Pennsylvania. Soon to be known as the Reading Formula, the procedure was as follows:

1.  the strike would end immediately;
2.  the employers would reinstate strikers without discrimination;
3.  the NLB would supervise a secret election by workers to determine whether or not they wished to have a union as their representative;
4.  the employer would agree to bargain collectively if the workers voted for a union;
5.  all differences not resolved by negotiation would be submitted to an arbitration board or the NLB itself for decision (Gross, 1974:20–21; Loth, 1958:228–29).

The crucial aspect of the formula was the provision of secret elections conducted by the NLB. Credit for the idea was attributed to Swope, the most prominent member of the corporate elite who believed that independent unions should be accepted.

However, most of the successes under the Reading Formula were with small businesspeople in coal delivery, laundry and cleaning, clothes manufacturing, and jewelry making. Their businesses were not big enough or organized enough to resist worker pressure and a government board. On the other hand, large industrial employers, especially those in steel and automobiles, refused to accept the efforts of the board:

> Despite its auspicious start, NLB's authority and prestige were sapped in the latter part of 1933 by the fatal lack of a legal underpinning. In October several companies refused to appear at its hearings. On November 1 the NAM launched a vigorous public attack upon the Board. In two major cases in December 1933, the Weirton Steel and Budd Manufacturing Companies openly defied the NLB and brought the agency to its knees (Bernstein, 1970:177).

The NAM attack claimed that the procedures of the board were unfair. It objected in particular to Swope's idea of representation elections, 75 percent of which were won by trade unions from August through December of 1933. NAM even objected to the business members of the board, claiming that "the representatives of the manufacturers are usually chosen from among those who are known from their expression of views to have a strong leaning towards labor" (Gross, 1974:44). The frequently occurring division between the sophisticated and practical conservatives of the internationalist and nationalist segments seemed to be emerging.

The strong opposition from steel, autos, and the NAM soon led to differences of opinion within the board itself, which had been enlarged from 7 to 11 members in October to deal with the heavy workload. One of those new members was BAC member Pierre S. du Pont, chairman of du Pont Corporation, and a member of the then closely knit du Pont family of Wilmington, Delaware. In addition to major ownership positions in du Pont Corporation and General Motors, the du Ponts had a large block of stock in U.S. Rubber and were a strong voice in the NAM.

The aforementioned general counsel employed by the NLB, Milton Handler, remembered du Pont as a person who tended to vote automatically for the business side in a dispute. This was in contrast to Teagle and Swope, whom he recalled as "very, very fair-minded men and they called the shots as they saw them" (Gross, 1974:44). Another member of the board's staff said:

> My experience with Pierre du Pont [was] that when he spent a little time in Washington subject to discussions with us, he would be well educated to the purpose of the act and interested in carrying out its functions . . . and then he'd go back to Wilmington for two weeks . . . (listening . . . to the people in his own organization who must have told him what a horrible thing the whole (7a) idea was) . . . and by the time he came back again, we'd have to go through the whole process all over again (1974:44–45).

These details on du Pont are worthy of mention because he became the key symbolic figure in the split that was about to emerge in the BAC and the NLB. du Pont made his first public dissent on March 1, 1934, when the majority on the board ruled that the union or organization chosen by a majority of the employees voting in a representation election had to be recognized as the sole bargaining agent for all the employees in the plant, factory, or office. This decision, if enforced, would have cut the ground from under one of the major tactics of antiunion employers, who insisted, based on a doctrine called "proportional representation," that they had the right and duty to bargain with their company unions and individual employees as well as trade unions. Although the industrialists' claim was based upon arguments about the rights of numerical minorities and individuals, it was believed by most observers to be a divide-and-conquer strategy that would allow them to avoid serious negotiations with unions. Corporate lawyer Lloyd K. Garrison, who chaired the reconstituted labor board for several months in 1934, later wrote that "I have never yet seen a case in which these arguments were advanced by a *bona fide* minority group generally concerned with negotiating a collective agreement applying to all" (Bernstein, 1950:103n).

Until du Pont's public dissent, the formulation of New Deal labor policy had taken place in much the fashion that might be expected from my other studies of the policy-formation process. Executives of the largest corporations, led in this case by the Rockefeller family and its foundations and think tanks, were organized into the Special Conference Committee and served as directors of IRC.

They were part of a new government policy advisory group, the BAC, and they held formal government positions as members of the Industrial Advisory Board and the NLB. The usual movement of both personnel and policy from corporation to policy group to government was complete.

However, du Pont's dissent, and the more general disagreement on labor policy uncovered by McQuaid within BAC records, signified a breakdown in the consensus-forming capabilities of the policy-planning network. The advice from experts was too diverse, and the conflicts among the business leaders too great. As McQuaid concludes, this failure to reach agreement spelled defeat for the sophisticated corporate conservatives. Top business leaders lost control of the issue to forces outside the corporate community:

> Business Advisory Council members were sure of only one thing. They must achieve a consensus for compromise among themselves—and among larger employers generally. Without such a consensus, the non-coercive mediation, conciliation, and arbitration efforts of the National Labor Board would be unsuccessful, and the Wilsonian compromise worked out between the BAC and the AFL would fall apart. If businessmen proved unable to accommodate relatively conservative leaders like [AFL president] William Green, labor policies would increasingly be made on the streets and picket lines rather than in conference chambers (McQuaid, 1979:691).

Since this failure by the sophisticated conservatives within the BAC to reach consensus among themselves is such a critical point in this story, it is worth pausing to consider why the issue of "majority rule" vs. "proportional representation" gave them so much trouble. I think the answer is a complex one, but I agree with Skocpol (1980:181) that it boils down to the fact that they did not want the state to have the power to help create a fully organized working class. At one level, this concern manifested itself in a desire to protect the company unions that the Rockefeller group had established in its various companies. Even after top business leaders lost control of the issue to Wagner and the lawyers at the labor board, Teagle and Rockefeller employees at IRC were writing to Wagner to urge him (successfully) to write his legislation in such a way that their company unions could persist. At another level, the corporate leaders were committed to proportional representation because it allowed them to deal with craft workers separately from industrial workers, thus maintaining the traditional segmentation of the working class. Proportional representation had been the basis for the agreement between big business and organized labor during World War I, and it had allowed the craft-oriented AFL to look after its workers while leaving industrial workers at the mercy of their employers. In suggesting a similar board in 1933, the business leaders were assuming that AFL leaders would accept the same sort of bargain (McQuaid, 1979).

The first sticking point in the new situation was that Lewis and Hillman wanted to organize industrial unions, so they refused to go along with proportional representation. In particular, Lewis was determined to organize the steelworkers because the steel companies would not allow him to organize the coal miners in the many mines owned by steel companies. These "captive mines," as they were called, left the United Mine Workers completely vulnerable to employers, who almost destroyed the union in the 1920s, and Lewis was determined that would not happen again (Dubofsky and Van Tine, 1977). Hillman also had strategic reasons to support industrial unions. He needed to organize textile workers to protect his clothing workers union.

If it were only a matter of Lewis and Hillman, perhaps the business leaders would have conceded the point on majority rule. However, for them there was a further issue—the growing unity and militancy among both craft and industrial workers. The business leaders simply did not want to see most workers organized into industrial unions, especially unions sanctioned by the state. In their minds the potential for eventual challenges to their usual power and prerogatives inside and outside the workplace was too great. The idea of collective bargaining was acceptable if it was voluntary and involved craft workers, but not if it was mandatory and contained the potential of uniting all workers.

The failure of the corporate moderates not only meant that labor policy would be made on the streets and picket lines, it also meant that labor policy would be decided by the President and Congress. Roosevelt's first reaction to the acrimonious split among his business advisers was to take an accommodating stance toward corporate policy preferences. As a member of the labor board for naval shipyards in World War I, and a participant in the NCF in the 1920s, he was most clearly identified with those within the power elite who favored a conciliatory approach toward workers and an acceptance of limited trade unionism. However, he made several temporizing decisions that encouraged the antiunion forces to believe their efforts might prove successful. This was particularly the case in late March, 1934, one month after the blowup on the NLB over majority rule. At that critical moment he moved jurisdiction over conflicts in the automobile industry to a separate labor board and endorsed the principle of proportional representation. It was a clear concession to the du Ponts of General Motors. His decision meant that company unions could flourish alongside trade unions, thereby undercutting serious negotiations by employers with independent unionists (Gross, 1974:61–62). If there had been any hope of restraining antiunion employers, this decision by Roosevelt killed it.

Even those business leaders like Teagle and Kirstein who had voted for majority rule in the March decision were privately pleased that the President had in effect overruled them and sided with du Pont. They believed the NLB now would fall by the wayside. They were in effect abandoning a government agency they had played a major role in creating. As Teagle wrote to Kirstein in a private note in April 1934:

> Just between you and me and the lamp-post it strikes me that the President's decision in the automobile controversy has put the Labor Board out of the running. I am sure that neither you nor I will shed any tears if such is the case (McQuaid, 1982:46).

However, as McQuaid rightly stresses, Roosevelt and the corporate leaders "reckoned without the determination of the congressional liberals—and the continuing labor insurgency that made such determination possible" (1982:46). The policy-planning network had helped to legitimate an idea—collective bargaining—and create a mechanism—the NLB—that were fast taking on lives of their own. Moderate big business had lost "ideological" control on this issue to liberals and industrial trade unionists. Senator Wagner, New Deal lawyers, Lewis, and Hillman were about to come to center stage to fight for an improved version of the board that corporate leaders had developed and then abandoned.

It is the opposition of even the most moderate of corporate leaders to Wagner's legislative proposals that I failed to comprehend in my first analysis of the Wagner Act in 1970, so it is worthwhile to pause here to explain how and why I went wrong. My methodological approach to policy questions is to search out the institutional affiliations of leaders within the upper class, corporate community, and policy-planning network to determine what seem to be the primary power-elite organizations or temporary committees involved in the given issue. I then study the policy positions of those organizations—that is, I get downright "discursive" in Plotke's terms—to see if those policy positions are similar to what is being proposed by various politicians or enacted by government. In the phrases I used in the introduction to this book, I do both a network analysis and a content analysis, and it is my claim that those two methodologies encompass everything we mean by "power structure research," even when it is done by structural Marxists and state autonomy theorists. By locating the key institutional clusters in general networks of power and then comparing their policy positions, it is possible to study conflicts among groups or classes and to see which group or class had its preferences implemented by comparing its policy statements to what the state finally did in the way of legislation, executive order, or agency finding. It is probably pretty simple-minded, but maybe not quite as simple-minded as Plotke thinks it is.

In the case of the Wagner Act, I did not find any committee or policy group that seemed to represent the sophisticated conservatives, and I only later learned why not. First, the crucial policy group, the by-now-familiar Special Conference Committee, turned out to be a secret one. It did not appear in any of the public records. I did not realize that this group stood behind the corporate leaders on the NLB of 1933, and I did not know that this group coordinated the opposition to the Wagner Act from behind the scenes, working closely with the NAM. However, this explanation is in another sense only an excuse. If I had been a better historian and taken more time to study this difficult case, I would have known that the papers of the Special Conference Committee had been subpoenaed by the LaFollette Civil Liberties Committee in 1936 and published by the Senate in 1939 (Auerbach, 1966). But I learned about these revealing papers too late to save me. Second, I did not find the indications that the BAC was opposed to the act. I did not pay enough attention to the conflicts within the BAC that were made clear in a series of resignations from it in June and July of 1935.

Beyond these two problems, I let myself be fooled by the fact that the majority of the BAC were in favor of the Social Security Act that was moving through Congress at about the same time. As demonstrated in the previous chapter, there was ample documentation in public sources and scholarly work for the strong influence of the BAC on that legislation. In effect, what I did was to generalize from the Social Security Act to the Wagner Act, using the involvement of BAC members on the NLB to convince myself that what Weinstein (1968) had shown for sophisticated conservatives of the NCF in the Progressive Era still held true. I assumed that if the members of the BAC were acting according to theory on the NIRA and the Social Security Act, then they must be acting that way on the Wagner Act, too, only more quietly. I made this overgeneralization because in corporate-liberal theory the lack of public opposition often means tacit consent (Weinstein, 1968:ix). If I had not been so wedded to the general tenets of the theory because it fit so many earlier cases, then I might not have misinterpreted what appeared to me to be the silence of the sophisticated conservatives on this extremely controversial issue.

What does this mistake mean from a theoretical point of view? Does the whole theory need to be scrapped? Hardly. It means, first, that the characterization of the sophisticated conservatives must be amended to say that their views may vary from issue to issue. The lesson is that each situation must be studied anew. Despite their opposition to labor legislation, however, the evidence continues to suggest that sophisticated conservatives will support some kinds of regulation and a wide variety of welfare measures, especially in the turmoil of the Progressive Era, the Great Depression, or the 1960s. Second, my mistake means that a more detailed account of the internal structure of the power elite needs to be developed, such as I am trying to do in this book. In the rest of this chapter I hope to show that a more nuanced view can provide a better explanation of how the Wagner Act was written and passed than any of the current alternatives.

## Who Wrote the Wagner Act?

Up to this point I have shown that collective bargaining in general and the specifics of early New Deal labor policy were developed under the auspices of top business leaders to a far greater extent than readers of my critics might imagine. In this section I am not going to continue with a primarily historical narrative because there is widespread agreement concerning the legislative history of the Wagner Act. We can stipulate that lawyers at the NLB, along with lawyer-economist Leon Keyserling on Wagner's staff, wrote the Wagner bills of

1934 and 1935, and even I can acknowledge that most corporate leaders opposed the act, as I also did way back when (Domhoff, 1970c:243–244).

Instead, in this section I want to focus on the notion that those who wrote the Wagner Act must be understood primarily as independent state managers, bureaucrats out to expand their empires, independent experts, or middle-class reformers. Although there are important differences in emphasis among the three critics in how they understand these officials, their main theme from my point of view is that such people are not part of any power elite.

Skocpol and Tomlins do not concern themselves with the social backgrounds or connections of the authors of the Wagner Act. Having shown that business leaders opposed the act, they focus on these people as autonomous politicians or government bureaucrats. However, Plotke (1989:118, 138) makes much out of the fact that there are no corporate executives or hired experts from the corporate community among them. He cites work by Peter Irons (1982:3–10) showing that New Deal lawyers in general were disproportionately young Ivy League graduates of minority religious backgrounds (Catholic and Jewish).

The data presented by Irons on the subsequent careers of the 82 New Deal lawyers he could trace into later decades looks to me like it contradicts the thrust of Plotke's argument. Two-thirds of them had gone into private practice, mostly with large firms in New York and Washington that sell their knowledge of government to large corporations. Indeed, Irons concludes that "Federal law practice has become a form of taxpayer-subsidized graduate education, with the benefits reaped by corporate clients" (1982:299). This would seem to support a theory of corporate dominance of the federal government, not refute it.

Only 6 of these former New Deal lawyers, mostly from the middle levels of the NLRB, went to work for unions. Another 12 returned to law school teaching or began academic careers at the schools—Harvard, Yale, and Columbia—from which they graduated. Fourteen ended up as federal judges at some point in their careers, sometimes directly from government, sometimes after returning to teaching. Most damning of all for state-centric theorists, only 12 of the 82 stayed in government as civil-service lawyers (1982:299). This is not impressive evidence that these people had any interest in being independent state managers or that they cared about creating regulatory boards or labor boards to advance their careers in government.

But if a few New Deal lawyers were young and liberal, and perhaps Jewish, this certainly did not hold for the men who were important in shaping the Wagner Act. They are hardly the "labor bureaucrats" of Howell Harris's (1985) florid fantasies any more than they are the heroic "intellecrats" and middle-class reformers that keep cropping up in the imaginings of Sipe (1981) and Plotke. Instead, they are staid and respectable corporate lawyers and law school professors for the most part, and several of them are members of the upper class. Plotke has committed the "ecological fallacy" that is warned against in introductory sociology classes by assuming that the generalizations about New Deal lawyers fit the authors of the Wagner Act.

In the remainder of this brief section I want to look at the nine men who played the major roles in fashioning the specific provisions of the Wagner Act. I will note their social, educational, and occupational backgrounds, their tenure in government, and their subsequent careers so that those who do not specialize in the New Deal can get a sense of just who the people are who are being called state managers, bureaucrats, and middle-class reformers. Two served as chairs of the pre–Wagner Act labor boards after Wagner left: Lloyd K. Garrison and Francis Biddle. Two filled the role of general counsel: Milton Handler and Calvert Magruder. Three were lawyers who worked under the general counsel: William G. Rice, Philip Levy, and Thomas Emerson. One, Charles Wyzanski, was the main lawyer in the Department of Labor. One, Leon Keyserling, worked as a legislative aide to Wagner; he was the "holder of the pen," the person responsible for the actual drafting of the Wagner Act (Keyserling, 1960; Casebeer, 1987).

Lloyd K. Garrison replaced Wagner when the NLB was transformed in 1934 into the first NLRB. Garrison was a member of a family that had been upper class since the eighteenth century. His mother was a descendant of John Jay, the first chief justice of the Supreme Court. His paternal grandfather was a famous abolitionist. A graduate of Harvard Law School, Garrison practiced on Wall Street from 1922 to 1932, when he became dean of the law school at the University of Wisconsin. Garrison ran the labor board for four months, then went back to Wisconsin. In 1946 he returned to Wall Street with Paul, Weiss, Rifkind, Wharton, and Garrison, where he was active for the next 30 years.

Francis Biddle was from an "old" Philadelphia family of considerable wealth. He attended Groton at the same time as Roosevelt. He graduated from Harvard Law School in 1911 and practiced corporate law in Philadelphia with the firm that handled legal business for the Pennsylvania Railroad. He was tapped for the labor board by Garrison when they were both vacationing at an exclusive summer resort in New England. He wrote in his autobiography that he thought Secretary of Labor Frances Perkins approved of his appointment because he was so "respectable":

> Miss Perkins liked the idea chiefly because I was "respectable." Our firm represented solid interests, and the country would have a feeling that the appointment was that of a man who had dealt with the practical affairs of business, an experience generally believed to make him "safe," particularly in a position where the diverging conflict between labor and industry was at white heat (Biddle, 1962:7–8).

Roosevelt's personal letter to Biddle on July 11, 1935, expressing his thanks for Biddle's service includes the following sentence: "It was particularly nice for me to have an old classmate in this position of responsibility, and I feel very certain the work of the board has done much to lead the country in the right direction in respect to problems of employment" (Wagner Papers, General Correspondence). "Problems of employment": the upper-class euphemism. Biddle returned to corporate law shortly after the act passed, then came back to Washington as Solicitor General in 1940 and Attorney General from 1941 to 1945.

Milton Handler, the general counsel of the first board in 1933, was the only lawyer employed by that board. He was from a Jewish background. He graduated from Harvard Law School in 1926, then became a professor of law at Columbia University, specializing in antitrust. He knew very little about labor law when he joined the board, but helped formulate some of the basic principles followed by the first board. He returned to Columbia after a year and doubled as president of the Majestic Corporation from 1937 to 1948. This $10-million real estate firm owned a city block of apartments west of Central Park. Handler later became a partner in the corporate firm of Kaye, Scholer, Fierman and Hays, but remained a Columbia professor all his life.

Calvert Magruder, the general counsel for the reconstituted labor board in 1934 and 1935, had an upper-middle-class background. He graduated from Harvard Law School in 1916 and was a law clerk for Justice Brandeis in 1917. He was an attorney for the United States Shipping Board in 1919–20 and became a professor of law at Harvard in 1920. His marriage into the Saltonstall family of Boston in 1925 brought him into upper-class social surroundings. He was vice dean of the Harvard Law School when he took a one-year leave to join the labor board. He returned to Harvard from the labor board in 1935 and stayed there until he became general counsel for the Wages and Hours Division of the Department of Labor in 1938. In 1939 he was appointed to the federal court of appeals. In a law review article he wrote in 1937 on the history of management–labor relations, he scolded corporate executives as follows:

> The conclusions from these laborious studies would seem to be that employees will not submit to a reign of industrial absolutism; that efforts by employers to suppress bone fide organization of employees are bound ultimately to fail and, meanwhile, to provoke the bitterest industrial unrest; that the sooner employers abandon the stupid battle over "recognition," and negotiate collective agreements with labor unions as a matter of course, the better will be the outlook for stabilizing labor relations on a healthy basis; that the policy of the law, therefore, should be to encourage the development of strong labor organizations (1937:1078).

William G. Rice, one of the people who worked directly with Keyserling on both the 1934 and 1935 versions of the Wagner Act, came from a prominent Democratic family. His father was secretary to Grover Cleveland when Cleveland was governor of New York, and was made chair of the National Civil Service Commission when Cleveland became president. Rice was a graduate of Andover and Harvard (B.A., 1914, LL.B., 1920). After serving as a law clerk for Brandeis in 1921–22, he became a professor of law at the University of

Wisconsin. In 1935 he became U.S. labor commissioner in Geneva and in 1937 he returned to Wisconsin as a law professor and special counsel to the Wisconsin Labor Relations Board. In 1939 he was a special legal consultant for the Wages and Hours Division of the Department of Labor, and he worked for the temporary National War Labor Board from 1942 to 1944 before going back to the University of Wisconsin again.

Philip Levy, a graduate of Columbia University Law School in 1933, came down to Washington with Handler, who had been one of his teachers. He was with the labor board in its various incarnations until he became a legislative aide to Wagner in 1937. He entered private practice in 1947, specializing in labor law, arbitration, and foreign claims settlements. He actually fits Plotke's image of an author of the Wagner Act: he was young, Jewish, and somewhat liberal.

Thomas Emerson, who helped with the final version of the Wagner Act, is described by Irons as having "venerable New England Puritan forebears" (1982:235). He graduated first in his class at Yale in 1931 and spent two years as a civil liberties lawyer before joining the labor board. In the late 1930s he became a professor of law at Yale and stayed there ever after, writing important books on freedom and civil liberties. Emerson clearly was young and very liberal during the New Deal.

Charles Wyzanski, the solicitor at the Department of Labor from 1933 to 1935, was a graduate of Exeter and Harvard (B.A., 1927, LL.B., 1930). He was a corporate lawyer with the distinguished Boston firm of Ropes & Gray from 1930 to 1933 and then again from 1938 to 1941, at which time he became a U.S. district judge for Massachusetts. In later years he married into the extremely wealthy Warburg family, served as a visiting lecturer at Harvard and MIT, and became a trustee of the Ford Foundation. When he joined the New Deal he was young, but not very liberal. Moreover, his Jewishness was old-line German-Jewish, and his employment at Ropes & Gray shows that he was not excluded from the inner circles, as some young New Deal lawyers were.

Leon Keyserling, the son of the largest cotton planter in South Carolina, received his B.A. in 1928 at age 20 from Columbia, his LL.B. at age 23 from Harvard, and then did graduate work at Columbia in economics with Rexford Tugwell, who took him to Washington when Tugwell joined Roosevelt's Brain Trust. His friendship with Senator "Cotton Ed" Smith of South Carolina, head of the Senate Agricultural Committee, got him an immediate job with Jerome Frank at the Department of Agriculture, but he joined Wagner a few months later as Wagner's only staff member. Keyserling was very liberal, but he was also a well-connected southern Democrat, which made him an ideal go-between within the Democratic party. In 1937 he became general counsel for the National Housing Agency and in 1948 Truman appointed him chair of the Council of Economic Advisors. He remained an active liberal Democrat in Washington all his life as an attorney and consultant. He was president of his own policy group, the Conference on Economic Progress, in later years.

It does not seem to me that very many of these men fit the mold of state manager, bureaucrat, or middle-class reformer. Most of them were in government for only a short time—their careers are in their professions for the most part. At least four of them can be described as conventional members of the upper class—Garrison, Biddle, Magruder, and Wyzanski. Emerson and Keyserling were young and liberal, but not what we usually mean by "middle class." Handler and Rice were professors, but not reformers, and Rice had many elite connections. Only Levy is young and "ethnic." I submit that Plotke has missed the boat once again.

However, I agree with Plotke about one important matter: these men have to be understood as acting as part of a political current. The question is whether that current is flowing in the power elite or merely the middle class. From my point of view, people like Garrison, Biddle, Wyzanski, and Magruder are members of the power elite as I always have defined it. By their backgrounds and their training as lawyers, they are classwide leaders who are not strongly tied to one or another class segment. Given their status, education, and occupation, I do not think corporate lawyers take a back seat to business executives within the power elite. Put differently, I think Skocpol, Plotke, and Tomlins assume that anyone not a business executive could not be part of a power elite, or at least not a very important part.

But none of what I have said in this section explains the passage of the Wagner Act. Government appointees have to be linked to a political argument before their presence takes on any importance. I will make that step for Garrison, Biddle, and the others in the next section.

## Why Did It Pass?

The Wagner Act passed the Senate by an overwhelming 63–12 in mid-May, 1935; it passed the House in mid-June on a mere voice vote. How could such a controversial measure pass so handily?

The explanation provided by Skocpol is that business lost power with the collapse of the NRA and the election of liberal Democrats responsive to the urban industrial workers who had switched their allegiance to the Democratic party (Finegold and Skocpol, 1984:177, 181–182). More specifically, they "had lost political influence and economic ideological hegemony because of the failure of the National Recovery Administration" (1984:183). Plotke's argument, it will be recalled from the introduction to this chapter, is very similar. Although he does not focus on the NRA, he does say that business lost power with the rise of the Democrats. His explanation also includes the militancy of the working class and the fact that the AFL no longer objected to state involvement in supporting unions.

I think the alleged "loss of power" by business is contradicted by the shape and fate of other legislation before Congress at the same time. If, as shown in the previous chapter, business-oriented conservatives within Congress could play a big part in shaping social security legislation to suit their desires, why was their power less on the Wagner Act? Furthermore, Congress dealt harshly with three other New Deal initiatives that were opposed by business. It altered the Federal Reserve Act so that New York bankers retained some of their traditional power through an Open Market Committee. It shocked Roosevelt by rejecting the "death sentence" in the Public Utility Holding Company Act not once but twice (Schlesinger, 1960:316). Patterson claims that the House was rebuking Roosevelt in this vote because its members were "annoyed at what they considered Roosevelt's undue hostility to free enterprise" (1967:56). Finally, the House made modifications in the proposed wealth tax to the point where Schlesinger (1960:324) calls it a "feeble measure." The Wagner Act, I am suggesting, was a unique piece of legislation even in a liberal congress, and if it is unique then it is not possible to explain it with generalities like "loss of business power." Business did not lose power, as I will show, but rather it lost its usual allies in another segment of the ruling class.

A second type of explanation for the passage of the Wagner Act concerns the disruptive power and radical potential within the working class, combined with the growing strength of radical political organizations and parties. As Goldfield puts it after marshalling a great deal of historical evidence: "Labor militancy, catapulted into national prominence by the 1934 strikes and the political response to this movement, paved the way for the passage of the Act" (1989:19). I think there is much to be said for this view if militancy is seen as providing the context that forced some kind of legislation. Business leaders and politicians clearly knew that the upheavals of 1933 and 1934 were not over. However, I am not as convinced that the radical political groups played a key role except in organizing the new industrial unions. In other words, I am not sure that they were seen as a political threat by either liberals or conservatives.

I now turn to my new fourfold explanation for the passage of the Wagner Act. First and most critically, the Wagner Act passed because it was acceptable to the southern segment of the ruling class, as it manifested itself in Congress, due to the exclusion of agricultural and seasonable labor from its protection. It is quite true that Wagner and Keyserling were responsible for the act and that the large number of northern Democrats in Congress supported it, but they were only able to pass it because they cut a deal with the southerners to remove the great bulk of the southern work force from its purview. Excluding farm labor also made it easier for the Progressive Republicans of the midwest to vote for the act.

Wagner understood exactly what he was doing in excluding the southern work force. He had seen his 1934 antilynching bill die without even getting out of committee. More generally, he fully understood that the southerners controlled the Democratic party and Congress, and that they were not above using the filibuster in the Senate if all else failed, as they did against a 1935 antilynching bill. In a statement that reveals the real story, Keyserling later said that Secretary of Agriculture Henry Wallace did not want to include farm labor because "He was entirely beholden to the chairmen of the agricultural committees in the Senate and House, who were all big Southern landowners like Senator Smith and Congressman Bankhead" (Casebeer, 1987:334). When socialist leader Norman Thomas wrote to Wagner to complain about the exclusion of farm labor, Wagner replied as follows on April 2, 1935, before the bill was voted on in the Senate:

> I am very regretful of this, because I should like to see agricultural workers given the protection of my bill, and would welcome any activity that might include them. They have been excluded only because I thought it would be better to pass the bill for the benefit of industrial workers than not to pass it at all, and that inclusion of agricultural workers would lessen the likelihood of passage so much as not to be desirable (Wagner Papers, General Correspondence).

The second reason why the Wagner Act passed is that it was acceptable to the upper-class centrists and liberals who controlled the executive branch, meaning Roosevelt and such appointees as Biddle, Garrison, Magruder, Wyzanski, and Secretary of Labor Frances Perkins. These were people who believed through long experience in the settlement house movement, the NCF, and other mildly reformist organizations that unions were a safe and sensible method for dealing with workers. I agree with the many analysts who say that unions were not Roosevelt's first choice, but the crucial point is that he was not antiunion. He was not prepared to use state violence to block unions. That is, it mattered who governed at this critical juncture in the labor struggle, for the use of state violence on workers was a time-honored tradition in the United States (cf. Dubofsky and Van Tine, 1977:324). I put the matter this way in 1970 in reaction to Schlesinger's (1959:402) classless analysis of Roosevelt as a mere politician poised between business and labor:

> Roosevelt was not a balance between business and labor, but an integral member of the upper class and its power elite. However, he was a member of that part of the power elite that had chosen a more moderate course in attempting to deal with the relationship of labor and capital. He was a member of the tradition reaching back to the heyday of the NCF and some of the most prestigious members of the power elite (including his uncle, the aforementioned Frederic Delano). While he did not encourage unionism, as his record during the thirties makes very clear, he was nonetheless unwilling to smash it in the way the NAM had hoped to do since 1902. I believe we see here the importance of the ideas developed within the NCF in the pre–World War I years, ideas which Roosevelt encountered as head of shipyards during World War I and as a member of the NCF. When the time came for choosing, he and the moderate members of the power elite chose bargaining rather than repression (Domhoff, 1970c:242).

My point thus far is that there was a very unusual lineup of forces within the power elite on the Wagner Act. Instead of the internationalist segment and the classwide moderates taking sides against the nationalist segment and the south-erners, as is very often the case, the southerners in Congress and the moderates who controlled the White House were lined up against the internationalists and nationalists. I will have more to say on these shifting intraclass alliances when I discuss congressional voting patterns as part of my analysis of the Democratic party in Chapter 9.

However, it was not merely within the power elite that things were different on the Wagner Act. There were also new developments within the northern white working class. Since the 1870s there had been important political divisions between the craft and industrial segments of this class, as convincingly demon-strated in a detailed historical analysis by Gwendolyn Mink (1986). Mink shows that craft workers opposed the immigration of industrial workers from the mo-ment that Chinese workers were brought to California and Massachusetts be-cause they saw the introduction of more workers and mass-production industry as the beginning of the end for their good wages and high status. Instead of trying to fight capitalists by siding with their fellow workers, they decided that their best hope was in limiting the number of available workers in order to keep their wages high. The fact that the immigrants were "different"—eastern and southern Euro-pean, Chinese—only heightened their resolve. Ironically, these attacks on immi-grant industrial workers actually played a role in creating union solidarity at the expense of class solidarity:

> 'Class feeling' fell to 'race feeling,' but race feeling considerably enhanced 'union feeling.' Indeed, the coincidence of episodic booms in the San Francisco labor movement and action against the Chinese suggested to labor leaders that race feeling was an important source of solidarity within old labor. The interaction of race feeling and union feeling encouraged the internal (organizational) development of old labor (Mink, 1986:72–73).

From the outset, then, the craft unions of the AFL were hostile to industrial unions with one or two exceptions, such as coal miners. Very little effort was made to organize industrial workers, and such efforts as were made were calcu-lated to enhance the power of the original AFL unions. In short, this is not a formula for working-class solidarity. The AFL ended up pursuing its nativist policies through the already-racist Democratic party. The Republicans, on the other hand, were proimmigration and courted the new industrial workers. The result was a political split in the working class, with immigrant industrial work-ers supporting the Republicans from 1896 to the late 1920s (1986:155).

Thus, the third reason for the passage of the Wagner Act is that the two major segments of the working class voted together for Democrats for the first time in the 1930s and then worked together for the passage of the Wagner Act. The AFL leaders had some reservations about the act because they knew it would put them at the mercy of state decisions on voting procedures and on the determination of the size of bargaining units, but they backed it even though none of their suggested amendments to the proposed legislation was incorporated (Tomlins, 1985:139–140).

Finally, the Wagner Act passed because Roosevelt had developed an alliance with the industrial segment of the working class as well as the southern segment of the ruling class. That is, the key labor leaders on this issue were Hillman and Lewis, precisely the people who created the Congress of Industrial Organizations (CIO) shortly after the passage of the act. Indeed, several close observers at the time believed that Roosevelt struck a deal with Hillman and Lewis in March 1935 to support the Wagner Act in exchange for labor support for the renewal of the NIRA. The executive secretary of the Special Conference Committee wrote as follows from Washington to his employers in his March 27, 1935, newsletter:

> There is much speculation over the question of whether or not Roosevelt has made a deal with Wagner and the American Federation of Labor, as a result of which the Administration will support the Wagner bill and receive labor's aid for some of its own projects in exchange. People who suspect a deal of this kind had been made point out that Wagner switched his vote on the prevailing wage amendment on the public works bill, and that a few days later William Green and John L. Lewis agreed to the appointment of Donald R. Richberg as head of NRA. For this concession the labor leaders ostensibly received no other consideration except the appointment of an additional representative on the NRA Board. Some people suspect, however, that there was an understanding about the Wagner bill (U.S. Senate, 1939:17017).

The Washington representative added that he was not certain the deal had taken place: "One point against this story is the fact that the Wagner bill was not included in the list of 'must' legislation which Roosevelt gave to Senator Robinson just before the President left for his Florida vacation this week" (1939: 17017). But an economist close to Hillman, George Soule, was confident that a deal had been struck. He reported to liberals and leftists in *The Nation* on April 3 that informal talks between Hillman and Roosevelt were going on about industrial unions to work with the government (Soule, 1935).

I would now put these four factors together as follows. The Great Depression led to both disruption and a united working class. The union leaders who spoke for the working class found allies in the liberal Democrats they had helped to elect to Congress and in the upper-class moderate they helped elect to the presidency. It was possible for the liberals and Roosevelt to work with labor on this issue because the southerners had been satisfied by the removal of their main work force from the package.

Plotke thinks we have to take the terms of the debate over the Wagner Act very seriously. My guess is that the debate was mostly rhetoric on both sides. The industrialists talked about individual freedoms and the constitution, but they were only interested in protecting their very great prerogatives, privileges, and profits. As for the pro-Wagner people, they were sick and tired of hearing the baloney about freedom from unctuous people whose profits had risen very nicely in the past two years. To take the extreme case, General Motors went from $48.1

million in profits in the first half of 1933 to $69.6 million in the first half of 1934, and then to $83.7 in the six months of 1935 when the Wagner Act was debated (*New York Times,* 1934, 1935a). True, the underconsumptionists wanted to put some of that money into the hands of workers so workers could be consumers. But these lesser capitalists also knew it was time to cut the industrialists down to size so that they wouldn't subordinate the rest of the ruling class as well as the workers (cf. Levine, 1988:104–106).

In my view, "business," meaning the nationalist and internationalist segments of the ruling class, did not suffer a drop in power in 1934–35. Similarly, working-class militancy was constant from 1933 through 1935 at a high level that forced action to be taken. However, two other factors changed to make it possible for the liberals to pass the Wagner Act: the southern segment deserted its northern counterparts on a labor question, and the craft and industrial segments of the working class were united for the first time. In this context it mattered that the White House was willing to opt for collective bargaining over repression, at least outside the South.

The plausibility of this new analysis is reinforced by looking at the way in which the Wagner Act was weakened in the 13 years after its passage. The details of the story are told extremely well by Gross (1981), who shows that the unusual alliances within both the power elite and the working class came apart, thereby undermining the legitimacy of the act and the effectiveness of the NLRB created by it. By 1939 the board was on the defensive, and by 1947 the Wagner Act was amended in such a way that its usefulness to labor was severely restricted.

First, the southerners were deeply upset by the sitdown strikes in the North in early 1937 and by attempts by the CIO to organize in the South in the same year. The fact that the CIO organizing drives were interracial only added fuel to the fire. The southerners began a series of actions within Congress that created problems for the board, ranging from passage of a "sense of the Senate" resolution that sitdown strikes were illegal to attacks on the board's budget (Patterson, 1967:135–137; Gross, 1981). At the same time, the AFL became extremely bitter toward the board because of a belief that its decisions favored the CIO. The board was using the very power that the AFL had feared before passage of the act to create large bargaining units that included workers in a wide range of occupations.

There had been very little conflict between the AFL and CIO in 1935 and 1936 over the NLRB for the simple reason that they were too busy fighting between themselves (the CIO having been formed as a committee within the AFL in late 1935) and too busy making sure that as many New Deal Democrats as possible, including Roosevelt above all else, were elected in 1936. They knew it would be impossible to organize if police power was in the hands of governors and a president who would send in the troops against labor if a strike became long and nasty. Once the elections were over, however, both sides began to do open battle with employers, and most of these battles were won by the CIO.

AFL leaders felt from early 1937 on that the NLRB was aiding the CIO, but the decision that "could not be forgiven" (Gross, 1981:56) occurred in June 1938, when the board ruled that the entire West Coast would be the bargaining unit for longshoremen and warehousemen. This ruling effectively eliminated the AFL in the four ports where it had small locals. This was followed by a decision in which the board voided an AFL contract because it was a sweetheart deal between the company and the AFL to head off the CIO (1981:59). AFL officials, showing their racism and their disdain for unskilled workers, also were upset by the ruling in the Mobile Dry Dock Company case in Alabama that allowed for plantwide elections even though the 500 "white, highly skilled mechanics" would be outnumbered by the 1,000 African-American laborers (1981:95).

The AFL retaliated by claiming that the board and the CIO were dominated by communists. It charged that Nathan Witt, a communist who had great power as the executive secretary of the board, had manipulated information in the West Coast longshoremen's case in favor of the procommunist CIO union, and that one member of the board, Edwin S. Smith, was a procommunist. It is highly likely that these AFL charges were true, but the important point is that the craft segment of the working class had gotten into a public political battle with the industrial segment. The communists in the CIO, and there were many of them in key positions (Stepan-Norris and Zeitlin, 1989), were primarily a useful rallying cry, an ideal scapegoat.

The result of southern and AFL disenchantment with the Wagner Act was a new alignment of class forces. The southerners now were in alliance with a united northern business community that had worked for amendments in the act from the day of its passage. The working class, on the other hand, now was split. More concretely, the most conservative segments of the ruling class and the working class entered into an unheard-of alliance after decades of hostility. From as early as July 1938, leaders of the NAM met in private with AFL lawyers to decide upon those amendments to the Wagner Act that would best serve their common interest in thwarting the CIO (Gross, 1981:67ff.). By 1939 further coordination was provided by a conservative southern Democratic congressman, Howard Smith, who also was chairman of a local bank in his hometown of Alexandria, Virginia. It was this NAM–southern–AFL coalition that greatly weakened the NLRB in 1939 and 1940 through damaging revelations in House committee hearings (1981:2). These hearings undermined the board's credibility and forced Roosevelt to make changes in its personnel. The personnel changes and the more cautious rulings that followed reduced the importance of the board to union organizers.

Moreover, it was the bill fashioned by this coalition that was the basis for the Taft-Hartley Act, a fact the AFL later tried to deny or ignore:

The Hartley Bill was written in Smith's office using Smith's 1940 bill as a model, and the Taft-Hartley Act of 1947 contained most of the more severe provisions of the Hartley Bill.

The AFL-business-conservative southern Democrat alliance during the first half of the twelve years between the Wagner and Taft-Hartley Acts has had a lasting effect on labor history and on labor law (1981:3).

The AFL muted its antagonism to the CIO in the postwar years because its situation had changed. It had gained greater strength than the CIO and the CIO had lost its momentum. Moreover, labor strife in the months after the end of the war had led a Democratically dominated Congress to pass restrictions on the Wagner Act in early 1946 that only a veto by Truman kept off the books. Then, in the election a few months later, the Republicans gained control of Congress, a clear sign that a majority of the electorate was not sympathetic to organized labor.

The AFL and CIO worked together to return strong Democratic majorities to both houses of Congress in 1948. With Truman in the White House as well, labor had every hope that it could reverse some of the changes wrought by the Taft-Hartley Act. In particular, labor wanted to remove clause 14b, which legalized antiunion "right to work laws" at the state level. Eleven states already had passed such laws, all of them in the South and Great Plains, and seven more in the same regions were to do so in the 1950s (Dempsey, 1961:25–27).

However, the union movement was stopped cold in its effort, and once again the power of the southern segment of the ruling class is the central issue. As Robert Zeiger points out, a united working class could do nothing against the southern Democrats, who of course had the support of most northern Republicans as well:

But despite labor's electoral and financial contributions and the Democrats' successes in 1948, the Eighty-first Congress failed to move energetically on Taft-Hartley. Although President Truman dutifully supported revision of Taft-Hartley, even under Democratic control Congress remained in conservative hands. Southern Democrats, almost uniformly hostile to the labor movement, dominated key congressional committees. While the tally sheets of labor lobbyists showed that most Democratic senators and congressmen from northern, eastern, and blue-collar districts loyally supported labor's goals, they also revealed that labor simply could not muster the strength to gain significant revision of the law (1986:119).

Both the passage of the Wagner Act and the failure to amend the Taft-Hartley Act point to the southerners as the tipping point in the power system. Their complete domination of workers in their region through segregation and other tactics translated into great political power in the Democratic Party and in Congress, giving them a virtual veto power over any legislation that threatened them. This situation was not to change until the massive disruption by the civil rights movement in the 1960s once again forced some unusual voting coalitions in Congress, only this time it was conservative northern Republicans who deserted the southern Democrats.

My emphasis on the importance of the southerners puts me in agreement with

Goldfield (1987:235), who makes the regional nature of the union movement the first point in his excellent overall explanation for the political weakness of American labor "in comparison to the labor movements in other economically developed capitalist countries." He also astutely points out that union involvement in a political coalition including Dixiecrats kept the CIO from being as militant as it needed to be in order to win (1987:240).

Having at last explained the Wagner Act to my satisfaction with a theory that emphasizes both intra- and interclass conflict, I turn to a few general thoughts about labor and class power in America in the final section.

## Implications and Conclusions

The first and major conclusion I draw from the battles over labor relations in the first five decades of the twentieth century is that the owners and managers of large businesses showed their great power quite dramatically in the way they were able to narrow the conflict between capital and labor to the limited matter of collective bargaining over wages, hours, and working conditions, and then to undercut collective bargaining with welfare capitalism, scientific management, and outright repression. Collective bargaining was the one area where the two sides had a little something in common, ideologically speaking, and it was the one area where their "power" was even vaguely comparable due to the ability of workers to strike. Still, that strike power was conditioned on the neutrality of the state. If the state used the law or the militia on striking workers, as it often did, then the workers were powerless. Once again, the domination of relevant institutions of the state becomes a crucial issue in understanding capitalist power in America.

The second conclusion I would draw is that the only victory for unions in the twentieth century of any major significance in the legislative arena, the Wagner Act, was due to three relatively rare conditions: the economy was in serious trouble, the ruling class was split, *and* the working class was united and militant. The emphasis on the split in the ruling class is another way of saying that the political power of the southern segment of the ruling class is demonstrated very graphically by comparing the legislative histories of the Wagner Act and the Taft-Hartley Act. When the southerners acquiesced in the New Dealers' solution to capital–labor conflict in the North, the act could pass. However, once they turned against the act, thereby uniting the three major segments of the ruling class, the handwriting was on the wall for organized labor due to its inability to organize in the South.

My third conclusion is that the decline of the union movement began in the late 1930s when the South turned against the Wagner Act and the craft and industrial segments of the working class split apart. The coming of World War II merely masked the weakness of the union movement, which failed in the spring of 1937 in its assault on "Little Steel" in Ohio, Indiana, and Illinois, states where the mayors and governors would not withhold the police and militia, and in its attempt to organize southern textile workers, where harsh repression again was used against it. The growth of the union movement during the war was due to the power elite's need for a united country in order to prosecute the war, leading the unions to develop the same kind of illusions about their strength that they harbored during World War I. It seems to me that the various defeats suffered by the unions in the early postwar years, including Taft-Hartley, are evidence for the illusory nature of union power during the war.

Finally, I conclude that all of us were wrong on the Wagner Act, except Goldfield (1987) on the importance of the South. We looked in the wrong places. We did not take seriously the power of the southern segment through its role in the Democratic party and Congress. In my own case, my long travail with the Wagner Act has forced me to think more systematically in terms of class segments and to understand more fully that there is no easy and direct relationship between the economic and political power of a class segment. The internationalist segment has the biggest and most profitable firms, but the southern segment had the most political power until the 1960s due to (1) its total domination of its major work force, and (2) the historically determined structure of the American state. That realization has forced me to take the necessity of power structure research even more seriously than I did in the past.

# 5

# DEFINING THE NATIONAL INTEREST, 1940–1942:
## A Critique of Krasner's Theory of American State Autonomy

### Introduction

Just as New Deal social legislation provides an ideal test of rival theories of the American state in relation to domestic issues, so too does postwar foreign policy planning in the years 1940–42 present an equally perfect challenge in the even more critical area of the nation's "national interest." The two previous chapters showed that my power elite theory of government domination better explains the Social Security Act and the National Labor Relations Act than various state autonomy theories. In this chapter I now intend to demonstrate that my theory also provides a better interpretation of key foreign policy issues than does the "realist" version of state autonomy theory cogently articulated and tested by Stephen Krasner in *Defending the National Interest* (1978).

Contrary to Krasner, I will show that the important issue is not the defending of a national interest said to derive from the goals of the state, but the defining by private citizens and state leaders alike of what comes to be accepted as the national interest. More specifically, I will show that in the years 1940–42 a new definition of the national interest for the postwar years so important to Krasner's thesis was in good part the product of power elites and their hired academic experts, working through a private organization and temporary appointments within the federal government.

While the focus of the chapter is on the work of Krasner, it has wider import because the theory he advocates is in fact the starting point assumed by the state-centric or "realist" paradigm in the field of international relations. As Krasner (1978:13) notes, this basic framework is utilized by many of the most prominent scholars who study international relations, including Robert Gilpin, Robert Tucker, and Kenneth Waltz. This chapter, then, is an attempt to call an entire paradigm in international relations into question, as least as it applies to the United States in the second half of the twentieth century.

The remainder of this chapter is organized in three sections: The first presents an overview of Krasner's theory and the evidence he provides for it. The section concludes he is right in saying the crucial evidence for his argument against other theories concerns American foreign policy after World War II, including the origins of the Vietnam War. The second section provides a detailed account of the origins of the new definition of the national interest that led to the expansion of American power all over the world. It concludes that the elite-based Council on Foreign Relations worked closely with the State Department and White House in creating and advocating a definition of the national interest that made American economic prosperity coterminous with global hegemony outside the Soviet Union and Eastern Europe. The final section uses the evidence developed in the second section as the basis for a critique of Krasner's emphasis on a disembodied "Lockean liberalism" as the motive for postwar American interventionism. Harvey Feigenbaum's (1985) surprising findings and insightful analysis concerning the role of ideology in relations between big business and the vaunted French state then provide a bridge from the critique of Krasner to a wider perspective on how a power elite rooted in private corporations dominates foreign policy.

## Krasner's Theory and Findings

Like other state autonomy theorists, Krasner is concerned to counter what he sees as the undue emphasis in pluralist and Marxian theory on the influence of outside societal forces on the goals of the state. He thinks stress should be placed on the distinction between state and society, and on the state as an independent actor that has purposes different from those of any social groups in the society. He calls this a "statist" or "state-centric" approach:

> A statist paradigm views the state as an autonomous actor. The objectives sought by the state cannot be reduced to some summation of private interests. These objectives can be called appropriately the national interest (Krasner, 1978:5–6).

Krasner, like any other theorist, must begin with a definition of the slippery concept of "state." As shown in Chapter 1, it usually means roughly what most Americans understand when they say "government," but it also can mean much more or much less in the hands of specific theorists. For the structural Marxists Poulantzas (1969:77) and Louis Althusser (1971), the "ideology apparatus" of the state includes schools, churches, political parties, the mass media, and most unions. In fact, it includes virtually every organization in a country except left-wing trade unions and Marxist-Leninist parties. Krasner goes to the other extreme, defining the state as "a set of roles and institutions having peculiar drives, compulsions, and aims of their own that are separate and distinct from the interests of any particular societal group" (1978:10). This definition becomes more concrete when he states that at least for foreign policy "the central state actors are the President and the Secretary of State, and the most important institutions are the White House and the State Department" (1978:11). These state actors are usually referred to throughout the book as "central decision-makers." As for the other departments of the executive branch, they are only part of the state to the degree they join with the White House and State Department in acting to promote collective goals as opposed to "specific societal and bureaucratic interests" (1978:11). Congress is not considered as part of the state, but as part of the government in general. It represents societal interests that tend to hamper the state in its pursuit of its goals (1978:63–66, 267, 295). In Krasner's view, then, the state is much less than "government" in terms of the institutions that are part of it. Something as mundane as "territorial regulation" is nowhere on the horizon. It is definitely a conception of the state well suited for social scientists who focus on international relations.

In making this argument about the autonomy of the state, Krasner is not claiming that it never serves the needs of society. Quoting an earlier state theorist, he notes that the state needs a satisfied people who are willing and able to fulfill the demands made on them. More importantly, the state's objectives and the needs of society are closely intertwined in a democracy (1978:11). Nor is he asserting that the state is never blocked in striving for its goals:

> Central decision-makers may be frustrated in their efforts to further the national interest by opposition not only from external actors but from domestic ones as well. The ability of state actors to deal with their own societies depends upon the political system in which they must act—more precisely, on the resources at the disposal of the state to overcome private resistance (1978:33).

The American state is a weak one in the sense that members of society often can prevent the adoption of a policy. The reasons for this weakness are numerous: no threat of foreign invasion for much of American history, great societal cohesion and value consensus, and a strong economy that can function well without much state involvement. Furthermore, the American state must "operate in a political culture that views the activist state with great suspicion" (1978:62). This political culture includes both a Congress concerned with localist interests and large corporations with great assets. Thus, for example, a coalition of independent oil companies acting through Congress stopped central decision-makers from creating a state oil company in the early 1940s to buy oil from Saudi Arabia (1978:189–97). None of this would come as any news to C. Wright Mills; the only surprise is the assertion of state autonomy in the face of these qualifications.

Once his theory of the state is made clear, the next step in Krasner's argument is to be more explicit about what is meant by a "national interest" that is no mere summation of the interests of groups within society. His defining statement is that the national interest concerns either "general material objects" or "ambitious ideological goals related to beliefs about how societies should be ordered" (1978:10). For research purposes, however, Krasner adopts an empirical type of definition: the national interest can be determined by the actions taken by the state and by the statements of central decision-makers. This position is very similar to the one suggested many years ago by the historian Charles Beard (1934) in *The Idea of National Interest,* one of the few lengthy treatments of the topic: "The question—what is national interest?—can be answered, if at all, only by exploring the use of the formula by responsible statesmen and publicists and by discovering the things and patterns of conduct—public and private— embraced within the scope of the formula" (Beard, 1934:26, as quoted in Krasner, 1978:42–43).

Krasner anticipates objections to this approach because some statements by state actors may be merely self-serving attempts to keep themselves in power. He therefore adds two specifications as to what statements and preferences will quality as the national interest: "these preferences do not consistently benefit a particular class or group, and they last over an extended period of time" (1978:43).

This formulation of the national interest allows Krasner to do the kind of empirical study that is seldom undertaken by those theorists who simply assume a statist paradigm and certain a priori national interests in their analyses of foreign policy and international relations. More concretely, this definition en- ables him to compare the statements and actions of central decision-makers on specific issues with the preferences on those issues stated by private interest groups, and in particular leaders of large corporations. If such a study demon- strates that the state acts in terms of its own interests and not the declared interests of the corporate executives, then both the idea of an autonomous state and the concept of a national interest are said to be supported.

The empirical body of Krasner's work concerns 15 case studies relating to international investments in raw materials between the years 1910 and 1975. Some cases involve state support or lack of support for new investments overseas by American corporations. Others involve the reaction of the state to the na- tionalization of American investments in foreign countries. Krasner had at least two good reasons for focusing his empirical test on raw materials. First, it is likely that raw materials would be a major concern of the state. Second, the American corporations involved in such investments are very large and consid- ered to be very powerful. They include all the major oil and copper companies, for example. As Krasner summarizes: "direct foreign investments in the exploi- tation of raw materials have involved powerful societal actors and a wide range of governmental institutions and have touched upon issues of major importance to the state" (1978:10).

The conclusion drawn from the case studies is that central decision-makers always sought three main objectives in a consistent order of preference. Their first and most important objective was promoting broad foreign policy goals. Their second objective was to insure the security of the supply of raw materials to the United States. Their third goal was to increase economic competition in the supplying of raw materials (1978:14). Thus, his approach to the national interest can be stated even more exactly: "an inductivist statist approach asserts that the national interest consists of a set of transitively ordered state preferences concerned to promote the general well-being of the society that persists over a long period of time" (1978:45).

Krasner also found a general difference in the nature of the broad foreign policy objectives that were sought before and after World War II. Before World War II, with the exception of the Wilson administration, the state acted primarily in terms of such concrete interests as "enhancing strategic security and furthering economic well-being by increasing competition or promoting security of supply" (1978:15). After World War II, however, the broader foreign policy objectives were primarily "ideological" in nature. That is:

> American leaders were moved by a vision of what the global order should be like that was derived from American values and the American experience—Lockean liberal aims and a nonrevolutionary, democratic, and prosperous historical evolution. They were more concerned with structuring the international system and the domestic policies of other countries than with readily identifiable economic and strategic interests. The shift from interest-oriented to ideological goals was the result of America's global power position (1978:15).

This distinction between interest-oriented objectives related to economic and strategic concerns on the one hand, and ideological objectives related to American values on the other, a distinction adapted from Franz Schurmann (1974), is a crucial claim in Krasner's overall argument. He sees it as the main way to distinguish his theory from that of the structural Marxists because the superiority of his theory only becomes clear, he believes, with those cases that involve noneconomic, ideological considerations. Since my own findings and argument will dispute this distinction between economic and ideological objectives, it is necessary to spell out Krasner's position in considerable detail. The first statement of it in the first chapter is as follows:

> The most powerful evidence I can offer in defense of a theoretical perspective that denies that state actions can be reduced to societal needs, even very general ones like preserving the coherence of capitalist structures, is that the behavior of the United States when it extended itself to the utmost—when it was prepared to use overt or covert force—must ultimately be understood not in terms of economic or strategic objectives, but in terms of ideological ones" (Krasner, 1978:6).

Krasner elaborates on this theme later in the initial chapter when he links the "ideological" actions of central decision-makers with "nonlogical" behavior, which he defines as "divergence" between "means-ends relationships" as perceived by the performer of the action and "an experienced outside observer" (1978:15–16). What this means in this context is that American leaders "persistently exaggerated the important of communist elements in foreign countries" and "sometimes made no clear calculations about means and ends" (1978:16). Put another way, the anticommunist fervency of state actors was pursued without regard for economic interests or the coherence of capitalist society as a whole. Krasner sees such actions as contrary to structural Marxism because they are not rational in terms of the capitalist system (1978:16).

Krasner returns to these points in the last two chapters, first in the context of the American use of force after 1950, then in his concluding theoretical discussion. He emphasizes that force was used in situations where U.S. corporations only had small investments and where the issue was communism, not interests:

> Structural Marxist arguments must ultimately relate state behavior to the economic interests of the ruling class, even though that class might not perceive where its own best interests lie. In addition, for structural Marxists, the state will strive to act rationally; there will be a clear relationship between means and ends, even though inherent contradictions may prevent policy-makers from ultimately accomplishing their goal. The cases in which the United States has used overt or covert force do not conform with structural Marxist expectations. They are better explained by ideological considerations than by materialist ones: American goals are more closely linked with a Lockean vision of how societies should be ordered than with any economic aims (1978:278).

Although Vietnam was not one of his cases because there were no U.S. raw materials investments there, he nonetheless devotes the final 6 pages of the penultimate chapter to the Vietnam War as the best example of the argument he is making. Indeed, I think his book is really an attempt to understand how the United States became involved in what he sees as a very nonsensical war:

> One stands out above all the others—Vietnam. In Vietnam there was an absence of any clear and direct American interests, either economic or strategic. The costs incurred were enormous in both political and economic terms (1978:320).

Still, it was not ideology alone that led the central decision-makers into a nonlogical war in Vietnam. Lockean ideology has a long history in the United States, and it "has clearly been compatible with a noninterventionist foreign policy" (1978:325). Thus, the crucial additional factor was the new position of the United States as the most powerful nation in the world:

> Only states whose resources are very large, both absolutely and relatively, can engage in imperial policies, can attempt to impose their vision on other countries and the global system. And it is only here that ideology becomes a crucial determinant of the objectives of foreign policy. Great power removes the usual restraints on central decision-makers (1978:340).

Since the postwar actions of the United States are "based implicitly upon an assumption of a hierarchy of goals" (1978:340–41), Krasner offers two analogies to make his general argument clear. One is drawn from the sociobiology of Edward O. Wilson (1975), which argues that human beings, unlike other species, are not constrained by basic needs. The second is with Abraham Maslow's (1954) claim that there is a hierarchy of needs in each human being, with more basic physiological needs having to be satisfied before higher needs like self-actualization can emerge.

Aside from the highly dubious analogies with Wilson's extrapolations from lower animals, which are disputed even by many sociobiologists, and with Maslow's speculative hierarchy of needs, for which there is no evidence from psychological studies, Krasner's claims about the goals of extremely powerful states are plausible ones. The Vietnam War and other postwar interventions do seem nonlogical in terms of both their economic and social costs, and Lockean-based anticommunism does appear to be an ideology that greatly distorts the threat of the "red menace." However, as the next section shows, the definition of the national interest that led to these interventions was conceived in the years 1940–42 by corporate planners in terms of what they saw as the needs of the American capitalist system, well before communism was their primary concern. Moreover, as the final section argues, the capitalist system, state goals, and ideology cannot be seen as separate issues. There is a "promiscuity of organizations and functions" in highly developed market societies (Mann, 1986:17). Leaders within the capitalist-based power elite helped create the global definition of the American national interest, but they shared with state actors an ideology that might well be judged "nonlogical," in Krasner's terms, by a disinterested and experienced outside observer.

Put differently, Krasner is wrong in saying that postwar foreign policy could not have been made by, or at the behest of, corporate capitalists and their planners because the policy was not rational in terms of the capitalist system. But he is right in saying that ideology is not a mask for the class interests of the capitalists. Following Feigenbaum (1985), I argue in the final section that ideology as a rationale and guide for a way of life is at work in everyone in the society, and that it may lead to nonrational policies even while aiding power elite domination of the American state. The powerful act in terms of what they think are their interests, but it is perfectly possible that they do not always know their interests better than anyone else.

Before discussing these general issues, however, it is necessary to show how corporate planners at the Council on Foreign Relations worked with central decision-makers in the state to create a new definition of the national interest between 1940 and 1942.

## The Council on Foreign Relations and the National Interest

It is my contention that the starting point for understanding the new conception of the national interest that was developed between 1940 and 1942 must be found in the work of the private Council on Foreign Relations, and particularly in its war–peace study groups that worked closely with the State Department in those years. This claim builds on the detailed historical studies of Laurence Shoup (1974, 1975, 1977; Shoup and Minter, 1977) and my own historical research, but it is grounded as well in discussions of the council's work in other accounts of postwar planning (Notter, 1949; Langer and Gleason, 1953; Divine, 1967; Oliver, 1971, 1975; Eckes, 1975).

In putting great emphasis on the council, I am not denying that other private organizations and internationally oriented mass media played a role in influencing central decision-makers and public opinion. As Robert Divine (1967) has shown, there were many such organizations supported by internationalists around the country. Moreover, the magazines of publisher Henry Luce pushed very hard for postwar planning from 1940 to 1944, often chiding the White House and State Department for failing to keep up with a public opinion that increasingly favored American involvement in the war and in postwar planning once France fell and Germany attacked Great Britain. As early as January 1940, for example, a 19-member *Fortune* Roundtable discussion group, consisting of a cross section of business leaders, lawyers, and association officials, called for United States participation in organizing for the postwar peace discussions.

Despite all this other activity, it is still the case that many of the leaders of these organizations were members of the council or its postwar planning groups, including Luce and the organizer of his roundtable discussion groups. Just as often, their published reports were versions of what academic experts were proposing to the State Department as part of their confidential work with the council. In short, the council was the elite core of the internationalist perspective that projected a very large role for the United States in the postwar world. Its function was to create and organize the policy goals of the internationalist segment of the ruling class.

The Council on Foreign Relations had its origins in the years after World War I when many American leaders returned from the Paris Peace Conference dissatisfied with both their preparation for the negotiations and the outcome of the conference. They also believed that the growing economic power of the United States should lead to greater involvement and leadership in world affairs than the nation previously had shown. The Council actually was founded in 1921 with the merger of a New York businessmen's discussion group and a fledgling Institute of International Affairs that consisted in good part of statesmen and academic experts. As Divine summarizes:

> Limited to 650 members, 400 from New York and 250 from the rest of the country, the Council's roster read like a Who's Who of American business and professional men. Partners from J. P. Morgan and Company mingled with Ivy League professors, international lawyers with syndicated columnists, State Department officials with clergymen (1967:20).

There is ample systematic evidence to support Divine's contention that the council is the province of internationally oriented bankers and corporate executives in New York and surrounding areas, as well as of academic experts and journalists. It also is well established that its funding for projects comes from large foundations directed by business leaders who are members of the council in significant numbers (Domhoff, 1970c:Chapter 5; Shoup and Minter, 1977:Chapters 1–3).

The council endeavors to realize its internationalist aims through discussion groups, research studies, book-length monographs on a wide variety of countries and issues, and articles in its prestigious journal, *Foreign Affairs*. In attempting to foster its perspective, the council has seen its primary adversaries as isolationists in Congress and nationally oriented business executives who do not want the United States to become entangled in European affairs. In the early 1930s, its leaders vigorously entered a national debate in opposition to "self-sufficiency" and greater government control of the economy, and supported such steps toward internationalism as the Export-Import Bank of 1933 and the Reciprocal Trade Act of 1934 (Gardner, 1964; Shoup and Minter, 1977).

Any private group seeking to influence central decision-makers in the White House and State Department must know who is making decisions, when secret decisions are likely to be discussed and made, and what kinds of arguments and information are being utilized in making these decisions. Furthermore, to influence decisions a private group must have legitimacy in the eyes of decision-makers and access to them (Shoup, 1974:16–17). There is reason to believe that the council has such information, legitimacy, and access. Its studies are conducted by respected scholars. Its leaders are known to be highly informed about foreign affairs. Many members had close social and business relations with central decision-makers when they were in private life. Government officials are often members of council discussion groups. Then too, many members have served in government positions or as government advisers. For example, council director Henry L. Stimson, a New York corporation lawyer for most of his adult life, had been secretary of war under Taft, secretary of state under Hoover, and was named secretary of war by Roosevelt in June 1940, a position he held until the end of the war.

However, perhaps the best single example of this point about access and legitimacy is banker Norman H. Davis, president of the council from 1936 until his death in 1944. His relationships with central decision-makers in the State Department and White House were long-standing and close, particularly with Secretary of State Cordell Hull and Roosevelt. The son of a successful businessman in Tennessee, Davis became a millionaire by means of financial dealings in Cuba between 1902 and 1917. Through his friendships with Henry P. Davison, an important partner in J. P. Morgan and Company and chairman of the American Red Cross, and Richard M. Bissell, president of Hartford Fire Insurance and a member of the National Defense Commission, Davis became a financial adviser to the secretary of treasury on foreign loans during World War I.

Davis also was a financial adviser to the American delegation to the Paris Peace Conference in 1919, where he worked with Thomas Lamont, another Morgan partner. He then served briefly as an assistant secretary of treasury and undersecretary of state before turning to a banking career in New York in March 1921. At this point Davis involved himself in the affairs of the Democratic party, where he became friends with fellow Tennessean Cordell Hull, then a congressman and chairman of the national party. It was during this time that he also became friends with Roosevelt. In 1928 Roosevelt had begun work as a private citizen on an international development trust to stimulate foreign trade, and Davis helped him with the project (Gardner, 1964:19; see also the letter from Roosevelt to Davis dated October 8, 1928, in the Davis Collection in the Library of Congress). In addition, Davis was a delegate to international conferences under Republican presidents in 1927 and 1932, and Roosevelt made him an ambassador at large in 1933 and head of the American Red Cross in 1938.

Outside politics, Davis was considered a "well-known friend of the Morgan Company," according to former Roosevelt adviser Raymond Moley (Moley, 1949:227, as quoted in Shoup, 1974:27; for Davis' own detailed account of his relation to the Morgan interests, see his undated memorandum to Hull in the Davis Collection in the Library of Congress). He had become its Cuban representative in 1912, and negotiated a $10 million loan from Morgan for the Cuban government in 1914. In 1926, when Sumner Welles, a friend of Roosevelt's who became his undersecretary of state, wanted a job with the Morgan-affiliated Guaranty Trust Bank, "he wrote Davis who offered to arrange for Welles to see the officials of the Guaranty" (Shoup, 1974:27). By the time he was elected council president, Davis also was a trustee of the Bank of New York and Trust Company.

Davis had direct and frequent access to Roosevelt and Hull in the years between 1940 and 1942, when postwar planning was in its crucial formative phase. For example, there were two telephones in Davis' office at the American Red Cross, one for normal calls, the other a direct line to the White House. As for Hull, his appointment calendar shows that Davis met with him in his office several times a week; he also played croquet with Davis most nights of the week (Shoup, 1974:30).

Similar relationships between council leaders and central decision-makers will become apparent as the story of postwar planning unfolds. However, the more important question for now is whether this access shaped the thinking of central decision-makers or whether they relied upon the information and recommendations of state planners to develop their own perspectives. It is to that critical issue that we begin to turn, showing that the postwar planners of the Council on Foreign Relations provided the bulk of the State Department's postwar planning in 1940 and 1941 from the outside, and became part of the State Department in 1942 when serious planning within the state finally was undertaken.

The second world war began in early September 1939. By September 12, council leaders were meeting with Assistant Secretary of State George Messersmith, a longtime member of the council, to offer their services on postwar planning. Messersmith spoke later in the day with Welles and Hull, both of whom expressed interest in the idea. Shortly thereafter Davis talked with Hull and received verbal approval of the plan (1974:64). The State Department also conveyed its approval of the plan to the Rockefeller Foundation, which gave the council $44,500 on December 6 to begin the work. This foundation support continued for the life of what turned out to be a five-year project, and it amounted to several million dollars in 1986 dollars.

Members of the State Department and the council met at Messersmith's home in mid-December to finalize the arrangements. The council would set up study groups to "engage in a continuous study of the courses of the war, to ascertain how the hostilities affect the United States and to elaborate concrete proposals designed to safeguard American interests in the settlement which will be undertaken when hostilities cease" (Council Memorandum, as quoted in Shoup, 1974:65–66). In short, the postwar national interest was to be the main concern of the Council's work.

"Studies of American Interests in the War and the Peace," as the project was officially named, began with five study groups: Economic, Financial, Security and Armaments, Territorial, and Future World Organization. However, the first two were quickly made into one Economic and Financial Group, and the Future World Organization Group became the Political Group. Later, in May 1941, a Peace Aims Group was created to ascertain the peace aims of other countries through private discussions in New York with their leaders and representatives.

Each group had a leader, or "rapporteur" in council language, along with a research secretary and 10 to 15 members. Three of the groups had corapporteurs. Almost 100 people participated in the groups between 1940 and 1945. They were a cross section of top-level American leadership in finance, business, law, media, universities, and the military, and they included academic experts in economics, geography, and political science as well as White House advisers and other government advisers:

Through these individuals at least five cabinet level departments and fourteen government agencies, bureaus, and offices were interlocked with the War-Peace Studies at one time or another. They collectively attended three hundred and sixty-two meetings and prepared six hundred and eighty-two separate documents for the Department of State and President. Up to twenty-five copies of each recommendation were distributed to the appropriate desks of the Department and two for the President (Shoup, 1974:68).

Isaiah Bowman, president of Johns Hopkins University and a director of the council, was the leader of the Territorial Group; he was one of the nation's leading geographers. Whitney H. Shepardson, a lawyer-businessman in New York, headed the Political Group; he had served as an assistant to Woodrow Wilson's closest adviser, Colonel Edward M. House, at the Paris Peace Conference and helped found the council. International lawyer Allen W. Dulles and *The New York Times* military expert Hanson W. Baldwin were coleaders of the Security and Armaments Group. Hamilton Fish Armstrong, editor of the council's *Foreign Affairs* and a major force in the overall war–peace studies as vice-chairman under Davis, was the leader of the Peace Aims Group.

The key figures in the Economic and Financial Group, which played the most prominent role in the issues of concern in this chapter, were two former presidents of the American Economic Association, Jacob Viner and Alvin H. Hansen. Viner, a professor at the University of Chicago, was the most highly regarded international economist of his era. He began his career of advising government and policy groups during World War I and was an adviser to the Council on Foreign Relations throughout the 1930s. Hansen, who had come to Harvard from Minnesota in 1938, was the most visible and renowned Keynesian economist in the country (Galbraith, 1971:49–50). He had numerous advisory roles with the federal government, serving as a consultant to the State Department, Federal Reserve Board, and National Resources Planning Board, among others, during the time of his involvement with the council project.

On the basis of their backgrounds, neither Viner nor Hansen could be considered a likely candidate for an important advisory position. Both were raised in modest financial circumstances far from the centers of American wealth and power. Viner was born in Canada and did not become a citizen until he was 22 years old; however, he did receive his Ph.D. at Harvard and rose quickly in the professorial ranks at the University of Chicago. Hansen was born and raised in South Dakota, the son of immigrants from Scandinavia, and he worked as a school teacher and school principal before earning his Ph.D. at the University of Chicago at the age of 32. He did not arrive at Harvard until he was nearly 50, about the same time he became a Keynesian. Both Viner and Hansen, then, are testimony to the social mobility that is possible in American academic circles.

Despite their differing theoretical orientations, Viner and Hansen worked closely in the Economic and Financial Group, and they were joined by other economists with a similar range of views, including Percy Bidwell, Winfield Riefler, Eugene Staley, and Arthur Upgren. William Diebold, Jr., served as research secretary. The fact that experts of diverse orientations were hired by the Council for its project suggests a flexibility and farsightedness said to be lacking in such circles by many state autonomy theorists.

The group had two direct connections to the White House. The first was economist Lauchlin Currie, an early Keynesian who had worked at the Federal Reserve Board in the mid-1930s and joined the White House in 1939 as Roosevelt's administrative assistant with special duties in the field of economics, a position he held until 1945. He was considered the White House liaison to the group (Roosevelt Papers:Official File 3719, November 27, 1941). He joined the discussion group officially in February 1943. The second was Benjamin V. Cohen, a New York corporation lawyer famous for his partnership with Thomas Corcoran in crafting important New Deal legislation, including the Securities and Exchange Commission Act and the Public Utilities Holding Company Act (Lash, 1988). Cohen joined the group in September 1941.

The Economic and Financial Group later developed ties with the new Committee for Economic Development (CED), a policy-discussion group formed in 1942 by sophisticated conservatives with close relationships to the Department of Commerce. One of the founders of the CED, business executive Ralph Flanders, joined the council study group in July 1942. Another important connection was provided by one of the aforementioned economists, Arthur Upgren, who had a major role through the Commerce Department in organizing the CED (Schriftgiesser, 1960:15–18).

While the council was organizing its study groups, the Department of State created its own internal structure for postwar planning. In mid-September 1939, after the meetings with council leaders, Hull appointed a special assistant, Leo Pasvolsky, to guide postwar planning. Shortly thereafter, on December 12, Pasvolsky drafted a plan for a new departmental division to study the problems of peace and reconstruction (Shoup, 1974:70). Then, in late December, the department formed a policy committee named The Advisory Committee on Problems of Foreign Relations, with Undersecretary Welles as chairman. All members were officers of the State Department except Davis of the council and lawyer George Rublee, a founding member of the council and the director of the intergovernmental Committee on Political Refugees.

It is important to look more closely at the State Department's planning structure and personnel in order to understand the central role played by the council. First, the special assistant to Hull, Leo Pasvolsky, had been an employee of a private think tank, the Brookings Institution, from 1923 to 1935, and then received his Ph.D. in international economics from Brookings in 1936. He also had been a member of the Council on Foreign Relations since 1938. After working for the Bureau of Foreign and Domestic Commerce in 1934–35 and the Division of Trade Agreements within the Department of State in 1935–36, he became a special assistant to Hull from 1936 to 1938, and then again from 1939 to 1946, when he returned fulltime to the Brookings Institution until his death in 1953. All this suggests that Pasvolsky was as close to private economic planners as he was to central decision-makers.

The study division envisioned by Pasvolsky in his memorandum of December 12, 1939, did not come into being until early in 1941 due to the lack of personnel in the department. Indeed, Pasvolsky's memorandum indicated that the division's own research would be minimal at first and stated that it "would stress assembly of materials and the attempt to influence the research activities of unofficial organizations" (Shoup, 1974:71, his paraphrase of the memorandum). In short, any early planning would come from the council under the general guidance of the State Department. Much of this guidance came from Pasvolsky himself, who regularly attended meetings of the Economic and Financial Group.

As for the policy-level Advisory Committee on Problems of Foreign Policy, it did very little before it became defunct in the summer of 1940. It was not replaced until late December 1941, after the United States had entered the war, when it was enlarged and renamed the Advisory Committee on Postwar Foreign Policy. The pressure of immediate events as the war in Europe grew in 1940 was too great for thinking about postwar problems in the understaffed department. It is in this context, then, that the council began its postwar planning efforts. It had a close liaison with Hull, Welles, and Pasvolsky, and it was functioning in a situation where the State Department had little or no research staff of its own and very little time for general postwar policy discussions. It was an ideal situation for an outside group to have great influence.

The earliest and most important council planning took place within the Economic and Financial Group. It began modestly with four papers dated March 9, 1940, that analyzed the effect of the war on United States trade, concluding that there had been no serious consequences up to that point. Similarly, five papers dated April 6 were primarily descriptive in nature, dealing with the possible impact on American trade of price-fixing and monetary exchange controls by the belligerents. Two papers dated May 11 began to give an indication of the direction of council planning. One warned that a way would have to be found to increase American imports in order to bring about a necessary increase in exports. The second concluded that high American tariffs had not had a big influence in restricting American imports. Although reducing tariffs would help to increase imports, boosting industrial activity and consumer income would do even more to increase them. Given the almost exclusive emphasis Hull put on reducing foreign and domestic tariffs to foster the international economy he single-mindedly sought, this conclusion is the first piece of evidence that the council was going to develop its own analysis rather than reinforcing the State Department's usual conception of the national interest. Indeed, because Krasner (1977) believes that State Department economic policy was based on an "amorphous Wilsonianism" between 1940 and 1947, any divergencies between Hull and the council perspective are evidence for council influence.

The Nazi invasion of France in May 1940 and the subsequent attack on Great Britain turned the attention of both the State Department and the council to the problem of stabilizing the economies of Latin American countries that previously had depended upon their exports to continental Europe. There were numerous meetings and exchanges of information between State and the council from May to October in relation to this work. At a plenary meeting of all council groups on June 28, the project's official contact with the State Department, Hugh R.

Wilson, urged that materials given to the department should be couched as practical recommendations (Shoup, 1974:91). Pasvolsky then outlined the close relationship that had developed, stating that:

> he had gone over many details with Mr. Hansen, had suggested some directions of work, and had pointed out to Mr. Hansen the great usefulness of the work already done. The relations between the groups and the State Department were such that, for economic matters, he might be asked at any time about the usefulness of a proposed investigation. He did not think lack of knowledge of general policies ought to prove a serious obstacle ("Memorandum of Discussions of First Plenary Session Council on Foreign Relations," June 28, 1940, as quoted in Shoup, 1974:91).

On June 10, State Department planners suggested it might be necessary to set up a single trading organization to market all surplus agriculture production in the Western Hemisphere. This would make it possible to bargain in the face of Germany's great economic power. However, it was realized that this kind of solution was not in keeping with American values and would be criticized by the business community. When Roosevelt asked on June 15 for a recommendation by June 20 on what to do about the economic problems of Latin America, it was decided that as an interim measure the government's Reconstruction Finance Corporation should supply the money to buy the surplus products. On September 26, Congress gave the Reconstruction Finance Corporation $500 million to carry out this policy.

But the council's Economic and Financial Group had concluded in a paper of June 7, three days before the first State Department memorandum, that a "Pan-American Trade Bloc" would not work because it would be weak in needed raw materials and unable to consume the agricultural surpluses of Canada and the southern half of Latin America. There were too many national economies in the hemisphere that were competitive with each other rather than complementary. Furthermore, economic isolation in the Western Hemisphere would cost the United States almost two-thirds of its foreign trade (Shoup, 1974:102). As if that were not enough, council planners shortly thereafter concluded that any Western Hemisphere cartel for selling to Germany was doomed to failure because the self-sufficiency of the German bloc was such that it could not be forced to trade with the Western Hemisphere (1974:106).

It was in analyzing this problem that the council began to define the national interest in terms of the minimum geographical area that was necessary for the productive functioning of the American economy without drastic controls and major governmental intervention. A report of June 28, entitled "Geographical Distribution of United States Foreign Trade: A Study in National Interest," showed both the increasing importance of manufacturing exports as compared to agricultural exports and the increasing importance of Asia and Oceania for both exports and imports. As Shoup summarizes, "They concluded that the Far East and Western Hemisphere probably bore the same relationship to the United States as America had to Europe in the past—a source of raw materials and a market for manufactures" (1974:107–8). Equally important, and essential in understanding the hegemonic role undertaken by the United States, other studies soon concluded that the economies of Great Britain and Japan could not function adequately in harmony with the American economy without a large part of the world as markets and suppliers of raw materials. It was emphasized that Japan's trade needs could be accommodated as part of a larger solution to world economic problems, but that United States problems could not be solved if Japan excluded the American economy from Asia. This economic argument, I believe, provides the starting point for the policies that later led to the application of containment policy to Southeast Asia and then to war in Vietnam. While strategic and ideological dimensions were later added to concerns about Southeast Asia, it is the critical economic issue in relation to the British and Japanese economies that is usually overlooked in most standard accounts of American postwar foreign policy, including Krasner's.

The council refined its analysis from July through September with "detailed study of the location, production, and trade of key commodities and manufactures on a world-wide basis and within the framework of blocs [of nations]" (1974:109). The four blocs were (1) the Western Hemisphere, (2) continental Europe and Mediterranean Basin (excluding the Soviet Union), (3) the Pacific area and Far East; and (4) the British Empire (excluding Canada). Due in good part to the export competition between the southern countries of Latin America on the one hand and Australia, New Zealand, and India on the other, Great Britain itself was seen as an essential market for dealing with agricultural surpluses. Only with Great Britain included was there a non-German area that was self-sufficient and harmonious, as a memorandum of September 6 concluded (1974:110).

These economic issues were embodied in a memorandum of October 19 that was the first full statement of the national interest from the council. It "set forth the political, military, territorial and economic requirements of the United States in its potential leadership of the non-German world area including the United Kingdom itself as well as the Western Hemisphere and the Far East" (Memorandum E-B19, as quoted in Shoup, 1974:111). After summarizing changes in the nature and direction of American trade, it stated that "the foremost requirement of the United States in a world in which it proposes to *hold unquestioned power* is the rapid fulfillment of a program of complete re-armament" (Memorandum E-B19, as quoted in Shoup, 1974:113, emphasis added). The maintenance of British resistance to the Nazis would have to be supported through new forms of aid, as had been suggested in a brief memorandum of October 15. Also necessary was the "coordination and cooperation of the United States with other countries to secure the limitation of any exercise of sovereignty by foreign nations that constitutes a threat to the minimum world area essential for the security and economic prosperity of the United States and the Western Hemisphere" (Memorandum E-B19, as quoted in Shoup, 1974:113). Finally, there would have to be new monetary, investment, and trade arrangements.

The introduction to this document makes quite clear what the American interest is in aiding Great Britain in its war with Germany: political concessions by the British and more favorable economic arrangements for the U.S. economy:

> The most important features of the immediate war situation—the continued resistance by Britain and certain military and naval implications growing out of it—are considered. These relate to the extent to which the United States, by more extensive expenditures in both a geographic and a financial sense, some of which may be actually a *quid pro quo* for desired political arrangements, may secure a larger area for economic and military collaboration, thus minimizing costs of *economic* readjustments that would be greater for a smaller area (E-B19, 1940:1, italics in the original).

This breathtaking memorandum was discussed by members of all four study groups then in existence as well as Pasvolsky on October 19, the date it was issued. When the question of Japanese expansion arose, Pasvolsky suggested a study of economic warfare with emphasis on the effectiveness of the American trade sanctions against Japan that were beginning at the time. The result was a memorandum of November 23 detailing the great vulnerability of Japan to such sanctions by the United States. [Secretary of War Stimson and several other cabinet members already were advocates of an oil embargo, but military leaders feared the United States was not yet prepared militarily for any hostilities (Langer and Gleason, 1953:34–35).]

Members of the Political Group present at the plenary session doubted that Germany would settle for a stalemate in the war, so Pasvolsky suggested that the Political Group might

> suggest blocs that it thought might result from the war, and then see what could be done in economic terms within each area. There would be two cores to start on; the first, Germany and the minimum territory she could be assumed to take in the war; the second the United States. Working outward from these cores, one could build up several possible blocs on a political basis, and then examine their economic potentialities (Discussion Memorandum E-A10, as quoted in Shoup, 1974:115).

State Department planners at the staff level, inactive from July to October on postwar questions, resumed their meetings on October 15. They had been organized as an Interdepartmental Group to Consider Postwar Economic Problems and Policies because they now included representatives from the Tariff Commission, Federal Reserve Board, and Agriculture, Treasury, and Commerce departments. Pasvolsky, as chair of the group, proposed a series of commodity studies that paralleled those already completed by the council (1974:124–25). In fact, Pasvolsky gave all members a set of the council studies (1974:127). Shoup writes that the group's work on commodity issues was more extensive than that of the council because of the greater resources of the departments and agencies represented within it, but that "the Council's initial goal of giving direction to the work of the government had clearly been achieved" (1974:128). I think he is right. But neither Shoup nor I is claiming that the council's plans had been adopted as the national interest at this point.

As the State Department resumed its planning studies, the Political Group at the Council on Foreign Relations refined its questions about several of the assumptions in the October 19 report of the Economic and Financial Group. It reaffirmed its belief that Germany would not cease its efforts against Britain under any circumstances, meaning that the prolonged coexistence of a German bloc and an American-led bloc was politically unlikely even if it were economically feasible. The Political Group also questioned the political viability of one non-German bloc dominated by the United States; such a large area might bring charges of imperialism and perhaps alienate some Latin American countries. The Political Group therefore raised the possibility of two democratic blocs in the non-German world, one led by Britain, one led by the United States, with close coordination between the two. Finally, the Political Group raised the possibility that economic sanctions would not make Japan more open to negotiations (1974:132–34). In short, there were differences in perspective between planning groups that needed to be ironed out.

Members from all council planning groups attended a general meeting to discuss these issues on December 14, 1940, still a full year before American entry into the war. While some disagreements remained after the meeting, a general consensus was reached on three key issues. First, most thought there was a need to plan as if there would be a Germanized Western Europe for the immediate future; however, everyone agreed they preferred the defeat of Germany and the integration of Western Europe into the Western Hemisphere–Asia–British Empire bloc that was now being called the "Grand Area." Second, there was general agreement that the Grand Area could not be broken into two democratic blocs because of the danger that Great Britain might try to maintain its empire and exclude the United States from free trade and investment within it. Third, it was agreed that important American economic and strategic interests in Asia were being threatened by Japanese expansionism. The conclusions concerning American interests in Asia were considered so pressing that they were embodied in a memorandum dated January 15, 1941, under the title "American Far Eastern Policy." Using one quote from within this policy report, Shoup summarizes its statement of the American national interest in Asia, and in the process demonstrates the strategic factors that combined with economic issues in shaping postwar policies toward Southeast Asia:

> The main interests of the United States in Southeast Asia were dual in nature. The first was purely economic. The memorandum stated that the "Philippine Islands, the Dutch East Indies, and British Malaya are prime sources of raw material very important to the United States in war and peace; control of these lands by a potentially hostile power would greatly limit our freedom of action." The second concern was strategic with political and psychologi-

cal, as well as economic, aspects. A Japanese takeover of Southeast Asia would impair the British war effort against Hitler, threatening sources of supply and weakening the whole British position in Asia. Many would view it as the beginning of the disintegration of the British Empire. In addition Australia and New Zealand might well decide to concentrate on home defense (1974:137).

The report then suggested that the United States should take the initiative by (1) giving all possible aid to China in its war with Japanese invaders, (2) building up the defenses of countries in Southeast Asia, and (3) cutting off American exports to Japan of such materials as steel armor, machine tools, copper and zinc under "the excuse of our own defense needs" ("American Far Eastern Policy," E-B26, January 15, 1941:3).

In late February 1941, when trade sanctions already were being imposed on Japan, the State Department began its own studies of the possibilities of full economic warfare with Japan (Shoup, 1974:139–40). Sixteen commodity committees were created "to determine which United States exports to Japan were essential to that country" (1974:140). Two reports were completed by late March and early April, and thirty-eight additional studies by August 1. Ironically, these studies led to the abandonment of postwar planning by the aforementioned Interdepartmental Group because they required the services of all available staff. The council was once again left with the main planning capability on postwar issues.

In early 1941, two closely related issues dominated the planning of council leaders now that the conception of the Grand Area had been firmly established in general discussions at the end of 1940. The first was to gain the acceptance of the Grand Area strategy by both American and British central decision-makers; this concern was pursued by pressing for a joint British–American statement of war aims. The second issue concerned the planning of the economic and political organizations that would be needed to integrate the Grand Area; this problem led to a report on tariffs and preferences as integrating mechanisms in February 1941 and to several reports in the second half of 1941 on new international monetary, investment, and development organizations. The issue of war aims turned out to be an immensely tangled one for a variety of reasons that will be explained shortly. The issue of economic integrating mechanisms is not central to my purpose here, so it will be dealt with in the next chapter.

Before turning to the problem of establishing war aims, it is also worth mentioning that council planners began to take positions in government in 1941, a process that was to be intensified greatly a year later. When an Economic Defense Board headed by Vice-President Henry Wallace was established on July 30, 1941, to consider postwar economic issues, Wallace appointed Riefler of the Economic and Financial Group as his chief adviser. About the same time, Upgren of the same planning group became head of the newly created National Economics Unit within the Department of Commerce. It was from this position that he performed staff functions in creating the CED. Finally, Hansen was appointed the United States chairman of the Joint Economic Committee of the

United States and Canada (Shoup, 1974:160). It is likely that these positions provided new avenues for arguing the council perspective. At the least, they were further listening posts about state activities on postwar planning, making the state even more vulnerable to penetration by private elites.

The first report from the Economic and Financial Group concerning war aims, dated April 17, 1941, began with an analysis of what government leaders in various countries had said up to that point relating to war aims. After characterizing the main themes, it noted that both Churchill and Roosevelt had avoided specific statements because they believed that defending freedom by defeating the Nazis was war aim enough. Rather than recommending specific war aims at the time, the report ended with several suggestions for the "tenor" of war aims. These suggestions were based on the assumption "that the United States and Great Britain have a somewhat similar interest in a more closely integrated world economic order" ("Economic War Aims: General Considerations," E-B32:13).

First, national self-determination should be qualified because "a more closely integrated world economic order will almost certainly require some restrictions on sovereignty." Second, "stress should be laid on economic harmony as basic to political liberty and national security." Third, the economic security of individuals should be guaranteed by government. Fourth, specific aspects of reconstruction should be discussed. Fifth, "the benefits of a world economy should be contrasted with autarchy." Finally, no war reparations should be demanded of enemy countries, and aims should apply to the whole world (E-B32:14).

Council leaders pushed their concern for a war aims statement more vigorously at the dinner meetings held by Vice-President Wallace to discuss postwar goals. A meeting on May 3, 1941, was especially important because it produced a lengthy memorandum to the president. Thirteen of the nineteen people present at the dinner were connected with the council, including such important figures in the war–peace studies as Armstrong, Bowman, Dulles, Hansen, Riefler, and Viner. The most detailed history of the Atlantic Charter of August 1941, the first public statement of American–British war aims, treats this memorandum at great length and concludes that "It is notable that a good many of the phrases in the 'Memorandum' recur in the Atlantic Charter" (Wilson, 1969:299, footnote 12).

The memorandum urged a conference between the president and Churchill. It stated as a first principle that America "should and would take much more responsibility in the coming peace than in the peace which is now past" (1969:176, quoting the memorandum). It said the United States should claim a dominant position in the postwar world. It stressed that "it is important to come to agreements while Great Britain is willing to deal" and that there should be "an immediate opening of conversations leading to the establishment of common institutions" (1969:176, quoting the memorandum). Further:

A suggested agenda for such discussions included plans for immediate and joint action, and for postwar cooperation throughout the world. The issue of access to raw materials also belonged on the agenda. These questions could not be postponed much longer; and in fact some participants indicated impatience with the current rate at which the "fusion" of America and British interests was taking place (1969:177).

Finally, the memorandum suggested "a statement of our alternative to Hitler's new order," and reminded the president that "the need for a vigorous lead was repeated over and over. . . . Without outspoken leadership, we are in the position of fighting something with nothing" (1969:178, Wilson's ellipses in the quotation from the memorandum).

The council made a formal recommendation concerning war aims on June 22 in a document that is also seen as background for postwar planning by Eckes (1975:37–38). It began with the two functions of war aims—propaganda and the definition of the national interest—and analyzed the relationship between them:

> Statements of war aims have two functions: propaganda and definition of national interests. The latter is undoubtedly the more difficult and is of basic importance, as a failure of propagandistic and promissory war aims to correspond to the accepted view of national interests might jeopardize the entire peace settlement. Therefore, our national interest must first be defined so that promises incompatible with it may be avoided. It is with this aspect of war aims that the present memorandum is concerned ("Economic War Aims: Main Lines of Approach," E-B36, June 22, 1941:1).

It then defined the national interest:

> (1) the full use of the world's economic resources—implying full employment and a reduction in business cycle fluctuation; and,
> (2) the most efficient use of the world's resources—implying an interchange of goods among all parts of the world according to comparative advantages of each part in producing certain goods (E-B36, 1941:1).

Based on these interests, it called for postwar international antidepression policies, new policies on monetary stabilization and investment, international commissions for special purposes, and a lowering of trade barriers. It concluded:

> One clear and explicit statement must accompany any such list of American war aims: A declaration that the United States, because it recognizes that its interests are in the proper functioning of a world economy, has worldwide responsibilities, and will take part in schemes of international economic cooperation, whether involving new international institutions or only negotiations between governments and will make concessions in its own economic policy to help establish the new requirements—provided, of course, that other countries will do the same (E-B36, 1941:5).

The Political Group added the political dimension to the issue of war aims on July 10. It said that the most important aim was "the decisive defeat of the Axis aggressors as rapidly as possible," calling for total American mobilization and full military collaboration with Great Britain, "regardless of risk." The second aim was the restoration of civil order, including the political reconstruction of Germany to make it an "acceptable member of the international community." Third, there was a need for the establishment of an effective system of international security, essentially through a joint policing effort by the United States and Great Britain ("Basic American Interests," P-B23, July 10, 1941:1–2).

The council statements on war aims are also notable for what they do not emphasize as a panacea: the simple doctrine of free trade espoused by Hull. In the April 19 memorandum, the emphasis on a world economy is coupled with a criticism of making free trade the central focus. "Positive measures of government policy," meaning the kind of international economic organizations envisioned by the planners, are essential:

> This should not be cast in terms of free trade versus autarcky. It is doubtful if the idea of free trade now has very much appeal save to a small group of businessmen and economists. Nor is it likely that anything approaching free trade will be achieved for a long time to come. Rather, we should stress the value to all concerned of a greater interchange of goods, to be brought about in part by a removal of trade barriers and in part by positive measures of government policy ("Economic War Aims: General Considerations," E-B32, 1941:14).

Similarly, the report on war aims of June 22 contains a paragraph on free trade that is even more openly critical of Hull's approach:

> (4) Old shibboleths should play no part in a statement of war aims. For instance, "free trade" sounds attractive to relatively few people and conveys an idea of reversion to the past rather than a willingness to accept a flexible approach to new problems. Such phrases also tend to paralyze the thinking of those addicted to them, by appearing as cure-alls. When used, these ideas should be conjoined with other proposals indicating awareness of the new techniques required by complex difficulties ("Economic War Aims: Main Lines of Approach," E-B36, 1941:3).

Council planners also emphasized their criticisms of the free-trade approach in published statements. For example, the research secretary for the Economic and Financial Group, William Diebold, Jr., in his book on *New Directions in Our Trade Policy,* stated the larger and more power-oriented view of council planners as follows: "The war has made it crystal clear that trade policy is an instrument of foreign policy which must be made to serve the national interest as a whole rather than the limited ends implied in the slogan 'to promote foreign trade' " (Diebold, 1941:111). What the council leaders had in mind for the postwar world, then, was far more than an "amorphous Wilsonianism" based in Lockean liberalism. They saw the United States as a nation that should use its political and military power to create the international economic and political institutions necessary for the expanding world economy they believed essential for the proper functioning of the American, British, and Japanese economies.

However, two problems faced council planners in trying to establish this outlook as the national interest, and it was not until 1942 that these obstacles were fully overcome. The first was that Roosevelt did not want to go beyond general statements of objectives because he did not want arguments with allies, and in particular the British, over specific policies and institutions (Dobson, 1986:65). He also wanted to avoid arousing the strong isolationist voices in Congress who were speaking against any statements or steps that might commit the United States to join the actual fighting. The second problem was that the British wanted to delay discussions of common economic actions as long as possible with the hope they would be able to obtain better terms if the United States entered the war.

Persuading Roosevelt to make the aims explicit was not an insurmountable task, for he already shared an internationalist vision. For him such a statement was a matter of timing, which is the province of a brilliant political leader in the role of head of state. Persuading Britain was another matter. It was greatly weakened financially by American demands that it pay cash for goods from 1939 to 1941, sell off assets in the United States to pay for goods, and limit commercial exports, which made it difficult to develop financial reserves. Great Britain thus feared it would be totally subordinated after the war by the United States, as indeed it was. Furthermore, the British were not confident the Americans would adopt the economic policies that would be needed to prevent another world depression. Although their planners were in fairly close formal and informal contact with council planners, there would still be the problem of dealing with Congress after the war. There even was doubt that Hull was serious about his emphasis on free trade. The American position in talks in 1941 over trade in wheat, for example, was highly discriminatory in favor of American farmers, and completely contradicted Hull's grand principles even though he claimed otherwise (Dobson, 1986:80–84, and Chapter 4).

It is therefore not surprising that the British–American statement on postwar economic aims in the Atlantic Charter was satisfactory to neither Hull nor the council leaders. The statement had an escape clause on free trade that disappointed Hull, and its lack of any statement beyond free trade and equal access to raw materials was not enough for council leaders. The upshot of several days of cagey bargaining between American and British leaders, recounted in detail in Wilson (1969:Chapter 9) and Dobson (1968:Chapter 3), was a laudatory general statement of war aims that only spoke as follows on key economic issues: "They will endeavor, with due regard for their existing obligations, to further the enjoyment by all States, great or small, victor or vanquished, of access on equal terms to the trade and raw materials of the world" (Wilson, 1969:200).

The council reacted to this statement with five brief reports that analyzed its implications and suggested ways to spell out economic cooperation more fully. The fifth of these reports, formally dated January 3, 1942, but discussed and shared with State Department officials in the fall, suggested a joint British-American declaration devoted to economic issues. It was similar to what State Department officials had been proposing to the British in the context of other negotiations to be discussed in the next paragraph, but it emphasized positive government measures and international collaboration as well as freer trade:

> A just and durable peace requires that governments make it their purpose to collaborate on an international basis for the promotion of full employment, increased production, higher living standards, improved labor conditions, social security, and economic stability, in their own countries and throughout the world.
>
> In recognition of this fact, the two Governments declare that:
>
> (A) In their relations with each other and with other countries, they intend to pursue appropriate and coordinated economic policies, in which all countries are invited to participate, that have as their objective the effective world-wide use of the world's productive resources of men and material, to further the purposes set out above.
>
> (B) In order to achieve and maintain the full and most effective world-wide use of the world's productive resources of men and material, they intend to pursue within their respective countries on the basis of international collaboration, appropriate internal economic policies that have as their objective the full use of each country's domestic productive resources of men and material ("Tentative Draft of a Joint Economic Declaration by the Governments of the United States and the United Kingdom," E-B45, 1942:1).

Dissatisfaction with the Atlantic Charter as a statement of war aims also strengthened the resolve of central decision-makers to obtain a more explicit statement of British cooperation in the ongoing lend-lease negotiations. These negotiations were an attempt to establish what "considerations" Great Britain would provide after the war in exchange for the vast amount of free war aid the United States had been providing since March 1941. Here a brief historical reminder may be in order. The congressional bill providing what was termed lend-lease aid to Britain had given the president a free hand in deciding the nature of any future British repayment. In early discussions of the issue, in March and April, central decision-makers in the Treasury Department had thought in terms of such noncash repayments as returning undamaged military equipment and providing raw materials. When the State Department took over the negotiations in May, however, the emphasis switched to "considerations" relating to the ordering of the postwar world. The idea was to use the Lend-Lease Agreement to force the British to open up their empire to the American economy and to join the United States in creating a multilateral world economy (Dobson, 1986:41–46).

It was in part British resistance to these demands that had led the State Department to try to use the meeting between Roosevelt and Churchill in August 1941 to realize its objectives. When that approach was only partially successful, the battleground returned to the Lend-Lease Agreement. Finally, in February 1942 (and here I am telescoping an extremely complicated set of negotiations that will be discussed again in the next chapter), Roosevelt insisted on closure on the issue (Dobson, 1986). Shortly thereafter, the British agreed to a statement more acceptable to the State Department. Hull later called the statement the "foundation" for "all our postwar planning in the economic field" (Hull, 1948:1153, as quoted in Eckes, 1975:40). Council planners also were satisfied with it because it did not begin and end with free trade, and clearly incorporated some of their thinking. The key statement contained several echoes of the council's proposed joint statement cited above:

> In the final determination of the benefits to be provided to the United States of America by the Government of the United Kingdom in return for aid furnished under the Act of Congress of March 11, 1941, the terms and conditions thereof shall be such as not to burden commerce between the two countries, but to promote mutually advantageous economic relations between them and the betterment of world-wide economic relations. To that end, they shall include provision for agreed action by the United States of America and the United Kingdom, open to participation by all other countries of like mind, directed to the expansion, by appropriate international and domestic measures, of production, employment, and the exchange and consumption of goods, which are the material foundations of the liberty and welfare of all peoples; to the elimination of all forms of discriminatory treatment in international commerce, and to the reduction of tariffs and other trade barriers; and, in general, to the attainment of all the economic objectives set forth in the Joint Declaration made on August 14, 1941, by the President of the United States of America and the Prime Minister of the United Kingdom (Gardner, 1956:58–59).

It is not only this statement that reveals a considerable congruity between council statements and official state aims. Other public statements, reports, and actions by central decision-makers during 1941 also present a view of the national interest that is very similar to that found in council memorandums in 1940, thus suggesting the influence of private planners on central decision-makers. On February 21, for example, Assistant Secretary of State Dean Acheson spoke on "World Crisis and the American Farmer" to a farm audience in Des Moines, Iowa. He began by saying that

> Future solidarity of the Americas in the interest of hemisphere defense involves economic problems of a long-range character. The Western Hemisphere, as its economy is organized today, produces vast surpluses of agricultural and other extractive products which have hitherto been disposed of in markets outside the Western Hemisphere (Shoup, 1974:142, quoting Acheson).

While some steps could be taken to deal with these surpluses within the hemisphere, Acheson went on, the fact was that these economies were closely related to those in other parts of the world. Because the hemisphere "does not contain the essential characteristics of a self-contained economic area," it had to

> look elsewhere for market outlets for large surpluses of extractive products. Above all, this hemisphere must continue to have unrestricted access to the great British markets (1974:142, quoting Acheson).

Lynn R. Edminister, a special assistant to Hull, gave a speech similar to Acheson's on May 21. Three key paragraphs relating to the councils Grand Area analysis read as follows:

Every possible advantage would be taken by totalitarian dictatorships of the dependence of this hemisphere upon over-seas markets for the sale of its vast surpluses of agricultural and other extractive products.

It follows from all this that our country should exercise leadership, in policy and action, in an endeavor to establish and maintain the largest possible sphere in the world within which trade and other economic relations can be conducted on the basis of liberal principles and of cooperation to the mutual advantage of all nations which are willing to participate.

In laying the groundwork for future international economic cooperation, it is essential that we take all possible immediate steps to assure that the largest possible grouping shall be formed as the nucleus of such cooperation. To that end the closest possible cooperation between the United States and British empire is indispensable (Shoup, 1974:167–68, quoting Edminister).

Reports from the department's Division of Research, which finally had been created in February 1941 with a three-person staff, also reflected similar postwar goals. Shoup summarizes a report of September 11 as follows:

Trade barriers had to be reduced and discrimination abolished to give all countries equal access to world markets and to increase trade generally. International monetary structures had to be set up, free from exchange controls and in such a way as to allow balancing of international payments with stable exchange rates. Also necessary were adequate facilities for international investment of capital and action to avoid depression (1974:186).

Most striking of all is the rationale that was used in preparing for possible military action with Japan in late 1941. After Japan moved into Southeast Asia in July of that year, central decision-makers imposed an immediate embargo that led to lengthy and tense negotiations. The negotiations broke down in late November because Japan would not agree to the key American demand that it evacuate Chinese territory. The three central decision-makers who functioned as the War Council, Hull, Stimson, and Secretary of Navy Frank Knox, then decided that "Roosevelt should inform Congress and the American people that if Japan attacked Singapore or the East Indies the security of the United States would be endangered and war might result" (Shoup, 1974:196). In a declaration that was preempted by the Japanese attack on Pearl Harbor on December 7, they stated the national interest in terms of assumptions very similar to those developed by council planners in the latter half of 1940. The first and sixth paragraphs read as follows:

This situation, precipitated solely by Japanese aggression, holds unmistakable threats to our interests, especially our interest in peace and peaceful trade, and to our responsibility for the security of the Philippine Archipelago. The successful defense of the United States, in a military sense, is dependent upon supplies of vital materials which we import in large quantities from this region of the world. To permit Japanese domination and control of the major sources of world supplies of tin and rubber and tungsten would jeopardize our safety in a manner and to an extent that cannot be tolerated.

If the Japanese should carry out their now threatened attacks upon and were to succeed in conquering the regions which they are menacing in the southwestern Pacific, our commerce with the Netherlands East Indies and Malaya would be at their mercy and probably be cut off. Our imports from those regions are of vital importance to us. We need those imports in time of peace. With the spirit of exploitation and destruction of commerce which prevails among the partners in the Axis Alliance, and with our needs what they are now in this period of emergency, all interruption of our trade with that area would be catastrophic (Shoup, 1974:197, quoting the document).

Indeed, even the wording in this statement by the War Council has similarities to the "American Far Eastern Policy" report by the council's Economic and Financial Group dated January 15, 1941. The memorandum began with the words "It is to the interest of the United States to check a Japanese advance into southeastern Asia," and then provides the following explanation in the second paragraph:

The Philippine Islands, the Dutch East Indies, and British Malaya are prime sources of raw materials very important to the United States in peace and war; control of these lands by a potentially hostile power would greatly limit our freedom of action. Toward the Philippines we have special obligations of a historical and moral nature. A Japanese occupation of the countries of southeastern Asia would further injure our interests by weakening the British war effort against Hitler, as it would threaten the chief source of supply for the war in the Near East, lead the Australians and New Zealanders to concentrate on home defenses, and would have serious psychological repercussions throughout the world—particularly in Asia, since it would appear to many as the beginning of the disintegration of the British Empire. Conversely, the frustration of Japanese plans for expansion would appear as a defeat for the totalitarian partners in the Tripartite Pact ("American Far Eastern Policy," E-B26:1).

Once the United States entered the war with a definition of the national interest that at the very least can be called consonant with the aims of the council, council leaders worked closely with central decision-makers to intensify planning efforts inside the state and to assure that these efforts were controlled within the State Department, not some other agency or department. On December 28, 1941, the president agreed that "all recommendations on postwar problems of international relations from all departments and agencies of the government should be submitted to the president through the Secretary of State" (Shoup, 1974:200). This put the Department of Treasury and Vice-President Wallace's Economic Defense Board, now renamed the Board of Economic Warfare, in subordinate roles.

On the same date the president also approved a new 14-member Advisory Committee on Postwar Foreign Policy. Council president Norman H. Davis had a large hand in its formation:

The immediate origins of the Advisory Committee on Postwar Foreign Policy can be traced to a September 12, 1941, memorandum drafted by Leo Pasvolsky in consultation with Norman H. Davis. Pasvolsky, acting on directions from Secretary Hull, proposed an Advisory Committee structure, noting that this suggestion was "the result of a recent conversation between Mr. Norman Davis and myself, arranged in accordance with your desires in the matter. It has been read and approved by Mr. Davis" (Shoup and Minter, 1977:148).

The members of the Advisory Committee came primarily from the State Department and the Council on Foreign Relations. Nine were government officials and five were private citizens chosen "because of their high personal qualifications for policy consideration and because of their capacity to represent informed public opinion and interests" (Notter, 1949:72–73). Four of the five private citizens—Armstrong, Bowman, Davis, and former United States Steel chairman Myron Taylor—were members of the Council on Foreign Relations. The fifth, *New York Times* journalist Anne O'Hare McCormick, could not be a council member because it was a male-only organization until the 1970s. Of the government officials, four were members of the council or the war–peace groups, including White House adviser Cohen and planner Pasvolsky. In early 1943, as the Advisory Committee faded in importance, six of the members—Hull, Welles, Davis, Taylor, Bowman, and Pasvolsky—took the main responsibility for political issues and became known as the Informal Political Agenda Group. Roosevelt called them "my postwar advisers" (Shoup, 1974:203). All but Hull were members of the council, and two—Davis and Bowman—were highly involved in the war–peace studies.

The Advisory Committee worked primarily through a series of subcommittees. Bowman, rapporteur of the Council's Territorial Group, chaired the Territorial Subcommittee. Davis chaired both the Security Subcommittee and the Coordination Subcommittee, whose function it was to provide "contact with private organizations actively discussing postwar problems" (Notter, 1949:80). Welles chaired the Political Subcommittee. When a Special Subcommittee on European Organization was created in May 1943 to consider boundary questions and regionwide organizations, it was chaired by Armstrong. Of the eight members of the special subcommittee drawn from other subcommittees, five were members of the council or the war–peace groups. As for the two members from outside the already established subcommittees, they were Percy W. Bidwell and Jacob Viner, revealing once again the importance to the state of experts from the Council's Economic and Financial Group. Notter explains that Bidwell and Viner "were drawn from outside the subcommittee structure for reasons of special technical competence" (1949:147).

The Advisory Committee and subcommittee appointments provided a close liaison between the council and the State Department at the policy level, but council leaders nonetheless sought similar coordination at the research level as well. The issue was discussed at a meeting between council leaders and department officials on February 21, 1942:

> Early in this meeting Armstrong proposed that a decision about liaison and coordination between the Council on Foreign Relations and the Advisory Committee should be made. Welles then asked if the Advisory Committee could take over the research staff of the Council without disrupting its endeavors. Armstrong replied that the Council's labors might be seriously impaired and proposed instead that the research secretaries of the Council should work in the Department two or three days each week, attending the subcommittee meetings. The

Council would thus be in "close relation to the actual functioning of the Advisory Commit-tee." Welles agreed, stating that he "wished to have the most effective liaison that could be devised" (Shoup, 1974:208, with internal quotes from the minutes of the meeting).

Under this arrangement, council discussion groups held their meetings early in the week, freeing the research secretaries to meet with the departmental subcom-mittees later in the week. This allowed the secretaries the opportunity to commu-nicate the research needs of the department to the council groups. They were given the title of "consultants" and received travel expenses and a per diem allowance from the government.

Based on my arguments in Chapter 2, I believe the combination of appoint-ments at both the policy and research levels of the department's postwar planning structure is in itself powerful evidence that the council played a major role in defining the postwar national interest. Moreover, additional evidence for the importance of these appointments arises from the fact that some regular staff members believed that the consultants were dominating the research work through prior consultation with each other and council leaders. In particular, Harley Notter, who later wrote the official departmental history of postwar plan-ning, complained bitterly of the council takeover in several memos to Pasvolsky in early 1942 (Shoup, 1974:247–49). Finally, in September, Notter drafted a letter of resignation stating his situation was no longer tenable for two reasons. The first was that he was receiving one set of instructions from Welles and another from Pasvolsky, which reflected a power struggle between Hull and Welles that included both personal conflicts and complex issues concerning the structure of the projected United Nations. The second concerned the power of the Council on Foreign Relations within the department's Division of Research:

I have consistently opposed every move tending to give it increasing control of the research of this Division, and, though you have also consistently stated that such a policy was far from your objectives, the actual facts already visibly show that Departmental control is fast losing ground. Control by the Council has developed, in my judgment, to the point where, through Mr. Bowman's close cooperation with you, and his other methods and those of Mr. Armstrong on the Committee which proceed unchanged in their main theme, the outcome is clear. The moves have been so piecemeal that no one of them offered decisive objection; that is still so, but now I take my stand on the cumulative trend (Shoup, 1974:250, quoting the letter from the Notter File in the National Archives).

Notter apparently changed his mind about resigning, for the letter was never sent even though nothing changed in the relationship between the council and the department. In his official history Notter (1949) gives no real sense of how large the council's role was nor of his dissatisfaction with it. But his superficial account is a major source for many inadequate histories of postwar planning.

It is also possible to show that this evidence relating to personnel changes in 1942 paralleled expressions of the national interest that were compatible with the council perspective. First, Shoup (1974:Chapter 8) summarizes a number of reports and speeches that provide evidence of this nature that is congruent with evidence I mentioned earlier in this paper for 1941. Second, council planners inside and outside the State Department were the earliest and strongest proponents of an unconditional surrender by Germany and Japan, which was considered essential by council planners if their plans for a new world economic and political order were to be realized. The difficulties of a mere armistice with Germany in World War I were emphasized repeatedly by members of the council's Political and Security and Armaments groups. The issue of armistice versus unconditional surrender was debated within the State Department in the Security Subcommittee headed by Davis. His call for unconditional surrender was supported by the army and navy representatives on the subcommittee, both of whom had been active in council groups and were selected for the subcommittee by Davis (Shoup, 1974:232). According to a memorandum from Notter to Pasvolsky dated April 8, 1943, Davis and the two military officers dominated the proceedings of the subcommittee (Shoup, 1974:233; cf. Gaddis, 1972:8).

Third, the planning for international organizations to integrate the postwar world also provides evidence that the substance of the council's earlier concerns was being taken as part of the national interest. The plans for the United Nations, worked out within the Informal Political Agenda Group with the aid of Pasvolsky and others, reflected the council's interest in the political integration of the postwar world (Shoup, 1974:238–46). However, it is true that such an organization was sought by other private groups and Hull as well (e.g., Divine, 1967). It also can be shown that the council's monetary objectives were embodied in the planning by the Treasury Department for the International Monetary Fund, as will be demonstrated in great detail in the next chapter in a critique of Fred Block's theorizing.

There is much more than could be said about the scores of planning problems that had to be faced on economic, transportation, political, territorial, population, and reconstruction issues in the years between 1942 and 1945, and the council produced hundreds of reports relating to them. The task of analyzing these reports and their impact is one for future researchers. However, I believe enough has been said here to show that the postwar imperial policies of the United States grew out of economic and strategic considerations that reflect the concerns, analyses, and goals of the war–peace study groups in the years 1940 and 1941. The council's definition of the postwar national interest had been firmly established in the state by the end of 1942 at the latest. The only new policy issue of major import that faced council planners and central decision-makers between 1943 and 1946 was the incorporation of the German economy and Western Europe into the Grand Area. Council planners worked diligently on this issue with State Department officials to defeat a last-minute Treasury Department plan to deindustrialize Germany that Morgenthau slipped into the appendix of a Roosevelt-Churchill meeting where the State Department was not represented. It turned out to be a tempest in a teapot, with the Morgenthau plan having no chance of being adopted (Shoup and Minter, 1977:189–95).

It is in the context of Grand Area planning between 1940 and 1942 then that we should look at how central decision-makers viewed Vietnam from 1943 to 1968. If we keep in mind that Southeast Asia was considered essential to the Grand Area from as early as the summer of 1940, and that council planners were prepared by the winter of 1940 to advocate war to keep Japan out of that area, then we can begin to appreciate the remarkable continuity that is found on this issue in the postwar reports and books of the council and in the official position papers of the state's National Security Council created in 1947. True enough, as all sources stress, the Cold War and the resultant containment policy, along with a fear of appearing "soft on communism" in the eyes of voters, came to dominate the thinking of postwar central decision-makers. But only the specific enemy had changed, not the policy. The primary concerns remained, first, healthy Japanese and British economies that could function in harmony with the American economy and, second, the ability to limit the power of nations that threatened this economically based conception of the American national interest. Since this Grand Area definition of the national interest preceded the advent of the Soviet threat, it cannot be attributed to a Lockean dislike of communism.

Before turning to the issue of the Vietnam War, however, it might be useful to mention briefly the concerns of council leaders in relation to communism in the early 1940s. While it is clear that none of them liked communism, the issue was discussed primarily in connection with Eastern Europe. Recognizing the weak and underdeveloped nature of the fragmented economies in the small countries of that region, some council planners suggested the creation of an Eastern European customs union. Such a customs union might lead to a regional economy that could serve as a market for Western Europe and as a buffer against the Soviet Union (Shoup, 1974:241).

Council leaders and central decision-makers were divided as to the possibility of such an outcome. When Armstrong argued at a State Department subcommittee meeting on March 7, 1942, that steps should be taken to keep those countries from becoming communist, Assistant Secretary of State A. A. Berle, Jr., "immediately reminded Armstrong that Russian help was indispensable for a United Nations victory and that the Department should be cautious about moves to put hostile states on that country's borders" (Shoup, 1974:241, paraphrasing State Department minutes). When Armstrong pressed the same point at a meeting of the department's Territorial Subcommittee on October 9, 1942, Bowman thought there was no choice but to accept it if the Soviets took over those countries (1974:242). Historian John Gaddis (1972:137) also uses comments by Bowman to suggest that by 1943 American decision-makers were prepared to acquiesce in Soviet hegemony in Eastern Europe. In short, there was neither strong emphasis nor great unity on the question of Eastern Europe, the primary area where there was a threat of communism. Germany and Japan were the dangers to the Grand Area conceived as the necessary living space for the American economy, and neither the Soviet Union nor Eastern Europe was a part of that area. Southeast Asia, however, was a part of the Grand Area, and I believe that is a major reason why communism was resisted so vigorously in that region.

To demonstrate the original basis of later policy in Southeast Asia, it is necessary to return to council and State Department planning for colonial areas between 1942 and 1945. The first council deliberations on Southeast Asia took place in the Territorial Group on March 18, May 20, and July 6, 1942. Armstrong and Bowman were the main figures in the discussions, a point of major significance because of their subsequent impact on colonial policies within the State Department. Providing the starting points for these discussions were reports by group member Owen Lattimore, an expert on Asia who had recently returned to the United States after serving as a political adviser to Chiang Kai-shek.

As the "Digests of Discussion" for these meetings make clear, the question of freedom for the native peoples of Southeast Asia was constantly balanced with the need to secure American interests. Thus, in the context of anticipating what China might want in Indochina, Bowman drew some conclusions about power that seem to reflect the bottom line for later American strategizing about the area:

> The course of the discussion led Mr. Bowman to observe that a general idealized scheme, as, for example, of complete Asiatic freedom, sometimes runs counter to proposals which were more practical. He was not opposed to the aspirations of the Chinese, but he did not think we could proceed from victory to the ideal, but must go from victory to that security which is a prime condition for the realization of the ideal. Security must take first precedence. It is, in the first instance, a matter of power—power exercised from critical points. The problem is how to make the exercise of that power international in character to such an extent that it will *avoid conventional forms of imperialism.* The eventual question will be how to provide for a later period of genuine international collaboration on a wider basis. All of the ideal principles of the Atlantic Charter, for instance, will be empty words without a prior guarantee of security through power. We should come out and say this openly and frankly. At the same time, we can point to our Latin American good neighbor policy of the last decade as proof of our contention that the possession of overwhelming power need not result in that abuse of power characteristic of imperialism ("Digests of Discussion," T-A25, 1942:9, emphasis added).

On July 6 the group discussed a memorandum on French Indochina (Cambodia, Laos, and Vietnam) prepared by Lattimore. The members were highly critical of French administration of the colony and thought it best to postpone any decisions on how it should be governed until after the war. Based on the discussion, the group sent the State Department an outline for further studies in relation to Southeast Asia and China, entitled "Political, Territorial, and Strategic Elements of a Settlement in the Far East." As will be seen in the context of State Department planning in 1943, the Territorial Group returned to its discussions of Indochina and Southeast Asia at that time.

The most detailed study of official postwar planning for Southeast Asia can be found in the work of historian Gary Hess (1987). He reports that the State Department's Subcommittee on Territorial Problems, chaired by Bowman, and including Armstrong and Taylor among its members, gave early attention to colonialism in Southeast Asia. However, he writes that "the most extensive discussion and the significant recommendations emerged later from the Subcommittee on Political Problems" (1987:62). This subcommittee was chaired by Welles, and included Armstrong, Bowman, and Taylor among its nine members. The membership of the two subcommittees actually overlapped almost entirely except that Welles and one other person were not on the Territorial Subcommittee (1987:62).

At the outset, both subcommittees hoped to push the European colonial powers into a worldwide anticolonial policy based on the principles of the Atlantic Charter. As the idea was crystalized in the Subcommittee on Political Problems in August 1942, there would be a trusteeship arrangement whereby the major powers would oversee a gradual movement to independence by former colonies. However, the bad French record in dealing with Indochina might require a special arrangement there, at least in the first thoughts of Welles:

> Welles drew an important distinction between the French colony and those of Britain and the Netherlands. While international administration of Indochina was necessitated by the French record, the British and Dutch could be restored to authority in their colonies provided they agreed to general supervision of, and to report to, the regional international trusteeship council. Hence the Southeast Asian trusteeship council, as envisioned in August, 1942, would have an overall responsibility for assuring the development of self government, but would exercise direct control only in Indochina (Hess, 1987:66).

But this solution, which also reflected Roosevelt's views on French policy in Indochina, pleased no one. Hull and others in the State Department did not like the plan because the department had claimed it would treat all colonies the same, and they did not want to weaken France in Europe (e.g., Kattenburg, 1980:13–14). The British did not like it because it forced them to give up some sovereignty over their colonies, and divided them from their French allies. The French didn't like it because it took away their colony.

In an attempt to deal with the emerging tangle over Indochina, it was Bowman who wrote the memorandum that led to the eventual American position. Not surprisingly, it reflected his earlier thinking and that of other members in the war–peace Territorial Group. Dated October 29, 1943, Bowman's statement listed four alternatives for dealing with Vietnam that ranged from independence to complete French control without supervision. Independence was ruled out because of a fear of instability in the region (Hess, 1987:75). Complete French control was considered unacceptable due to France's past failures. A trusteeship such as Welles and Roosevelt favored was ruled out because, as Hess summarizes, such a plan "depended upon all colonial powers accepting similar international control of their possessions" (1987:74). Thus, Bowman argued that the area had to be returned to French control through British–American power, but with "an international system providing for review and inspection of colonial areas" (1987:74). When Britain and France wouldn't even agree to that much oversight, the United States in effect had no choice but to support France because of its fear of an independent Vietnam.

According to Hess, Bowman's conclusions were "reinforced" by a report dated November 16, 1943, from an expert on Southeast Asia who was working for the Territorial Group:

> The conclusions of the Territorial Subcommittee were reinforced by a detailed report on Indochina by Rupert Emerson, who like [Amry] Vanderbosch [a political scientist advising the State Department] was a recognized authority on Southeast Asia. Emerson's study, completed for the Council on Foreign Relations, analyzed the prewar conditions in Indochina and the various postwar options. He held that French rule should be continued but subject to international review, and the expectation that it would lead to self-government (1987:76).

In fact, Emerson had been a member of the council's Territorial Group since August 1943 and had discussed these issues with Bowman before Bowman wrote his official memorandum. In September 1943, he also wrote a council memorandum, "Regionalism in Southeast Asia," in which he had floated the idea of a regional council "to establish non-discriminatory trade policies" and to place "political and economic control in hands likely to be friendly to the United States" (T-B67, 1943:6). In other words, the combination of Bowman and Emerson meant that the council view had carried the day.

Two years later, with a nationalist movement fighting for independence in what was by then called Vietnam, American leaders were faced with a decision about supporting the French once again. They decided they could not risk granting independence to Vietnam because of the communist leadership of the nationalist movement, despite the close ties between the nationalist movement and the handful of American government officials in Vietnam. The United States would support nationalists, as shown in Indonesia in 1947–48, but not communist-nationalists (Kattenburg, 1980:5–8). In deciding to oppose the communist-nationalists, American leaders knew from the start that they were likely to lose. Their policy goal became one of denying the area to communism for as long as possible. Given that minimal goal, their policy was successful between 1945 and 1975, as Gelb and Betts (1979) argue. They did not deceive themselves about Vietnam, but only the general public. The policy advice they received was accurate about the great strength of the communist-nationalists, and the decision to fight for a stalemate was made with their eyes wide open. For that reason Gelb and Betts give their book the title *The Irony of Vietnam: The System Worked;* it is a hymn to the rationality of the American elite and the U.S. state.

Once the decision was made to support France in Vietnam, American leaders had to follow French policy even while providing indirect financial support through the Marshall Plan from 1948 to 1950 and direct military support from 1950 to 1954. The Americans could suggest, cajole, and even threaten, but the French now had the ultimate weapon: the threat to leave. If the Americans ever were tempted to deal with the Vietnamese leadership in the 1940s, and it is highly unlikely that they were, that temptation disappeared when the communists won in China in 1949, followed shortly thereafter by the Korean War. From that point forward, according to historian Robert M. Blum in his study of postwar policy in Southeast Asia, "The American containment policy in Southeast Asia arose from the ashes of its failed policy in China" (1982:214).

But yet, despite the importance of the revolution in China in shaping subsequent American policy in Southeast Asia in general, there is still a problem in terms of Vietnam specifically. As Gaddis (1987:89) has pointed out, the inclusion of Indochina within the American "defensive perimeter" in Asia in the late 1940s actually was an "anomaly." The military suggested a defense rooted primarily in islands stretching from the Aleutians, Midway, and Okinawa to British and Dutch islands in the southwest Pacific (1987:74). Nonetheless, a study by the State Department's Policy Planning Staff in March 1949 and a National Security Council review in December of the same year both concluded that Southeast Asia was more vital than either Taiwan or Korea. Gaddis, basing his analysis on official government documents, but without the benefit of information on earlier council planning for the area, explains American concern with Southeast Asia in the late 1940s as follows:

> American officials appear to have made an exception to their general rule of not regarding mainland areas as vital, in the case of Indochina, for several reasons: (1) the conviction that Ho Chi Minh was a more reliable instrument of the Kremlin than Mao Zedong; (2) the belief that the Soviet Union had designated Southeast Asia as a special target of opportunity; (3) concern over the importance of Southeast Asia as a source of food and raw materials; and (4) in an early version of what would come to be known as the "domino theory," fear of the strategic and psychological consequences for the rest of non-communist Asia if Indochina should fall to communism (1987:90).

Drawing on the work on the American occupation of Japan by Michael Schaller (1985), Gaddis stresses that the concern with food and raw materials involved support for the Japanese economy as well as keeping needed supplies from the Chinese communists. Then too, the importance of Southeast Asia at the time as a source of raw materials and markets for Europe as well as Japan is stressed in an account of an aid mission to Southeast Asia in 1950 written by its deputy chief (Hayes, 1971:21–22). In short, we can see here great continuity between American policy toward Southeast Asia in the early postwar period and the council's prewar conception of the future Grand Area. Once again, that is, there is a deep concern with Japan and its economy that is as important as the ideological need to "draw the line somewhere" in explaining the American desire to protect Indochina.

The council itself devoted little direct attention to Southeast Asia in the post-war years until March 1950, when it formed a study group to reconsider the region. During the next year it created a joint study group with Great Britain's parallel organization, the Royal Institute of International Affairs, to discuss the same area. The view of council leaders resulting from these discussion groups is best revealed in the book that came out of the joint study group. Shoup and Minter summarize the book as follows, with the internal quotes coming from the book:

> The book produced by the joint study group in January 1953 defined the American national interest in Southeast Asia almost exactly as had the War and Peace Studies Project—in economic and strategic terms. The book argued that 'Southeast Asia contributes some of the most critical raw materials needed by Western Europe and the United States. It also makes an essential contribution to the food supply of India.' Strategically, the 'loss of any further portion' of the Far East in general 'could well have decisive effects on the balance of world power in the years ahead.' (1977:226).

The first full statement of the American national interest in Southeast Asia in over a decade by a central decision-maker was written in January 1952 by W. Averell Harriman, a director of the council and Truman's director of mutual security. Shoup and Minter (1977:234) call Harriman's memorandum "identical" with the council view on why the area was of importance. Six months later, the National Security Council approved a statement of policy concerning Southeast Asia that had the usual emphasis on raw materials and the strategic role of the region, adding that "the loss of any single country would probably lead to a relatively swift submission to or an alignment with communism by the remaining countries in this group" (1977:234, quoting NSC memorandum 124/1). In addition, and in keeping with the now-familiar Grand Area conception of the American national interest, the statement concluded that "the loss of Southeast Asia, especially of Malaya and Indonesia, could result in such economic and political pressures in Japan as to make it extremely difficult to prevent Japan's eventual accommodation to Communism" (1977:235, quoting NSC memorandum 124/1).

In October, 1953, the council organized a 40-person discussion group on Southeast Asia. Its research director, William Henderson, wrote a pamphlet for the closely related Foreign Policy Association in March 1955, based on his work for the group. It called Southeast Asia an "economic and strategic prize" that was "worth fighting for" (1977:227–28). A 1954–55 study group on the area resulted in a book by the group's research director, John K. King of the University of Virginia, that claimed the area was "of global strategic importance roughly comparable to Panama and Suez" (King, 1956:7, as quoted in Shoup and Minter, 1977:229). Raw materials and the importance of the area to Japan also were part of his argument.

During the Eisenhower years, with John Foster Dulles and Allen W. Dulles of the war–peace study groups serving as secretary of state and director of the CIA, respectively, National Security Council statements of 1954, 1956, 1958, and 1960 continued to define the national interest in Southeast Asia in terms of concepts similar to those of the council and the Truman administration. The last paragraph was almost identical in language to the last paragraph of the policy statement under Truman: "The loss of Southeast Asia, especially of Malaya and Indonesia, could result in such economic and political pressure on Japan as to make it extremely difficult to prevent Japan's eventual accommodation to communism" (Shoup and Minter, 1977:236, quoting NSC memorandum 5405).

The council established another study group on Southeast Asia in 1959 that met over a two-year period. Among the 43 members were several people who had been in the earlier studies of the subject, including Henderson and King, and one person, Philip Mosely, who had been a research secretary in the war–peace studies and a State Department adviser on Southeast Asia after the war. The research director, Russell F. Fifield of the University of Michigan, in effect summarized the group's outlook in his *Southeast Asia in United States Politics* (1963). He repeated the same themes found in the work of council leaders and research scholars since the early 1940s. He also called for military involvement and supported the interdependency theory that had come to be known as the "falling-dominoes" principle: "Military defense against direct and indirect aggression must be a fundamental United States objective in Southeast Asia, for without security all other goals collapse like a row of dominoes when the first is pushed over" (Fifield, 1963:407, quoted in Shoup and Minter, 1977:232).

With this definition of the American national interest firmly established over nearly a 20-year period, the Kennedy administration had little discussion of basic assumptions as it gradually involved itself in Vietnam. Many commentators at the time had the impression that United States involvement in the war was unthinking and almost accidental, with no real understanding of the risks and costs, and it was not until the publication of the *Pentagon Papers* (1971) that most people began to understand otherwise. As political scientist John C. Donovan later wrote in his study, *The Cold Warriors: A Policy-Making Elite* (1974):

> The Kennedy administration did not question (even privately) the *purposes* of the American intervention in Vietnam. Kennedy and his advisers went along with the inherited assumption that the perpetuation of a non-Communist regime in Saigon was vital to United States interests (as quoted in Shoup and Minter, 1977:237, his italics).

More recent accounts of decision-making in the 1960s, based upon previously classified documents, provide support for Donovan's analysis. Gelb and Betts conclude that for the Kennedy years, "Vietnam policy debates from the beginning of the administration centered on how to save Vietnam, not whether to save it" (1979:73). Political scientist Larry Berman reports for the Johnson administration that "the documents show that the principals accepted containment of communism and the domino theory as basic premises for formulating policies and not as hypotheses for analysis" (1982:130). Berman also quotes a government study of Vietnam decision-making that emphasizes that the basic commitment to defend Southeast Asia was made early in the postwar era and never really challenged thereafter (1982:131).

There is also ample evidence that the "wise men," the group of former government officials who informally advised Johnson, were highly supportive of government escalation of the war until the Tet offensive in February 1968. At that point the group advised Johnson not to send more troops, and the gradual switch in war strategy was underway. According to Shoup and Minter (1977:242), 12 of the 14 men present at this crucial turning point were members of the Council on Foreign Relations.

The rest is history, as the saying goes, a terrible war and a terrible tragedy (Berman, 1982). There is no need to repeat that story here. This chapter is about how the national interest came to be defined by the Council on Foreign Relations and central decision-makers, not about the consequences of that definition. It is to the implications of this defining process for state theory that I now turn.

## Discussion

I think the foregoing account establishes several key points that do not fit with Krasner's general theory of state autonomy or his claims about the reasons for American interventionism after 1945.

First, the definition of the national interest that animated postwar foreign policy was created in good part by leaders and planners within the private and elite-based Council on Foreign Relations in the years 1940 and 1941. These private elites also worked very hard within the state in 1941 and 1942 to see that their goals were adopted as the national interest. This material suggests that the state as defined by Krasner was not autonomous from the larger society on what he regards as a critical issue for his theory.

Second, the new definition of the national interest was in good part economic in the sense that it was concerned with the full functioning of the American capitalist system with minimal changes in it. The goal was to avoid depression and social upheaval, on the one hand, and greater state control of the economy on the other. True enough, capitalists and state decision-makers shared these common goals. However, this establishes that state goals were not separate from capitalist goals, but compatible with them. Both corporate planners and central decision-makers were defending the American way of life, a way of life in which the state has the smallest possible role. Acceptance of the idea of the smallest possible state by central decision-makers further suggests that private capitalists are at least equal partners in the arrangement.

Third, the focus of central decision-makers was on providing raw materials and markets for other large capitalist countries as well as on the security of American supply. Thus, raw material goals are not exclusively state goals, but shared goals of capitalists and central decision-makers. This claim is in keeping with Krasner's own observation on the issue: "While the United States is still relatively self sufficient in most natural resources, its major allies, the Western European states and Japan, are very dependent on foreign mineral resources" (1978:220). This is exactly how council planners saw the matter in 1940, and this helps to undercut Krasner's claim that postwar interventionism around the world was primarily ideological.

Fourth, the national interest defined by council planners was far more than Hull's "amorphous Wilsonianism" based in Lockean liberalism, which Krasner claims to be the basis of American foreign policy from 1940 to 1947 in an article related to his book (Krasner, 1977). Two wartime planners who later wrote on their experience, one British (Harrod, 1951:528), one American (Penrose, 1953:19), have made this point, and council planners made it not only in documents I have quoted, but in contemporary books as well (Diebold, 1941:111). This fact further undermines Krasner's claim that American foreign policy only took on its imperial form after the war as an ideological reaction to communism.

Fifth, I believe that anticommunism became a key aspect of foreign policy only after the Soviet Union, China, and their Communist party allies within many nations became the new challengers to the Grand Area conception of the national interest. In a certain sense, as stated in the previous section, they merely replaced the fascists of Germany and Japan as the enemies of the international economic and political system regarded as essential by American leaders. Communism is indeed anathema to the Lockean liberal ideology that permeates the United States, but that only made it easier to mobilize the country for the challenge. Moreover, fascism also was abhorrent to Lockean liberalism, as demonstrated in opinion polls in the United States in the late 1930s, and it too was defined as an implacable enemy that must be forced to surrender unconditionally. The special emphasis on anticommunism as an ideological reaction is misguided. Indeed, I would argue that the Americans were prepared to live and let live with both the Soviets and the Chinese Communists until communist threats arose within Western Europe and Southeast Asia, a claim that is borne out by good relations with China since the 1970s and better relations with the Soviets when they backed off in the Third World and Eastern Europe in the 1980s.

Sixth, it is striking how consistently the council leaders and central decision-makers defined American interests in Southeast Asia in terms of conclusions that were reached in 1940 and 1941. They were always concerned with the raw materials and the strategic importance of the area of which Vietnam is a part, but perhaps even more with the area as a market for Japan, Britain, and the United States. Nor was their concern with "falling dominoes" nonrational and ideological, for they did end up losing Cambodia and Laos when they lost Vietnam, and they were fighting in Vietnam at a time when Indonesia had the third-largest

Communist party in the world. It is not a trivial fact that President Lyndon Johnson proudly mentioned the defeat of the Indonesian Communist party in the 1968 speech in which he announced that he would not run again. The geopolitical rather than simply ideological basis for the actions in Southeast Asia by central decision-makers also is revealed in a remarkably clear fashion in this paragraph from a piece that former Kennedy and Johnson adviser Samuel P. Huntington wrote for the *Washington Post* in 1977:

> My support for American involvement in Vietnam declined significantly in 1966 because changes in Asia greatly reduced the communist threat to Southeast Asia: China became engulfed in the Cultural Revolution; the dimensions of the Sino-Soviet split became clearer; the military take-over in Indonesia eliminated the likelihood of Communist control of that country; and so on. I changed my views accordingly (Huntington, 1977:Feb. 1, A-17).

It would seem that these six conclusions do not leave much room for a state-centric theory such as Krasner's when it is applied to the United States. However, a proponent might argue that council planners and other private interests were being used by the state for its own purposes. They did not influence the state, but rather the state influenced them and only used those plans which fit with its goals. In reply to any claim that the state merely used the council, I would argue in the following way.

First, the council planners made many of their suggestions before the central decision-makers began to think about postwar issues. Priority certainly does not automatically show influence, but it leans in that direction. Second, the state had very little postwar planning capability of its own. Attempts at both staff-level studies and policy-level discussions were made in fits and starts between 1940 and 1942, but they were interrupted by immediate issues that required all the time and energies of central decision-makers and their small staffs. Third, and here I am slightly repeating one of the general conclusions I made earlier, it does not fit with the idea of the state using the council that so much emphasis was placed on economic matters, particularly on the question of leaving intact the present economic structure of the society. While central decision-makers with a Lockean ideology certainly would not want to control the economy, their lack of interest in independent political and state goals seems excessive even given that ideology. Fourth, I would argue that the ability to place members in key positions as central decision-makers is evidence that the private interests at the council were not being used by the state. Since state autonomy theorists put no weight on the social and occupational backgrounds of central decision-makers, this argument will not wash with them. I hope it will make sense to other readers in light of the analysis presented in Chapter 2.

Proponents of a state-centric theory also might try to rebut the account in the previous section by saying that all the economic analyses were just so much rationalization. Central decision-makers wanted to control the world for Lockean reasons once that they had the power to do so. They therefore gladly accepted economic arguments so that they could defend and then take over the British empire, or so they could protect the British because they shared a somewhat common ideology with them (Locke, after all, was British). But once we enter into an argument over "real" reasons that go beyond the written and spoken record, we are on a very slippery slope as far as empirical studies. Short of some very subtle content analysis system for inferring motives, we soon lose the possibility of doing research because a critic can say the studies don't deal with the "real" reasons. Put another way, if the kind of empirical analysis presented in this chapter does not go deep enough, then the case studies by Krasner are brought into question as well, for he too relied on the statements and actions of private leaders and central decision-makers.

Assuming that the empirical findings presented in the previous section are accurate, what are their implications? What all this adds up to, I believe, is that distinctions among rational economic interests, state goals, and a general ideology are false ones, as others also have argued (e.g., Smith, 1974; Randall, 1980, Mann, 1986). Indeed, Stephen J. Randall, who has written his own book on American foreign oil policy between the years 1919 and 1944 (Randall, 1985), makes this point about artificial distinctions in a review of Krasner's book: "This distinction between ideology and economic-strategic objectives tends to be artificial and overly restrictive, suggesting a compartmentalization of values that bears little relationship to reality" (Randall, 1980:414).

Now, Krasner is fully aware that central decision-makers are cognizant of the needs of the economic system, and that they often take actions to benefit that system. Where his compartmentalization causes problems in my view is in the narrow vision that he in effect attributes to private corporate leaders and economic planners, implying they are not aware of the fact that business takes place in a nation-state system. His view gives the impression that the power elite are only concerned with narrow economic issues, not with ideology or the power of "their" nation. It does not easily accommodate the fact that corporate planners in the war–peace study groups concerned themselves with strategic, political, and ideological interests as well as economic ones. That they were concerned with "the national interest" is almost a contradiction from a state-centric perspective.

A small example of this narrow view of corporate leaders can be seen in Krasner's (1978:50–51) brief discussion of the 1951 presidential commission on raw materials known as the Paley Commission. As Krasner notes, the report of the commission begins with a ringing ideological attack on the machinations of the "barbarous" communist nations. It then makes various recommendations that Krasner claims were ignored once the Korean War ended and prices on raw materials stabilized.

But Krasner's account is deficient on two counts concerning the perspective of corporate leaders on ideology and the state. First, this ideological report was written by a commission that was made up in good part of corporate leaders and private planners who were appointed at the behest of a corporate leader serving in government for a brief time. The most conspicious, of course, was Paley himself as the owner and chief executive officer of CBS (and a member of the Council on Foreign Relations), but others were almost as prominent. Second, it is not quite correct to say that nothing came of the recommendations. In fact, the private institute suggested by the report to develop new ways to think about raw materials was organized shortly thereafter as Resources for the Future with a generous grant from the Ford Foundation. Paley became chairman of its board, and there is reason to believe that it has had a significant impact in shaping how planners think about raw materials and in providing experts for government service (Alpert and Markusen, 1980).

In short, this example shows that corporate leaders can be as "ideological" and anticommunist as central decision-makers, and that they can use presidential commissions to help legitimate nonprofit institutions that develop close connections to both the corporate community and the state. This chapter has made the case for such a linkage only in terms of the Council on Foreign Relations, but I have argued elsewhere (Domhoff, 1970c, 1974a, 1979) and in earlier chapters of this book that such nonprofit, bipartisan organizations form a policy-planning network that is the true "political organization" of big business and in some ways part of "the state" as well. In my view, then, the Paley Commission and Resources for the Future are a microcosm of the more general point that the separation of ideology, economy, and state is not a good foundation for theorizing about power in the United States.

Beyond the Paley Commission and the United States, there is recent evidence that separating ideology, economy, and state may not be a good idea for any advanced capitalist country. This evidence appears in Harvey Feigenbaum's (1985) detailed study of the relationship between oil companies and the French state in the twentieth century. The case is particularly appropriate in this context because Krasner (1978:58) believes that France and Japan probably have the "strongest states" among developed market-economy countries. He claims the French state has used a variety of policy instruments, including control over credit, to "exercise public control over private actors," choosing the interests it prefers to deal with (1978:58). In addition, the political culture accepts an activist state, unlike the United States, and "the best graduates from the most elite universities are likely to choose the central administration over the private sector" (1978:60).* Considerable control over the oil industry is outlined as one prime example of the strength of the French state (1978:58).

---

*Krasner here suddenly concedes that it might matter who governs and inadvertently provides another argument for the Council on Foreign Relation's influence over the state on postwar policy, for the best graduates of elite American universities go to work in the private sector, not the state sector. It is hard to imagine that the often young and often second-rate staff members within the State Department were not deferential to the likes of Hansen of Harvard and Viner of the University of Chicago. Council planners certainly understood this issue. In the summary of a discussion with British planners on January 24, 1942, it is stated that the people in government service with the time to plan ahead are the "washouts." To have a plan with the prestige to be taken seriously by the

But archival and interview research by Feigenbaum has revealed a very different story. The efforts of the French state, even its creation of public-supported oil companies, mostly have served the interests of the oil industry. The major result of French oil policies has been higher prices for all consumers and a loss of competitiveness for some industrial sectors where energy costs are important. This is hardly an outcome that consistently benefits society in general, thus contradicting one aspect of Krasner's definition of the national interest. Even security of supply has not been assured, for French oil companies did not act differently from private oil companies during oil shortages. In the final analysis, claims Feigenbaum:

> the actual behavior of these firms has been to defend sectoral interests at the expense of the public interest. This suggests that parts of the French state have been captured in much the same way that McConnell described the supposedly weak United States bureaucracy (1985:25).

This fragmentation of the state has made it very difficult for central decision-makers to pursue an overall policy that is rational in terms of state interests, consumer interests, or even general capitalist interests in France. How is such an outcome possible? Feigenbaum attributes it to the acceptance of a liberal market ideology by all concerned, and I think his argument is a convincing one:

> Ideology reinforces institutional linkages of state to society. Thus the ideology of neoclassical economics dominates the solutions of French officials. This is reinforced by networks of dependence. In the French state, the political representatives depend on the bureaucracy for expertise and the bureaucracy depends on the private sector both for information and for the careers of its personnel. Those who do not accept the doctrine are not "serious," and are treated accordingly (1985:167–68).

Or, as he puts the argument within the context of an economic starting point:

> Said another way, market forces fragment capitalist interests (e.g., into buyers and sellers, oligopolists and competitive industries) and become reflected in the state through a division of labor in the policy process. This fragmentation is reinforced by competition among elites whose corps have colonized different sectors. The dominant ideology of "efficiency-promoting" profit centers justifies independent firms and thus reinforces the fragmentation of the state. Thus, even when some sectors pass into public hands, the doctrines of profit maximization and managerial autonomy serve to keep the state from posing any real threat to the private sector as a whole (1985:173).

*(continued)
"operational" people in government, it would have to be developed by people outside government who were in touch with key positions in government ("Digests of Discussion," E-A25, Part II: 10–11).

Although Feigenbaum is arguing that ideology disarms the state, he is not claiming that it is a clever plan to mystify the workers. To the contrary, it mystifies everyone, and makes it difficult if not impossible to solve practical problems:

> A caveat, however: ideology may be the mechanism that both unifies diverse factions and ensures the predominance of the private sector, but it does not necessarily follow that economic beliefs will function in the long-term interests of those who hold them. The evidence presented here seems to indicate that although the ruling ideology is based on an idealization of the market, its effect in terms of practical policy is to obscure solutions to the problems of advanced capitalism. Ideology does indeed mystify, but what many writers seem to ignore is that ideology mystifies the rulers as well as the ruled (1985:168).

Feigenbaum thus shows that the state does not pursue a national interest that is independent of capitalist ideology, but instead cannot pursue a separate national interest because it has a capitalist ideology:

> It is a final irony that the ideological sinews which bind the state to capitalist society also inhibit it from solving the economic problems of advanced capitalism. Neither the private sector nor the state capitalist public sector seems to have an incentive structure that promises an easy solution to the problems of energy, reindustrialization, and inflation (1985:171).

Feigenbaum concludes with a critique of both Krasner and structural Marxists concerning their theories of state autonomy. Krasner's view, assuming a unified state pursuing a unified interest, is contradicted by the lack of unity in both the society and the state. In a fragmented state, as noted in Chapter 2, the various bureaucracies are "vulnerable to the demands of the already privileged," and various elites thus penetrate those parts of the state of concern to them (1985:172). As for the structural Marxists:

> The theoretical intentions of these writers seem to be governed largely by embarrassment at the continuing ability to capitalist economies to endure. Yet their implicit conclusion is that the autonomous state ensures capitalism's durability. The conclusions of this study are quite the opposite. It is precisely because the state is not autonomous that the problems of capitalist economies become intractable. Potentially powerful state institutions become neutralized. Strong states become weak states precisely because they are captured states (1985:173).

The detailed case study presented in this chapter strongly supports Feigenbaum's generalizations based on the French case, for it has shown the ways in which private elites affiliated with the Council on Foreign Relations were able to penetrate a state that shared their liberal, capitalist ideology and thereby help create an expansionist economic definition of the postwar national interest. This new definition of the national interest had ramifications throughout the society because it called for an international economic and political system that would include the Western Hemisphere, the British Empire, and Asia as a "Grand

Area" to be protected politically and militarily at all costs. The analysis therefore reveals a blending of political, economic, and ideological networks in a way that contradicts Krasner's emphasis on an autonomous state and disembodied Lockean liberalism.

Krasner's case studies concerning raw materials in the postwar era must be understood within the context of the Grand Area, as must the Vietnam War. More generally, any case study of issues in postwar America, foreign or domestic, must take into account this new definition of the national interest because it reinforced the "corporate liberalism" of the internationalists, as will be seen in my reanalysis of the Employment Act of 1946 in Chapter 7.

Clearly, it is time for those international relations experts cited by Krasner as sharing his theory of state autonomy to take a closer look at a theory such as mine that combines class and institutional perspectives. A power elite shapes foreign policy in the United States, where the state is more fragmented and open to elite outsiders than their previous studies have indicated.

# 6

## THE RULING CLASS DOES RULE:
The State Autonomy Theory of Fred Block,
and the Origins of the International
Monetary Fund

### Introduction

Two hard-hitting papers by the then-Marxian sociologist Fred Block, "The Rul-ing Class Does Not Rule" (1977a) and "Beyond Corporate Liberalism" (1977b), had considerable impact over the years in helping to isolate the views I am alleged to hold. In particular, as demonstrated in Chapters 3 and 4, they were used by Theda Skocpol (1980), Jill Quadagno (1984), and Christopher Tomlins (1985) to clear the way for their theoretical claims about American state autono-my based in studies of New Deal social legislation.

The critical burden of "The Ruling Class Does Not Rule" is that some people called "instrumentalists" adhere to the reductionistic view that farsighted and completely class-conscious capitalists directly dominate the American govern-ment by telling government officials what to do. Now, Block does admit that this personal access is supplemented by other direct influences and by ideology in the theory. He also acknowledges that business leaders themselves are appointed to government. However, the latter point is explained away because the business appointees are members of general policy-discussion groups that help them be-come more sophisticated than the usual shortsighted business person. The fact that "instrumentalists" first pointed out these groups and said much the same thing about their functions as training grounds for potential government appoint-ees is not mentioned.

Block further reduces the significance of these business appointees in the government by saying they "are forced to look at the world from the perspective of state managers" (1977a:13). Thus, at one level his theory is similar to tradi-tional role theory, rejecting any emphasis on social background, previous oc-cupational experience, or future career plans. On a more positive note, Block then advances his own theory. New government policies are said to be the outcome of conflicts among interest-conscious business leaders, the working class, and all-important independent state managers who try to manage class struggle without losing business confidence. It is a form of state autonomy theory that he develops by building on the structural Marxism of Nicos Poulantzas (1969) and Claus Offe (1974).

"Beyond Corporate Liberalism" provides a more empirical argument against "instrumentalism" by claiming with a few examples from mass-media accounts that the theory could explain neither mid-1970s discussions about government–business planning by a few business leaders and liberal economists that went nowhere, nor social spending cutbacks by Nixon, cutbacks the theory never denied were possible when the pressure was off, and that we now can see never really happened anyhow. Block's critique, of course, only culminated an attack begun earlier by *Kapitalistate* Marxists (Lehmann, 1975; Gold, Lo, and Wright, 1975; Mollenkopf, 1975a), but he did finish the job in the eyes of many social scientists.

However, it now turns out that the problem that led Block to his new theoretical perspective on the ruling class and the state was neither failed planning nor spending cuts in the 1970s. Instead, it was the alleged independent origins of the International Monetary Fund (IMF) in the early 1940s that started Block in a new direction. This belief, not apparent in either of the 1977 articles, is discussed in the introduction to a more recent book by Block (1987:16–17) that brings together the papers he wrote between 1976 and 1986. This introduction gives more careful attention to those of us he now calls "business dominance" theorists, even though he now thinks we underestimate the independent role of academic experts and middle-class reformers in addition to our other mistakes.

The introduction also is of interest because Block states he is now a "post Marxist," abandoning historical materialism as too economistic. He now believes that politics is "irreducible" and that race, gender, and other social struggles cannot be understood as aspects of class struggle (1987:17–18, 34–35). This change of position brings him to the same starting point as those of us he previously made into scapegoats for the failures of the American Left, a point he is yet to acknowledge. However, he retains his great emphasis on state autonomy as compared to those he finds limited in their theorizing, so he sees his views as closest to what he calls the "soft" version of state-centric theory that he discerns as one tendency in the work of Skocpol. Unlike Skocpol, however, he emphasizes the interaction of societal and state factors rather than making the state primary in all times and all places (1987:20–21).

But it will not be my purpose in this chapter to discuss the evolution of Block's views. Instead, I want to focus on the actual process through which the IMF was created in 1944 as an institution to facilitate currency exchanges, encourage stability in exchange rates, and sustain world trade through currency loans to countries with temporary deficits in their balance of payments. My goal in making this effort is to show the inadequacy of the analysis of the IMF that led Block to think in terms of state autonomy in the first place. I will attempt to demonstrate through an analysis of various historical documents that his paradigm case does not fit his emphasis on state autonomy in the United States, either in its past Marxian version or its present modified version. Instead, this case fits a business dominance view in which the ruling class does rule in corporate America. The chapter thus can be viewed as a challenge to state autonomy theorists in general as well as to Block's theory in particular.

The next section of the chapter presents Block's claims about the origins of postwar plans for the IMF. Following that, there is a lengthy and detailed section on my historical findings, which show how corporate planners from the war–peace study groups of the Council on Foreign Relations helped to create the IMF as one part of their larger economic plan for the postwar world. There is then a concluding section wherein I turn to more general issues, including the role of experts within a business-dominance perspective.

## Block's Theory

Block's claims about the origins of the IMF appear in the third chapter of his book on international monetary policy between 1945 and 1972 (Block, 1977c). These claims are only one small part of the book, and his general thesis does not stand or fall with the validity of his views on the IMF's origins. Block's primary concern is with understanding the impediments to the creation of a new international monetary order in the 1970s. He aims to shed light on this issue by understanding the rise and fall of the new monetary system that was created in 1944, implemented with changes in the 1950s, and largely dismantled in the early 1970s.

Block emphasizes that the nature of an international monetary system is related to the power of specific nations and classes. The projected postwar system, featuring the IMF at its center, reflected the power of the United States and its desire to create an open world economy. To make his point, Block (1977c:9) quotes none other than Jacob Viner, the international economist who played such a large role in the war–peace study groups discussed in Chapter 5. In 1944 Viner wrote that the United States was now creating a new international economy almost singlehandedly and in opposition to the strong nationalist pressures that had obtained a strong grip on most capitalist countries after the crash of 1929. Little did Block know that Viner himself, as we shall see, had a major part in planning the organization Block sees as a product of an autonomous state.

As shown in Chapter 5, I agree with Block that the main aim of the United States in the early 1940s, before the beginnings of the Cold War, was to create an open world economy in order to save the American economy from further depressions. This is an especially crucial agreement to emphasize in a time when the new conventional wisdom in Cold War historiography, called "postrevisionism," claims that "there is little evidence that they [policy-makers] saw a crisis of capitalism as the most pressing issue facing the country at the end of World War II" (Gaddis, 1983:173). The issue between Block and me, then, only concerns the who and how of the new foreign economic policies, not their importance. Block thinks that independent state managers inside an autonomous state made these policies with little or no pressure or coaching from corporate leaders and their associated expert planners. I think he is wrong.

More specifically, Block believes that the IMF, as one of the key institutions of the postwar economic order, was created by "idealistic internationalists" within the state, who favored the creation of separate national economies in the various capitalist countries rather than an international economy. These idealistic internationalists are also called "national capitalists" by Block, and he notes that they favored increased planning and government social spending. The idealistic internationalists were opposed by the "business internationalists" who wanted a truly internationalist capitalist system with free trade and direct capital investments overseas. The idealistic internationalists were located primarily in the Treasury Department, the business internationalists in the State Department. Those in the Treasury Department were especially free of outside influences, but even the business internationalists received very little help from corporate leaders outside the state. Corporate policy groups are seen as relatively impotent because they did not have any serious policy alternatives to those being discussed in the state (Block, 1977c:35, 231, footnote 9). Moreover, many representatives of large banks, and especially large New York banks, opposed the plan for the IMF in its entirety or sought changes in it.

President Roosevelt tolerated the battle that developed between State and Treasury over plans for the IMF for several reasons. First, he allowed the Treasury to be involved in postwar economic planning because of his close friendship and good working relationship with Secretary of Treasury Henry Morgenthau. Second, Roosevelt liked to have a variety of policy alternatives before him to keep his options open and strengthen his own hand. Finally, he wanted to maintain his political coalition with "national-capitalist" planners such as those inside the Treasury because they were supported by middle-class liberals and organized labor (Block, 1977c:42).

According to Block, the national-capitalist planners were successful in creating the IMF over the opposition of the business internationalists in the State Department. However, there is an irony in this because the Treasury plan helped to strengthen the business internationalists:

> It is one of the stranger ironies of international monetary history that the men who actually dominated U.S. international monetary policy during World War II were far more sympathetic to national capitalism than to the idea of an open world economy. In fact, the International Monetary Fund, designed to be a central institution of the postwar monetary order, was shaped initially by national capitalist assumptions (1977c:32).

Moreover, the goals of the business internationalists were "hidden by the skillful invocation of the rhetoric of the idealistic internationalists" (Block, 1977c:37). The rhetoric he is referring to concerns domestic policies to create full employment:

> The clearest example of this was the International Monetary Fund itself. It was originally conceived as an instrument to facilitate expansionary domestic policies, but it eventually became another means to impose the deflationary discipline of the gold standard (1977c:37).

The main author of the plan for the IMF was Harry Dexter White, an economist in the Treasury Department. Block claims White's influence "was enormous because of the monopoly of technical knowledge that he and his associates held" (1977c:43). Block uses a partial quote from White to suggest that White's economic orientation was national-capitalist. This quote concerned the fact that White thought a high level of domestic economic activity "would do far more for our foreign trade than a complete wiping out of our tariff rates, or 100 trade treaties" (1977c:232, footnote 15).

Block concedes that there is little direct evidence for his claim of a policy split between State and Treasury. He thus must make inferences on the basis of various secondary sources:

> While the secondary sources rarely acknowledge that there was more at stake in the conflict between State and Treasury than a jurisdictional dispute, there is evidence that fundamental policy issues were at stake. Hints at the conflict can be found in passim, in [he then lists four books and an article] (1977c:232, footnote 19).

Block further claims that the plans agreed upon for an IMF were ignored by the State Department after Roosevelt died and Morgenthau resigned his position at the Treasury. At this point State took control of postwar planning and bypassed the IMF agreements: "The State Department planners were not happy with the IMF, both because of its departure from the gold standard and because the Bretton Woods agreements had let the British off too easily" (1977c:56).

The early history of the IMF has many levels and aspects. Some of these aspects include highly technical questions. In this chapter I will deal only with those aspects which contradict three claims by Block that are crucial to his theory of state autonomy. First, and most importantly, there is the alleged absence of outside influence by corporate planners armed with an alternative economic vision. Second, there is the alleged struggle within the state between State and Treasury over substantive issues. Third, and finally, there is the alleged State Department takeover of postwar monetary planning after the death of Roosevelt, which led to the bypassing of the IMF in the immediate postwar years. I will try to show that all these claims are incorrect.

Before turning to these issues with new empirical information, however, it should be noted that Block's claims about substantive differences between State and Treasury are at variance with most of the authorities on the subject (e.g., Blum, 1967:233; Gardner, 1956:72–76), who see the differences as jurisdictional and procedural. John Gaddis, for example, concludes that

> Although relations between the two departments were not cordial—[Secretary of State Cordell] Hull with some justification suspected Treasury Secretary Henry Morgenthau, Jr., of trying to usurp State Department responsibilities—their plans for the postwar world complemented each other neatly, both looking toward restoring the free flow of world trade within a capitalist framework (1972:20).

Alfred Eckes (1975), the author of the most detailed account of the origins of the IMF available when Block wrote, directly contradicts Block's claim about White's orientation. He writes that although White was pro-Keynesian, "there is no evidence, however, that White found autarky an acceptable second-best alternative to multilateralism" (1975:4).

The conclusions of the sources available to Block carry some weight in this dispute because Block relies solely on secondary sources in making his strong claims. As he frankly states in his preface, "I did not, however, make use of archival materials because the time-consuming nature of such work would have forced me to abandon the project of analyzing both the rise and fall of the post–World War II monetary order" (Block, 1977c:x). This is hardly a solid basis for far-reaching changes in basic theory about the state.

The problems of such an approach can be seen very clearly in his use of the aforementioned quote from White concerning the importance of domestic economic activity in boosting international trade. Richard Gardner (1956:15), his source for the quote, sees White as a strong internationalist. He uses the quote in the context of a discussion of the fact that free trade might not, in and of itself, have unalloyed economic benefits or reduce the likelihood of international political conflict. Actually, White's point in his comment is that the United States would have to increase its imports if other countries were to have a way to pay for increased American exports. This argument is in keeping with international expansionism, not national capitalism. As shown in the previous chapter, this issue was emphasized constantly by the international corporate planners of the early 1940s, who were in effect White's mentors and who aided him in formulating the specific plans for the IMF.

However, it is not an adequate refutation of Block to pit one secondary source against another, or his interpretation against my interpretation. We need to go back to archival sources because the accounts Block draws upon were not focused enough on the origins of the IMF to provide detailed evidence on his claims one way or the other. The account by Eckes (1975) is excellent as far as it goes, but it needs to be supplemented.

## The Who, Why, and How of the IMF

Recalling Chapter 5, it will come as no surprise when I claim that the starting point for understanding American postwar monetary policy is in the policy discussions in 1940 and 1941 in the war–peace study groups of the Council on Foreign Relations. My general background case for this kind of claim already has been presented, but I should note again that it builds on the work of Shoup (1974) and Notter (1949) for postwar planning in general, and add that the work of Alfred Eckes (1975) and Robert Oliver (1971, 1975) demonstrates the role of council planners in the case of the IMF and World Bank.

For the purposes of this chapter the most important of the study groups is once again the Economic and Financial Group, led by Viner and Hansen. As noted in the previous chapter, Viner was active in the Council on Foreign Relations throughout the 1930s. Here it can be added that he also was an adviser to Secretary of Treasury Henry Morgenthau during the New Deal; in 1934 he helped create and manage the exchange stabilization fund within the Treasury that was a precursor of the IMF. In 1935 he helped Morgenthau in negotiating a pact with Great Britain and France through which national exchange stabilization funds were used to stabilize currency values (Blum, 1959:Chapter 4). This Tripartite Pact, which grew to include several smaller democratic countries as well, was only a step or two from an international stabilization fund. Not insignificantly, Viner also happened to be the person who first brought White into the Treasury Department in the summer of 1934. He hired White to write a summary report on American monetary and banking legislation "with a view to planning a long term legislative program for the Administration" (Rees, 1973:40, quoting Viner's letter to White). White then joined the department on a full-time basis, resigning his professorship at Lawrence College.

Hansen, as the leader of the liberal Keynesians, was best known for his emphasis on public spending for domestic projects, but he was knowledgeable about monetary issues as well. His several government appointments included an advisory position at the Federal Reserve Board. Other economists from the Economic and Financial Group who were introduced in the previous chapter, and especially Winfield Riefler and Arthur Upgren, also were active on the IMF project.

Working under the auspices of the council, Viner, Hansen, and their co-workers provided the rationale and context for White and other experts in State and Treasury to create the plans for the IMF. More than providing context, however, they also played a mediating role between American and British government experts on monetary issues and between Treasury and other agencies in the American government. Later, Viner worked directly with White on the original IMF proposal, and Hansen played a critical role in improving the plan through his advisory position at the Federal Reserve Board and his membership on the interdepartmental technical committee that approved the final draft.

The starting point for the deliberations of the Economic and Financial Group on international monetary questions can be found in report E-B34, dated July 24, 1941. It was meant primarily as a general framework for studies of the international monetary, investment, and trade organizations that would be needed to integrate the Grand Area. It provides a good summary of the council vision and strategy presented in the previous chapter. Entitled "Methods of Economic Collaboration: The Role of the Grand Area in American Economic Policy," it began with an overview of the war situation at that moment, stressing defense needs over postwar issues:

*Purpose*

The purpose of this memorandum is to summarize the concept of the Grand Area in terms of its meaning for American policy, its function in the present war, and its possible role in the postwar period. The memorandum is the introduction to a series concerned with the methods of integrating the Grand Area economically.

*The Grand Area and American Defense*

The economy of the United States is geared to the export of certain manufactured and agricultural products, and the import of numerous raw materials and foodstuffs. The success of German arms from the invasion of Poland onward brought most of Europe under Nazi domination and threatened the rest of the world. Faced with these facts, the Economic and Financial Group sought to determine the area (excluding continental Europe, which for the present was lost) that, from the economic point of view, was best suited to the defense of the United States. Such an area would have to: (1) contain the basic raw materials necessary to the full functioning of American industry, and (2) have the fewest possible stresses making for its own disintegration, such as unwieldy export surpluses or severe shortages of consumers' goods.

With this end in view, a series of studies was made to ascertain the "degree of complementarism" in trade of several blocs: the Western Hemisphere, the British Empire (except Canada), the Far East. (The memoranda are listed in the Appendix.) From the point of view of the United States, the Western Hemisphere is an inadequate area because it lacks important raw materials which we get from southeastern Asia, and it is burdened with surpluses normally exported to Europe, especially the United Kingdom. An extension of the area in opposite directions to take in these two economically important regions thus becomes necessary. The extension brings new problems, but it was found that the United States can best defend itself—from an economic point of view—in an area comprising most of the non-German world. This has been called the "Grand Area." It includes the Western Hemisphere, the United Kingdom, the remainder of the British Commonwealth and Empire, the Dutch East Indies, China, and Japan (E-B34, 1941:1).

After a discussion of the German-controlled bloc and the relative unimportance of the Soviet Union to the American economy, it stressed the role of the Grand Area in military preparedness and in avoiding adjustments in the American economy:

The Grand Area, then, is the amount of the world the United States can defend most economically, that is, with the least readjustment of the American economy. To maintain a maximum defense effort, the United States must avoid economic readjustment caused by constriction of the trading area if the military cost of defending the area is not too great. What such constriction might mean in weakening the defense economy can best be seen by imagining the strain on American supplies of labor, materials, and industrial capacity of the attempt to manufacture substitutes for or to do without rubber, tin, jute, and numerous vegetable oils, instead of importing these products from southeastern Asia. Similarly, to the extent that the United States and other countries can continue to export their surpluses, some dangerous stresses in the domestic economy are prevented from developing.

It is important for the United States to defend the Grand Area and to prevent the capture of any of its parts by the Germans. Similarly, the Grand Area must be defended from defection from within, (1) by making it economically possible for all member countries to live in the area, and (2) by preventing any country—particularly Japan—from destroying the area for its own political reasons. Some studies of the economic aspects of these problems have been made, others are projected. It is not the role of the Economic and Financial Group to determine how the area is to be defended nor to assess whether such a defense is feasible, though broad military considerations have of course played some part in determining the area, and it has been assumed that keeping the area intact is not patently impossible from a military viewpoint. Similarly, the methods of political collaboration needed to integrate the area, and the diplomacy required for keeping it intact, do not fall into the Group's sphere, except insofar as economic weapons and enticements are part of that diplomacy and the institutional structure for solving economic problems is called political. Economic collaboration within the area, however, is an important field of study for the Group. Such collaboration to secure integration is necessary to transform the economic potential of the area into military power, and is at the same time a part of the defense of the area. By creating a working economic organization for the Grand Area, we make that area more viable and stronger both economically and, presumably, politically (E-B34, 1941:2–3).

Two pages later, the document turned to the importance of collaboration with Great Britain in integrating the Grand Area, emphasizing that this economic collaboration must begin during the war, not after:

Anglo-American collaboration is the key to the integration of the Grand Area, both as a wartime measure and in forging an enduring peace on the lines desired by the two countries. Many of the problems facing the peace-makers will be determined by wartime policies and the developments of war economics. It is likely to be easier to continue economic collaboration begun in wartime than to start anew at the peace settlement. It seems important, then, that the United States and British Empire countries work together within the framework of the Grand Area economy in wartime, and plan their policies—so far as is compatible with the immediate war effort—to provide the best possible basis for coping with problems of the peace (E-B34, 1941:4–5).

The document went on to say that there would be problems in integrating the Grand Area. There would be a need for a "conscious program" to insure that it did not come apart:

The statistical neatness of the Grand Area will not cause it to function automatically simply because Germany controls most of Europe although the blockade and its consequences stimulate this development. The condition of "buying first from one another," on which it is based, would itself require a considerable degree of trade readjustment and raise certain problems of transportation. The Grand Area was defined on the basis of peacetime trade; the conditions of war change demand patterns and create hazards, such as the destruction of shipping and production capacity. Japan's expansionist policy continues to threaten the integration of the Grand Area. These problems may not be ignored; some have already been the subjects of study (see Appendix). Above all, it appears certain that the integration of the Grand Area requires a conscious program of broadly conceived measures for (1) knitting the parts of the area closer together economically and (2) securing the full use of the economic resources of the whole area.

The integration of the Grand Area is based on American-British collaboration. At the same time, America and British interests are neither identical nor entirely parallel. Not only will there be disagreements as to what policy is best, but also real clashes of interest which can be resolved only to the hurt of certain groups within one or the other country. In wartime the tendency is for such clashes of interest to be submerged and subordinated to the single goal of winning the war. At the peace and after it, they tend to re-emerge, sometimes more sharply than ever. With outside pressure of a common enemy removed, such conflicts of interest can easily destroy the whole program of continued international cooperation. One of the most important tasks of the Grand Area studies will be to detect present and prospective clashes of interest, define them so far as possible, and seek means of eliminating, alleviating, or compromising them (E-B34, 1941:5).

Finally, there was an outline of proposed studies relating to the economic integration of the Grand Area. Those concerning "Financial Collaboration" and "Monetary and Exchange Problems" are relevant to the issues of this chapter. They show that at least some business internationalists with access to the White House and State Department were proposing a dramatic alternative vision for the American economy:

I. Financial collaboration
   A. international financial institutions
   B. postwar financial structure of the world: role of governments and of private investment
   C. international anti-depression measures
   D. development programs
      1. backward areas
      2. special areas: e.g., the Yangtze Valley
      3. regional developments involving several countries
   E. defraying the cost of the war
   F. effect of changes in the United Kingdom's balance of payments resulting from the war
II. Monetary and exchange problems
   A. stabilization of exchanges
   B. role of gold
   C. international banking institution
   D. synchronization of national credit policies (E-B34, 1941:6)

I have quoted at length from what I think is a rather amazing and comprehensive blueprint for the American future not only because it is a direct challenge to anyone like Gaddis (1983) who thinks that the creation of a postwar international economy was a minor item on the American agenda, but also because it reveals the actual framework within which monetary planners worked. The blueprint is of further interest because it warns of the problems with Great Britain that were to make the creation of the IMF very difficult. Merely generating a plan for an international exchange stabilization fund, as Viner (1942:174) pointed out, was in fact a "comparatively easy" task. Moreover, there also was a good chance that such a plan would gain general acceptance in the world community because the expected differences of opinion did not "particularly follow national lines" or reflect "important and conscious conflicts of vested interest" (1942:173). Nonetheless, there were major problems in creating a plan that suited the British, and negotiations with them were to be highly complex and seemingly endless over a three-year period.

To understand the work of British and American planners that led to the IMF, it is necessary to recall the British perspective presented in Chapter 5 through the work of historian Alan Dobson (1986). Britain's economic and financial position had not only been greatly weakened by its war with the Nazis, which is obvious, but by its financial dealings with the United States as well. Due to the neutrality laws passed by Congress in 1935 at the insistence of isolationists, British purchases of war-related materials between 1939 and 1941 had to be on a cash-and-carry basis. This arrangement rather quickly drained British reserves of American dollars. As the pressure on Great Britain's finances increased, the American Treasury insisted that the British sell their assets in the United States to make their payments. While these asset sales made further immediate payments possible, they also meant that Great Britain would be less able to earn American dollars in the future.

American officials in the Treasury Department kept a sharp eye on the British gold supply as well. They wanted to be sure that the British were not hoarding gold before they would try to bring about changes in the neutrality laws. When Morgenthau learned in December 1940 that the British had $42 million in new gold waiting in Capetown, South Africa, he immediately recommended that Roosevelt ask for it. The gold was picked up a few weeks later with much fanfare. The British were deeply insulted by what they saw as a crass maneuver by a nation already in possession of most of the world's gold supply (Dobson, 1986:25–28).

Finally, in March 1941, with Great Britain nearing bankruptcy in terms of dollars and gold, Roosevelt was able to push a Lend-Lease Bill through Congress that made possible unrestricted aid to the British in exchange for future repayments or "considerations." The bill gave the president remarkable freedom in deciding what the repayments or considerations would be, and this freedom was to become very important in negotiations for the IMF.

However, lend-lease did not solve all of Great Britain's immediate problems. The American Treasury quickly insisted on restrictions on British commercial exports that were in competition with American exports. Officially, these restrictions were demanded in order to maintain American public support for the lend-lease program; however, there was considerable suspicion in Great Britain that these restrictions also were meant to further diminish Britain's declining economic power (Dobson, 1986; Gardner, 1956:173–75). Whatever the intent, the restriction on its exports did help to keep Great Britain on a short financial tether.

British leaders also were very wary of American pronouncements in favor of free trade, which had been a staple of the State Department under Hull. There were two reasons for this wariness, as noted in the previous chapter. First, the British were not at all sure that the Americans would accept free trade in practice. Second, free trade by itself was seen as a very antiquated and dangerous doctrine by a British government influenced by the experience of the Great Depression and the thinking of the economist John Maynard Keynes. Simply put, the British firmly believed that free trade without commitment to antidepression fiscal, monetary, and social policies in the United States would drag the world economy into any future depression that began in the United States. They believed American policy failures had contributed to the abandonment of relatively free trade in the early 1930s, and they did not want to see those failures repeated at their expense.

Although British officials realized that many leaders in the State Department, Treasury Department, and Council on Foreign Relations understood this point, they were not at all confident that the reactionaries, nationalists, and isolationists so prevalent in Congress would accept the New Deal and Keynesian policies necessary to safeguard an open world economy. Indeed, Keynesianism was openly hated in the classical laissez faire thinking of American conservatives, and even by conventional New Dealers such as Secretary of Treasury Morgenthau.

Given the antipathy Morgenthau and many members of Congress had toward Keynesian economics, it is ironic that Keynes himself was one of the chief British advisers and negotiators in relation to lend-lease repayments and a future international monetary stabilization fund. I say ironic because Keynes not only saw the large economic problems better than most officials, making him a brilliant adversary for the American negotiators, but he instinctively generated resistance in many key American leaders due to his polished and arrogant style.

Keynes arrived in the United States in May, 1941, to negotiate the details of the lend-lease agreement that had been passed by Congress two months before. It was right at the time when council leaders and officials in the State Department were thinking about how to gain British acceptance of the Grand Area strategy. Anticipating that there would be British resistance to these ideas because they implied Great Britain's subordination to the United States, the American negotiators hit upon the idea of linking the lend-lease agreements with their plans for the postwar world. That is, the "consideration" they sought from the British in exchange for vast amounts of war material and other supplies was acceptance of the American plan—nothing more, nothing less.

The lend-lease negotiations were focused on the issue of lowering tariffs and removing other trade barriers, which meant in practice that the British empire, protected by "imperial preferences," would be opened up to American trade and investment. But Keynes kept pointing out that Great Britain would have a balance of payments problem after the war, and that the Americans therefore would have to accept more imports and give loans to the British if they expected to increase trade with the British Empire. Furthermore, the acceptance of more imports might necessitate Keynesian policies in the United States to increase the level of activity in the domestic economy. Thus, any plan for international economic cooperation would have to include more than simple trade agreements.

Keynes also was aware of the fact that there were important people in London who would oppose American postwar plans because the plans would undermine the empire and hasten Britain's decline as a world power. Eckes provides a graphic summary of the issues involved in the negotiations:

> John Maynard Keynes, England's leading financial negotiator, realized that, without parallel arrangements to assure an expansionary world economy, to reconstruct war-debilitated nations, and to erase currency imbalances, Britain could not adjust to the cold shower of American competition. Thus, on one visit to Washington in 1941, Keynes bluntly dismissed the "lunatic proposals of Mr. Hull," and warned that without American financial assistance Britain might be compelled to select an autarkic course in the postwar period. Of course, more than economic considerations shaped the British position. Advocates of imperial preference argued vigorously that nondiscrimination spelled the death of Britain's historic empire and England's decline as a world power (1975:39).

Not surprisingly, then, there was very little meeting of the minds during the spring and summer of 1941. The British knew the Americans would not cut off aid in the midst of the war. They also hoped that the United States eventually would come into the war on their side, and that the terms of the lend-lease could be made less onerous for the British in that event. As for the Americans, they did not want to become more specific than acceptance of the general principles of the Grand Area strategy. This was partly because officials of the executive branch did not want to make promises until they were sure Congressional opinion had become more internationalist. However, it also involved the fact that the State Department had very little planning capability at the time, and that Treasury had not begun to develop any plans for monetary policy. Then too, Roosevelt had not yet decided whether State, Treasury, or Wallace's Economic Defense Board would take the lead in coordinating postwar planning.

When Keynes returned to London in July, the negotiations were at an impasse and officials in the State Department were extremely annoyed. The American negotiators, as explained more fully in the previous chapter, therefore turned their attention to gaining British acquiescence to their plans through the creation of the joint British–American statement of war aims called the Atlantic Charter. These war aims included a call for equal access for all nations "to the trade and raw materials" of the world; however, the statement also said that this economic freedom would be practiced "with due respect for existing obligations," which leaders in the State Department and the council saw as an escape clause for British protectionism (e.g., Gardner, 1956:46). They were disappointed that Roosevelt had not pressed harder on this point with Churchill, and they were more determined than ever to realize their goals through the negotiations over lend-lease considerations.

It is in this context, then, that planning for what came to be called the International Monetary Fund actually began in the fall of 1941. Most commentators on the origins of the IMF believe that the planning began independently in the United States and England, with White taking the lead for the Americans and Keynes for the British (e.g., Gardner, 1956:71; Van Dormael, 1978:Chapter 4). However, the situation was more coordinated than that, with Hansen and Viner playing a mediating role between experts from the two countries. For example, the Economic and Financial Group initiated a series of four off-the-record meetings with British economists on September 20 to discuss general issues of collaboration. Also present was the secretary of the Royal Institute of International Affairs, the London counterpart to the Council on Foreign Relations. According to the summary of the discussion, a wide range of economic topics were covered in a general way ("Digests of Discussion," E-A20, September 20, 1941).

Shortly thereafter, Hansen traveled to London, where Keynes was thinking about methods to implement American proposals in a way that would be satisfactory to Great Britain. Despite his anti-internationalist assertions while in the United States, Keynes realized that it would be very hard to resist the economic and political power of the Americans. He also knew that Britain's recovery would be slow and painful without American trade and loans. He therefore began working on a plan for international currency stabilization that could lead to the liberalized expansion of international trade that the Americans sought. The essence of his plan was the establishment of a very large international currency exchange and credit-granting institution that could be drawn upon relatively easily by any country that was temporarily short of any given foreign currency due to trade imbalances. Functioning on the principle of a friendly and trusting bank, the "international clearing union," as the projected institution was called, would make it possible for countries to "overdraft" their accounts for a period of time so that expansionary trade could be continued. In effect, it was a bank that made temporary loans of foreign currencies from a fund that was based on no more than the promise of the member countries to provide the needed currencies when called for. Each country would provide the clearing union with a line of credit, but would not have to provide the currency until it actually was needed. As will be seen, the Americans were very nervous about this plan. They were afraid that some countries would not provide the currency when it was asked for. Even more, they feared there would be an unlimited call for American currency with no assurance that the countries needing the loans were living within their means.

It was during this time that Hansen arrived on the scene in London to confer personally with Keynes. Keynes's first major biographer, economist Roy F. Harrod, explained the visit as follows, noting that Hansen's "mandate" from the government was "obscure":

> At this period there occurred a useful visit by Professor Alvin Hansen, the well-known economist, and Mr. Gulick, a consultant of the National Planning Board and expert on the TVA. Although sponsored by the State Department, the nature of their mandate was obscure. They advocated Anglo-American cooperation to prevent world depression, and proposed the establishment of an International Economic Board to advise collaborating governments with respect to internal policy designed to promote full employment, economic stability, and world trade. . . . They also advocated an International Resources Survey and an International Development Corporation, with a view to promoting wise development overseas (1951:527–28).

The British were somewhat surprised by these progressive proposals, according to Harrod, who also recalled that the proposals were on a higher level of political sophistication than the simple Wilsonian trade doctrines of Hull: "These proposals were cordially welcomed; the doctrine seemed to belong to a different world of thought from that which took the elimination of discrimination in foreign trade to be the panacea for the world's ills" (1951:528).

Hansen wrote to Viner about his discussions with Keynes as soon as he returned to the United States, noting that the suggestions he had made to Keynes followed lines that had been talked about in the Economic and Financial Group. He also reported that he already had discussed the new proposals and his visit to Keynes with Hull and Wallace, and that he would be talking with Morgenthau the next day (Viner Papers: Hansen to Viner, October 20, 1941). Viner replied enthusiastically in a letter of October 24. He also suggested that Hansen get in touch with Riefler, who had been in the Economic and Financial Group from the outset and was now working with Wallace at the Economic Defense Board. He made this suggestion because Riefler "is working intensively along the same lines and has a very interesting draft of a specific Anglo-American post-war financing organization" (Viner Papers: Viner to Hansen, October 24, 1941). Hansen replied on October 28 with news that he had a revised draft of his plan based on "numerous conversations." He reported that he had been unable to contact Riefler as yet. He then suggested that the next meeting of the council planning group might be the place for further discussions:

> I see no reason why our Council on Foreign Relations, *in view of its confidential relations with the State Department,* might not have a full discussion of this draft, as well as of Riefler's proposals. Possibly you, Riefler, and I might have a special discussion of it at lunchtime on Saturday (Viner Papers: Hansen to Viner, October 28, 1941, emphasis added).

Unfortunately, this particular trail of paper ends at this point, a problem that will recur at other crucial junctures in the archival record because none of the principals was a compulsive record keeper. In this instance, however, the line of thought can be picked up to some degree in other documents. On November 28, for example, the Economic and Financial Group summarized the proposals by Hansen and Riefler in a memorandum entitled "International Collaboration to Secure the Coordination of Stabilization Policies and to Stimulate Investment" (E-B44). The emphasis was once again placed on the need for expansionary domestic policies in order to make possible open or "multilateral" international trade. A few days later, Hansen was able to make this general point again through another avenue, the governmental-sponsored Canadian–American Committee that he cochaired. On December 5, the committee sent the White House and State Department a proposal for an International Stabilization and Development Board that would make suggestions about how the United States, Great Britain, and Canada could coordinate their economies. Hansen also sent a letter directly to Roosevelt dated December 15, which contained the resolution of the Canadian–American Committee in favor of the joint stabilization board. However, none of the documents or resolutions discussed in this paragraph deals with the specific problem of monetary policy. As will be shown, Viner was carrying this issue in conjunction with White.

It was at this point, of course, that the Japanese attack on Pearl Harbor brought the United States into the war. While American involvement focused official attention even more on day-to-day issues, it also led to decisions on postwar planning that had been delayed for over a year. Morgenthau consolidated Treasury responsibility for foreign economic planning in White's hands early in December. A week later, on Sunday morning, December 14, Morgenthau called White to ask him to begin work on a monetary stabilization fund. This call was summarized the next day by White in a memo for the files (Morgenthau Diaries: Treasury Department Order No. 43). Then, in late December Roosevelt gave the order putting State in charge of postwar planning and assigning a secondary role to Treasury and the Economic Defense Board.

I was unsuccessful in determining why Morgenthau decided to call White about monetary policy on that particular Sunday in mid-December. There are no hints in his detailed records for the two previous weeks, nor in White's papers. On the basis of retrospective accounts by White's associates (Eckes, 1975:46), there is some reason to believe that White actually had been working on monetary plans throughout the fall, and that Morgenthau's call only made official what had been going on unofficially. Such a possibility would not be surprising because White's longstanding involvement with monetary policy began with his work for Morgenthau and Viner on exchange stabilization in 1935 and 1936 (Blum, 1959:Chapter 4).

Whatever the exact origins of Morgenthau's order, the more general issue is the possible influence of council planners on White's plan. As the Treasury Department's liaison with the State Department on postwar planning issues in the previous two years (Notter, 1949), White was well aware of the internationalist proposals being sent to State by the council study groups. We also know from

Harrod (1951:539) that White had direct conversations about foreign economic issues with Hansen and from the Morgenthau Diaries that he "continually supported the fiscal proposals of Alvin Hansen" (Blum, 1970:430).

However, the most important linkage between the war–peace project and White was Viner, who worked regularly as a consultant within the Treasury Department during this period. The Morgenthau Diaries reveal that he was present for general meetings at the Treasury on December 1, 2, 11, 12, 22, and 23. Moreover, there is documented evidence from his reappointment letter of January 1, 1942, and subsequent memos by White and another department official, that he aided in the drafting of the original proposal for an International Monetary Fund. Given Viner's earlier relationship with White and his deep involvement in the council's postwar planning, the documentary evidence concerning Viner's work with White at Treasury is the "smoking gun" that demonstrates the influence of elites outside the American state on monetary policy. True enough, there are class and state "structures," as suggested by structural Marxists, and there is a general ideological "atmosphere," as proposed by many types of theorists, but in addition there is also direct input from an outside expert on a specific decision in a situation of potential conflict and great uncertainty (Zeitlin, 1984). It is the necessity of this level of interaction in a volatile capitalist society with a fragmented state that is missed in analyses such as Block's, and in those of all state autonomy theorists, for that matter (cf. Feigenbaum, 1985).

The first direct evidence of Viner's involvement is his letter of appointment for 1942, which states that he will be paid from the "Exchange Stabilization Fund":

January 1, 1942

Sir:

You are hereby appointed Special Assistant and Consulting Expert in the Office of the Secretary, with compensation at the rate of nine thousand dollars per annum, payable from the appropriation "Exchange Stabilization Fund." In addition to your salary, you will be allowed five dollars per diem; in lieu of subsistence while on duty in Washington, D.C.

> Signed, Henry M. Morgenthau
> (Morgenthau Diaries, Book 483:180)

In the first week of January, when the first plan seems to have been finalized, Viner was at the Treasury Department on the fifth, sixth, and seventh. On January 6 White asked Undersecretary of State Sumner Welles if he would be interested in introducing a resolution in favor of an "interallied" stabilization fund at the conference of American ministers in Rio de Janiero later in the month. When Welles responded positively, White sent a memo to Morgenthau on January 8. It included the plan and reported that White had asked Viner to approve it:

In the event Mr. Welles decides at Rio to propose a resolution on the establishment of a Stabilization Fund, I have in mind submitting the appended draft for his consideration. This draft was prepared in this Division, and is a much shorter draft than the one I showed you before. I have asked Mr. Southard to go over it with the Legal Division and Mr. Viner, and after they have approved, to submit it to you for your tentative approval (Morgenthau Diaries, Book 483:222).

One week later, on January 15, Southard sent a copy of the proposal to Undersecretary of Treasury Daniel Bell with the following preface that asserts the role of Viner in creating the plan. It is the clincher, so to speak:

Mr. White discussed the proposal for such a Fund with the Secretary early in January and received the Secretary's approval of the idea in principle. The draft prepared by Mr. White grew out of several discussions within the Treasury which included Mr. Bernard Bernstein [a department employee] and Jacob Viner (Morgenthau Diaries, Book 486:1).

On the same day as the Southard memo, White contacted Morgenthau from Rio, where White was assisting Welles at the Inter-American Conference. He asked permission for Welles to submit the proposal to the meeting. Before making a decision, Morgenthau called in Bernstein to brief him on the issue. Bernstein wrote the following memo to the file after the briefing. It is quoted here because it once again shows the central role played by Viner:

I told him that there was one point which Jacob Viner thought should be cleared with him [Morgenthau] and that was whether the subject of this resolution should be cleared first with the British before it is presented down there, and if presented, whether it should be done by the British and Treasury representatives in Washington or by the President to Churchill (Morgenthau Diaries, Book 486:4).

Morgenthau thought the issue over, and decided to wait on introducing any resolution rather than bothering the president. Two days later, however, Welles himself wired Morgenthau asking him to reconsider. Welles argued that he did not think it was necessary to check with the British. He also enclosed a simplified statement of the possible resolution. On January 19, Morgenthau telephoned White, asked him if Welles felt strongly about the issue, and then gave the go-ahead when White replied in the affirmative (Morgenthau Diaries, Book 486:179, 208).

There are other reasons to believe that Morgenthau relied heavily on Viner. On January 21, for example, Morgenthau asked Viner and Lauchlin Currie, the White House economist who kept track of the war–peace studies for the President, to suggest ways to raise money for the war in all 12 Federal Reserve Districts. Even more intriguing is the following conversation about Viner that appears in the Morgenthau Diaries for February 1. (The "diaries" are in reality the transcriptions of Morgenthau's telephone tap and office tape recorder.) In this instance the tape recorder captured the following conversation that involved (1) a possible new employee and (2) a loan to China. Just when it comes to the point where we might learn something about White's personal feelings toward Viner, the tape recorder fails or the transcript has been censored. However, I believe enough is said to suggest that White had personal reasons to play down Viner's role in the department:

**Morgenthau:**   Harry [White], get Viner to help you.

**White:**   Mr. Secretary, anything at all that is even in Mr. Viner's field, I always ask him to help me. I am always glad of his help.

**Morgenthau:**   Well, that hasn't always been so.

**White:**   That has always been true except where we have—questions where I know we are opposed on domestic policy and in which I didn't think it would be a help but a hindrance, as far as I was concerned, but on foreign policy—

**Morgenthau:**   Well—

**White:**   Or monetary matters.

**Bell:**   It is always better to have Jake in after something is prepared, because he will argue for two hours before he gets started.

**White:**   He is helpful and I am always glad to have him.

**Bell:**   It is very helpful to get his criticism on documents that have been prepared.

**White:**   But again, thinking of somebody for Haas' division, you know, Viner is in a little different position than he would be if Haas had somebody in his division. There are men who might come in the same capacity as Viner, but who might or might not come in a—

**Morgenthau:**   Well, the man I had in mind would be in the same relation to the rest of us as Viner is. Now, if you ask me who Viner is responsible to, I don't know. He has never raised the question. He is here to help all of us.

**Bernstein:**   Well, he is responsible to you, but we all use him.

**Morgenthau:**   Including Harry.

**White:**   Very definitely, and I am very glad to.

**Bernstein:**   He really sits in on most of our conferences.

**Foley** [another department official]:   He has been in on all this China thing.

**White:**   Whenever he in the Treasury he is always in.

**Foley:**   He was in Harry's office on all of this [the loan to China].

**Morgenthau:**   I believe Harry. I don't know why Harry is suddenly sensitive on that one.

**White:**   Because three times in the last week you have reminded me to get him in. I always do. I don't know whether that was an indication that you think I don't.

**Morgenthau:**   Well, sometime when we are alone I will tell you why.

**White:**   O.K. I will try to give you some names of those [possible employees] I hear about and I will ask other men about Hardy. Maybe I got a peculiar notion about him [Hardy].

**Morgenthau:**   Well, you men needn't wait. I will just tell Harry now and get it off my chest, that is all.
(Morgenthau Diaries, Book 491:72)

And there the dialogue abruptly ends!

The 12-page plan drawn up by White and Viner in either late December 1941 or early January 1942 can be compared with the Keynes plan at this point as background for the later role of Hansen and Viner. Briefly, the plan called for a fund of $5 billion, considerably less than what Keynes envisioned. The fund would be "subscribed," unlike Keynes's plan, meaning that each country would put in a certain amount of its currency and gold beforehand so that the fund would have currencies to lend and exchange. The size of the subscription would depend on the size, power, and trade volume of the country. The voting arrangements on policy issues were structured in such a way that the United States would have 60 percent of the votes as long as its friendly Latin American neighbors voted with it (Eckes, 1975:49).

Generally speaking, the differences between the American and British plans reflected the economic situations of the two countries. Great Britain, as a debtor nation, wanted an institution that could make currency loans without putting any restrictions on the borrowing countries. As a country without much gold, it did not want gold to have the large role proposed for it by the Americans. Britain also wanted to be sure that creditor nations such as the United States would be forced to loan out their currency rather than holding onto it in times of economic downturn or trade imbalance. The United States, as a creditor nation with a huge gold supply, wanted the fund to be able to insure that borrowing countries were not headed for financial disaster or using the currency loans as disguised investment loans. It wanted a role for its gold as a restraint on overborrowing and as an assurance to conservative bankers and members of Congress.

The negotiations over the two plans proved to be long and difficult, but the British ultimately had to concede to the Americans on almost every basic point. British acquiescence became easier when the Americans agreed to a mechanism by which other countries would be assured that the Americans could not limit the supply of their currency without suffering some penalty. Despite the American dominance, however, Keynes was not totally disappointed by the outcome because he thought the American plan was far better than nothing at all, and far more than he had expected from the American government. In a confidential letter to fellow British negotiators of April 19, 1943, before the most intense debates had taken place, Keynes concluded that the White plan "represents a big advance," but added that "it is a long time too soon to even breathe a suggestion of compromise" (Van Dormael, 1978:75).

The draft IMF plan of early 1942 was finalized in late April. A clean draft was typed for presentation to Morgenthau on May 8, but was backdated to March for some unknown reason (Van Dormael, 1978:45). The final draft was quickly accepted by Morgenthau, who then strategized with White about the next step to take. Both hoped to move quickly; White wanted to avoid the State Department by sending the plan directly to the White House. Morgenthau compromised on that suggestion by sending the plan to the president and the State Department at the same time, but Roosevelt put a stop to any unilateral moves by sending his copy to Hull and telling him to work on the project with Treasury. At the same time, Roosevelt lodged responsibility for carrying through the project with Treasury. In actuality, Roosevelt's decision reflected arrangements for inderdepartmental cooperation on monetary issues that went back to early 1940, and that respected the large role on foreign economic issues that had developed for the Treasury Department in the 1930s (Notter, 1949: Chapter 2; Blum, 1967).

At this point an interdepartmental committee was created to discuss White's proposal and make alterations if necessary. White was named chairman. The main conflicts within the committee were between State and Treasury, but they were not over substantive matters. Rather, the main issues were the timetable and format for international discussions (Eckes, 1975:60–62). The State Department wanted to move slowly until other international economic issues with Britain were resolved and public opinion and Congress were sure to be favorable. The department also wanted to honor Britain's insistence that it have agreement with the United States before other nations were consulted. Treasury, on the other hand, wanted to move more rapidly and consult widely with other nations. It was not nearly as concerned with British sensibilities as was the State Department, a fact understood by the British (Dobson, 1986).

Morgenthau had a tendency to interpret State's concern as a dislike for the plan, but it seems more likely that Hull, and then Roosevelt, decided on a more cautious course for sound political reasons: "Hull seemed genuinely convinced that the administration must prepare the public for the United States' global responsibilities, and he was certain that premature disclosure would only polarize the public, damage the Democratic Party, and shatter the prospects for international cooperation" (Eckes, 1975:63).

Although Hull resisted high-level and visible negotiations on monetary stabilization issues, he finally agreed in July 1942 to preliminary talks if they were confined to experts from a few major nations. He did so because the two officials in his own department involved in monetary planning, international corporation lawyers Dean Acheson and A. A. Berle, Jr., argued that further delay might weaken British supporters of international economic cooperation and increase the possibility that other countries would turn to unilateral decisions to solve their economic problems (Eckes, 1975:63). The efforts by Acheson and Berle undercut Block's claim that the State Department was opposed in any substantive way to the creation of the IMF.

In addition to preliminary discussions with a few countries, the Americans continued to argue among themselves about the relative merits of what came to be called the White Plan and the Keynes Plan. But for all the disagreements over the two plans, they were in fact more similar than they were different. This fact became clear in a lengthy discussion of them in the Council on Foreign Relations' Economic and Financial Group on March 6, 1943. The discussion also is of interest because it reveals differences between Viner and Hansen, with Viner favoring the fund approach and Hansen favoring Keynes' overdraft proposal. However, Viner won the day by pointing out that many countries do not recognize a line of credit as a real obligation. He therefore argued that it was better to have the money (and gold) beforehand:

Mr. Viner thought that the memorandum [by Hansen] overemphasized the case in favor of the overdraft method of stabilization as opposed to the fund arrangement. Both require the same basic commitment to be made in the first instance, that a country will provide a certain amount of money—whether as a direct contribution to the Fund or as a line of credit for the Clearing Union—for use in connection with exchange stabilization. Under the Fund plan, the money is made available from the start and there is never any question that the Fund has access to it; under the overdraft plan, however, subsequent legal action may be necessary actually to make available money that has been nominally set aside for this purpose. If a Central Bank claimed it had no free assets when the Clearing Union wished to draw on the line of credit, no money might be forthcoming unless a priority had been legally arranged for. A country wishing to avoid its obligations might find it easier to cancel a line of credit than to seize a deposit of the International Fund ("Digest of Discussions," E-A24, 1943:4).

By the end of the discussion, Hansen said that "the difference between the two stabilization plans was less than he had believed" (E-A24, 1943:5). He therefore made changes in the memorandum on the two plans that he was preparing for circulation in the White House and State Department, and from that point on he worked to improve the fund concept and to convince the British to accept it. Viner clearly had the upper hand on the issue in council discussions, and probably at the Treasury as well.

Hansen and Viner continued to mediate between Keynes and White in the spring and summer of 1943. Keynes and Viner corresponded (Gardner, 1956:86, footnote 4). Hansen sent an advanced copy of the memorandum altered in the discussions with Viner to Keynes through Redvers Opie, a British economist who served as his country's liaison with the American Treasury, and especially with White. Opie replied with a lengthy letter marked "personal and private" to Hansen on May 19 regarding Keynes' reactions. It shows that Hansen was trying to shape the American proposal to deal with Keynes' concerns, and that he was being kept abreast of Keynes' latest thoughts. It also reveals that parts of the negotiations were considered "difficult points" that Opie could not "deal with in writing." This kind of problem, of course, makes it harder to reconstruct the decisional process to the total satisfaction of either pluralists or state-autonomy theorists, but the thrust of the negotiations is nonetheless quite clear:

Just before I left for the Food Conference I received a letter from Keynes thanking me and you for sending him an advance copy of your memorandum on "International Adjustment of Exchange Rates." As you expected Keynes was very glad that you stressed the need for getting creditor countries to share responsibility for making adjustments to restore international equilibrium. There are one or two points arising out of Keynes' letter to me that I should like to take up with you orally on the first opportunity but, since that is unlikely to be until after June 3, perhaps I had better raise one or two points now.

The first is interesting in the light of your revised figure of $12 billion for the resources of the Fund. Keynes suggested that it would be easier to reach acceptable quotas if the total were raised to $15 billion leaving the United States at $4 billion, on the assumption that the whole world has to be covered.

The second point refers to the limitation on the obligation of creditor countries. Keynes surmises that a maximum obligation will have to be accepted and he believes that $4 billion for the United States should be reasonably adequate. The real problem which then arises is the same in the Stabilisation Fund as in the Clearing Union, namely what to do when a currency becomes scarce. We have the same difficulty in understanding what the processes would be in the Stabilisation Fund solution. I should like very much to discuss this with you off the record when I return.

Thirdly, Keynes agrees that the source of funds for long-term foreign investment should be a different institution and also that for the Commodity Control the case for separation for the reasons which you give is not equally clear.

I should be most grateful if you could treat this letter as a personal exchange between you and me and I look forward to discussing one or two more difficult points which I cannot deal with in writing (Hansen Papers: Opie to Hansen, May 19, 1943).

The final American plan was honed by a technical committee formed in May 1943. Among the 24 experts from 5 different departments and agencies were 2 members of the council's Economic and Financial Group, Benjamin V. Cohen, representing the White House, and Hansen, one of the representatives from the Federal Reserve Board. As might be expected by now, it was Hansen and the Federal Reserve delegation that raised the most serious questions. Hansen continued to push to make the plan more acceptable to Keynes, and the other Federal Reserve participants raised concerns relating to the amount of gold each country had to contribute and the way it would be utilized. The thrust of these recommendations can be found in several letters and outlines, but the main points and their political implications are best stated in a personal letter from Hansen to White on June 11:

Since we had our conference with you, the staff at the Federal Reserve has again gone over the whole matter and Goldenweiser is sending you a summary statement of the main points.

I am sending you this personal note since I can't come Monday so that you will know my own point of view. It seems to me that our suggestions can quite easily be incorporated into your plan. You have frequently stressed the importance of having a plan that could get the approval of Congress. In my judgment, the modifications which we have suggested would help very much to get this approval, for the following reasons:

1. The American contribution would not be increased beyond the $2 billion you have suggested.

2. The contribution of other countries would be very greatly increased to $13 billion.

3. The Fund would be stronger in its gold holdings under our proposal. This, I think, would be pleasing to Congress.

4. The American voting power while small (rightly so with our relatively small contribution) would rapidly grow if we purchased large amounts of gold from the Fund.

5. The plan looks toward future limitation by the Fund of new gold production. This meets one type of opposition to gold purchases.

Our proposal suggests that decision can be made by majority vote. While this may not be pleasing to many Congressmen, I think they can be sold on our suggestion since if in fact we buy a large amount of gold, our voting power would rapidly rise. Thus, the ultimate control by the United States would become very great if in fact we were called upon to supply a large amount of the credit.

It seems to me that these suggestions would really greatly strengthen your plan and I hope

that you will give them, as I am sure you will, earnest consideration. I regret that I cannot be
at your meeting on Monday (Hansen Papers: Hansen to White, June 11, 1943).

The general similarity in outlook between Hansen and White did not mean that
these suggestions were gracefully accepted. In fact, White became annoyed with
Hansen and the Federal Reserve experts when they raised their fears about the
consequences of unlimited American gold purchases during a 3-day conference
later in June with monetary specialists from 19 countries:

> When Alvin Hansen openly questioned the wisdom of an American commitment to accept all
> gold mined in the world, White lost his patience. Such theoretical ideas sound good at an
> economic conference, he retorted, but that group does not determine government policy. To
> allay fears that Washington might do as Hansen proposed—restrict its gold purchases—White
> vigorously reaffirmed the Treasury's longstanding promise to buy and sell gold at $35 per
> ounce. From White's standpoint this commitment to interconvertibility was imperative if
> others were to have confidence in the postwar system (Eckes, 1975:95).

Still, White made some of the changes suggested by Hansen, the Federal
Reserve, and experts from other nations. The size of the fund was increased to $8
billion, the amount of gold in each country's quota was increased to 50 percent,
and countries were given more flexibility in adjusting their exchange rates during
the first three years of the fund's operation (Eckes, 1975:95–96; Van Dormael,
1978:86).

The new draft became the basis for formal technical discussions between the
United States and Great Britain in September 1943. With both countries now
eager for agreement, for their separate political reasons, the discussions moved
along very easily compared to the past. Keynes abandoned his plan for a clearing
union based on an overdraft principle, asking in return for a fund of $10 billion,
not $8 billion, and agreement that countries would not be deprived of their
flexibility in altering their exchange rates. Although White and Keynes continued
to argue and trade for three weeks over technical issues, it was understood once
the clearing-union concept was dropped by the British that there were no differences that could not be compromised (Eckes, 1975:97–98).

The stage was not set for a meeting of 44 nations in Bretton Woods, New
Hampshire. In terms of the international harmony and cooperation the meeting
symbolized, including participation by the Soviet Union, the Bretton Woods
Conference was the historic occasion it is usually called. It also provided the
opportunity to bring congressional leaders of both parties and pressure-group
leaders into the process. All such people who were present at the conference
became enthusiastic supporters of the outcome, including Republican Senator
Charles Tobey of New Hampshire, who had been feared as a potential isolationist
opponent. Another positive outcome of the meeting was the enormous media
coverage for the idea of international monetary agreements, which was seen as
the opening round in shaping elite public opinion in favor of the agreement.

In terms of substance, however, very little was changed in the draft proposal for the IMF that had been agreed to by the American and British negotiators (Gardner, 1956:110). Most of the arguments among nations concerned the relative size of their contributions to the fund, with countries lobbying for larger contributions than their rivals and neighbors for two reasons. First, they wanted to look like greater powers in the eyes of their own citizens and other countries than they in fact were. Second, the larger a nation's contribution, the more it could draw upon the fund for the currencies of other countries.

In addition to ratifying the plan for the IMF, the Bretton Woods Conference also agreed to plans for an International Bank for Reconstruction and Development (the World Bank in common parlance). Plans for such a bank had been discussed in both the Treasury Department and the Economic and Financial Group of the war–peace studies from 1941 onwards. However, they had been put to the side during the disputes over the exchange stabilization fund because the bank was relatively noncontroversial in the eyes of government officials and American bankers. Originally, however, as Block (1977c:Chapter 3) emphasizes, there were aspects of White's suggestions for such a bank that were highly liberal and controversial. But these aspects were removed in informal discussions within the government at a fairly early stage, as explained in a very detailed history of the bank by Robert W. Oliver (1975:110–25, 138–44). In short, Block makes far too much of very tentative plans in presenting his case for state autonomy.

The plan for the bank endorsed at Bretton Woods was written by Keynes and other European experts on the cruise to the United States for the conference, but it was very similar to a moderate plan drafted by White and sent to Keynes. It was little more than a fund for guaranteeing foreign investments (Eckes, 1975:132), and there was no opposition to it in Congress even from those who vigorously opposed the IMF.

The final hurdle facing the Bretton Woods agreements was approval by a majority in the House and Senate. Contrary to Block, all accounts agree that the State Department fully supported the plan and worked closely with the Treasury to win its acceptance (Gardner, 1956; Eckes, 1975; Oliver, 1975; Van Dormael, 1978). Taking no chances, officials in the Treasury and State expended an enormous amount of effort getting their message out through speeches, endorsements, and favorable newspaper and magazine articles. Most of those in the general public who knew anything about the plan were positive, but only 23 percent of the respondents in one poll "could even relate Bretton Woods to world affairs" (Eckes, 1975:196). As is so often the case, the battle would be fought out among highly interested partisans in the "attentive public" and Congress (e.g., Rosenau, 1961).

There was widespread business and agricultural support for the IMF and World Bank. The American Farm Bureau Federation testified in favor of it, and a Business and Industry Committee for Bretton Woods was formed that included officers from such major corporations as General Mills, American President Lines, Bristol-Myers, and Hilton Hotels (Paterson, 1973:151, footnote 15). Significantly, the support committee included two prominent leaders of the highly conservative NAM, Charles Hook of American Rolling Mills and James H. Rand of Remington-Rand.

The main opposition to the plan came from the banking community, especially from big banks in New York. It needs to be stressed that this opposition was not anti-internationalist. It was based first of all in a desire to maintain the large influence on monetary policy that traditionally had been enjoyed by large banks, and second on a fear that overly liberal currency policies might lead to postwar inflation (Eckes, 1975:176). Working through the American Bankers Association and the Federal Reserve Bank of New York, the bankers' alternative was an approach based on British–American collaboration in currency stabilization. Called the "key currency" approach, it would first stabilize monetary relations between the United States and Great Britain, partly through a large loan to the British, and then build out to other nations. An international organization such as White and the council planners envisioned would come later if at all (Eckes, 1975:88–89). Neither the Canadian nor the British government liked the plan (Williams, 1944:234; Eckes, 1975:90, 176–77), which reinforced the opposition of American officials and their advisers to it.

The author of this alternative plan was economist John H. Williams, vice-president of the New York Federal Reserve Bank and dean of the Harvard Graduate School of Public Administration. He also had been a member of the Economic and Financial Group from February through November of 1940. Like Hansen, he recognized that the success of any monetary plan was dependent on avoiding depression in major countries. His ideas were discussed within the Economic and Financial Group and published in the council's journal, *Foreign Affairs* (Williams, 1943, 1944). Clearly, then, there were differences over the IMF among members of the Council on Foreign Relations, with Williams and major commercial bankers fighting a proposal that had been shaped and supported by the war–peace project.

The board of the Federal Reserve Bank of New York urged the key currency plan on the board of governors of the Federal Reserve in Washington, but its pleas were rejected by the Washington board in favor of the White Plan. Revealing once again the degree to which this battle was within the in-group, Hansen played a major role as an adviser to the board of governors in defeating Williams' plan:

> Consultant Alvin Hansen, who was instrumental in shaping the Federal Reserve position on this issue, asserted that, if Bretton Woods failed, there was little hope for supplementary economic agreements on investments, commodities, and commercial policy. And, without a network of international ties, parallel political agreements designed to assure future peace would surely fail. "Having become internationalists on political lines," Hansen claimed, "there is the gravest danger that the United States will remain isolationist on economic lines." Unless the United States provided the leadership and demonstrated its commitment to perma-

nent international arrangements, "nationalistic policies tending toward economic isolation are almost certain to prevail. Economic nationalism and isolationism, rival economic blocks, and international friction will likely be intensified" (Eckes, 1975:119).

But Williams and the New York bankers did not speak for all bankers, by any means. For example, Edward Brown, president of the First National Bank of Chicago, who had been at Bretton Woods, joined the aforementioned Business and Industry for Bretton Woods Committee (Paterson, 1973:150–51). He claimed that many other bankers throughout the country agreed with him (Van Dormael, 1978:254). Erle Cocke, an Atlanta banker, wrote of his approval of the agreements because the IMF would increase export sales of southern cotton, tobacco, and peanuts (Eckes, 1975:170). Since southern Democrats were great believers in free trade until the 1950s, as will be shown in Chapters 8 and 9, they needed little prompting from Cocke in the 1940s.

Although the New York bankers were relatively isolated within the corporate community in their opposition to the Bretton Woods agreements, and were seen as engaging in a special-interest kind of pleading by other business leaders, they nonetheless were an important factor in the legislative struggle because they gave great moral support to the isolationist Republicans on the House Banking and Currency Committee. In particular, they had a close relationship with Congressman Charles Dewey of Illinois, the main isolationist spokesperson. Until two weeks before the final vote, it looked like Dewey had organized a majority on the committee to block the plan (Eckes, 1975:192–94).

The coalition between internationalist New York bankers and isolationist House Republicans was held together in good measure by the claim that the IMF would be wrongly used by needy countries to provide themselves with short-term reconstruction and transition loans under the excuse of monetary adjustments. The answer to this argument came in a "Hegelian compromise intended to satisfy both the government and the bankers" (Eckes, 1975:191). Its sponsor was the relatively new organization of big-business moderates, discussed briefly in the previous chapter, the Committee for Economic Development (CED). The CED had been formed in 1942 by business leaders working with Secretary of Commerce Jesse Jones, himself a Houston entrepreneur of great wealth and influence. Its stated goal was to plan for the transition to a postwar economy in a cooperative way in conjunction with the government and other groups, but its unstated goal was to minimize government involvement in the economy (Eakins, 1966; Collins, 1981). In 1943 it hired Viner, Upgren, and John H. Williams to help fellow economist Calvin B. Hoover with a major study of international policy, the conclusion of which was the need to develop mechanisms to avoid depressions and advance free trade (Schriftgiesser, 1960:118–19). Its members and expert advisers were similar in perspective to leaders of the Council on Foreign Relations, and in the postwar years the committee became the domestic parallel of the council, sharing a great many members with its older counterpart (Domhoff, 1970c:124; Salzman and Domhoff, 1983).

The compromise was fashioned within the CED in good part by Beardsley Ruml, a long-time social-science adviser to John D. Rockefeller, Jr. He suggested that any possibility of the fund being used wrongly for short-term loans could be dealt with by authorizing the proposed World Bank to make short-term stabilization loans as well as long-term loans for reconstruction and development:

> With the bank taking a more active role in the abnormal postwar period, the fund, designed primarily to cushion short-term fluctuations in an orderly world where international transactions tended to balance, would not have to assume the burden of financing unstable conditions. According to the CED analysis, if the bank engaged in stabilization lending, the fund would not misuse its resources and become frozen with unwanted currencies, as the bankers feared (Eckes, 1975:191).

This proposal, along with the addition of a high-level government advisory committee to advise American appointees to the fund and bank on how to vote, satisfied the bankers. Some observers argued at the time that the Hegelian compromise was largely symbolic, giving the bankers a way to save face and accept the inevitable (Eckes, 1975:192). However, the important point here is that big-business supporters of the fund had found a way to assuage banker opposition. This capitulation by the bankers, along with the ascendancy of Truman to the presidency, led to a "remarkable turnaround" on the House Banking and Currency Committee; the majority who had opposed the bill was now reduced to three isolationist "irreconcilables" from the Midwest (Eckes, 1975:197). The bill authorizing the president to accept membership in the IMF and the World Bank sailed through both the House and Senate by wide margins when the vote finally came after the usual apocalyptic and/or grandiose speechifying.

There was one more battle to be fought once the fund and bank were legislated. It was with the British at a conference of all member nations at Savannah, Georgia, during March 1946. The British lost on the location of the two institutions and on the degree to which the experts would be hedged in by political overseers. By the end of the conference the fund and the bank were clearly dominated by the American government and American bankers. Keynes left the conference very embittered by the American high-handedness.

American leaders were indeed less generous in their sharing of power than either White or council experts had envisioned. Still, as Hansen later wrote, "No one familiar with the political realities of the time is likely to argue that a more ambitious scheme could have been realized" (Hansen, 1965:177, as quoted in Eckes, 1975:279). In that sense, the final outcome demonstrates the great power of conservative business leaders and bankers through Congress. But the very existence of international financial and monetary organizations that would play the role planned for them by the council demonstrates the even greater power of the moderate internationalists on this issue.

And yet, after all this, the IMF did not come into its own until the 1950s.

Block believes this was because the State Department chose to bypass the IMF to deal directly with the British, but most commentators think otherwise (e.g., Gardner, 1956:191, 196–97). As one expert on the era summarizes, "the United States participated enthusiastically only in those international organizations it could control and circumvented or weakened those which did not serve its purposes" (Paterson, 1973:147). He goes on to note that "the United States held a distinct advantage in the International Bank for Reconstruction and Development and the International Monetary Fund and so added them to its arsenal of Cold War weapons" (Paterson, 1973:147).

The real problem with the IMF, as everyone agreed at the time, was that it was not designed to handle the transition to peacetime. It always was understood that there would have to be a loan to the British. Even with this understanding, the planners went wrong in underestimating the devastation of the British economy and the time that would be needed to reconstruct it. Block's analysis goes astray when he argues that the Americans were bypassing the IMF in granting a direct loan to the British. Actually, the Americans linked the granting of the loan to Great Britain's ratification of its participation in the IMF (Gardner, 1956:191, 196–97, and Chapter 11; Van Dormael, 1978:274–75). The loan was carrot, stick, and necessity, not an end run of the IMF.

So much, then for what I think are the main features of the creation of the IMF. As always, there is more detail that could be provided, and much more that could be learned, but I think enough has been said about the power and influence dimensions of the case to allow some general conclusions to be reached in the final section.

## Discussion and Conclusion

Fred Block and other state autonomy theorists say the ruling class does not rule in capitalist countries. I say it does in the United States. They mean that the ruling class itself does not create the policies adopted by the state and does not provide the state with personnel to carry out the policies. For them, the need for new policies arises out of conflicts between the dominant capitalist class and the working class, but the new policies are created by independent state managers who have interests of their own and cannot be considered representatives of the capitalist class. Block now would amend his formulation to include a role for independent experts and middle-class reformers as well.

I dispute Block and other state autonomy theorists because policy organizations of the ruling class articulate policies that are brought to the government in a variety of ways. Furthermore, these organizations provide much of the top personnel that implements the policies. This perspective does not deny intraclass policy differences that are often fought out within the arena of the state, nor does it deny that many policies are formulated in reaction to conflicts with the working class or middle-class reformers. But it does say that the ruling class, or a segment of it, has won most of these battles, at least since the United States became a corporate America.

In this chapter certain points contrary to Block's paradigm case for a structuralist theory have been established as well as they can be with the available archival evidence. Only more thorough file-keeping or diary-keeping by White, Viner and Hansen, or a new find in American, Canadian, or British papers, could improve the case. But the inadequacies of the record at certain points are hardly an argument against the preponderance of evidence that the ruling class did rule on the IMF. The burden of proof would clearly be on anyone's shoulders who wished to deny the following points:

1.  Through the Council on Foreign Relations, there was a large ruling-class involvement in the postwar planning that lead to the creation of the IMF, White's important role in writing the specific plan and seeing it through lengthy negotiations notwithstanding.
2.  The degree of substantive conflict between State and Treasury over postwar foreign economic planning was minimal. To the degree that White represented a highly liberal or even radical view, to that degree his plans were trimmed back by ruling-class experts in the State Department and British experts. This point is demonstrated more fully on the World Bank, which was given little attention in this chapter, than on the IMF (see Oliver, 1975, for details).
3.  Any lack of communication between the two departments was filled in and mediated by the outside experts from the Council on Foreign Relations.
4.  The State Department supported the IMF as part of its overall vision for the functioning of the postwar world economy. Any postwar subordination of the role of the IMF was due to an underestimation of the time and money it would take to make the transition to peacetime.
5.  More conservative internationalists in the ruling class, and in particular New York bankers, were able to bring about changes in the plan that made it more acceptable to them. They joined with isolationists in the House to accomplish their goal.
6.  Corporate leaders gave strong support to the plan and leaders within the CED created the final compromise that satisfied both the New York bankers and the ultraconservatives within Congress.
7.  Conservative opposition in Congress collapsed once the New York bankers compromised their differences with other internationalists within the ruling class. Only a few unreconstructed isolationists opposed the final bill.

In making these strong points, it is not my intention to say that the state is without power, or that politicians do not matter, but to insist that none of this adds up to the creation of the IMF by an autonomous state, let alone by "national capitalists" within that state. None of it suggests a lack of classwide vision on the part of the corporate leaders and planners who took responsibility for this major policy issue. Nor do we see very many independent state managers aside from White.

True, there were disagreements within the ruling class. Then too, experts played a very large role, including liberal Keynesian experts. Moreover, final decisions and compromises were made and legitimated inside the state. In the end, just about everybody was happy, including middle-class reformers and union leaders, who played supporting roles. But again, none of this means that the ruling class does not rule. Pluralism happens within a ruling-class framework.

There is one aspect of the preceding paragraph that I would like to discuss at greater length because Block now alludes to it, and Skocpol (1986/87) now puts stress on it as a "third force" in American politics. I refer of course to the role of experts. In this particular case study, as in many, we see very clearly the large role of experts, mostly economists in this instance. But the experts involved in the policy issue were not working independently. They were working for a ruling-class organization that had hired them to provide corporate leaders with the best possible advice they could suggest for making corporate capitalism function more smoothly and expansively. There is nothing new in this finding or in my statement. Experts have been helping the corporate community by means of participation in policy-planning organizations since at least 1900, and as far back as 1970 I wrote as follows in introducing three policy-related essays:

> Moderate leaders within the upper class, somewhat restrained by their more conservative brethren, have made the key decisions of the twentieth century; these moderate leaders have been helped in every area—foreign policy, domestic policy, propaganda and espionage—by a small number of highly-respected academic experts who are situated in a handful of prestigious and richly endowed universities (Domhoff, 1970c:108).

This does not mean such experts are doing the "bidding" of the capitalists. They are not "puppets" or "front men." To the contrary, they have an independent role in educating the business and banking officials on general issues, and they often argue with them or disagree with them. For me, though, the important thing is that the corporate leaders are the dominant interest within this relationship. They decide whom they will ask to advise them, and they decide which suggestions to accept and which to modify. Many colleagues have told me over the years that the academic experts are "smarter" than the corporate leaders, and hence the "real" power figures, but the corporate leaders seem to be smart enough to keep the experts working for them to realize corporate goals. Power is not a matter of giving advice, or of being intelligent in the academic sense, but of setting policy (Mills, 1956).

We do not have rich empirical examples of this give-and-take within the work of the Council on Foreign Relations' war–peace studies. The kind of interview and archival evidence we would need to make the point does not seem to be available. However, we do have such evidence in the case of the CED for the same period, thanks to the work of the committee's historian, Karl Schriftgiesser (1960, 1967). His books attest very nicely to the natural and understandable way in which the process works, including a very careful screening to find acceptable advisers. He shows there are limits to what corporate leaders are willing to listen to. Since they are the people who have access to government, I believe that is another indication that they have the power in the relationship.

But, it can be argued, the experts also have interactions with elected officials and high-level government appointees in the executive branch. We have excellent examples of how this works in the activities of Hansen and Viner, who seemed to be consulting for the whole government at one point or another. However, we have to remember that government officials are talking directly with corporate leaders, too. We have to remind ourselves that banker Norman Davis, president of the Council on Foreign Relations, was a close confidant of the president and secretary of state, and that other directors of the council had similar contacts with the same men and many other government officials. It is this direct business–government connection, I contend, that helps place general constraints on what ideas government officials are willing to consider from experts. Even more importantly, these experts are legitimated in the eyes of government officials because they are employed by respected organizations like the council. This is what provides their access. It is not just any old expert off the streets who can make an appointment with secretaries of state and place plans on their desks.

Still, my point can be overstated in the sense that disagreements among businesspeople give experts leeway in trying to sway government officials. In the case of monetary issues, for example, we have seen that internationalist leaders had disagreements among themselves that were reflected in the varying opinions of Harvard professors John H. Williams and Alvin Hansen over how to proceed. New York bankers favored Williams' key-currency approach, while leaders of the Council on Foreign Relations favored the Hansen–Viner–White approach. In this type of situation, a Williams and a Hansen both have their chance to influence government officials, and government officials have flexibility as to which corporate-sponsored expert they will decide to believe. In this case, Hansen won out over Williams at the Federal Reserve Board, because the millionaire banker who chaired the board, Marriner Eccles, had Keynesian-type ideas before he ever heard of Keynes. A Mormon from Utah with his own chain of banks, he also disliked New York bankers (Greider, 1987:Chapter 10). Once again, that is, we see that it does matter who governs in a democratic society with a volatile capitalist economy.

There is, then, a certain independence for experts, but it is a highly selective and constrained independence. It is not an independence that accords equal access to all experts, free of the existing realities of the power structure. Here I think of historian Robert M. Collins' (1981) account of how Keynesian thinking in the United States was gradually whittled down to a narrow "business Keynesianism" that was seldom breached by either Democrats or Republicans in the years between 1945 and 1964, when his study ends. My point is that the corporate dominance of the United States is very great for a variety of historical reasons, and this greatly restricts the policy options that experts can put on the political agenda.

All that said, this still does not deny that there are experts who are outside the corporate fold and the power structure. These experts work for unions, middle-class reform groups, universities, and the government. Some of them are very liberal, as in the case of Harry Dexter White. Such experts do widen the public debate, and to some extent the debate in government circles as well. They sometimes add momentary uncertainty to the final outcome of ongoing policy conflicts, but I do not think that a range of case studies would show that they have much impact. The failed attempt by pluralist Nelson Polsby (1984) to show otherwise is the best demonstration I know of this point.

Experts and all then, I do not think the story of the IMF, or any other case study I know of, provides any support for any version of state autonomy theory for the United States, structural Marxist or otherwise. Instead, the American state is dominated on major policy issues by a corporate-based ruling class, just as we might expect of a state that is fragmented by its existence within a market economy and that is suffused with the classic liberal market ideology (Feigenbaum, 1985:169–74).

There are conflicts within the fragmented American state, but they primarily concern conflicts among segments of the ruling class, or among special interests within the ruling class. Middle-class reformers and working-class leaders often create pressure for change, especially on domestic issues, but they usually sign up on the side of one ruling-class segment or another. Farmers had their moments in the now-distant past (McConnell, 1966), and trade unions had their innings in the 1930s before beginning a long decline that continues to this day (Goldfield, 1987). However, most evidence suggests that the American ruling class has had more influence over its government in the twentieth century than any counterparts in other advanced European capitalist nations. Perhaps there is irony in the fact that the most celebrated pluralist nation may be the least pluralist of the major democracies when it comes to political power on major issues (Flacks, 1988:Chapter 2).

I used the term "major issues" in the previous sentence, but perhaps I should have said "policies that relate to economic issues and class rule," for I do not believe that the ruling class has any class interest in abortion, busing, capital punishment, gay rights, gun control, school prayer, the teaching of evolutionary theory in southern high schools, or any other such social, religious, or personal issues considered major by pluralists and many middle-level interest groups.

Even racism and sexism are mostly secondary issues for the ruling class; only classism matters, unless the racism or sexism leads to serious social disruption (Zweigenhaft and Domhoff, 1991).

Of course, I can agree that there may not be a ruling class in other times and places. The state is a separate organizational network with the unique social role of regulating social life in specific areas (Mann, 1984, 1986), and as such it is always potentially autonomous (Skocpol, 1979:29–30. But not here, not now.

# 7

# STATE AUTONOMY AND THE EMPLOYMENT ACT OF 1946:
## An Empirical Attack on a Theoretical Fantasy

### Introduction

In this combative little chapter I am going to challenge an alleged insight about the relationship between the corporate community and "the state" that became fashionable among pluralists, elitists, and structural Marxists alike during the 1970s. I am going to do so by holding it up to the mundane light of empirical reality. The new idea to which I refer is that big business does not have to bother to influence or dominate government because it has a "privileged position" due to the fact that only private corporations can invest and create jobs in a market economy. The mundane reality that it cannot explain is the bitter defensive struggle businessmen and their allies had to wage over the original version of the Employment Act of 1946, which was in good part fashioned inside the state.

The simple idea in question, which I will explore fully in a moment, was immediately seized upon as one of the most penetrating insights of recent decades. Best of all, the idea could be used to refute the "conspiratorial" and "instrumentalist" theories of people such as me. There was no longer any need to determine whether or not capitalists dominated government. Of course they didn't. But government did their bidding anyhow because it has no choice. Government has to give capitalists most of what they want or else there will be economic depression and political instability. Then elected and appointed government officials might lose their jobs.

Among the first people of note to put forth this idea in the early years of the dreary decade were political scientists Kenneth Prewitt and Alan Stone in an avowedly elitist book appropriately titled *The Ruling Elites* (1973). They present the idea in the context of criticizing my emphasis on the business-financed policy-discussion groups that I have shown to connect the corporate community and government. Instead of corporate domination of government, there is a

"perceived mutuality of interest" between corporate leaders and high government officials (1973:68). Because the giant corporations have a great impact on
the health of the economy, it is necessary for government officials to formulate
policies that will maintain "business confidence and encourage the large firms to
invest, employ large numbers of people, and transact a considerable volume of
business with supplier and customer firms" (1973:68). According to Prewitt and
Stone, this formulation is useful because it explains the important role of big
business "without resorting to the notion of businessmen engaging in a surreptitious conspiracy to manipulate or dominate the government" (1973:69).

Shortly thereafter, and apparently quite independently, the argument appeared
as a key element in the revisionist Marxist work on the relationship between the
state and the ruling class by Fred Block (1977a), whose claim that the ruling class
does not rule was explored in the previous chapter. Instead, state managers do
that. Moreover, "the idea of a division of labor between non-class-conscious
capitalists and those who manage the state apparatus can be found in Marx's
writings." Even when Marx implies otherwise, it is because of his "polemical
intent to fix responsibility for all aspects of bourgeois society on the ruling
class." Using an argument that makes it difficult to know when to take Marx
seriously and when to conclude that he is merely being political, Block concludes
that "Marx used the idea of a conscious, directive ruling class as a polemical
shorthand for an elaboration of the structural mechanisms through which control
over the means of production leads to control over other aspects of society"
(1977a:10).

Having satisfied himself that Marx meant other than what he wrote and is in
agreement with Block's theory, Block goes on to argue that the state managers
pretty much have to do what capitalists want because the development of the state
and their own tenure as its managers "are dependent on the maintenance of some
reasonable level of economic activity" (1977a:15). This is first of all due to the
state's need to maintain its tax revenues at an adequate level and second of all due
to the fact that "public support for a regime will decline sharply if the regime
presides over a serious drop in the level of economic activity with a parallel rise
in unemployment and shortages of key goods" (1977a:15).

Thus, the problem for the independent state managers is to create conditions
under which capitalists will feel inclined to invest, and the key to calling forth
this necessary investment is the cultivation of "business confidence":

> The most useful concept is the idea of business confidence. . . . The sum of all of these
> evaluations [by capitalists] across a national economy can be termed the level of business
> confidence. As the level of business confidence declines, so will the rate of investment
> (1977a:16).

The idea next appeared in a revisionist work by one of the most prominent
pluralists of the 1950s and 1960s, Charles Lindblom. The appearance of the new

insight in *Politics and Markets* (1977) made it respectable for everyone. Here is one quote among many that summarizes it:

> Any government official who understands the requirements of his position and the responsibilities that market-oriented systems throw on businessmen will therefore grant them a privileged position. He does not have to be bribed, duped, or pressured to do so. He simply understands, as is plain to see, that public affairs in market-oriented systems are in the hands of two groups of leaders, government and business, who must collaborate and that to make the system work government leadership must often defer to business leadership (1977:175).

Once again, the new insight is followed one paragraph later with a criticism of views such as mine, which are described as "crude allegations of a power elite established by clandestine forces":

> Thus politics in market-oriented systems take a peculiar turn, one largely ignored in conventional political science. To understand the peculiar character of politics in market-oriented systems requires, however, no conspiracy theory of politics, no theory of common social origins uniting government and business officials, no crude allegations of a power elite established by clandestine forces. Business simply needs inducements, hence a privileged position in government and politics, if it is to do its job (1977:175).

Lindblom's conversion to this view is surprising. For him to conclude his book with the words "The large private corporation fits oddly into democratic theory and vision. Indeed it does not fit" was a real shocker, and he was attacked vigorously by many mainstreamers and neoconservatives while being applauded by Marxists. But his theory remained as economistic as ever because it focuses exclusively on why government has to pay heed to business, never stressing that political power is necessary to guarantee economic power in the face of rebellious workers. Thus, it did not take state power seriously, but structural Marxists overlooked this shortcoming because he had come around on the power of capitalists.

Lindblom claims that his view is new, something that has not been put together in quite this way before. He explains: "Every step in the analysis will refer to a familiar aspect of these systems, the implications of which, taken together, have been overlooked by most of us" (1977:172). But is this formulation new? Has it been "overlooked" in the past? Hardly. This viewpoint is so obvious, so taken for granted as part of the definition of the capitalist system, that in the 1960s it would have been an embarrassment to put it forth as new. Moreover, it is only one dimension of the overall situation, one tendency, and a tendency that can be challenged, as the original thrust of the Employment Act of 1946 will demonstrate.

For myself, I first remember reading this argument in the early 1960s in political scientist Michael Reagan's overlooked book, *The Managed Economy* (1963). There, however, it is presented as one of several factors that add up to very great corporate influence on government. In a chapter on the sources of business power and influence, Reagan writes: "When we come to examine business's position in relation to government, the first fact that emerges is government's dependence on business" (1963:86). But he is not only talking about the privileged position of business when it comes to investing. First of all he notes that "the national government is heavily dependent upon business cooperation in fulfilling the most basic of all government responsibilities: national survival," and he points out that just before World War II big corporations held back on conversion "until their conditions were fulfilled—the major condition being a virtual guarantee of profits" (1963:87). He then goes on to present the new idea as one part of a two-pronged process:

> The President's most notable domestic role is that of "manager of prosperity." By the provisions of the Employment Act of 1946 he has been made responsible for analyzing the economic state of the union and for devising a program to promote "maximum employment, production, and purchasing power." Whether these goals are realized, however, depends heavily on the behavior of business firms over whom the President has no authority. The dependence is both direct and indirect. Directly, prosperity depends upon private-sector decisions regarding such factors as the rate of business investment, the rate of innovation, and the movement of prices. Indirectly, business influences, or indeed determines, the ability of the government to take appropriate steps to improve the nation's economic performance. That is, through lobbying in Congress in opposition to a President's antirecession program, business organizations impeded the President's ability to compensate for the original inadequacies of private-sector decisions—as was the case with President Kennedy's 1961 program for full employment and a higher growth rate (1963:87–88).

To make my point clear, let us turn in detail to a famous Marxian alternative to pluralism, Miliband's *The State in Capitalist Society* (1969). This is the book that was defamed and distorted in a widely cited review by French structural Marxist Nicos Poulantzas as claiming the opposite of what is actually said (Poulantzas, 1969). It is an alleged prime example of the dreaded "instrumentalism." Here is Poulantzas at his elegant worst, attacking Miliband for bothering to refute the pluralist claim that there are not very many capitalists within the state:

> If Miliband had first established that the State is precisely *the factor of cohesion of a social formation and the factor of reproduction of the conditions of production of a system* that itself determines the domination of one class over the others, he would have seen clearly that the participation, whether direct or indirect, of this class in government *in no way changes things*. Indeed in the case of the capitalist State, one can go further: it can be said that the capitalist State best serves the interests of the capitalist class only when the members of this class do not participate directly in the State apparatus, that is to say when the *ruling class* is not the *politically governing class* (1969:73, his italics).

Poulantzas does not present any empirical evidence for his claim that the governments without capitalist in them do best by capitalists, nor have any of those who quote him. Following his reasoning, the United States government, with undoubtedly the most capitalists in it, is the worst of all capitalist governments and American capitalism the least successful of all capitalisms.

Instead, Poulantzas goes on to say that "a long Marxist tradition has considered that the State is only a simple tool or instrument manipulated at will by the ruling class" (1969:74). He says that Miliband does not quite "fall into this trap" (1969:74), but that is not how it came out six years later in the article discussed in Chapter 3 by David Gold, Clarence Lo, and Erik Wright (1975) based on discussions of the matter in the *Kapitalistate* Group.

First, the American critics of Miliband define an "instrumental theory" of the state: "What we mean, therefore, by an 'instrumental theory' of the state is a theory in which the ties between the ruling class and state are systematically examined, while the structural context within which those ties occur remains largely theoretically unorganized" (1975:31). They then label Miliband on the basis of a misinterpreted quote for which they give the wrong page number: "In the Marxist scheme, the 'ruling class' of capitalist society is that class which owns and controls the means of production and which is able, by virtue of the economic power thus conferred upon it, to use the state as its instrument for the domination of society" (1975:32). There is nothing in there about having to have "ties" to the state to dominate it. It is just as likely that the "economic power conferred upon it" means exactly what the theorists of the 1970s mean by the "privileged position of business."

Did Miliband really overlook the great idea of the 1970s? If not, what was it about his book that got him so badly misinterpreted, leaving the way clear for young American Marxists and Lindblom to claim so much for themselves? Let me look at these questions carefully, for it is high time that someone set the record straight and put the big insight into a proper context.

In an early chapter, "The State and the State Elite," Miliband sets the stage for his later discussion by asking whether the capitalist class controls the state directly or rules through other means. He then gives an historical answer that should have been a warning to those who later distorted Miliband:

> But it is obviously true that the capitalist class, as a class, does not actually "govern." One must go back to isolated instances of the early history of capitalism, such as the commercial patriciates of cities like Venice and Lubeck, to discover direct and sovereign rule by businessmen. Apart from these cases, the capitalist class has generally confronted the state as a separate entity—even, in the days of its rise to power, as an alien and often hostile element often under the control and influence of an established and landowning class, whose hold upon the state power had to be broken by revolution, as in France, or by erosion, as in England in the nineteenth century, that process of erosion being greatly facilitated, in the English case, by the constitutional and political changes wrought by violence in the seventeenth century (Miliband 1969:55).

However, Miliband then turns his attention to countering claims by Max Weber, Raymond Aron, and others that very few businesspeople are involved in the state. It is here he gets in trouble with the critics, for in the changed climate of the 1970s they were so put off by his empirical challenge to the now passé pluralists that they failed to see that he is unfolding his full theory in step-by-step fashion over the range of several chapters. Still, after presenting the facts on the large numbers of business leaders in government, he then points out that not too much should be made of this information:

> Notwithstanding the substantial participation of businessmen in the business of the state, it is however true that they have never constituted, and do not constitute now, more than a relatively small majority of the state elite as a whole. It is in this sense that the economic elites of advanced capitalist countries are not, properly speaking, a "governing" class, comparable to pre-industrial, aristocratic and landowning classes (1969:59).

In short, Miliband is saying there is more to the matter. He takes the next step in the argument in the following chapter, "The Purpose and Role of Governments." There he emphasizes that most state leaders have an ideological commitment to the capitalist system:

> This consensus between political office-holders is clearly crucial. The ideological dispositions which make the consensus possible may not, because of various counterpressures, finally determine how governments will act in every particular situation. But the fact that government accept as beyond question the capitalist context in which they operate is of absolutely fundamental importance in shaping their attitudes, policies and actions in regard to the specific issues and problems with which they are confronted, and to the needs and conflicts of civil society (1969:72).

However, Miliband is still working on the level of ideology and bias. Later in the chapter he signals that his view is going to be one that includes both "ideological dispositions" and "structural constraints":

> Thus 'bias of the system' may be given a greater or lesser degree of emphasis. But the ideological dispositions of governments have generally been of a kind to make more acceptable to them the structural constraints imposed upon them by the system; and these dispositions have also made it easier for them to submit to the pressures to which they have been subjected by dominant interests (1969:79).

Once again, however, Miliband pauses in his theoretical argument to deal with empirical issues, this time of an historical nature. He even interposes a chapter titled "Servants of the State" before he goes on to score a direct bullseye on the overlooked idea. The purpose of the interposed chapter is to argue that "the dominant economic interests in capitalist society can normally count on the active good-will and support of those in whose hands state power lies" (1969:145).

Finally, we reach what must be the most overlooked chapter in any book so widely footnoted. It is called "Imperfect Competition" because it shows, contrary to pluralist theory, that business is an "interest" like no other in capitalist society. The previous chapters only showed that large-scale business "did enjoy such an advantage *inside* the state system, by virtue of the composition and ideological inclinations of the state elite" (1969:146, his italics). In short, his alleged "instrumentalism" is one part of the picture. Now he is going to argue that "business enjoys a massive superiority *outside* the state system as well, in terms of the immensely stronger pressures which, as compared with labour or any other interest, it is able to exercise in the pursuit of its purposes" (1969:146, his italics).

But Miliband is talking in terms of pressures, and the critics from the 1970s deride the need for any pressures by big business. However, Miliband means by pressures precisely what more recent theorists mean with their talk about structures and autonomy and privileged position. He starts the first section with what certainly sounds like the new idea to me:

> One such form of pressure, which pluralist "group theorists" tend to ignore, is more important and effective than any other, and business is uniquely placed to exercise it, without the need or organization, campaigns and lobbying. This is the pervasive and permanent pressure upon governments and the state generated by the private control of concentrated industrial, commercial and financial resources. The existence of this major area of independent economic power is a fact which no government, whatever its inclinations, can ignore in the determination of its policies, not only in regard to economic matters, but to most other matters as well (1969:147).

As if this were not enough, Miliband goes on to write directly about "business confidence," the very phrase used by Prewitt and Stone, Block, and Lindblom. Lest it be thought he only touched on the matter in passing, or perhaps meant something different than his detractors, I hasten to quote him as he begins about four pages of discussion on the idea:

> These difficulties and perils [facing governments that might attack business] are perhaps best epitomized in the dreaded phrase "loss of confidence." It is an implicit testimony to the power of business that all governments, not least reforming ones, have always been profoundly concerned to gain and retain its "confidence." Nor certainly is there any other interest whose "confidence" is deemed so precious, or whose "loss of confidence" is so feared (1969:150).

That this loss of confidence has to do with investment, among other things, is made clear in a quote Miliband uses from *The Times* of London concerning the attempts of the Labor government of the late 1960s to restore business confidence:

> Labour came to power with a large fund of good-will among the business community [says *The Times*]. It is perhaps a recognition of its subsequent disillusion that the Prime Minister is now ready to intervene in the constant Whitehall-industry dialogue to restore confidence

necessary for promoting higher investments and changing practices (*The Times*, October 3, 1967, as quoted in Miliband, 1969:152).

Miliband also quotes *Fortune* as follows, a quote that shows that *Fortune* had a hold on the new idea long ago:

The chairman of the editorial board of *Fortune* magazine said in 1952 that "any president who wants to seek a prosperous country depends on the corporation at least as much—probably more than—the corporation depends on him. His dependence is not unlike that of King John on the landed barons at Runnymede, where Magna Carta was born" (1969:147).

Where did Miliband get this quote? From his friend C. Wright Mills in *The Power Elite* (1956). It turns out that even an allegedly crude and conspiratorial power elite theorist of a radical neo-Weberian stamp knew the great secret. But so did a conservative elitist, Andrew Hacker, whom Miliband quotes (1969:148) as making the same kind of point against "Parsons and other liberals" in 1961. Maybe everyone knew it.

Some noted leaders from the New Deal era certainly knew the theory. None other than Franklin D. Roosevelt believed that business had caused the recession of 1937–38 in order to "force a retreat from the New Deal" (Hawley, 1966:389). He was reinforced in this belief by several of his anti-Keynesian advisers, and the theory "that capital was on a sitdown strike was soon to become the official version of the recession" (1966:389). But it was not only the Roosevelt administration that blamed a capital strike. The Communist party did, too, because it was supporting Roosevelt at the time and did not want to attack him for the spending cuts and budget balancing that were the real cause of the recession. "Monopoly capital has gone on a sitdown strike," the party leader said. "It is trying, by direct action, to cancel the mandate of the people of November, 1936" (Klehr, 1984:2188). So the ancestors of the "privileged position of business" theorists include not only Michael Reagan, Miliband, Mills, and Hacker, but a great president of United States and a leader of the Communist party as well.

But is the privileged position of business an all-important idea? I think not. Given the tensions and uncertainties of a dynamic and volatile capitalist economic system, and the possibilities for social change in a democratic state system where elected legislatures can greatly influence the functioning of administrative agencies and businesses themselves, it is just a fairy tale to think that it does not take continuous efforts on the part of the corporate community to dominate the state structure. No American capitalists ever have been so serene and confident as to rely on underlying "structural imperatives" to insure that people in decision-making positions will do what needs to be done for the sake of capitalism.

Still, all this is only assertion. What about some evidence that bears on the importance of the privileged position of business in the relationship between class and state in the United States? It is fortunate that one of the best-documented legislative struggles of recent decades relates to this question. The original Employment Act, formulated almost completely by elected officials and state employees, was meant to deal with underinvestment by capitalists, among other problems. Yes, right here in the U.S.A., in the ideological stronghold of free-market worship, there actually was a move afoot to give the state the capability to invest in productive facilities and to create jobs as a matter of course. It was not a blueprint for socialism, but it would have reduced the dependency of government and ordinary workers on the decisions of private capital. It would have changed the way in which American capitalism operated in dramatic ways.

Not surprisingly, then, most businesspeople didn't like the government investment and expenditure provisions in the proposed Employment Act. They said things like "there is an implicit threat that if 'free enterprise' cannot supply jobs, then the task will be taken over by the government" (Bailey, 1950:130). They even said that the spending provisions of the bill would undermine business confidence. Moreover, the big commercial farmers who were the businesspeople's friends and allies said they opposed the bill because it might undercut their supply of cheap farm labor (1950:148).

Contrary to our privileged-position theorists, these corporate bigwigs may have been right to worry a little bit. After all, the Great Depression was still fresh in everyone's minds in 1945. Despite several years of wartime prosperity, many working people feared a sudden return to unemployment, and they wanted government to make sure that did not happen. Understanding these concerns full well, Roosevelt had campaigned in 1944 on the need for a new economic bill of rights that included the right to a job. And there were still many liberals in Congress, not to mention liberal and socialist employees in state agencies and bureaucracies who thought major changes were needed in the business system. Although Lindblom has made a big contribution by showing that a market system is essential if a successful egalitarian movement is going to avoid the authoritarian state structure that seems likely with a centrally planned state economy, that does not mean the usual relationships between private property, the market, and the state are immutable in a context such as existed in 1945 when the Employment Act was formulated and debated.

It is clearly time to consider events leading up to the Employment Act of 1946 in greater detail. There is nothing like a little empirical data after all this hot air. This is especially so since it is not obvious to me how privileged-position theorists would explain the following case history except by explaining it away, that is, by claiming that the policies embodied in the act really were in the interests of business, or would have been abandoned eventually if business refused to function, or would have been nipped in the bud by high-level state managers even without all the frenzied activity by capitalists.

## Conflict over the Employment Bill

The origins of the Employment Act of 1946 are complex and diverse (U.S. Senate, 1965). Certainly the many converts to Keynesian economics in the universities were strong advocates of compensatory government spending and budget deficits, with the most liberal of them calling for direct government investment as well as other types of spending. There also had been a series of reports from the president's National Resources Planning Board that were legitimating the use of planning and fiscal policy to shape the economy; in fact, the board's 1943 report dealing with postwar policy, *Security, Work, and Relief Policies,* was considered so radical by a majority within Congress that the board was abolished by congressional action three months after the report appeared (Bailey, 1950:27). Then too, as the two previous chapters showed, the corporate moderates and their hired hands in policy groups like the Council on Foreign Relations and the CED had been issuing reports concerned with ways to avoid a return to depression after the war ended, with a special emphasis on increasing foreign trade and investment (Eakins, 1969; Shoup and Miner, 1977). Here I can add that they were aided in this effort by the National Planning Association, an organization that included labor and farm leaders as well as corporate officials and experts.

However, the origin of the Employment Act that was to cause so much stir in the corporate community can be traced to notes written in April 1944 by Russell Smith, a legislative representative for the liberal National Farmers Union. The basic idea was that "the federal government would underwrite the total national investment necessary to insure full employment" (Bailey, 1950:23). Smith, who previously had worked as a newspaperman and an appointee in the Bureau of Agricultural Economics and the Board of Economic Welfare, showed his draft to a number of friends in government who helped improve it. He also spoke with the ubiquitous Harvard economist, Alvin Hansen.

After further refinement, and with the encouragement of government employees from several agencies and legislative committee, Smith's plan was introduced as an amendment to Senate legislation concerned with reconversion to a peacetime economy. The amendment called for the government to make loans available to private industry and local and state governments if it were determined there would be shortfall in the amount of investment needed for full employment. Most importantly for our purposes here, the amendment stated that "if such loans were not applied for or utilized in sufficient quantity to bring about full employment, Congress would then appropriate for public works and other federal projects the amount of money needed to accomplish this end" (Bailey, 1950:24).

There was no thought by its sponsors that the amendment to the reconversion legislation had a chance to pass at that time. Offering Smith's handiwork as an amendment was merely a way for the legislative strategists behind the bill,

Senator James E. Murray of Montana and his chief legislative aide, Bertram Gross, to build support for the ideas among liberal and labor constituencies and to solicit opinion from other government officials. The real legislative test was to come later.

The bill that originally was called the Full Employment Act first appeared as an appendix to the Year-End Report of Senator Murray's War Contracts Subcommittee. It was drafted by Gross over a two-month period in late 1944 with the help of a wide range of government experts, including one of the most eminent political scientists of recent years, V. O. Key. Based on the comments sent to Gross about the Smith proposals, the new bill put as much emphasis upon creating consumer demand through compensatory government spending as it did on the more narrow concept of government investment. In short, these very liberal government employees realized that "investment" was not the sole basis for the "privileged position of business," and they aimed to take a more comprehensive approach to undermining that privileged position. Contrary to what I implied in my earlier accounts of the drafting process, moderate business leaders at the National Planning Association did not take any part in this process and were not enamored of the result (Domhoff, 1970c:188, 1979:110). Their input came later.

Nor did the National Farms Union or any other liberal pressure group play a very great or independent role in formulating this act, contrary to the impression that can be gained from a pluralist reading of Bailey (1950). The main action was created and coordinated from inside the office of Senator Wheeler. I have been convinced of this fact during lengthy discussions with Bertram Gross himself, who was not at full liberty to discuss with Bailey and others everything about the formulation of the act while he was still in a sensitive political situation because he served in government at the pleasure of Democratic politicians and appointees.

From the point of view of many of the bill's supporters, the guarantee of the right to a job and the authorization of spending to fulfill that guarantee were essential to the act. A key sentence read: "There are hereby authorized to be appropriated such sums as may be necessary to eliminate any deficiency in the National Budget" (Bailey, 1950:48). However, the authorization of spending was one of the first things that had to go when Senator Murray set out to find cosponsors for the bill in the Senate.

The process of compromise leading to changes in the bill began even before it reached the Senate floor. This bothered some members of the original drafting committee "who felt that the bill was being hopelessly emasculated" (Bailey, 1950:59). The most investment oriented of the Keynesians among the advisers to Gross felt that everything but the authorized spending was mainly window dressing. Senator Murray and Gross, on the other hand, agreed to the changes in order to gain the moderate support they knew would be necessary if any measure calling for economic planning and forecasting by the government was even to get out of committee when it arrived at a House dominated by the conservative coalition. Whatever the merits of the two sides in this argument over compromises, the important point in terms of the so-called privileged position of business is that some members of the state had put forth a way to begin to neutralize that privileged position.

The bill that passed the Senate by a vote of 71 to 10 on September 28, 1945, was a very satisfactory one from the view of the sponsors despite all the compromises that had to be made. Although there was no obligation to government spending, the possibility of it was retained in the following successful amendment:

> (4) to the extent that continuing full employment cannot otherwise be attained, [the Federal Government shall] consistent with the needs and obligations of the Federal Government and other essential considerations of national policy, provide such volume of Federal investment and expenditures as may be needed, in addition to the investment and expenditure by private enterprises, consumers and State and local governments, to achieve the objective of continuing full employment (Bailey, 1950:122).

It was in the House that the NAM, local and state Chambers of Commerce, and the American Farm Bureau Federation aided the conservative coalition in stopping the bill cold. It was in this context that corporate moderates came into the picture in a big way. In what I would call the classic fashion on such issues, the sophisticated conservatives broke ranks with the practical conservatives and agreed to a small economic forecasting capability within the state. Working through a moderate conservative from Mississippi, Representative Will Whittington, the moderates were able to fashion an acceptable compromise that created a Council of Economic Advisers (CEA), an annual economic report issued by the President, and a joint committee of Congress to receive and analyze the report. Schriftgiesser (1960) presents an early account of the important role played by corporate moderates in both the Senate and House, and the details on how the last stages of this process operated have been provided by Robert Collins (1981:Chapter 4). Collins's account includes the surprising fact that experts from the Chamber of Commerce of the United States, normally a very conservative organization, joined with business leaders in the CED in providing critical support in the final negotiations.

The sophisticated conservatives' support for a modified version of the Employment Act must be understood at least in part in relation to their internationalist postwar planning. In terms of the assurances that American postwar planners in the Council on Foreign Relations and CED had to give to Great Britain and other allies to convince them to open up their economies, the Employment Act can be seen as a down payment on the promise to insure that the new international economic order would not be pulled into a worldwide depression by a decline in the American economy. Put another way, the Employment Act was not the creation of the Council on Foreign Relations and CED, but as finally formulated it was completely compatible with the new world economy they wanted to build. Contrary to the sanguine liberal views of the Keynesian economist John K. Galbraith, who says that the Keynesian ascendancy was a "revolution without organization" (1971:54), Alvin Hansen and the other Keynesians did not simply have a better idea that won the day in an open discussion (cf. Jones, 1972). They had an idea that supported the goals of the internationalist segment of the capitalist class, whose organizations tried to make sure that the ideas were implemented in the limited fashion in which they were useful to this segment.

Still, the liberals in the government were able to influence the final shape of the sophisticated conservatives' bill when it arrived in the conference committee appointed to iron out differences between the Senate and House versions. In particular, they insisted that the CEA be a part of the president's office, as called for in the House bill, rather than an independent commission (Bailey, 1950:226–27). More generally, they insured that the bill made the presidency responsible in principle for the overall functioning of the economy even though later events showed that his reports are not always reacted to by Congress (Gross, 1953:178–79).

The final bill also has implications about the nature of the American state itself, and about its alleged autonomy. As I first argued in a more detailed account of this policy conflict in *The Powers That Be* (Domhoff, 1979), the compromise supported by the sophisticated conservatives had the effect of formally linking policy-planning groups to the state apparatus. This was due to the inclusion of a specific mandate for the CEA and the Joint Committee on the Economic Report to utilize the work of "private research agencies" (Bailey, 1950:231–32). Thus, the Brookings Institution, the National Bureau of Economic Research, and similar private organizations assumed a more formal standing. The act helped to insure that much of what little planning there was to be in postwar America would take place outside the state in organizations closely related to the corporate community in terms of their financing and top-level governance.

The close relationship the Employment Act created between private policy groups and the state is demonstrated very dramatically in a study I did of the 41 people appointed to the CEA between 1945 and 1983 (Domhoff, 1987b). In all, 11 of the 13 CEA chairs during that time span had worked for a policy-discussion group or think tank. Six had been advisers to the CED, 6 had an affiliation with the National Bureau of Economic Research, 4 were associated with the Brookings Institution, and 3 had an affiliation with the American Enterprise Institute. There were very few career differences between the 7 Republican and 6 Democratic appointees, although the 2 men not from the policy network, Leon Keyserling of Wagner Act fame and Arthur Okun, were appointed by the Democrats.

Half of the regular (nonchair) members of the CEA were affiliated with the policy-planning network, half were not. Among the 14 regular members not from the policy network, 6 came from a primarily academic background, 7 from a mixture of academic and governmental positions, and 1 from a government career. Four had experience in the corporate community. As with the chairs, there were few career differences between Republican and Democratic appointees.

The findings on regular members suggest that other networks as well as the policy-planning one are operative in these appointments. My belief is that the chairs are tapping into their academic and governmental connections to find members to serve with them. There is some basis, then, for Skocpol's view that some governmental experts come merely from the "general stock of higher-educated specialists," but they are being appointed by people who are part of the corporate network (Skocpol and Ikenberry, 1982:31).

The post-CEA affiliations of both CEA chairs and regular members demonstrate the integration of corporate and governmental institutions. Previous members of the policy network often left the CEA to go on to even more important positions within policy groups than they had held previously, and three of the fourteen not previously in the policy network became prominent figures in it after they left government. The aforementioned Arthur Okun, a Yale professor and CEA staff member before his appointment, became a fellow of the Brookings Institution and a member of the CED's Research Advisory Board. Ezra Solomon, a Stanford professor before his appointment as a member under Nixon in 1971, joined the Research Advisory Board of the CED after he left government. The post-CEA careers of eight former chairs and members also included appointments to boards of directors of large corporations. Five of these people had been in the policy network previous to their CEA appointment, three had not. Six were Republican appointees, two were appointed by Democrats.

In short, agencies such as the CEA become part of a general circuit that includes corporations, policy groups, and government. Thus, the CEA is not only a recipient of appointees from the policy network, but an entry point into the policy network and the corporate community for some of those who previously moved only in academic or government circles.

The integration of corporate networks with the government can be seen most directly in the overall relationship between the CED and the CEA. In all, 20 of the 41 people in this study were advisers to the CED either before or after their CEA appointments. If we were to count the three people who wrote reports for the CED-sponsored Commission on Money and Credit that had a strong influence on governmental thinking in the 1960s, then the number would rise to 24 for that one policy group alone (Schriftgiesser, 1974:164–65).

The similarity of the CEA's advice under both Republican and Democratic presidents also suggests the importance of its linkage to the policy-planning groups and think tanks. The CED played a central role in helping to create a consensus around the "business Keynesianism" that was acceptable to both parties (Collins, 1981). The story is told best by Herbert Stein, the chief econo-mist for the CED for many years and then CEA chair under Nixon, in his *The Fiscal Revolution in America* (1969). In particular, he describes well "the devel-opment of consensus, 1945 to 1949" (1969:Chapter 9). This consensus also reveals itself very nicely in a book of interviews with former CEA chairs, especially those with Stein and Charles Schultze, the chair during the Carter administration (Hargrove and Morley, 1984:363ff., 484–99).

The meager planning capability within the American state contrasts sharply with the situation in many Western European countries. I believe this reflects both the greater strength of the organized working class and the statist traditions in those countries with planning agencies. However, in the state with the most fabled planning agency, France, something more may be going on, namely, support from the American power elite. In his account of this agency, Stephen Cohen (1977:101–2) says that he believes but cannot prove that it was money from the Marshall Plan that gave this agency its postwar power. However, he does not draw any theoretical implications from his comment.

If Cohen is right, he has shot a big hole into theorizing about the French state. He also has demonstrated the pragmatism of the internationalist segment of the American power elite as well, for everyone agrees that CED trustees ran the Marshall Plan. Thus, the same CED capitalists who wanted limited planning within the U.S. government were willing to back state planning in France in the face of a militant, Communist-led union movement, a history of statism, and the socialization of corporations owned by pro-Nazi sympathizers. Moreover, as if to emphasize the importance of American money, Cohen (1977:273–79) reports in a postscript to the paperback edition of his book that the power of the French planning agency has faded in recent years. A lengthy interview I conducted in Paris in spring 1979 with an economist for the French counterpart to the CED (l'Institut de Entreprise) led me to the same conclusion (Domhoff, 1981).

## Conclusion

This account of the Employment Act has several implications for theories of state autonomy. First, it shows that it is fully possible to conceive of plans that challenge the alleged privileged position of business. The Employment Act as originally designed could have started a transition to a very different relation between business and the state. If the state could create demand and make investments, it would be very hard for capitalists to withhold investments; they would be forced by the expand-or-die logic of capitalism to compete for the potential profits being dangled before them. Thus, business leaders concerned about their power and privilege are unlikely to believe they are so privileged that they do not have to worry about dominating the state through all possible avenues.

Second, this little tale shows that even some people inside the "state apparatus" are sometimes willing to challenge that privileged position. Electoral victories by liberals can provide critics of big business with a base inside the state. The "independent state managers" are not of a piece in terms of their values and ideology. In short, politics does matter, which is why I always have put so much emphasis on the importance of corporate "fat cats" within the electoral process (Domhoff, 1967:Chapter 4; 1972; and Chapter 9 of this book).

Third, this story shows that capitalists have to remain vigilant in order to insure that challengers inside the state do not succeed. They have to be certain that they have representatives who can fight such initiatives as the Employment Act from inside the state, and they have to be organized to exert pressure from outside.

Fourth, we encounter again the role of experts within the legislative and policy processes. Contrary to Block, Skocpol, and Plotke, we see that we can distinguish between the independent liberal and radical experts who formulated the original Full Employment Act and the business Keynesians with network connections to the CED and the think tanks who predominate as chairs of the CEA. We can see the role that the policy-planning network plays in creating, selecting, and elevating those experts who make the most sense to the business leaders. Block, Skocpol, and Plotke have created a straw man in saying that I treat all experts the same, and they have failed to understand the role of the policy-planning network in bringing the right experts to the fore for governmental positions.

Finally, the outcome of this act shows that it is very difficult to tell where the supposedly autonomous state begins and ends in the United States. The private policy-planning and research groups are so intertwined with government in terms of personnel and policy inputs that the line is a hazy one. The policy groups and think tanks are strictly private in terms of citizen access, but they are part of government in terms of some of their financing and to the degree that state agencies must rely on them for information and expert personnel. In other words, the battle over the Employment Act has led to a policy-planning network that is both inside and outside the state, formally speaking, and that has no mandate to authorize spending to deal with a downturn in private investment. In that sense, the corporate community was very successful in defending its privileged position, but the important point is that it did have to defend that position. The final result was a strengthening of its position in terms of keeping a close eye on government.

Even when it comes to the idea of the "privileged position of business," considered one of the great insights of the 1970s, we must face the fact that the potentially autonomous state in the United States is dominated from the inside and outside by a power elite rooted in the upper class, the corporate community, and their associated policy-planning network of foundations, think tanks, institutes, and policy-discussion groups. We have to understand that the "privileged position" has to be defended when the state system is "permeable," to use the euphemism adopted by Skocpol (Skocpol and Ikenberry, 1982:31).

Thus, it is necessary to move away from Prewitt and Stone, Block, and Lindblom, and get back to C. Wright Mills and power structure research if there is to be any chance of understanding the complex phenomenon of power in corporate America.

# 8

# CLASS SEGMENTS AND TRADE POLICY, 1917–1962:
# A Challenge to Pluralists and Structural Marxists

Few studies have tried to document the case for pluralism at the national level in a systematic way. Most of the books or articles cited in support of a pluralist view, if any evidence beyond ordinary common sense is thought necessary, are textbooks or quick little studies of legislative issues that are not deeply connected to larger theoretical issues. There is no equivalent at the national level of Dahl's study of New Haven that everybody can point to as definitive proof. One of the few attempts, by Arnold Rose (1967), was an easy target (Domhoff, 1970c: Chapter 9).

But there is one study that is very often cited by those who wish to deny that there is a power elite or ruling class. It is a detailed account of public opinion, business lobbies, and Congressional decision-making in relation to foreign trade policy between 1953 and 1962 by Raymond Bauer, Ithiel Pool, and Lewis Dexter (1963). Although the book was primarily concerned with communication processes, not power structures, it was nonetheless seized upon by pluralists as evidence for the dispersion of power in the United States. After all, the authors do say it is their "suspicion" that the relative power of big business has declined in the last fifty years. Not only that, but what power big business has left is wielded in a more responsible fashion (1963:488). Moreover, the book provides the most detailed case yet for the independence of Congress from pressure groups and lobbyists, making it a favorite for some types of state autonomy theorists as well.

Because the book was so popular among pluralists, I provided a brief critique of it in my chapter in *The Higher Circles* on how foreign policy is made, stating what I thought to be serious weaknesses in conception and empirical fact. The book made no attempt to explain the change from protectionism to freer trade within the business community between the 1930s and postwar years. The individuals and ad hoc pressure groups mentioned in the chronology were not embedded within a larger organizational or class context. Most importantly, there

205

was no understanding that the battle was between what I then called the internationalist and isolationist wings of the corporate community (Domhoff, 1970c: 143–45).

The critique didn't make the slightest dent in the credibility of the book, of
course, and it didn't even get a rise out of anybody until the structural Marxist
Alan Stone (1984) saw it as an opportunity to criticize my views as well as those
of Bauer–Pool–Dexter. According to Stone, there are fewing saving graces to
my analysis aside from its greater emphasis on the executive branch in understanding the Trade Expansion Act of 1962. He even says that I mischaracterize
the Bauer–Pool–Dexter study by allegedly calling it "pluralist" when its authors
are merely out to show that Congress passed trade legislation independent of
pressure groups. He thereby forgets that pluralism is a word for a family of
theories that say power is dispersed; there are variants of pluralism that are not
pressure-group theories. What they all share in common is an emphasis on
elected officials who are at least the compromisers among the many conflicting
interests. Moreover, I did not say the book was an example of pluralism. I said
the book was often cited as evidence for pluralism against views such as mine
(Domhoff, 1970c:144). There is a difference.

More importantly, Stone also falsely claims that I see the power elite acting
from personal motives that are independent of the social system. He thinks my
analysis provided no basis for understanding why this or any other public policy
might be "of concern to the power elite" (1984:302). He wants to be shown that
it matters whether or not members of the power elite are involved in a decision:
there is a need to explore "whether the decision needed the involvement of a
power elite to lead to the same substantive result" (1984:302). These are the
usual laments of the structural Marxists who want every page to start with a little
reminder on the nature of capitalism and the power of the state. To say that the
power elite is the leadership arm of an upper class rooted in capitalism is not
direct and redblooded enough for a sophisticated Marxist.

In this chapter then, I will take on pluralists and a structural Marxist with the
same analysis. I will show that the situational level of the pluralists and the
systemic level of the structural Marxist both miss the very real battle between
class segments that went on over trade policy between 1917 and 1962, a battle
that came to be personified by a few organizations and individuals at the time the
Trade Expansion Act passed in 1962. I will show that it is absurd to imply that I
do not imbed organizations and classes within the context of political economy,
but that it is equally absurd to make the economy an all-powerful system of
objective structures and constraints. Before plunging into the case study, I will
present a brief overview of the general viewpoints espoused by Bauer–Pool–
Dexter and Stone.

## The Pluralists

As a study of communication processes as they relate to Congress, the analysis
by Bauer–Pool–Dexter casts a very wide net. Conceptually speaking, it starts

with a national survey of public opinion on tariffs, turns to interview studies in communities that might be affected by tariff legislation, and then focuses on interviews with several hundred business leaders chosen through sampling procedures. Only then does the study look at how business, Congress, and the White House interacted on trade and tariff policies between 1953 and 1962.

The survey of public opinion revealed that most people did not know or care much about the trade issue. Workers were sometimes enlisted on one side or another by their companies, but there was little or no class conflict on the issue. The pluralism was almost exclusively within the business community and government. Similarly, there was a lack of interest in the issue within the communities that were studied, except for a few people. This suggests that leading protectionists in Congress could pretty much say what they wanted to as far as any possibility of public backlash at the polling booths.

The interviews with business leaders showed that they were not much more informed or concerned than the general public, although the strong majority had abandoned protectionism as a principle since the early 1930s. Taxes, wages, and unions were of far greater concern to them (Bauer et al., 1963:125). As for the business lobbies, they were found to be often underfinanced, understaffed, or even "woefully ignorant" (1963:484). They only talked to the converted, avoided opponents, and were usually ineffective.

In this kind of mess it is small wonder that Congress reigns supreme. Bauer–Pool–Dexter argue that members of Congress can choose the issues they will respond to. Members can project an image that invites "pressure" from some lobbies and keeps others from even bothering to contact them (1963:415–21). Because there are so many groups demanding different things, members are in effect free to choose among the groups they will support. Further, they know that much of their mail is stimulated by pressure groups and they often ignore it while pretending otherwise. The biggest pressures are actually from inside the Congress as a social and communication system, but the leadership will allow members to make symbolic negative votes as long as it knows it has enough votes to win anyhow. More generally, a member of Congress has independence because "Congress is so complex that it is easy for him to hide where he stands on any issue and what he has done about it" (1963:424).

Bauer–Pool–Dexter (1963:39) make clear that trade issues between 1953 and 1962 were not a life and death struggle as far as members of Congress were concerned. While members disagreed on tariff levels and import quotas, they all accepted the present system of decision-making on tariffs, which involves deliberations and negotiations on specific items by the executive branch. This system took direct pressure off members of Congress, but gave them the opportunity to fight for changes for specific industries by hectoring the executive branch.

When it is recalled that Bauer–Pool–Dexter believe that the relative power of big business has declined and become more responsible since the bad old days, it is easy to see why pluralists love this book. It demonstrates that the business community is divided, that big-business groups are often inept or unconcerned, and that elected officials are independent decision-makers. It may not be a pluralist book by Stone's standards, but it certainly makes the idea of a power structure or a power elite seem highly unlikely.

## The Structural Marxist

The contrast between the tale told by the pluralists and the structural Marxist could not be more complete. Where the pluralists see only individuals, specific industries, trade associations, and ad hoc publicity committees, the structural Marxist sees only constraints set by the logic of the system. He proudly states that "my intention very simply is to avoid the 'constant diversion from the objective structures and laws of the system to the personal motivations of their agents,' " with the internal quotation coming from yet another structural Marxist, Ernesto Laclau. Stone asserts confidently that there are "implications" that follow from the "stage of capitalism in which a particular society is located;" there are even "functional requisites." Once this is understood, there is no need to study people or their social background because of "the constraints and demands imposed on policy makers by virtue of their roles as caretakers of the nation's economic system" (1984:310).

Due to these constraints, it is neither here nor there whether businesspeople are involved in decisions. Just about anybody will do as long as they are rational, as in the following:

> The range of choice exercised over such "important" decisions, whether through elite choice, interest-group activity, or public opinion, is thus dependent upon the constraints imposed by the socioeconomic system. The latter is the critical consideration, and, depending upon its intrinsic needs, policy options are wider or narrower. Thus, with respect to the core of a policy, there is no particular need for business groups to exert pressure on political decision makers. The latter—assuming that they are rational—know full well what the problems are, and share with outside interests a common framework within which to solve them (1984:305).

It is far more important, then, to determine the needs of the system, which Stone does by taking seriously the reports and speeches of those involved in the decision. In the case of the Trade Expansion Act of 1962, it was dictated by the fact that the United States was having a balance of payments problem and faced possible exclusion from the newly forming European Common Market. The need was to expand domestic production and increase exports. These systematic imperatives lead to common assumptions among those who are the "caretakers" of the economy:

> Given the widely shared ends of U.S. economic policy, the basic policy embodied in the Trade Expansion Act was a logical proposal, irrespective of the social background, career patterns, or interlocking associations of the policy makers. No evidence exists to show that

these background factors had any direct input into the policy decision. Far more persuasive is the logic embodied in the policy, which motivated the responsible policy makers (1984:309).

In going on and on about social backgrounds, Stone joins the long list of structural Marxists who cannot understand the use of social background as a power indicator in some studies and as an indicator of class segments in other studies. Rather than try to explain this in the abstract once again, I will demonstrate it by looking at how the battle over trade policy unfolded between 1917 and 1962. The greatest emphasis will be on the final nine years of that time span, leading to the Trade Expansion Act of 1962.

## Trade Policy in the Interwar Years

As Jeff Frieden (1988) forcefully demonstrates, the years between 1917 and 1930 present a major problem for those who think of "the economy" or "the state" as the determinant of tariff and trade policies. Following World War I the United States by all measures was the leading economic, political, and military power in the world. It had supplied most of weapons for the allies. It was the leading financial leader in the world, and it had more direct foreign investments than any other country. It was the largest trading power in the world even though foreign trade was only a very small part of its huge economy (1988:59–61).

The logic of the situation seemed to dictate an increasing internationalization of the economy, and Europeans looked toward the United States for economic leadership, but the general trend during the 1920s was toward protectionism and isolationism. This protectionist tendency reached its climax in the early stages of the depression with the infamous Smoot-Hawley Tariff Act of 1930, which raised tariffs to all-time highs in an orgy of logrolling that had industry representatives writing their own tickets in the halls of Congress.

Bauer–Pool–Dexter dismiss the Smoot-Hawley legislation as a kind of bizarre exception, "an episode in the legislative drama during which selfish interests treated the halls of Congress as their own" (1963:25). Nor does Stone make any effort to explain why high tariffs were logical in the 1920s but not in the 1960s. This silence is in fact a major problem in Stone's theoretical framework, for the economic tendencies of that particular stage of American capitalism clearly called for internationalization. As Frieden argues:

For those who look at economic affairs first and foremost, America's unchallenged position as the world's leading capital exporter should have accelerated the trend towards trade liberalization and international monetary leadership begun before World War I; instead, the pendulum swung back towards protectionism and little public U.S. government involvement in international monetary issues (1988:61).

I agree with Frieden when he explains this seeming anomaly in terms of the greater political strength of the nationalist segment of the capitalist class. This segment was far stronger then the internationalist segment because only a small part of American industry and finance was involved in the international economy. The internationalist firms were very large and expanding rapidly, and they had access to the White House, but they failed again and again in the interwar years in their attempts to influence Congress, or even Republican presidents, when nationalist manufacturers and agricultural interests opposed them. On foreign policy issues, they found their few friends among southern Democrats, long-standing opponents of high tariffs.

According to Frieden (1988:83), the Great Depression began the reversal of the protectionist tendency by undermining the economic, political, and ideological strengths of the nationalist segment. With their industries in shambles, low-tariff Democrats in charge of Congress, and doubt cast on the efficacy of their high-tariff claims by the collapse in world trade after the passage of Smooth-Hawley, the nationalist segment was unable to oppose what Frieden calls a gradual and halting move toward economic internationalism between 1932 and 1940 (1988:83).

One of these halting steps was the passage of the Reciprocal Trade Act of 1934, granting the president the right to negotiate mutual tariff reductions on specific items. Although the Act had very little impact in terms of dollars and cents, it did institutionalize a new executive-based system for determining tariffs (Haggard, 1988). Characteristically, Bauer–Pool–Dexter manage to reduce the Act to the level of personalities, arguing that the Act "owes more to the accident that a gentleman of traditional Southern views was secretary of state than it does to the economic policies of reformers" (1963:26, note 4). Although there is no detailed study of the involvement of private groups in the creation of the Reciprocal Trade Act, there is evidence that internationalist business leaders enthusiastically supported the Act (Haggard, 1988:98) and also worked to increase trade through the creation of the Export-Import Bank in the same year the Act was passed (Adams, 1976). Then, too, the information I presented in Chapter 5 on the close relationship between Secretary of State Cordell Hull and bankers such as Norman Davis in the Council on Foreign Relations suggests to me that Bauer–Pool–Dexter are very wrong in their glib analysis of the act.

## Postwar Trade Policies

If the Great Depression started the move toward freer trade, it was the outcome of World War II that made free trade the principle and protectionism the exception. After this war it was even more obvious than in 1917 that the United States dominated the world. Moreover, the failure of the New Deal to rebuild the economy despite what then seemed like massive expenditures made it clear to most people that there had to be serious changes in the economy to maintain the wartime prosperity. It is in this context, of course, that the efforts of the Council on Foreign Relations and related organizations described in Chapters 5 and 6 take on their full significance. It was these efforts both inside and outside the government that made it seem "natural" to think in terms of freer trade and greater international political involvement. What seems to Stone to be an inevitable logical consequence of the functional requisites of capitalism is in fact the result of the internationalist segment's successful effort to convince people of the believability of their argument for how the economic system should function. Backed by the economic muscle that war spending built into big corporations, they had been able to create a new "conventional wisdom," or what Marxists call "ideological hegemony."

Although there is in many ways a seamless web that runs through the trend toward freer trade in the postwar years, the year 1953 does provide a somewhat unique juncture because it was the first time since the Smoot-Hawley Tariff Act was passed that the Republicans controlled the presidency and both houses of Congress. This was of significance because there were still many protectionist Republicans in powerful positions in Congress. The question was whether the Republicans would move in a free-trade direction or revert to protectionism, and it is here that Bauer–Pool–Dexter pick up the story in detail.

At this point, as a counterpoint to both the pluralists and Stone, I want to focus on the role of the CED as the "personification" of the internationalist segment in the postwar years and as the key factor in bringing about the Trade Expansion Act. This does not mean that the Council on Foreign Relations suddenly dropped out of sight or that other organizations were uninvolved. It only means that the CED provides the most continuous and visible window into trade conflicts between 1953 and 1962. It allows me to show that the businesspeople involved in the issue were not as disconnected and inept as Bauer–Pool–Dexter imply and at the same time to demonstrate to structural Marxists like Stone how a handful of central "personalities" can come to stand for class segments. It also gives me a chance to show how Stone distorted my argument and to explain once again how power structure research can use its empirical focus on individuals and organizations to talk in sophisticated terms about class segments and their policy preferences.

The CED, as I noted in Chapter 5, had its origins during World War II and, as shown in Chapters 6 and 7, had a part in the decisions leading to the IMF and Employment Act. Its members had even bigger roles in the Marshall Plan and other events of the postwar era, but the important point for this narrative is that many of its members were among the early backers of Dwight D. Eisenhower for president. Indeed, they had convinced Eisenhower to become a trustee of their organization while he was president of Columbia University, and they helped him to found a more general discussion group called the American Assembly (Eakins, 1966:463–65).

Members of the CED were anathema to ultraconservative Republicans as "eastern internationalists," which was their term for the internationalist segment of the capitalist class. While many CED trustees were easterners, it was more accurate to say that they were internationalists from all over the country. They included among their trustees James Zellerbach, president of Crown Zellerbach in San Francisco; John Bullis, chairman of General Mills in Minneapolis; John Coleman, chairman of Burroughs in Detroit; Reuben Robertson, chairman of Champion Paper in Canton, North Carolina; and Stanley Allyn, president of National Cash Register in Dayton.

The CED trustees were not merely supporters of Eisenhower, they were determined to have an influence on his policies as well. To steal a march on their opponents, eight of them met with Eisenhower in New York six days before he was to leave for the White House. They urged the general CED program on him, including a liberalization of such aspects of trade policy as tariffs, shipping restrictions, and "Buy American" legislation (Schriftgiesser, 1960:162–64).

Shortly thereafter, CED came out with a policy statement on foreign economic policy entitled *Britain's Economic Problem and Its Meaning for America* (1953). As the title implies, the report focused on the need to strengthen the British economy by making it possible for the British to sell more products in the United States. A strong British Empire was seen, just as it had been in the 1940s by Council on Foreign Relations planners, as important to the United States for both economic and geopolitical reasons. That is, a strong British economy would make it possible for more American exports to go into the British empire, but it also would insure that Britain would remain a strong political ally. However, the report is of more general significance here because it called for lower tariffs and the removal of other trade restrictions for all American allies, not just Great Britain.

But it turned out that legislation for freer trade was going nowhere in a Congress controlled by old-guard Republicans, most of whom were protectionists. The Eisenhower administration, to the dismay of the internationalists, had to settle for a one-year extension of the Reciprocal Trade Act and a special investigatory commission, the Commission on Foreign Economic Policy, which was supposed to come up with trade recommendations for the next legislative session.

The Commission on Foreign Economic Policy included ten Congressional members and seven private citizens. There were three Republicans and two Democrats from each house, five businessmen, one economist, and one labor leader. Several of the Republicans were archprotectionists. All four Democrats were low-tariff but otherwise conservative southern Democrats. The chair, Clarence Randall, was the former head of Inland Steel and a strong advocate of freer trade. One of the other businessmen, Cola Parker, a leader in the NAM, was staunchly protectionist. The remaining businessmen—Lamar Fleming of Anderson, Clayton; Jesse Tapp of the Bank of America, multimillionaire investor John

Hay Whitney—were for lower tariffs. Harvard economist John H. Williams, who figured in the story of the IMF and became a regular adviser to the CED, also favored lower tariffs, as did labor leader David McDonald, president of the United Steel Workers. Fleming, Whitney, and Williams were members of the Council on Foreign Relations, and the immediate superiors of both Fleming and Tapp were trustees of the CED. Rather clearly, the idea was to lock the warring parties into a room and let them fight it out.

Bauer–Pool–Dexter (1963:40–50) tell of the all-too-human grousing and maneuvering that went on within what came to be known as the Randall Commission, named after its imperious chair, the aforementioned Clarence Randall. However, I dare not repeat such gossip here lest the structural Marxists use my expansiveness as ammunition against me. The only important point is the outcome, a report that further legitimated the freer-trade forces but made numerous concessions to the protectionists. Still, it must be said that Bauer–Pool–Dexter delight in telling how the wily old Republican politicians allegedly ran circles around the inept business leaders.

Paralleling the Randall Commission, the CED formed its own study group on the issue at the same time as the commission was appointed. It included top officers from General Electric, Standard Oil of New Jersey, Bankers Trust, and H. J. Heinz Company, among many major companies. One of its three technical advisers was Jacob Viner, by now a professor at Princeton. Most interesting of all as far as later events in this story, the committee was chaired by Howard C. Petersen, the chairman of Fidelity Philadelphia Trust Bank. Petersen's first job was as a lawyer with Cravath, Swaine, and Moore in New York in the 1930s. During the war he served as an assistant to the undersecretary of war and then the secretary of war. From 1945 to 1947 he was assistant secretary of the army, where he had a role in helping to revive the German economy. It was after the war that he joined Fidelity Bank and became active in the CED.

As head of the subcommittee, Petersen spent a considerable amount of time talking with leading spokespersons for protectionists industries (Schriftgiesser, 1960:182). One of them, William C. Foster, president of the Manufacturing Chemists Association, was on the subcommittee. In other words, Petersen was becoming a generalist on trade policies who shared the views of other internationalists and understood the concerns of the protectionists in the business world.

The report by Petersen's subcommittee, called *United States Tariff Policy* (CED, 1954), made the case for expanding both imports and exports in a familiar fashion. It claimed that economic specialization by countries tends to raise the standard of living in all countries through more efficient use of resources. It argued that the United States needs to encourage more imports if other countries are to have the money to buy American exports. Finally, in a noneconomic argument, it insisted that low tariffs are necessary to help our allies, and especially Great Britain, which relies far more on trade than the United States. That is, geopolitical concerns entered into the argument once again.

   Still another business committee appeared about the same time as the Randall
Commission and the CED subcommittee were formed. This one was an advocacy committee to urge freer trade through publicity and lobbying. Called the
Committee for a National Trade Policy, it is one of the groups seen as rather
bumbling and ineffective for the most part by Bauer–Pool–Dexter (1963:380–
87). Although they identify some of the members by profession or corporate
affiliation, they give no indication that these people were part of larger organizations that had an ongoing role in disseminating the internationalist position. In
fact, all six officers and directors were members of either the CED or the Council
on Foreign Relations. The executive director to the committee, lawyer Charles
Taft of Cincinnati, was selected because he was the obvious checkmate to his
protectionist brother, Senator Robert Taft. He also had worked closely in a battle
against oil import quotas in 1951 with another lawyer, George W. Ball, who
helped found the new committee (1963:380). Ball, whose credentials as an
internationalist went back to government service in the war years on foreign
economic policies, is another person who will figure prominently later in this
story.
   When these three committees are looked at as part of a larger picture, the
efforts of the internationalists are not quite as disorganized as Bauer–Pool–
Dexter imply. But even with the Randall and Petersen reports, and the publicity
work by the Committee for a National Trade Policy, the Eisenhower administration probably lost ground in the 1955 legislative session. It received permission
to lower tariffs by only 15 percent over the next three years, and it had its hands
tied slightly by a number of protectionist amendments that there is no need to
outline here (Pastor, 1980:103).
   These setbacks were somewhat unexpected in that free-trade Democrats had
taken control of both the House and Senate after the 1954 elections. The key
committees were headed by low-tariff southerners, not Republican protectionists,
and their strong efforts had been essential in holding the losses to the protectionists to a minimum. But something else had changed between 1953 and 1955.
The textile industry, now largely located in the South, began to clamor for
protection for the first time. After dominating the American market in the years
when American allies were still rebuilding from the war, the textile manufacturers were now feeling a slight pinch from foreign imports. Less than 10 percent of
the market had been captured by lower-cost imports, but the trend was such as to
make the southern textile owners fearful for the future.
   Working through their longstanding trade association, the American Textile
Manufacturers Institute, industry leaders put on a vigorous campaign throughout
the South. They held scores of meetings with other businessmen, encouraging
them to contact their Congressional representatives. They enlisted the support of
textile workers. They sponsored letter-writing campaigns. They ran ads. And
they lobbied everywhere in Washington. As Bauer–Pool–Dexter (1963:359)
readily admit, here was one business group that was very effective.
   But Bauer–Pool–Dexter did not realize just how effective the textile owners

were because they did not know that a very detailed study of how the power structure operated on the textile issue already had been published by Floyd Hunter (1959:Chapter 10). It was one part of a larger study of the national power structure that identified several hundred "top leaders" for the 1950s. Whereas Bauer–Pool–Dexter had large-scale surveys, research grants, and research assistants at their disposal, Hunter did his study by himself, using spare time and pieces of small grants that were awarded for applied studies. Although an excellent book, it was buried by the political science establishment the minute it appeared because the earlier attack on *Community Power Structure* (1953) had discredited his research method.

Perhaps the most damaging statement on the new book was a disgraceful review by Robert A. Dahl, which claimed that the book was a "grab-bag of names and organizations" and a "morass of ambiguities and unexamined contradictions" (1960:148–49). Dahl made sport of the fact that Hunter's method had lead him to believe that Senator Ralph Flanders of Vermont was a top leader when everyone at the time knew that he was a minor Senator from a minor state. However, what everyone didn't know except Hunter was that Flanders was a major figure in the business community thanks to his deep involvement in the CED and his quiet role in facing down Senator Joe McCarthy (Schriftgiesser, 1960, 1967). Even worse, Dahl's snide comments about a "dubious" methodology include no hint that Hunter had in fact made a very detailed case study of the textile issue, interviewing textile leaders in North and South Carolina, sending a questionnaire on the subject to 33 top national leaders, and even traveling to Tokyo in 1957 to interview Japanese textile and government leaders. The result is a far better, and far more focused, explanation of the textile issue from a power perspective than can be found in Bauer–Pool–Dexter's highly acclaimed book.

For my purposes here, the most important point is that Hunter documents the constant communication between textile officials and other top leaders in the business community. Contrary to the Bauer–Pool–Dexter finding that the lobbyists only preach to the converted, Hunter shows that the textile representatives were in direct contact with top leaders who favored freer trade. Moreover, some of these top leaders reported that they had supported a recent compromise whereby Japan "voluntarily" limited its imports of textiles into the United States. This preserved the general policy stance of freer trade while at the same time responding to the textile industry:

> The non-textile men who had called upon the administration and Congress, particularly a number of national non-government leaders who were identified as communicators on the question, were satisfied with the compromise. They had spoken forthrightly in favor of keeping trade channels open, and had stressed the need to keep Japan in the Western allied policy orbit (Hunter, 1959:241).

Then, too, Hunter's study shows how the power structure can deal with an issue without most people or even average business leaders knowing or caring very much about it. He estimates, based on his interviews and questionnaire, that at most six or eight people from the textile industry did most of the work with government officials and other business leaders (1959:234), but concludes that the industry campaign was nonetheless thorough and successful. In other words, the general chaos and confusion portrayed by Bauer–Pool–Dexter are not a prima facie case for lack of business power. This is an age of specialization even within the power elite, with only a few hundred people specializing in general leadership (Moore, 1979; Higley and Moore, 1981; Useem, 1984, for excellent empirical evidence on this point).

Hunter's study of the textile issue also is of great relevance in this chapter because he comes to exactly the same conclusions on the independence of members of Congress from mere "pressure" that Bauer–Pool–Dexter arrive at with great fanfare 4 years later. Indeed, he says in one paragraph what it takes them several chapters to say:

> Policy makers are not as amenable to pressure as the average citizen is led to believe by press stories. Government officials accede to the pressure that fits their own frame of reference, be that frame of reference personal, professional, or commercial. Many legislators are not dependent for a living on political office, or they can straddle issues, or the people forget. At any event, they do not capitulate quickly to mere pressure (Hunter, 1959:239).

Parenthetically, it should be noted that Mills (1956:251–56) also anticipates that Bauer–Pool–Dexter analysis of Congress, but he too goes unmentioned by them. If there are social scientists who need to be disabused of certain illusions about the importance of "pressure-group" tactics, they are not the power structure researchers ignored by the mainstream social scientists who gain great reputations as scholars even though they do not study the extant literature on their topic.

Both Bauer–Pool–Dexter and Hunter report that the efforts of the textile owners apparently had an impact on southern Democrats. In no time at all, they changed from philosophic free traders to cautious protectionists. For all the talk about the independence of members of Congress, Bauer–Pool–Dexter do show that several southerners in the House, and particularly those from Georgia and Alabama, made rather rapid conversions in their tariff beliefs (1963:60, 359–60).

Put more generally, the conversion of the southerners to a protectionist stance on textiles meant that the three national-level class segments were now aligned on foreign trade in the same way they were on labor and social welfare issues. That is, the protectionist coalition was an instance of the more general conservative coalition, defined as a majority of southern Democrats and Republicans voting together on an issue (Shelley, 1983:20). Now the nationalist industrialists of the North and the southern segment were lined up against the internationalists on trade issues.

The power of the conservative coalition in Congress will be discussed fully in the next chapter. Suffice it to say here that it usually wins when it forms (Manley, 1973), and that it did not come to include foreign policy issues until the 1950s (Sinclair, 1982:85, 110). Given the power of this coalition, especially in the 1940s and 1950s, there was no contest when it decided to take on the internationalists. The internationalists had gained in strength since the interwar years discussed by Frieden (1988), but they were in trouble in Congress when they could not count on the southern Democrats.

Not surprisingly, then, the legislation for renewal of the Reciprocal Trade Act in 1958 was hardly a victory for the Eisenhower administration. While renewal was granted for four years, the protectionists hemmed the executive branch in a little further by granting Congress the right by a two-thirds concurrent vote to "force the President to implement a recommendation of the Tariff Commission" (Pastor, 1980:103). It also rewrote a national security escape clause "so that virtually any domestic industry could obtain protection from foreign competition if it were determined that such competition were weakening the internal economy and thereby impairing national security" (1980:103–4).

## The Trade Expansion Act

Despite this stalemate, the efforts of the CED and other internationalist organizations continued unabated during the late 1950s. The CED published several reports that continued to call for liberalized trade policies, chaired by leading corporate executives like Thomas Cabot of the Cabot Corporation in Boston and T. V. Houser of Sears, Roebuck. Cabot's 1959 report on the new European Common Market sounded warnings about possible U.S. exclusion from European markets that anticipated those that would be heard in the Kennedy campaign for the Trade Expansion Act (Schriftgiesser, 1967:123–24). The emerging balance of payments problem was the theme of *National Objectives and the Balance of Payments Problem* (CED, 1960), a report produced by a subcommittee chaired by Emilio Collado, treasure of Standard Oil of New Jersey (1960:125). Collado earlier had served on the staff of the Randall Commission. In 1960 the CED put together a new subcommittee to prepare *A New Trade Policy for the United States,* a document that appeared in 1962 while the legislative struggle over the Trade Expansion Act was in progress. The report recommended many of the provisions that were included in the Kennedy legislation.

In 1956 the Rockefeller Brothers Fund joined the battle with a series of panels whose reports recommended an expansion of American military and economic commitments abroad. In good part meant to legitimate Nelson Rockefeller as a presidential candidate, as well as to further the internationalist agenda, the reports were published as *Prospect for America* (Rockefeller Brothers Fund, 1959), and they received considerable attention in the New York and Washington press.

Three of the business leaders and two of the academic advisers on the panels also were involved with the three CED reports mentioned in the previous paragraph. Among the 83 people who took part in one or more of the panels, 26 became members of the Kennedy administration. Although most of them were consultants or advisers, the list also included the Secretary of State, Dean Rusk, who had been president of the Rockefeller Foundation, and 7 other state department appointees (Johnson, 1978).

However, the internationalist intentions of the Kennedy administration in the trade area were most clearly signaled by the appointment of George W. Ball to head a preinauguration task force to recommend new initiatives in foreign policy, and then to serve as the assistant secretary of state for economic affairs. Ball's appointments related to his political connections as well as his corporate ones, for he was an early and stronger supporter of fellow international lawyer Adlai Stevenson for the presidency in 1952. Whatever the reason for the appointments, they were obviously a good omen for the internationalists.

Kennedy then took another step that demonstrated his seriousness about liberalizing trade legislation. He appointed banker Petersen as his special trade adviser in the White House. Newspaper reports described Petersen as a Republican banker who had been a major fund-raiser for Eisenhower before his nomination in 1952. He was said to be in charge of drafting new legislation and to have a staff of 10 people he would be directing. Bauer–Pool–Dexter (1963:74) suggest that his proposed legislation was cautious, but Pastor (1980:106) concludes otherwise from later accounts (e.g., Preeg, 1970:44–45).

Bauer–Pool–Dexter barely mention Petersen. After talking about the importance of Ball, they merely say that "Howard Peterson was appointed presidential aide for the task" (1963:74). They provide no information on him, not even his occupation, and they spell his name incorrectly. They do not attempt to find out why he was appointed. Thus, he is just another individual, not a widely recognized and respected Republican banker with a considerable expertise on the issue at hand.

Nor was Petersen a mere drafter of legislation and organizer of staff. Just as he had done in his work with the CED, he was the leader of the negotiations between the Kennedy administration and the protectionist industries. As Bauer–Pool–Dexter report in their only other mention of him, this time spelling his name correctly, "The campaign by the administration on the chemical industry was carried as far as a private meeting between Howard C. Petersen, the President's special assistant on trade policy, and industry leaders in February at a session of the Manufacturing Chemists Association in New York" (1963:351). In the case of the even more crucial textile industry, the final negotiations apparently were carried out by another White House aide who worked with Petersen, lawyer Myer Feldman.

The negotiations with the textile industry are especially revealing in terms of what it took to gain the acquiescence of textile leaders in the new Trade Expansion Act. Among other things, the Kennedy administration had to impose import quotes for the industry and then sweeten the pot with an offer of an increased subsidy for cotton growers (Bauer et al., 1963:78, 362). Bauer–Pool–Dexter make much of the fact that neither the Kennedy administration nor the textile industry was effective through directly lobbying Congress. They conclude that the textile industry was successful because it convinced other southern elites to support its cause, and that the Kennedy administration was effective through cutting a deal with the textile people. While this claim may be of interest as a critique of a narrow pressure-group theory, it is not of great theoretical moment in terms of a class-based theory.

Still, Bauer–Pool–Dexter's conclusion concerning the negotiations with protectionist industries is somewhat startling: "It was the indirect effect of the administration's approach to and conversion of the textile lobby and to numerous other businessmen that indirectly affected Congress" (1963:422). This conclusion about the effects of specific deals on trade policy makes hash out of Bauer–Pool–Dexter's general claim about the independence of members of Congress. What they show in this case is that the avowed congressional protectionists simply folded up their tents once there was an agreement that satisfied aggrieved businesspeople. They might not have been pressured, but they stuck pretty close to business elites. Prudent politics, not pressure, no doubt.

Moreover, Bauer–Pool–Dexter's statement about the Kennedy administration entering into negotiations with protectionist industries is in some ways very misleading. The failure to identify Petersen in terms of his occupation, past history, and organizational connections makes it impossible to realize that the meetings he and his aides held with leaders of the protectionist industries were in fact between leaders of two major coalitions in the power elite: Petersen spoke for the internationalists, and the protectionists spoke for the southerners and the nationalist industrialists in the North. The great case study beloved by pluralists, with its endless discussions of the views of thousand of individuals and part-time lobbyists, boils down to a clash within the ruling class that is resolved when Congress rubber-stamps the agreement made between class segments.

But a conclusion that stresses only class segments is in one sense too strong. The bill as agreed to by the internationalists and the conservative coalition also included a provision for "adjustment assistance" that was not favored by either of them. The adjustment assistance amendment made it possible for the government to give compensation to those industries and workers that were directly harmed by import competition. This provision was first suggested by McDonald of the steelworkers union when he was on the Randall Commission. The idea had been rejected by the commission, but Senator John Kennedy and other Democrats picked it up as an amendment to the 1955 legislation. The idea also failed as an amendment, and it was explicitly rejected by the CED, but Kennedy and his aides insisted on it as part of the Trade Expansion Act. This is the element of pluralism in the legislation, for it is in part a concession to labor (Bauer et al., 1963:43–44).

Stone's analysis of the Trade Expansion Act, unlike that of Bauer–Pool–

Dexter, is not so much misleading as it is incomplete and inaccurate. He starts
with an emphasis on the serious implications of trade policy at that particular
juncture in the American capitalist system:

> Thus, in 1962 trade expansion was a policy area with implications too wide to be left in its
> important outlines to the bargaining and logrolling of Congress. It had to be developed by
> some central planning organization that could and would rise above the provincial interests,
> and a campaign had to be waged for it that would effectively tie Congress's hands and brand
> legislative opponents of the measure irresponsible, if not worse (1984:308).

From this vantage point Stone goes on to emphasize, contrary to Bauer–Pool–
Dexter, that the executive branch was the important actor on this policy, not
Congress. He says that "the genesis of the Trade Expansion Act can be traced to
a pre-inaugural task force under the leadership of George Ball (who was to
become Under-Secretary of State), which recommended a new trade program
keyed to the development of the Common market" (1984:308). He also mentions
Petersen at this point. However, no attempt is made to trace the "genesis"
beyond the task force and Petersen. This failure to link the authors of the act to
business organizations allows Stone to emphasize the role of the executive
branch as a "central planning organization" for capital, and to play down the
possibility that the people he names may embody the policy preferences of a
particular segment of the capitalist class.

Stone criticizes Bauer–Pool–Dexter for overemphasizing Congress, but his
criticism is misguided because it overlooks the fact that the textile industry, an
integral part of the southern segment of the ruling class, was able to extract far
more concessions through its influence in Congress than were warranted strictly
on the basis of the alleged imperatives of a capitalist system increasingly involved in foreign trade. Stone finesses the important point that Bauer–Pool–
Dexter make about the numerous concessions that the internationalists had to
give to protectionists in order to pass their legislation. He does so by dismissing
the industries that fought for protection as mere special interests, thereby privi-
leging the internationalists as representing the logic of the system. In effect, he
has been taken in by the internationalist arguments on the issue, seeing them in
hindsight as indicating the only logical direction for the economy to go.

But the protectionists were not swayed or cowed by this rhetoric, contrary to
Stone's implication that the White House won in part through a propaganda
campaign against Congress. They were swayed when they received the concessions they wanted through cold, hard bargaining. Like Bauer–Pool–Dexter, who
celebrate the brilliant and amazingly clever way that the Kennedy administration
supposedly "shredded" and "smashed" the protectionist coalition (1963:74, 77–
78, 321), Stone is writing from the point of view of the internationalists. Both the
pluralists and the structural Marxist end up as apologists for one side in an
intraclass conflict.

Stone emphasizes what he thinks are the main reasons why the Trade Expansion Act was so necessary in 1962: the decline in the balance of payments and a fear of being excluded from the Common Market. The underlying need was to expand domestic output (1984:309). Stone implies that these constraints can be deduced from the overall functioning of the economy, but in fact he infers them from statements by Kennedy and other government officials in relation to the legislation. He seems especially taken with statements by those he calls foreign trade and economic affairs "insiders," who are apparently the purest embodiment of what the system dictates (1984:303, 308).

Stone makes a great fuss over contrasting his emphasis on system constraints with the alleged search for "motives" in my work. He thus fails to realize that both the alleged system constraints and the alleged motives are the same thing in that they are inferred by all researchers from the same sources, that is, from the "output" from central organizations and key individuals within the power network. Everyone relies on the same reports, speeches, and documents, including the numbers, graphs, and trend projections that are generated by industries, government agencies, and economists. Stone doesn't know it, but he is doing "content analysis," one of the standard operations of any power study (Domhoff, 1978:Chapter 4).

But content analyses are by no means obvious and straightforward. By what criteria do we decide how important various arguments are? And whose numbers do we trust? Isn't there a book called *How to Lie with Statistics* (Huff, 1954)? Didn't Oskar Morgenstern write a detailed treatise on the inaccuracy of economic data in which he concluded that "decisions made in business and in public service are based on data that are known with much less certainty than generally assumed by the public or government" (1963:vii), and that foreign trade statistics are "arbitrary" and "accidental" (1963:137)? The solid facts offered up by Stone are at bottom mere weapons in a power struggle.

These points take on relevance for this case when it is recalled that the CED had been pushing for freer trade since at least 1953, before there was a balance of payments problem or fear of a Common Market. The possibility thus arises that these new arguments were emphasized because they were more likely to scare opponents and fencesitters, not because they were the real reason, as Bauer–Pool–Dexter (1963:78) rightly suggest. Indeed, contrary to Stone's certainty about economic imperatives, Ernest Preeg flatly states that most members of the administration understood that tariff reductions were unlikely to have any effect whatsoever on the balance of payments, "especially in view of its [the U.S.'s] consistently substantial trade surplus" (1970:50). Advisors cautioned Kennedy not to link the two issues, but he went on his merry way for his own reasons:

> When he was warned of the substantive and tactical reasons for avoiding a direct connection, he would answer, "Yes, I get it, I get it." But on the next occasion he was apt to bring up the subject again in much the same way (1970:51).

Stone's entire edifice of imperatives crumbles with Preeg's revelation that Stone was as fooled by Kennedy's rhetoric as the average Joe on the street, but he has the further problem that the CED statements I summarized earlier in the chapter express a concern for helping allies as well as with expanding American exports. Should we take these geopolitical claims seriously? A concern with geopolitical matters in relation to trade policies also was expressed to Hunter in his interviews with top leaders in 1957 and 1958 in relation to the textile industry and its conflict with Japan. The top leaders said that they had encouraged the Japanese to rebuild their textile industry after the war as one way to become self-supporting again, and they had encouraged Japanese exports to the United States, they claimed, to keep Japan as part of the international capitalist economy. They did not want Japan to have to orient itself toward China or the Soviet Union (Hunter, 1959:228).

However, Stone gives little weight to helping allies in explaining the Trade Expansion Act, mentioning only that one argument used against Congress had to do with national security and the dangers of communism (1984:309). Does he have a theory that tells him the national security concerns and the fears of losing allies to communism are mere rhetoric? You bet he does. The truth is that Stone's implicit economic biases have led him to ignore or play down any statements that don't fit his structural Marxian theory. He does not take seriously any fear of losing capitalist countries to the Communist Bloc. But since we already have seen this kind of concern expressed about Japan in the early 1940s by the postwar planners at the Council on Foreign Relations, perhaps I may be excused if I do not automatically assume that the reasons for the passage of the Trade Expansion Act are as economistic as Stone insists on the basis of alleged insights into "objective structures" and "socioeconomic constraints."

## Conclusion

I find myself in full agreement with Robert Heilbroner when he says that the constraints of the economy are "so wide as to be of little use for historical analysis" (1980:83). They allow a wide variety of outcomes that can be rationalized as sustaining capitalism. Economically speaking, countries can turn inward at key junctures, as the United States did in the 1920s, or they can turn outward, depending on the interaction of economic, political, military, and ideological power networks (Mann, 1986) and the relative power of classes and class segments (Zeitlin, 1980, 1984).

For me, then, it makes no sense to say, as Stone does (1984:302, 305, 311) that "capitalism" or the "particular stage of capitalism" sets the terms for policy discussion. Instead, we have to speak of "capitalists," and even of "international" and "national" capitalists, along with "workers" and other people organized into groups, classes, and networks. This is because capitalist structures and other structures are created in struggle and put in place, by and large, by the victors in those struggles (cf. Zeitlin, 1984). The length of the struggle may be days or years or centuries, but a good historical analysis, I believe, will always find the contending power groups that created the practices that are now called "objective structures" by the Stones of the world. There is no "it," but only us.

The one best example of this point for the United States concerns the way in which the "municipal reform movement" of 1890 to 1920 created a new "structure" for thousands of city governments. It is the best example because the time frame is brief and the data are abundant for a wide range of outcomes. The new system of council–manager government, accompanied by off-year, nonpartisan, citywide elections of unpaid officials, was the "conscious" result of planning by leaders of the growth machines who were threatened and annoyed by increasing working-class power in many cities. Liberals and the Socialist party were winning too many elections in too many of the districts that were used in electing city councils, and party labels seemed to be helping workers to vote for Socialists and liberal Democrats even though the voters knew nothing of the "character" and "record" of these candidates. The result, according to the established elites, was a "corrupt" government by nasty "machines," meaning that ethnic Americans were making off with some of the government contracts and offering a few more benefits to ordinary workers (e.g., Erie, 1988). In some cities, workers and Socialists actually were sitting on city councils (Weinstein, 1967:93–118).

The developers and merchants who opposed this shift in power to ethnic machines and workers organized themselves as the National Municipal League in 1894 (Stewart, 1950). They gradually developed a "reform" program that could put city government in the safe hands of "experts" who would be efficient, free of graft, and of course procapitalist. The new program, as one of the founders of the AALL, Clinton Woodruff, put it in 1909, was based on "the belief that if the administrative system can be perfected upon the basis of business economy, and properly safeguarded, it makes little difference which kind of men are elected" (Rumbarger, 1989:112). That is, the reformers were for a structural Marxist solution to their problems if they could create it.

This and many other quotes from city business leaders and their expert friends of the Progressive Era establish beyond a doubt that these people were "conscious" and "farsighted" in attempting to change government structure. Not only that, they succeeded to a considerable extent. In 1965, over half the cities between 25,000 and 250,000 in population were functioning under council–manager government. The figure was 40 percent for all cities with over 5,000 citizens (Goodall, 1968:60–61).

This story was first told from a class struggle point of view by none other than a mere corporate-liberal Marxist, James Weinstein (1962), who then expanded his account in his book on corporate involvement in a wider range of Progressive Era reforms (1968:Chapter 4). The story has been told more generally in other places (e.g., Hays, 1964; Scheisl, 1977; Domhoff, 1978:160–69; Davidson and

Korbel, 1981; Rumbarger, 1989:110–16). One systematic study even shows the way in which these reforms decrease voter turnout (Alford and Lee, 1968), which is hardly a progressive step.

This class-conflict theory of local government structure is strengthened by the fact that the municipal reform movement did not succeed in all cities. There were places, especially larger cities with industrial working classes and organized machines, where the campaigns of the businessmen and experts were defeated at the ballot box by Democrats or even Socialists (Goodall, 1968:34–35; Wolfinger, 1974:Chapter 11). Thus, if we look at the variety of state structures at the local level in the United States we can see an array of outcomes that only can be understood through historical studies. The theory is thus a dynamic one, allowing for a variety of outcomes depending on the relative strength of probusiness reformers and their opponents in the ethnic middle class and the working class.

But structural Marxists or state autonomy theorists like Skocpol never seem to see any need to refute these "comparative" historical studies of local state structures, or to provide an alternative explanation, even though the varying outcomes of these obvious struggles seem to refute their theory. Perhaps the local level does not count for them, except for the important exception of the autonomous mayor in New Haven, of course.

So, when Stone writes of the general agreement in the 1960s on the importance of foreign trade he is not stating an imperative that follows from system logic or structures, but is ignoring the defeat suffered by a once-ascendant segment of the capitalist class that wanted to solve America's problems through "self-sufficiency," not internationalism. In 1930 Congress raised tariffs in the face of a drastic depression in spite of desperate pleas from governments all over the world. Hoover signed this legislation even though dozens of international bankers begged him not to and 1,028 economists sent him a petition saying that the act would lead to disaster (Bauer et al., 1963:25). Congress didn't listen, Hoover didn't listen, and the result was another push downward in the complex chain of events that drove the system into even deeper depression. I can see no capital logic in all this, but only conflict and struggle among willful individuals organized into various groups, class segments, and classes.

Power, not economic logic, decides such issues. That is why in 1962, and here is my punch line, it once again mattered who governs when the internationalists George W. Ball and Howard C. Petersen made a deal with the textile and chemical manufacturers to create the Trade Expansion Act. That is, the mere "individuals" I focus on empirically are the "personifications" of capitalist class segments on this particular issue.

But I have talked about politics long enough without explaining how political parties fit into the larger power structure. That slight will be remedied in the next chapter.

# 9

## WHICH FAT CATS SUPPORT DEMOCRATS?

The importance of campaign finance in understanding power in America in the twentieth century is largely ignored or downplayed by grand theories in the social sciences. For pluralists, big money is at best one "resource" among many in the electoral arena, not an essential ingredient. They revel in pointing out that the person with the most money doesn't always win, thereby obscuring the fact that there is no possibility of even being a candidate without a certain necessary minimum. As "constraints" go, this would seem to be a formidable one in protecting wealthy capitalists from the will of the propertyless, but it gets no attention from the structural Marxists or state autonomy theorists either.

From my point of view, then, it may not be irrelevant that Theodore Roosevelt, William Howard Taft, Franklin D. Roosevelt, John F. Kennedy, and George Bush were from wealthy families, or that Lyndon Johnson, Richard Nixon, and Ronald Reagan had a coterie of very wealthy backers who financed their political careers and helped them become millionaires in the process. It would seem that politics truly is a "rich man's game," but such crude facts must be "theorized," i.e., put into an acceptable framework, before they can be given their due weight.

It is the great virtue of Thomas Ferguson and Joel Rogers's *Right Turn* (1986) that it calls attention to the importance of campaign donations and related resources of the wealthy that aid politicians. Indeed, this well-written and sharply argued book brings together a wide range of information to claim that such resources are not only crucial in the electoral process, but also in shaping public policies as well. On this basis it presents a whole new interpretation of the New Deal and of more recent policies of the Democratic party, an exciting prospect for those who have doubts about the oft-repeated claim that the Democrats are the party of "the common man" that does battle with the business-dominated Republican party.

Unfortunately, Ferguson and Rogers challenge pluralist wisdom about the Democratic party as the party of liberals, labor, and minorities within such a superficial framework that structural Marxists and state autonomy theorists will ignore it entirely, or see it as confirmation of their worst suspicions about theories emphasizing campaign finance. Ferguson and Rogers not only claim that big donors "invest" in politicians in the same way they invest in stocks, always seeking specific payoffs in terms of policy changes, but they further argue that these investments actually have a direct and fairly immediate effect on politicians. Just as the officers of corporations respond to the signals they receive from buying and selling on the stock market by investors, so too do politicians respond to the signals provided by changes in investments in one or the other of the two political parties. Ferguson and Rogers thus take both "economism" and "instrumentalism," the two worst sins in the structuralist catechism, to new heights.

It will be the purpose of this chapter to challenge the Ferguson and Rogers analysis with arguments and empirical data that completely contradict their most important claims. I will argue that the relationship between electoral campaigns and policy options is not nearly as close as they claim and that they are wrong empirically about which fat cats support Democrats. The chapter begins with an overview of the Ferguson and Rogers analysis. It next explains why there is a large gap between politics (office filling) and policy-making in the United States, and then turns to systematic empirical evidence on campaign finance that refutes Ferguson and Rogers's anecdotal account of Democratic supporters during the New Deal and their flawed systematic study of Democratic contributors in 1984. Finally, the chapter presents my own analysis of the financial basis of the Democratic party. It saves a critique of the failure of Ferguson and Rogers to include social disruption in their analysis for the next chapter, when I deal with other inaccurate theories on the rise of Reaganism as well.

## Right Turn and the Decline of the Democrats

The purpose of *Right Turn* is to explain the decline of the Democrats in the 1970s and the 1980s. Before presenting their explanation in terms of changes in political investments by certain sectors of the business community, however, they describe and critique other theories. By and large, they are attacking the conventional wisdom of liberals, but in the process they are also denying that the working class and its allies, even when aroused and disruptive, have any independent effect on policies.

They begin by arguing on the basis of many different opinion polls that support for liberal positions on most economic and social issues did not decline in recent years. The conclusion they draw is that it was not the people who took a right turn in the 1970s. However, it is a big jump from opinion polls to the voting booth, and I will argue in the next chapter that in fact just enough Democrats and independents changed their voting ways to help tip the scales toward the Republicans. Indeed, they did so in the way that might be expected by the "realignment" theorists within political science who are found wanting by Ferguson and Rogers (1986:41–43).

Ferguson and Rogers then present survey data to suggest that Reagan's ratings on job performance were not unusually high. Most people liked him, but many did not like his policies (1986:24–28). The implication is that the Democrats might have won in 1980 if they had not managed to start a recession right before the election. Ferguson and Rogers acknowledge that Reagan would have been tough to beat in 1984 once he pumped up the economy in record fashion shortly before the election, but they point out that the Democrats lost all hope of winning when their platform emphasized a tax increase and did not include a job-creation program (1986:185–86). I believe there is much to be said for this part of their analysis.

So, the question becomes why the Democratic party moved away "from its traditional commitments to promoting employment gains and growth" (1986: 36). The answer is to be found, they say, in understanding the role of economic elites within the party. More generally, "what properly defines American party systems is not blocs of voters but patterns of interest-group alignment and coalitions among major investors (1986:44). That is, to rephrase what I said in the introduction, switches in political investment strategy by wealthy investors in the face of new economic or social problems lead to changes in the policy stances of one or both of the political parties, and to new policies by government.

However, Ferguson and Rogers stress that not all wealthy individuals and corporations need the same policies. There may be conflicts between real estate investors and manufacturers, for example, leading real estate investors to support one party and manufacturers the other. Political battles are real, but they primarily involve people at the top, and sometimes labor unions. The most potent "power bloc" in the community of investors uses its campaign money, research groups, foundations, media access, and prestige to bring about success for the candidates and policies of its choice: "the rise and fall of American party systems is thus best analyzed by examining the rise and fall of investor blocs" (1986:46).

This general approach is used to explain the rise and fall of the New Deal coalition. Based on a more detailed article by Ferguson (1984), the book argues that the New Deal reflects the consolidation of a new coalition of investors that included internationally oriented commercial bankers, investment bankers, capital-intensive manufacturers, and labor unions. The relative lack of concern with labor costs on the part of the financiers and capital-intensive manufacturers made it possible for them to join with unions in a Democratic coalition against the less international and more labor-intensive manufacturers who are the major investors in the Republican party. In addition, the capital-intensive manufacturers shared with the international bankers a strong commitment to expanded international trade: "Because most large capital-intensive firms (with the important exception of the heavily protectionist chemical industry, which did not belong to the bloc) were world, as well as U.S. pacesetters, they stood to gain from global free trade" (Ferguson and Rogers, 1986:47).

The new block is said to have represented only a small part of the corporate community in the 1930s, but to be nonetheless "immensely powerful" (1986:

47). Not only were the firms in it large, but their "professionalism and scientific advance" allowed them to "fire the imagination of large parts of American society in this period" (1986:47). Then too, it was people from this bloc who sat on the boards of the major foundations, and they were close to the owners of the country's most important newspaper, the *New York Times*. In short, Ferguson and Rogers are talking about the internationalist segment of the capitalist class.

The exemplar firms named as part of this new coalition include many of the fastest growing or largest companies of the 1930s: General Electric, IBM, Pan Am, R. J. Reynolds, Standard Oil of New Jersey, Standard Oil of California, Cities Service, Shell, Bank of America, Chase National Bank, Brown Brothers Harriman, Goldman Sachs, Lehman Brothers, and Dillon Read. They are said to have "broadly supported" the legislation of the second New Deal, including the Social Security Act, the National Labor Relations Act, and the Public Utilities Holding Company Act. Here Ferguson and Rogers hedge a bit, however, with a long footnote saying that "broadly supported, while carefully chosen, could be misleading" because there were "different levels of enthusiasm" for "different parts of this package" (1986:236). This is putting it mildly in terms of the National Labor Relations Act, as my analysis in Chapter 4 demonstrates, but the really important point is that support for a given piece of legislation, such as the Social Security Act, does not necessarily mean support for the Democratic party. Some of the people from the business community who supported the act, as we will see, wanted to elect Republicans in 1936.

Despite its successes over several decades, the New Deal coalition broke apart in the 1970s for several economic reasons. Most generally, increasing competition from Japanese and Western European multinationals forced the capital-intensive American companies to adopt policies to reduce the costs of labor and government regulation, putting them into conflict with labor unions and those Democrats who favored regulation. About the same time, the huge OPEC price increases of 1973 pushed the oil industry out of the Democratic camp because of battles over price controls and the oil depletion allowance (1986:90). Then, too, the multinationals' desire for lower taxes in the context of their profit squeeze meant that the Democrats would have to cut back on the social and welfare programs that were favored by their voting constituencies. These and other factors added up to pressure to move rightward: "By the mid-1970s the cumulative weight of all these factors—faltering domestic performance, lagging international competitiveness, the explosion of energy and commodity prices, and pressures for increased military spending, along with a cost cutting in labor, regulation, social programs, and taxes—was immense" (1986:103).

In short, the profit squeeze faced by the multinationals put the Democrats in a political squeeze, and the multinationals switched to the Republican party because it "appeared as a more efficient vehicle for realizing their aspirations" (1986:103). The result was a Reaganism of the center, not of some right-wing takeover artists. As for the Democrats, their remaining investors insisted on self-serving policies that further isolated the party from its natural base in lower-income Americans.

## Politics and Policies

As pleasant as it is to read a serious book that draws attention to campaign finance and other resources of the wealthy in American politics, and as much as I like its spirited description of the political and economic changes of the 1970s and 1980s, I do not think that *Right Turn* contains an accurate account of how campaign finance, elections, and policy are interrelated. Simply put, there is a more complicated relationship between politics and policy than the authors describe. Campaign finance and politics are concerned primarily with the filling of offices by particular individuals, which is related to policy in only a very loose way. There are many structural and historical reasons for this bifurcation, as is rightly emphasized by the many mainstream social scientists who contrast American parties with their more programmatic European counterparts. Since this analysis is so well known, and since I have made it many times myself (e.g., Domhoff, 1979:Chapter 4; 1983a:Chapter 4), I will not develop it at length here.

The important structural point is that a presidential system and single-member districts lead to a series of winner-take-all elections in which a vote for a third party is a vote for your least favorite candidate. This is a powerful inducement toward a two-party system in which policy differences tend to be blurred by the candidates as they appeal to middle-of-the-road voters in search of an electoral majority. What this means is that policy deals are made by politicians after the election, not before, as is possible in countries with parliamentary governments (especially if they also use proportional representation). I think Lipset's (1963:Chapter 9) comparative analysis is very compelling on these points.

If political structure essentially dictates a two-party system, the economic structure of the United States has widened the gap between politics and policy even further, for it has forced some strange bedfellows into the same party. I am going to try to demonstrate this at length for the Democratic party after demonstrating the empirical inadequacy of Ferguson and Rogers's analysis of Democratic party financial support, but for now the point is that the southern slaveholders/landlords and northern merchant/real estate interests who formed the business basis of the party from at least 1830 to at least 1980 have policy differences as well as the common interests that unite them. This in turn leads the southerners to join with the somewhat more homogeneous Republican party on some issues. What I have just said is hardly news to those who take analyses of voting patterns in Congress seriously (e.g., Mayhew, 1966; Clausen, 1973; Patterson, 1967; Sinclair, 1982; Shelley, 1983), but it does reinforce the point that politics and policies are often separated in the American system.

It is these structural and historical factors that make name recognition and image so important in American politics. Since it is risky to overemphasize issues, clever slogans and denunciations of the personal life of the opponent come to the fore. Modern-day Americans sometimes believe that this tendency is on the upswing due to television, but in fact it has been a staple of American politics since at least the 1830s, and may have been worse in the nineteenth century than it is now. At the presidential level, for example, both sides always have tried to claim that their candidate is from more humble circumstances or more "of the people" than the opponent, but this "log cabin" myth is belied by the large slave and land holdings of an Andrew Jackson or Zachary Taylor, the inherited wealth of a William Henry Harrison or John Tyler, and the important business clients of corporate lawyers such as Martin Van Buren and Abraham Lincoln (Pessen, 1984).

It is in this two-party, policy-blurring, image-building context that campaign finance can loom so large. When visibility and personal charisma can sway voters who do not necessarily share policy positions with the candidate, then large amounts of money are necessary for election to major offices, even if it is also true that the candidate with the most dollars doesn't always win. Campaign donations by businesspeople, who provide an overwhelming portion of the money raised in both parties, thus can enter into the power equation in a critical fashion to support friendly candidates or to eliminate candidates viewed as too liberal or (more rarely) too conservative. But the candidates usually are not of one extreme or the other, and that means most donations by wealthy individuals are linked to such mundane factors as friendship with the fund-raiser, a personal liking of the candidate, long-standing party identification, or general social outlook, not policy positions. Indeed, as will be shown, policy concerns in elections are so minor that many wealthy people and corporate officers don't even bother to "invest."

In a system where elections, parties, and policies are not closely tied, two other processes arise to connect society and state on issues of policy: First, the narrow and short-run interests of major economic sectors are handled within a "special-interest" or "interest-group" process by trade associations, committees of the U.S. Chamber of Commerce, lobbyists, and law firms. This process is the primary focus of pluralists, and the disagreements and complexities within it so bedazzle them in the context of the unprogrammatic political parties that they pronounce the overall system free of any class rule. Functionaries within the special-interest process understand that politicians often feel compelled to say one thing to win elections and then do another to keep the NAM and Chamber of Commerce from targeting them in the next election. Lobbyists develop contacts with members of both parties, and they usually give the bulk of their PAC money to incumbents, even Democratic ones, to the great annoyance of right-wing ideologues. What the lobbyists want is "access" to as many elected officials as possible and a voting majority on their particular issues. They do not care exactly where that majority comes from on any one issue, and they understand that even their best friends can't give them what they want on every issue and still win elections (e.g., Fenno, 1978:144).

More general policy issues, such as those analyzed in earlier chapters, are discussed and compromised within a different network of people and organizations that includes foundations, think tanks, policy-discussion groups like the Council on Foreign Relations and CED, presidential commissions, and specialized media outlets. Most of the people who operate within this more general policy-planning network are corporate lawyers, top-level executives, and academic experts who tend to stay aloof from party politics. They may or may not give large contributions to Democrats or Republicans, but there are both Democrats and Republican donors within all of the centrist policy-discussion groups.

A few people from this network are mentioned prominently by Ferguson and Rogers as key figures in the Democratic party by virtue of cabinet-level appointments. They include Robert McNamara, secretary of defense under Kennedy, W. Michael Blumenthal, secretary of treasury under Carter, and Cyrus Vance, secretary of state under Carter. However, my analysis of their past histories suggests that they were not heavy contributors or closely identified with the party before they were appointed. The Kennedy people didn't even know if McNamara was a Democrat or a Republican when they started to feel him out for a possible appointment; he had been recommend to Kennedy by a nominally Democrat investment banker, Robert Lovett, who had served in the cabinet in the Truman administration (Schlesinger, 1965:132).

Contrary to Ferguson and Rogers, my point would be that people like McNamara, Blumenthal, and Vance are appointed to government precisely because of the tenuous relation between politics and policy. The policy-planning network is indeed the political arm of the multinational corporations and international financiers, as Ferguson and Rogers recognize, but it is this network's nonprofit and nonpartisan image that gives it effectiveness within the government whichever party happens to be in power. Ferguson and Rogers are right, I believe, in their analysis of the policy changes that occurred within the internationalist segment in the 1970s, but they are wrong to identify that segment so closely with the Democratic party. Put another way, that segment is not the key to understanding the financial support for the Democratic party, nor did its alleged switch to the Republicans lead to the decline of the Democratic party.

In the following sections I will show that Ferguson and Rogers are dead wrong about the financial support of the Democratic party, and I will present an alternative analysis of the financial basis of the party. This alternative analysis will reveal the major reason for the decline of the New Deal coalition: southern white elites ditched it and then smashed it.

However, I will save the full explanation for the right turn in policy since the mid-1970s for the next chapter. There I will argue that it is the result of two intertwined processes within the lower, not higher, levels of the social structure:

on the one hand the decline in disruption and militancy by African-Americans, students, antiwar activists, and other social activists, and on the other the rise of a New Right rooted in a reaction to the civil rights and liberal gains created by the 1960s activists. The internationalization of the economy emphasized by Ferguson and Rogers plays a role by increasing the rate of unemployment and heightening job insecurity, but it is hardly direct exertions by the corporate community that precipitated the rollback of the 1960s. Instead, the right turn is another battle in the class war, made possible by the decline of the disruption that originally forced the sophisticated conservatives to act moderately until the storm subsided.

## Fat Cats and Democrats

*Right Turn,* for all its fine analysis and invective at the level of economic policy, has only two empirical bases when it comes to the Democratic party's campaign finances: anecdotes about alleged big-business support of Roosevelt in the 1936 elections, and an analysis of Democratic contributors in 1984. Its analysis may appear convincing at first glance because of its seeming wealth of detail, but for anyone who knows the campaign finance literature it comes as a shock, for it completely ignores the systematic findings that contradict it.

In the case of the New Deal, Louise Overacker's (1937) comparison of campaign finance reports for 1932 and 1936 showed that many of the major bankers and industrialists who supported Roosevelt in 1932 did not do so in 1936. She concluded that the Democrats were supported by smaller businesses, not big ones. Overacker's work is not without serious defects because it did not make full use of a Senate committee's list of big donors and did not identify the business connections of many donors (Webber, 1990), but these errors tend to underestimate big-business support for the Republicans, not exaggerate it.

Looking at only the very largest contributors for the two elections, Ferdinand Lundberg concluded in a somewhat similar but more detailed fashion that Roosevelt was supported by those "whose revenues derive primarily from direct exploitation of the retail market—department store owners, textile fabricators, cigarette manufacturers, independent industrialists, processors and distributors, and big real estate operators" (1937:450). This view receives some support from Overacker's (1941, 1945) studies of the 1940 and 1944 campaigns, where almost three-fifths of Republican money came from bankers and heavy industrialists, while almost half of big Democratic money came from retailers, light industrialists, and the entertainment industry. It is this view of the financial backing of the New Deal that has been picked up by Peter Friedlander (1987) and Steve Fraser (1984, 1989) with nary a nod to Overacker.

The discrepancies between these earlier findings and the claims by Ferguson and Rogers, along with the limitations of Overacker's work, led Michael Webber

(1990) to analyze all extant information on the 1932 and 1936 campaigns with the Ferguson and Rogers thesis as one starting point. The data for 1932 consisted of all those people who gave $1,000 or more according to Overacker's compilation from reports submitted to Congress. The data for 1936 consisted of all those people who gave $100 or more according to Overacker's compilation of House records, along with contributors of $500 or more who were listed by the Senate's special committee on campaign finance for that year.

Webber first looked at all the donations for 1936 by officers and directors of companies named by Ferguson and Rogers as exemplary of the internationalist/capital-intensive bloc. His first major finding was that very few of these people gave to either party. This is similar to the results for two different studies of dozens of large firms and trade associations in 1968 (Alexander, 1971:182–87; Domhoff, 1972:15), and somewhat similar to those for studies of donations by extremely wealthy families in 1968 (Alexander, 1971:187–88) and 1972 (Allen and Broyles, 1989), where 30–40 percent do not give at all. The cumulative impact of these several analyses is to suggest that many rich people and business leaders are not highly motivated to give to political campaigns. I concluded that in the 1960s even those few who gave money spent far more on their horses and dogs than they did on politics (Domhoff, 1972:15), and this conclusion seems to hold for the 1930s as well, except for a few well-publicized exceptions on the Republican side like the du Ponts, Pews, and Mellons. Thus, there are a great many unused resources within the higher circles that could be thrown into the political fray if necessary.

The small percentage of wealthy and corporate donors is paralleled by the great turnover in donors from election to election. From 1928 to 1932, for example, three-fourths of the Democratic donors of over $1,000 disappeared from the lists (Overacker, 1933:779–80). Between 1932 and 1936, two-thirds of the large donors dropped off the lists (Overacker, 1937:490). Similarly, Alexander (1971:169–70) reports there is no great continuity of big donors for the 1960s. Together, these findings suggest that donors are giving as much to the candidate as they are to the party, and that fund-raisers for different candidates have connections to different donors.

Webber also found that very few of the people from the bloc who gave in 1932 favored Roosevelt. Thus, their preferences could not have had much to do with the 1932 victory by Roosevelt, as Ferguson and Rogers probably agree. It seems more likely, then, that Roosevelt won because he was backed by traditional Democratic donors and because ordinary voters were upset by the growing depression and angered by Hoover's minimalist response to it. As for 1936, there was no shift to Roosevelt by members of this bloc. Despite the larger number of people listed as giving due to the expansion of the data base to include donations down to $100, the donations from the bloc remained overwhelmingly Republican.

Ferguson (1984) makes much of the fact that certain visible elite Democrats who had been supporting Landon, such as Dean Acheson and James P. Warburg, switched back to Roosevelt shortly before the election. He also notes such a last-minute switch by several hundred Wall Street bankers who attended a Roosevelt rally on October 31 supposedly because of their fears of Landon's increasingly isolationist speeches. But the campaign records show overwhelming Wall Street support for the Republicans. As Overacker concludes, Wall Street gave "even more generously than usual" to the Republicans in 1936 and "with fewer dissenting voices than in the past" (1937:484). And surely any few possible last minute switchers cannot be thought to have had any influence. If anything, they had decided to jump on a bandwagon.

Webber looked at every company in various industrial sectors such as oil said by Ferguson and Rogers to be favorable toward Roosevelt, usually because they were either internationally oriented or capital intensive. His results for all sectors show conclusively that regional factors were more important than industrial sector, meaning that the few examples Ferguson and Rogers give of pro-Roosevelt firms in these sectors—e.g., Reynolds Tobacco, several Texas oil companies—are an artifact of regional differences.

Webber analyzed the campaign contributions of all members of the Council on Foreign Relations, on the assumption that it is the embodiment of the internationalist segment of the ruling class, an assumption that Ferguson and Rogers seem to share from their allusions to it (1986:66, 149, 200). Contrary to the expectation that these internationalists would be predominantly Roosevelt supporters in 1936, he found that 89 of the 517 members gave to the Republicans, while only 28 gave to the Democrats, a 76–24 split. These findings are remarkably similar to what I found for 1968, when 144 members gave to the Republicans and 56 gave to the Democrats, a 72–28 split (Domhoff, 1972: 151).

Webber also analyzed the contributions of the members of the BAC, the advisory group to Roosevelt discussed at length in Chapters 3 and 4. He found that in 1936 there were 16 Republican donors and 16 Democratic donors among all those who served on the council between 1933 and 1936. Thus, even some of those who tried to work out policy arrangements with Roosevelt did not necessarily support his reelection. This point also is apparent in Webber's analysis of donations by 15 businesspeople who supported the Social Security Act and 10 who opposed it according to work by Jenkins and Brents (1989). He found that 5 of the 15 who supported the act nonetheless favored Landon in 1936. Not surprisingly, all ten who opposed the act were for Landon. It is this type of analysis that demonstrates my earlier point about the separation of politics and policy in America, for it is not insignificant that one-third of the Republican donors nonetheless supported Social Security.

Since there is no evidence to support Ferguson and Rogers's claims about who financed whom at the height of the New Deal, it is useful to return to Overacker (1937) for a new starting point. First, 37 percent of the donations of over $100 in

1936 that could be allocated by region came from the South, where the Republicans received virtually no contributions. Second, the Democrats received support from smaller businessmen in northern cities like New York, Chicago, and Philadelphia. Third, organized labor gave $255,000 of the $5.2 million collected by the Democratic National Committee and then spent another $515,000 through its Non-Partisan League, the American Labor party, and other outlets. Finally, government officials and lawyers differentially favored the Democrats. In all, then, the funding of the Democrats in 1936 is a far cry from what might be expected from a reading of Ferguson and Rogers. The need for an alternative analysis thus presents itself. Are the Democrats perhaps the party of the common person after all?

## The South and the Growth Machines

The power base of the Democratic party can be found through a look at the history of the party. Such a look reveals the obvious, that the Democratic party has been the party of the southern segment of the ruling class. This assertion holds true from the beginnings of the party in 1792—or 1828, depending on where you come down in disputes about the continuity between the "old" and "new" party—until at least the 1970s, when the effects of postwar economic changes, the upsurge of civil rights and antiwar liberalism, and the passage of the civil rights and voting acts of 1964 and 1965 started a gradual movement of the southern rich, and most other southern whites, to the Republicans.

This does not mean that all southerners were Democrats from the very outset. Up until the 1850s there were important southerners in both parties (Grantham, 1963; Potter, 1972). It was only after the Civil War that the South became solidly Democratic except for a few presidential elections. Nonetheless, those southerners who were in the Democratic party in the first half of the nineteenth century effectively controlled it on the issues of concern to them—states rights, minimal federal government, low tariffs, and most important of all, no tampering with slavery.

Southern control of the Democrats, especially after the Civil War, rested on procedural traditions developed by Congress and the parties early in the nineteenth century primarily for organizational reasons. These traditions included standing legislative committees with powerful chairmen, a seniority system for selecting chairmen, a rules committee to decide what legislation would be considered by the full House, a party caucus for selecting congressional leadership, the assignment of new members to committees by Democratic members of the Ways and Means Committee, and (until 1936) support from two-thirds of the party delegates to win the presidential nomination. David Potter (1972) elegantly traces the origins of these procedures and shows how they—along with the filibuster—gave the southern rich power in Congress from 1878 to 1964 far out of proportion to their wealth, their number in Congress, or their population base. Indeed, their ability to bring the machinery of the federal government to a complete halt made it necessary to accommodate them on any issue of great concern to them.

Still, the southerners always had to have coalition partners in the North. From the time of the "botanizing expedition" to New York in 1791 by Thomas Jefferson and James Madison to the reorganization of the party in the 1820s by Martin Van Buren of New York and the Richmond Junto, the southerners found their allies in the North among those who had their own disagreements with Federalists (1792–1812), Whigs (1832–1856), or Republicans, or who were tied economically to the South. At the outset these allies included a landed-merchant–banking faction in the New York elite led by the great landlord Robert R. Livingston and his lawyer, Aaron Burr, who had been fighting with Alexander Hamilton and the Federalists over bank charters (Hammond, 1957:Chapter 5; Young, 1967:Chapter 10). This faction also included Irish merchants and others hostile to the English or to Hamiltonian policies. Jefferson himself put the contrast fairly accurately when he said that the Federalists were "natural aristocrats" and merchants tied to the British, whereas his side consisted of "(1) Merchants trading on their own capital; (2) Irish merchants; (3) Tradesmen, mechanics, farmers, and every other possible description of our citizens" (Chambers, 1964:16).

Now, Jefferson may have been a little self-serving in claiming most of the northern farmers, many of whom were eager for the industrialization advocated by the Federalists (Genovese, 1965:162). He also was excessively modest in leaving out the southern slaveholders he represented, and the landed interests who backed him in the North, but his analysis nonetheless pinpoints the key to understanding the Democratic party from its beginning to the present. It always has been the party of the "out-group" within the power elite, of those who in some way differ from the wealthiest WASP bankers, industrialists, and retailers of their day. Even in the 1790s, when their states loomed large in the union, the southerners felt themselves to be outsiders on the inside because they were agrarians in an industrializing society and slaveholders in a land of free labor and free soil. Similarly, their partners in the North tended to be newer or small businessmen, or else immigrants, Catholics, Jews, or freethinkers. The differences with the Federalists–Whigs–Republicans on this score were not complete, as the leadership of a Livingston, a Stephen Van Rensselear, or even a son of Alexander Hamilton, who speculated in real estate and became a Jacksonian, reminds us (Benson, 1961:6; Hammond, 1957:9). However, such differences show up in most comparisons between leading northern Democrats and their counterparts in the party of the truly established and respectable (Fuchs, 1956:24–26; Hammond, 1957:329–30; Benson, 1961:144, 176–79; Goodman, 1964:75–78; Young, 1967:566–70).

For example, Jacob Crowninshield, a leading Jeffersonian in Massachusetts, disagreed with the pro-British policies of the Federalists because of a dislike he developed for the British while he was making a fortune trading in the Far East and on the European continent (Murrin, 1980:423). The southerners found friends among the Germans of western Pennsylvania, who didn't like Hamilton's land taxes or his policy toward immigrants. According to John Murrin, these two policies "forever alienated Pennsylvania from the party of Washington, Hamilton, and John Adams" (1980:417). When the Democrats reorganized in the 1820s after having absorbed the Federalists for a period of 15 or 20 years, they found allies among hinterland bankers who wanted some of the government's money kept in their banks (Hammond, 1957:419–20). Tennessee slaveholders, and those who wanted to sell public lands to farmers, such as Senator Thomas Hart Benton of Missouri, a lawyer for New York Democrat millionaire John Jacob Astor, also supported the reorganized Democrats.

The economic ties of northern Democrats to the South can be seen most clearly in Brian Danforth's (1974) detailed study of over 500 New York merchants between 1828 and 1844. Contradicting earlier studies of more limited samples, he found that the merchants were about equally divided in their support of the two parties, but that 83 percent of the merchants who traded solely with the South were Democrats, with the figure dropping only slightly to 75 percent in favor of the Democrats for those who did half their business with the South. Conversely, 73 percent of those who had little or no trade with the South favored the National Republicans and later the Whigs (Danforth, 1974:163–64).

There were eight Irish-born Catholics in the study. Seven supported the Democrats, and six of those seven did half or more of their business with the South (1974:176). According to Danforth, native-born Protestants from wealthy families were more involved in transatlantic trading routes, leaving an opening for the Irish and others of new wealth to become involved in the southern commerce that did not become important until after the War of 1812 (1974:174). Clearly, then, there is an interaction between economic interest and ethnicity at the material base of the Democrats.

The Jacksonian version of the Democratic party was new in that it contained some former Federalists leaders in many states (Benson, 1961; Haller, 1962; McCormick, 1964), but its backbone was the same southerners and New Yorkers who had been with the party from the beginning. The Jacksonian party also was new in the sense that the demands and pressures of the newly enfranchised small farmers and artisans now had to be accommodated within the framework of the two-party system. The parties became a way of limiting the independence of such voters as well as a way of fighting sectional battles (McCormick, 1964:29–30, 254, 349). In this context, control of the party became as important as winning the regular election. Historians have documented this point for many areas of the country in the later years of the century, showing the way in which "Bourbon Democrats" battled to nominate their kind of candidates who were likely to lose rather than trying to win the election with more liberal candidates (Grantham, 1963:29–37; Merrill, 1953; Hollingsworth, 1963).

For all the diversity of the new Democratic party, the most important and loyal

allies of the southerners in the post–Civil War era were those northern immigrants whose fortunes were tied to land development and related real estate
businesses rather than industry. They were people whose primary concern was
the intensification of land use in order to increase interest and rents. In modern-
day terms, they were members of the growth coalitions or "growth machines"
that constitute the power structures of American cities (Molotch, 1976, 1979;
Logan and Molotch, 1987; Domhoff, 1986a). They were part of the real estate
segment of the capitalist class.

These real estate elites were the basis of the better known political machines
that are focused on by some social scientists as the key to the Democratic party.
The myth and reality of machines can be seen in the oldest and most famous of
them, Tammany Hall, which became the focus of New York Democratic politics
in the early nineteenth century (Mandelbaum, 1965; Callow, 1966; Mushkat,
1971). Fabled as the organization of enlisted men from the Revolutionary army,
as opposed to the elitist Society of Cincinnati, where former officers gathered
together (Goldman, 1966:14), Tammany Hall was in fact based in landed and
commercial businessmen who were prepared to do business with the southerners
economically and politically in order to thwart the Federalists. It was this growth
machine that supplied the political machine with the money to bring out and/or
buy voters on election day. Tammany Hall even served as an employment bureau
for the growth machine, although Goldman (1966:15) puts the matter in terms of
the wonderful help the political machine was giving to unemployed workers:

> In an era when employment agencies and union hiring halls were rare and the United States
> Employment Service non-existent, unemployed laborers by the score and the hundreds could
> be found applying for work every morning at the doorstep of their Tammany captain. The
> Tammany leadership was geared to refer these unemployed to builders, contractors, and
> nearly every other business enterprise in the city. Satisfaction with these deals depended
> heavily upon regular and competent job performance by the Tammany stalwarts. In return,
> Tammany could do much for cooperating builders, contractors, and other business enterprises
> (1966:15–16).

By focusing the voting strength of the underclasses of the city into the Democratic machine, it became possible for the smaller rich to gain control of government and further enrich themselves. "To the victor belongs the spoils" became
the famous cry of machine Democrats, to the outrage of "good government"
Republicans, who did not like the idea that upstart real estate entrepreneurs were
taking over the city government and becoming rich through its building contracts
and myriad other goodies (Tolchin and Tolchin, 1971).

Contrary to the myth created by a novel and a movie, these machines did not
have their "last hurrah" in the 1930s, nor even in the 1950s and 1960s (Snowiss,
1966:637–39; Tolchin and Tolchin, 1971:22). Roosevelt worked closely with the
machine bosses and funneled the temporary largesse of the relief programs
through their organizations (Dorsett, 1968, 1977; Stave, 1970; Erie, 1988). The

case of the infamous Pendergast machine of Kansas City provides a particularly crass example of the link between the growth machine and the political machine, for Boss Tom Pendergast had acquired a share in several companies that did building and service projects for the city with federal government money. In all, Pendergast was involved with an asphalt company, a cement company, a concrete pipe company, a paving company, a construction company, and a sanitary service company (Dorsett, 1968:110, 149).

In the case of Tammany Hall, there also were close ties with the South because trade, shipping, and loans with southern businesses were a major basis for the rise of the port of New York to national eminence. This was especially so with the growth of the cotton economy after 1820, for the famous "cotton triangle" between Europe, New York, and the South meant that most southern cotton was marketed through New York merchants and most southern imports came by way of New York (Albion, 1939:10; Foner, 1941). In the nineteenth century, New York was known as the "prolongation of the South." Most of its businessmen worked very hard to find compromises on the slavery issue to keep the South in the union, even though only half of them were Democrats (Foner, 1941).

However, the relatively few Democrats in the burgeoning New York City business community were extremely important in the party's national finances. One such person was August Belmont, an immigrant who first came to the country in 1837 as an agent of the famous Rothschild family and married the daughter of an American naval hero, Commodore Matthew Perry. Belmont gave the party tens of thousands of dollars in the second half of the nineteenth century (Alexander, 1976:62–63), and served as its national chairman between 1861 and 1872. Along with merchants Abraham Hewitt and Augustus Schell, and southern-oriented corporate lawyers Samuel L. Barlow and Samuel Tilden, he helped to rebuild the party's southern ties after the Civil War (Katz, 1968, Mushkat, 1981). Years later his son by the same name followed in his footsteps by joining the Virginia-born financier Thomas Fortune Ryan in paying off the party's $500,000 debt after the 1904 presidential campaign (Overacker, 1932:141, 152). And it was from a New York merchant family with ties to Tammany Hall and the South that the most important figure of the New Deal emerged, Franklin D. Roosevelt (Schriftgiesser, 1942).

From the very beginning, the strategy of the Democratic party was to have a presidential candidate who was sure to win in the South and New York, then to look around for a vice-presidential candidate who might help them win in one of the nineteenth century swing states: Pennsylvania, Ohio, Illinois, and Indiana (e.g., Mushkat, 1981:16). Thus, the year 1932 was only a slight historical exception when Franklin D. Roosevelt appeared at the head of the ticket and Jack Garner of Texas joined him as the vice-presidential candidate who would win the South and Southwest. It was a ticket that all southerners dreamed about and fought for against the Catholic Al Smith and the California newspaper magnate William Randolph Hearst. It was people from Texas banking, oil, and ranching who provided the big southern donations in 1936, and people from New York who provided the largest Northern donations.

The economic basis for the alliance between southern and northern Democrats can be discerned in the patterns of congressional voting since the New Deal (Mayhew, 1966; Clausen, 1973; Sinclair, 1982; Shelley, 1983). These studies focus on party and region, not class or economic interests, but it is safe to assume that the southern region is a stand-in for a class segment in the case of the South (Key, 1949; Brinkley, 1984; Sinclair, 1985), and that many northern Democrats are rooted in the machines (e.g., Snowiss, 1966; Miller, 1970). These studies show that most legislation clusters into five separate and consistent dimensions. "Civil rights" has to do with such rights as voting and free speech. "Social welfare" concerns labor legislation and government payments to individuals who are in need due to poverty, unemployment, poor health, or old age. "International involvement" is a mixture of foreign aid and defense issues. On these three dimensions northern and southern Democrats came to differ greatly after agreeing most of the time in the early New Deal. From 1933 on, a majority of northern Democrats supported civil rights, social welfare, and international involvement, but a majority of southerners opposed civil rights and labor legislation by 1937, other social welfare legislation by the early 1950s, and international involvement (foreign aid and low tariffs in this instance) by the mid-1950s. How, then, could the Democratic party cohere?

It is on the other two dimensions, "government management" and "agricultural assistance," that the Democratic party really rested. The government management dimension is a complex one that encompasses a number of issues, including business regulation and workplace protection, but the core of it as far as the Democrats themselves are concerned is spending to support public works projects, urban construction, and other projects favoring their key constituents (e.g., Sinclair, 1982:21, 61, 77). Similarly, "agricultural assistance" means above all else large subsidies that go to the big plantations and ranches in the South and rural West now known collectively as agribusiness. In short, the old alliance between the southern planters and the northern ethnic real estate developers became a prospending alliance that used its control of Congress to further its own economic interests against a tight-fisted Republican party based almost entirely in the industrial and bank capital of the internationalist and nationalist segments.

This does not mean that all northern Democrats voted for agricultural subsidies and all southern Democrats supported the grants and subsidies built into the government management dimension. It means only that a majority of both groups voted for each other's programs while a great majority of Republicans were opposing both types of spending. From 1961 to 1968, for example, an average of 92 percent of northern Democratic votes supported government management legislation. The solid South voted for such measures 69 percent of the time, and the Republicans only 17 percent of the time (Sinclair, 1982:145).

Between 1953 and 1960, to take another example, southerners voted for agricultural assistance measures 93 percent of the time, northeastern Democrats 64 percent of the time, and Republicans only 18 percent of the time (1982:108). This dramatic split between Democrats and Republicans, I believe, reveals the economic basis of the party even though there are some government management measures having to do with regulation of business and support for labor that are opposed by a majority of southern Democrats and Republicans (Shelley, 1983:51–52).

The differences between southern Democrats and northern machine Democrats on certain aspects of government intervention makes the point that their policy needs are not completely the same. Instead, the southern planters and the southern industrialists in textiles, tobacco, and lumber are as concerned as their Republican industrialist counterparts to control their labor force, and to limit unionism in particular. These concerns are embodied within the civil rights and social welfare dimensions, for much of the legislation in these areas helps labor. The civil rights dimension also includes legislation that would provide greater political freedom for African-American tenant farmers and laborers in the South, for example. The social welfare dimension not only includes legislation directly related to unions, but often legislation that would raise the "social wage" of all workers, therefore making unionization somewhat easier in both North and South. Broadly speaking, then, I believe the social welfare and civil rights dimensions contain within them the axis of class struggle in the United States as it manifests itself in the legislative process.

More generally, opposition to civil rights, union rights, social welfare, and business regulation is the substance of the conservative coalition in Congress, which is defined as a vote where a majority of southern Democrats and a majority of Republicans are in agreement (Shelley, 1983:20). This conservative coalition developed slowly at the end of the New Deal (Patterson, 1967) and then appeared on 20–30 percent of all votes after the mid-1940s; it won 91 percent of the time from 1939 to 1956, then its average fell to 55 percent from 1957 to 1968 (Manley, 1973:239). At this point some political observers of the day claimed that its power finally was broken, but during Nixon's first term its appearance reached all-time highs and its victories approached the level of the 1939–1956 period. Moreover, these findings do not include the many pieces of legislation that were watered down by northern Democrats to hold on to the southerners, nor the legislation bottled up in committees (1973:239).

The conservative coalition supposedly was fading away in the 1970s, but once again such announcements of its demise were premature. Work by Mack Shelley showed that between 1970 and 1980 the coalition materialized in the House on 20–30 percent of all votes and was successful from 50 to 80 percent of the time (1983:24–25, 34–35). The coalition played a crucial role in the Reagan tax cuts of 1981, but then it declined in its appearance throughout the rest of the 1980s. By then many southern Democrats had to be more cautious in dealing with their

African-American constituents. Besides, Republicans won the seats in the most conservative southern districts, which meant that it didn't take a majority of southerners for conservatives to win (*Congressional Quarterly,* 1981a, 1981b, 1981c).

For 30 years members of the conservative coalition liked to deny its existence as a conscious effort, and some analysts came to believe that it was simply a product of independent voting based on similar interests. However, one of its retired leaders, Howard Smith of Virginia, told John Manley (1973:231) that informal coordination among a few leaders on both sides did take place. The Republicans would meet in one building, the southern Democrats in another, and the leaders of one group would go to see their counterparts. Then both leadership groups would return to their caucuses. "It was very informal," said Smith. "But we met in small groups. There were no joint meetings of conservative Republicans and Southern Democrats" (1973:231–32). So, as we might expect from our general understanding of power networks, a few central individuals did tie things together.

However, disagreement between northern and southern Democrats over civil rights and social welfare issues was not nearly as divisive as it might appear to be from the great differences in voting records. This is because the machine Democrats in the North were willing to vote with the southerners inside the party caucus on such crucial questions as party leadership and the seniority system (Miller, 1970; Potter, 1972). This made it possible for the southerners to block or modify progressive social legislation within committees while at the same time ensuring the continuance of agricultural subsidies and a large share of defense spending for the South. When weakened social, labor, and civil rights legislation did reach the floor of the House or Senate, the machine Democrats always voted for it, of course, thereby preserving their liberal images for their labor and ethnic voting constituencies. Norman Miller, who covered the House for the *Wall Street Journal* in the 1960s, summarized this cozy little arrangement as follows in one of the more insightful articles on the power structure of the Democratic party:

> The organization Democrats have largely escaped notice because, until recently, liberal opinion judged Congressmen only by their voting records. On this score, most of the organization men were in an unassailable position: year after year they won "liberal" ratings of up to 100 percent from Americans for Democratic Action. Yet, in terms of "democratic action," they produced little or nothing. By voting right, they satisfied liberal opinion at home; by doing nothing effective, they satisfied their Southern allies in the House (1970:71).

Thus, as long as these 70 or so machine Democrats voted with the 80–90 southerners against the 70–80 liberals to uphold the various rules and traditions summarized from Potter (1972) earlier in this chapter, it was possible for the southerners and the machine Democrats to maintain the prospending alliance that satisfied their major backers and financial supporters. They had found a way to keep labor issues from destroying their alliance even while using labor votes (and money!) to defeat the Republicans. It is here that we see the real power nexus of the Democratic party at the political level, just as campaign finance and congressional voting patterns revealed that power nexus at the economic level.

But northern machine Democrats shared another interest with their southern friends that they couldn't talk about openly. They too wanted to minimize voting by African-Americans because they did not want their machines disturbed by the growing proportion of African-Americans in the inner city. The more African-Americans who voted, the more likely it was that some of them would replace the old machine Democrats in Congress, and that they would ask for a fair share of the subsidies besides. Piven and Cloward (1971) point to this problem as one of the reasons that the War on Poverty was structured by liberals and the White House to bypass local government; a pitched battle soon followed, however, and in 1967 Congress decreed that any federal money going into the city had to pass through local government.

Pinpointing the power structure of the Democratic party between 1792 and 1980 in an alliance between southerners and machine Democrats also receives support from the histories of crucial nominating conventions. It was southerners and machine Democrats who forced vice-president Henry Wallace off the Democratic ticket in 1944 and replaced him with a small-town senator from the border state of Missouri (Allen, 1950:123–36; Hinchey, 1965:19–20). In 1952 it was the Chicago machine that organized the coalition in favor of Adlai Stevenson over the liberal, integrationist senator from Tennessee, Estes Kefauver, after Kefauver scared the party by attacking organized crime in northern cities and winning a string of primaries. Part of the compromise to eliminate Kefauver involved putting southerner John Sparkman on the ticket as the vice-presidential candidate (David, Moos, and Goldman, 1954). And it was southerners and machine Democrats who insisted that Hubert Humphrey be at the top of the ticket in 1968 despite the fact that Eugene McCarthy had won numerous primaries and consistently outdistanced both Richard Nixon and Nelson Rockefeller in opinion polls. When the old party power structure lost control of the nominating process in 1972, it began the bellyaching about minorities, women, and "special interests" that has been going on ever since.

As we all know by now, the basis for domination of the Democratic party by the southern rich is disappearing gradually, contrary to what I originally predicted (Domhoff, 1972:Chapter 3). The southern economy finally was integrated with the northern economy after two centuries as a colonial economy—defined by Gavin Wright (1986) as a separate economy within a larger political entity. This integration began with New Deal agricultural support programs that pushed African-Americans off the land and mechanized agriculture (Daniel, 1984). Accelerated by the labor shortages and defense spending of World War II, these changes destroyed the separate southern economy rooted in a separate labor market and political resistance to outside capital. Southerners now actively sought industry and capital from the outside, and northern factories moved south

to avoid unionization and high wages. Then, too, the defense and space industries primed the southern pump in the fertile crescent that ran from northern
Florida to Texas. At the same time as African-Americans were moving north-
ward or into the inner cities of the South, a white suburban middle class was
developing in the new industries and in urban centers; it became the activist and
voting base for the Republican party.

The battles over civil rights and social welfare accelerated the disintegration of
the old party alliance. Gradually, elites in some southern districts turned to
supporting Republicans when House and Senate seats became available, partly
because they felt more in common with their northern counterparts, who were
now eager for states rights and defense spending, partly because they no longer
could control those Democratic primaries where African-Americans voted in
large numbers. The result is a two-party system in the South (Lamis, 1984; Black
and Black, 1987) in which African-Americans and a few white liberals make up
the new voting base of the Democratic party, while conservative whites of all
social classes tend to support the Republican party.

At long last, in the 1980s, the Democratic party was on its way to becoming
what liberals always thought it was, the party of liberals, labor, and minorities.
Hispanics, African-Americans, and Jews were the only social groups that gave a
majority of their votes to the Democrats at the presidential level in both 1984 and
1988, and union households and people who made below $12,500 a year were
the only economic categories that gave the Democrats a slight majority of their
votes in both of those elections. Sixty-three percent of white men and 56 percent
of white women, who together made up about 85 percent of those who voted in
1988, voted for the Bush–Quayle ticket, a figure that would be higher if Jewish
voters were excluded (*New York Times,* 1988:A16).

This analysis of the breakup of the North–South coalition within the Democratic party is also the primary explanation for the decline of the New Deal
coalition: the South deserted the coalition (cf. Reider, 1989). This mundane point
completely eludes Ferguson and Rogers, who focus on the multinationals, organized labor, and minorities as the heart of the coalition, and therefore as the place
to look for any decline or disintegration:

> If, as the investment perspective suggests, one looks first of all to switches in allegiances of
> organized groups and elites, then the New Deal party system could break down in only a
> limited number of ways. The peculiar coalition of the Democrats—multinational, capital-
> intensive industry and finance, organized labor, and now increasingly well-organized minor-
> ities—could disintegrate either because labor and the minorities disappeared or because the
> multinationals left the party (1986:57).

It is as if the South did not exist for Ferguson and Rogers. But both public
opinion data and studies of congressional voting patterns show that southerners
were more supportive of the New Deal coalition than any other region (Sinclair,
1982:71) until they began to undo it starting in the 1940s. From 1938 to 1972

they blocked or weakened its liberal initiatives in Congress and voted Republican in four presidential elections, even weakening the Civil Rights Act of 1964 more than most people now realize (Potter, 1972:81–84). Since 1972 they have moved into the Republican party as new social issues like abortion, busing, and school prayer join with their antiunion sentiments and virulent racism to solidify their Protestant-based conservatism. Some observers now paint the postwar years as an idyllic time of liberal ascendancy, but this is just another liberal self-deception that was more useful to the conservatives of the 1980s than it was to liberals. The southerners ruled America at the level of concern to labor, liberals, and minorities.

## Jews and Democrats

Ferguson and Rogers not only miss the role of the South and its allies during the New Deal, they are blind to the great importance of Jewish contributors to the Democrats in every large city and at the national level since the 1960s. The material base of the party is now in a religious group that gives primarily to Democrats whatever the donor's particular business sector may happen to be.

In this section I am going to marshall evidence to show that Ferguson and Rogers mistake religion for business sector in explaining Mondale's 1984 contributions. But several caveats must be registered before proceeding in order to head off potential misunderstandings. First, the only reason Jewish donors are so important to the Democrats is that most of the rich, northern gentiles have defected to the Republicans. Second, there is no mystery as to why most wealthy Jews remain Democrats, as I confirmed for myself in interviews with major Jewish donors in 1970 and 1971 (Domhoff, 1972). Not only are their family roots in the Democrats, and their community values more sympathetic toward helping the poor (Fuchs, 1956; Lipset and Raab, 1984), but they fear antisemitic Christians as well. As long as there is a fanatical evangelical and reactionary right in the Republican party, it is likely that the Jews will remain Democrats (cf. Isaacs, 1974; Cohen, 1989). Third, Jews remain Democrats in part because they do not fully trust rich gentiles. After all, those upstanding Episcopalians and Presbyterians have kept Jews out of upper-class social clubs in most cities until very recently, if any change has been made at all (Baltzell, 1964; Zweigenhaft and Domhoff, 1982). Finally, it needs to be said that not all Jewish donors give to Democrats. Twenty to 30 percent may give to Republicans in a typical election, and an even higher percentage in an atypical election where the Democratic nominee is perceived as anti-Israel, tolerant of antisemitism, or identified with the evangelical right-wing.

It is also important to note that the majority of Jews were not always Democrats. The German Jews who immigrated in the middle of the nineteenth century and prospered first as retailers were mostly Republican, unless they originally settled in the South. These Jews did not become Democrats until World War II, and some of them never switched. As for the Eastern European Jews, many of them voted Republican in the early years of the century because of Theodore Roosevelt's open immigration policy and courageous stands against antisemitism (Fuchs, 1956). Although Woodrow Wilson received a majority of Jewish votes in 1916, Jews did not become Democrats en masse and for good until 1932, when they abandoned both the Republicans and third parties. Their shift to the Democrats paralleled that of other recent urban immigrant groups (Fuchs, 1956:73–74; Mink, 1986).

In 1936, Jews in New York city joined Catholics, people with southern connections, and lawyers in differentially funding the Democrats. Webber (1990) found that 57 percent of the New York donors in his sample who were listed in *Who's Who in American Jewry* gave to the Democrats. In an analysis using names that are 95 percent likely to be those of Jews (Himmelfarb, Loar, and Mott, 1983; Larewitz, 1986), Webber found that 68 percent of New York Jewish donors favored the Democrats. However, Jews from outside New York had an equally strong preference in the other direction, favoring Republicans.

By the 1940s, as the horrors of the holocaust became more apparent and the hopes for a Jewish state greatly increased, most Jews were supporting the Democrats with their donations. Five of the eight families listed by Overacker (1945:910–911) as giving $15,000 or more to the Democrats in 1944 were Jewish. Many of the prominent Jewish donors of the next 20 years appeared as major contributors for the first time in that year. In an analysis of distinctive Jewish names, Webber discovered that the split in favor of the Democrats was 85–15 in 1944 and 70–30 in 1956.

The role of Jewish contributors within the Democratic party in the 1950s can be seen in a study of the 105 largest donors for 1952 and 1956 (Domhoff, 1967:94). Religious affiliation could be determined for 65 of these people, and 32 percent of them were Jewish.

The relative importance of gentiles and Jews in the 2 parties since 1960 can be seen in my study of those who gave $10,000 or more in 1960, 1964, and 1968. There were 60 known Republican contributors of $10,000 or more in 1960; 10 percent of those identifiable as to religion were Jewish. On the other hand, 55 percent of all identifiable Democratic donors of $10,000 or more in that year were Jewish. The percentages drops slightly for both parties in 1964: Jewish contributors made up 4 percent of 47 big Republican donors, 44 percent of 67 Democrats.

The high-water mark for Jewish involvement in Democratic campaign finance between 1944 and 1980 came in 1968, the year for which there is also extensive data for the first time thanks to the efforts of Herbert Alexander at the Citizens Research Foundation (Alexander, 1971). About 14 percent of the identifiable Republican donors of $10,000 or more were Jewish, compared to an impressive

61 percent of the knowables among 64 large donors to Humphrey. The findings are equally striking for the 43 people who lent Humphrey $5.9 million in sums ranging from $5,000 to $250,000. Twenty-two of the 43 were Jewish; among those in the group loaning Humphrey $95,000 or more, 14 of the 22 (64 percent) were Jewish.

The low point for Jewish giving to Republicans in the 1960s was 1964, when many Jewish donors deserted Goldwater because he was so extremely conservative. However, Jewish financiers and executives were not the only wealthy businesspeople who switched to the Democrats in 1964. Alexander (1971:183) analyzed the campaign contributions for members of the Business Council for the years 1956 to 1968, finding that a great majority backed Republicans in every year but 1964, when 36 gave $187,100 to the Republican and 33 gave $135,450 to Lyndon B. Johnson.*

Although it is not generally known, the most extensive efforts to link campaign donations to various sectors of the business community were made for the 1968 election (Alexander, 1971:176–87; Domhoff, 1972:Chapter 2). Looking first at those who gave $10,000 or more, Alexander found that Republicans receive far more than Democrats from insurance, oil, and manufacturing, that Democrats receive more from real estate and entertainment executives, and that the two parties do equally well in the investment, electronic, computer, and legal categories (1971:176). His study of all officers and directors of various trade associations, industrial corporations, oil companies, and defense companies showed that the top companies in these sectors gave overwhelmingly to Republicans. This finding holds for 1956, 1960, and 1972 as well, with an occasional exception such as is caused when a southern corporate lawyer gives $15,000 to his son's Democratic senatorial campaign (Alexander, 1976:108–12). In 1964, reflecting the general business defection from Goldwater, Democrats received slightly more than Republicans from these groups as a whole.

Similarly, I looked up the officers and directors of dozens of firms on campaign contribution lists for 1968, and searched out the corporate connections of donors of $500 or more in biographical dictionaries. I was expressly interested to learn if Wall Street investment bankers who gave to Democrats tended to do business with other checkbook Democrats, and especially with southerners. I also interviewed 75 people either in person or by telephone to determine who the biggest fund-raisers were in major cities and to see if they shared business connections with the donors that appeared in official records. Finally, I sent a questionnaire to political reporters at several newspapers in the South to uncover possible donors who did not appear on official lists.

When all was said and done, I had only a few differentiating factors. One was region, with the southerners still Democrats in 1970 despite a strong tendency to

*The Business Advisory Council changed its name to Business Council in the early 1960s.

support Republicans at the national level. Another was ethnicity, with Jews and Catholics favoring Democrats, which mirrored the well-known voting statistics of the 1960s (e.g., Hamilton, 1972). A third factor was liberality: there were a few rich Protestants with very liberal views whom I could only define as mavericks because they had no business connections among themselves nor with other Democratic donors.

Any relationship between ethnic or regional factors and business groups or business sectors was very weak. Many of the Wall Street investment bankers who backed the Democrats did come from the investment banks started by Jews (Supple, 1957; Wise, 1957, 1963, 1968; Carosso, 1970). However, there were Republicans in all these firms as well, including several gentiles who had become partners. What differentiated these investment firms from the non-Jewish ones was that the latter were almost entirely Republican—and still completely gentile at the time.

I did find through a study of interlocking directorates and stock offerings that the investment banks with Jewish origins had business ties to some Jews and Texans who were Democrats. But I also found gentile Democrats in the South and Texas who did business with Republican gentiles in the North. None of the people I interviewed thought there were any parts of the corporate community that were particularly Democratic. Put another way, I once tried to support a theory along the lines of the one proposed by Ferguson and Rogers, but I could find no evidence for it.

The dramatic difference between gentile and Jewish businesspeople in their support for the Republican and Democratic parties also can be seen by studying the donations of those who belong to exclusive gentile and Jewish social clubs. For example, only 5 of 159 donors from the all-gentile California Club in Los Angeles gave to Democrats in 1968. The situation was the same at two similar clubs for which I had membership lists at the time, the Pacific Union in San Francisco, where only 5 of 89 donors gave to Democrats, and the Detroit Club in Detroit, where 5 of 110 gave to Democrats. Since there is every reason to believe that these clubs include a cross section of the entire business community, it is hard to see how a Democratically oriented business sector could exist.

By way of contrast, Jewish clubs contained both Democratic and Republican donors. Within the Harmonie Club in New York, the oldest of Jewish men's clubs in the country, with a very strong contingent of German Jews, there were 36 Republican and 36 Democrat donors. At the Standard Club, the Harmonie's equivalent in Chicago, but with fewer German Jews, there were 23 members who gave to the Democrats and 11 who gave to the Republicans.*

---

*In 1965 a wealthy Jewish scion of the Macy family, R. Peter Straus, who was working as a strategist for Robert F. Kennedy, criticized Kennedy in-law Stephen Smith for staying at a club "which is known to discriminate against Jewish people." In 1968, when Smith flew into Chicago to discuss a last-minute draft of Teddy Kennedy, he judiciously set up his headquarters at the Standard Club.

Perhaps the best indication of the political inclinations of successful Jewish businesspeople whatever their business sector can be seen in the donations of the delegates and governors of the American Jewish Committee, the most prestigious Jewish organization in the country. In 1968, 43 delegates and governors gave to the Democrats, 27 gave to the Republicans. Four gave to both parties, and almost all of them gave to Republican Senator Jacob Javits of New York, at the time the most prominent Jewish elected official in the country.

Just as the overwhelmingly Republican donations from members of gentile social clubs militate against any claims about some business sectors being more Democratic, so too do declines in Jewish support for Democratic presidential candidates in some election years deny that economic self-interest could be affecting their giving. In 1972, for example, many Jews were very disturbed by McGovern's views on Israel. According to Isaacs (1974:1), he lost the support of most traditional Jewish supporters of the party when he gave the wrong answers about Israel at a meeting in New York with major Jewish fund-raisers.

The differences in Jewish donation patterns between 1980 and 1984 also argue against an economic interpretation of their political preferences. In a study of over 500 donors with distinctive Jewish names, we found that in 1980, 63 percent favored Democrats, 28 percent favored Republicans, 6 percent favored Anderson, and 3 percent gave to both Republicans and Democrats. However, in 1984, 88 percent gave only to Democrats, 10 percent gave to Reagan, 1 percent gave to third parties, and 1 percent gave to both Democrats and Republicans.

It seems highly unlikely that the economic interests of 25 percent of Jewish donors would change as dramatically as their donations changed in the space of four years. It seems more likely from exit polls of Jewish voters that the retirement of the evangelical southerner, Jimmy Carter, along with the increasing identification of Ronald Reagan with the evangelical right, led Jewish donors to support Walter Mondale, a person whose civil rights record and cultural pluralism made him very attractive to Jews (Lipset and Raab, 1984:408). This interpretation is reinforced by other findings on differences between Jewish and Christian voters. Jews were much more likely to be concerned about the separation of church and state, to support civil rights legislation, to support welfare spending, and to oppose military spending. More generally, a wide range of findings showing that affluent Jews have more liberal social and political attitudes than their Protestant counterparts weighs against an economistic interpretation of their campaign finance donations (Cohen, 1989). This is especially so, as we will see, when their gentile counterparts in the same businesses are giving to Republicans.

It is in this context, then, that we should look at the few pieces of evidence that Ferguson and Rogers present for their interpretation of Democratic party financing in 1984. They first provide a list of 25 big supporters from businesses like investment banking that are said to be "natural opponents of Reaganism" (1986:163–64). Thirteen of the 25 people are of Jewish background. This includes 9 of the 11 investment bankers. Since there is good reason to believe that there are more Jews in investment banking than most other businesses because of antisemitism in large corporations, there is thus the possibility that the sectors allegedly inimical to Reagan are in reality merely those with more Jews in them.

Ferguson and Rogers present more systematic data on 1984 in their appendix. Indeed, it is the only systematic data in the entire book, so much is riding on the analysis. They studied hundreds of real estate developers, investment bankers, and corporate executives in industrial and service corporations. Overall, only 26 percent of these people gave to Democrats, and in most sectors "comparatively few major investors contributed anything to the Democratic Party" (1984:224). However, 36 percent of the investment bankers and 52 percent of the real estate developers gave to Democrats. Obviously, investment banking and real estate will be the focus of my attention.

Ferguson and Rogers point out that there were problems in doing their study of investment bankers. They decided to study only the top 4 partners in the 20 largest firms, but they often had trouble determining who the top partners actually were (1984:223). Because many of these firms have dozens of partners, this is a very inadequate sample of investment bankers. Fortunately, the basis for a much more complete study of the donations of individual investment bankers has been provided by Public Data Access, an organization that painstakingly matched government data on election donations with the officers and partners of 700 firms in business, accounting, and law.

When I compiled the figures provided by Public Data Access for Democratic and Republican donors from the investment firms, a very different pattern emerged than what might be expected from reading Ferguson and Rogers: There are great variations from firm to firm in the percentage of Democratic and Republican contributors. Unless there are very subtle distinctions within the investment banking community that Ferguson and Rogers did not mention, such variations refute the notion that investment banking as a whole is a natural opponent of Reaganism. For example, Ferguson and Rogers mention Richard Fisher of Morgan, Stanley as a Democratic contributor, but my analysis shows that 19 of the other 21 members of Morgan, Stanley who gave individually at the presidential level gave to Reagan–Bush. Conversely, the early 1980s incarnation of the venerable German-Jewish investment banking firm of Lehman Brothers had three partners who were considered major Democratic fund-raisers and supporters by Ferguson and Rogers. In this case, 36 of the 42 partners who gave individually did support Mondale or one of the other Democrats, with only 5 giving to Republicans and 1 giving to both parties.

Still another pattern emerged with Goldman, Sachs, a German-Jewish firm of the past once very close to Lehman Brothers, but since gone its separate way. The dominant partner in the firm in the 1930s was Sidney Weinberg, often claimed to be a major Democratic fund-raiser of the era. Although one of the two present comanagers of the firm is John L. Weinberg, one of Sidney's sons, the firm now probably has as many gentile as Jewish members. It is of special interest here because Ferguson and Rogers identify Weinberg as a Democratic supporter and add that another partner, Robert L. Rubin, raised $1.8 million for the Democrats in 1984 (1986:164). This surely gives the impression that Goldman, Sachs is a "Democratic" firm.

The data from Public Data suggest three problems with the Ferguson and Rogers analysis. First, 32 of the 51 partners who gave individually gave exclusively to Reagan–Bush—5 gave to both parties, and 14 gave only to Democrats. Second, John L. Weinberg is listed as giving to Reagan–Bush, not the Democrats. His brother, Sidney Weinberg, Jr., another partner, did give to Democrat John Glenn, but then he gave to Reagan–Bush as well. Third, the comanaging partner with John Weinberg, John C. Whitehead, by far the largest donor in the firm to all Republicans, was serving as the undersecretary of state at the time. One may wonder what a natural opponent of Reaganism was doing in such an important government position. And how come Robert Rubin did not hit up his partners for more of the $1.8 million he purportedly raised if common economic issues are so crucial?

I quizzed Rubin about these matters in a brief telephone interview on August 24, 1989. I asked him if he thought investment bankers were natural opponents of Reaganism; he replied that investment bankers were natural friends of Reaganism. I asked him if the debt was bad for investment bankers. He said that the debt was good for investment bankers, but bad for the economy. I asked him if John Weinberg was a supporter of Democrats, and he said no. I asked him why Sidney Weinberg, Jr., had given to the Democrats as well as the Republicans, and he said it was probably because somebody asked him, meaning that he was being polite to a Democratic friend by writing a check for a mere $1,000. I asked him why he is a Democrat, and he responded that he is comfortable in the middle of the spectrum as a general social viewpoint. I asked him if he had raised $1.8 million for Mondale and if so, did he raise the money from people with common economic interests. He replied that he and his friends probably ended up raising much more than $1.8 million, and that he raised money from people with common political views, only some of whom were close business friends. Perhaps I am naive and Rubin is putting me on, but the variability in donation patterns from investment firm to investment firm and the large number of Republicans at his own firm fit better with his analysis than that by Ferguson and Rogers.

The general findings on investment banking firms from the Public Data Access data are presented in the table below. The table ranks the firms by the percentage of all firm donors who gave exclusively to one or more of the Democratic presidential candidates. The firms founded by gentiles are asterisked; the others

| Democrat Percentage | Firm | Democrats | Both Parties | Republicans |
|---|---|---|---|---|
| 100 | E. M. Warburg Pincus | 6 | 0 | 0 |
| 100 | Hambrecht & Quist* | 3 | 0 | 0 |
| 96 | Salomon Brothers | 26 | 1 | 0 |
| 92 | Allen & Co. | 22 | 1 | 1 |
| 86 | Lehman Kuhn Loeb (Shearson Lehman Hutton) | 36 | 1 | 5 |
| 77 | Prudential-Bache | 23 | 2 | 5 |
| 75 | Oppenheimer & Co. | 9 | 1 | 2 |
| 75 | Paine, Webber* | 9 | 0 | 3 |
| 71 | LF Rothschild Unterberg Towbin | 15 | 1 | 5 |
| 70 | First Boston* | 7 | 0 | 3 |
| 67 | Wertheim & Co. | 6 | 0 | 3 |
| 59 | Bear, Stearns | 17 | 5 | 7 |
| 57 | Donaldson Lufkin Jenrette* | 16 | 1 | 11 |
| 50 | Lazard Freres | 5 | 2 | 3 |
| 50 | Kidder Peabody* | 14 | 0 | 14 |
| 50 | William Blair & Co.* | 11 | 0 | 11 |
| 45 | Merrill Lynch* | 15 | 0 | 18 |
| 42 | Dean Witter Reynolds* | 5 | 0 | 7 |
| 37 | EF Hutton* | 10 | 1 | 16 |
| 36 | Drexel Burnham Lambert* | 8 | 2 | 14 |
| 27 | Goldman Sachs | 14 | 5 | 32 |
| 20 | Brown Brothers Harriman* | 1 | 0 | 4 |
| 18 | Smith Barney Harris Upham* | 2 | 0 | 9 |
| 12 | Morgan Stanley* | 3 | 0 | 19 |
| 9 | Dillon Read* | 1 | 0 | 10 |

were created by Jews. The table shows that the gentile-founded firms are more likely to have Republican supporters.

The real estate people in the Ferguson and Rogers analysis were taken from the 1984 *Forbes* list of the 400 wealthiest Americans. There were 71 people in all. Since they are the only group where a majority—52 percent—gave to Democrats, they seem to be a particularly interesting group for comparing Ferguson and Rogers's analysis with mine. I therefore restudied these people, finding 42 of them listed as donors on the final records of the Federal Election Commission (available to one and all on microfilm at a very nominal fee). Of the 26 Democratic donors, 20 are Jewish; 4 of the other 6 are either southerners or Catholics. Of the 20 Republican donors, 12 are gentiles and eight are Jewish. When those people who gave to both parties are put in a separate category, the findings look like this:

| | Contribution to | | |
|---|---|---|---|
| Religion | Democrats | Both Parties | Republicans |
| Jewish | 16 | 4 | 4 |
| Christian | 6 | 0 | 12 |

It seems pretty clear to me what these findings reveal. The real estate business looks like it is a "natural opponent" of Reaganism only because there are more Jews in it, not because there is some economic reason for real estate developers to be natural opponents of Reaganism.

Although anything from this point on for the 1984 election is anticlimactic, the Public Data Access compilation does allow us to do further analyses. For instance, we can look for those companies where a great many officers or partners gave primarily to Democratic candidates at the federal, state, or district levels. There are dozens of such companies, but most of them are small except for a few movie and television companies, and many of them are southern companies giving to one or two candidates in their home state. Such an analysis also turns up the one part of the corporate community that has a majority of Democratic donors to candidates at all levels of government—law firms. Moreover, many of these law firms are exclusively Democratic in their donations.

Democratic law firms and Democratic partners in other law firms are part of the answer to those who might wonder how the predominantly Republican corporations keep in direct contact with elected Democrats—they hire Democratic lawyers to deliver their messages. Many of these lawyers are people of middle-class origins who came to Washington as part of a Democratic administration or as an aide to a congressperson, then stayed on to use their background with a regulatory agency, executive department, or congressional committee as a way to attract corporate clients (cf. Auerbach, 1976; Irons, 1982). In some cases these lawyers are making their fortunes by helping corporations circumvent the very laws or regulations they wrote while serving in government.

In my earlier study of the Democrats I found that Washington lawyers played a far larger role as Democratic fund-raisers and contributors than did Wall Street lawyers, who tended to be Republicans. By 1984, however, there were Democratic donors in just about all the top Wall Street firms. In that sense, some things do change a little bit. But the role of lawyers in Democratic finances is a very old story; Overacker wrote that lawyers are "usually more Democratic than Republican," and that this was true in 1936 as well (1937:488–89).

In my view, the big role of corporate lawyers in both parties helps render party identification meaningless when it comes to the day-to-day business issues of the corporate community. As all my interviews with such lawyers made clear in 1970, business comes first, and there are few compunctions about undertaking problematic cases for clients of a different political persuasion. Clark Clifford, Truman's right-hand man in the 1940s, and a secretary of defense under Johnson, was happy to make a million dollars helping the reactionary du Ponts steer a special capital-gains law through Congress. The law saved them tens of millions of dollars in taxes when they were forced to divest themselves of General Motors stock. One of the most famous of New Deal lawyers, Thomas Corcoran, became one of the most highly paid and notorious lobbyists in Washington after his government days were over (Zalaznick, 1969; Pearson and Anderson, 1968; Goulden, 1971).

To put it gently, I think my many findings on 1984 add up to a disaster for the economistic analysis presented by Ferguson and Rogers. There are no "Democratic" business sectors unless you want to count law firms, and there do not seem to be any economic factors that could lead a majority of the Jews in different business sectors to be Democrats and a majority of the gentiles to be Republicans. This in turns supports the idea that many investors in the two parties have other motives in addition to economic ones. Thus, I find myself in agreement with the conclusions of Alexander (1971, 1976, 1983, 1987), whose work on campaign finance, little used by Ferguson and Rogers, provides the soundest foundation for theorizing on this issue. Alexander has shown that some Republican business contributors will switch their financial support and prestige to a Johnson over a Goldwater when centrist policy arrangements are challenged in a context of social turmoil, and that Democratic business donors will prefer a Nixon over a very liberal McGovern, especially when some of them also are Jews who are not happy with McGovern's stance on Israel. However, he emphasizes that the motives for individual support of candidates often include social issues, status needs, or the desire for personal involvement in the political process as well as strictly economic ones. In the case of recently rich donors, who are a significant number in both parties, albeit from very different regional and religious backgrounds for each party, he suggests that they are often buying themselves into the "political register" as a substitute for inclusion in the "social register" (Isaacs, 1974:125, 138; Alexander, 1976:80).

Once "extremist" candidates are eliminated, then, other motives may come into play for campaign donors. Some seek appointments in government. Some seek glory for region or religion. Others are looking for a little excitement. Still others want to help out an old friend running for office. Contrary to the groaning I can hear from economistic and structuralist readers at this point, there is no necessary contradiction between personal motives and the functioning of the capitalist system. Businessmen are going to think like businessmen on business issues whatever their motives for being Democrats or Republicans.

In conclusion, I want to stress that my alternative analysis of the material basis of the Democratic party does not deny the great importance that Ferguson and

Rogers give to campaign finance in the electoral process. In that sense I am firmly in their camp in opposition to pluralists and state-centric theorists even though I do not share their economism. Further, my analysis does not deny that business donors to both parties fight for probusiness policies, reflecting their shared consensus on certain fundamentals of the capitalist system. Nor does my analysis downplay the role of foundations, policy-discussion groups, and think tanks in shaping policies for both parties; it merely says that they are not part of either political party.

More generally, I am saying that campaign finance and parties are only a part of the story of how a power elite rooted in a segmented capitalist class dominates government in the United States. Things are not as simple and straightforward when it comes to money and policies as Ferguson and Rogers imply, and there are times when the underlying population has more influence on policies than their theory allows. One of those times was the 1960s, and it is to the great importance of the rise and fall of militancy in explaining the Reagan ascendancy that I will turn in the final chapter.

# 10

## THE DECLINE OF DISRUPTION AND THE
## RETURN OF CONSERVATISM

Political sociologists and corporate-liberal historians of the 1960s and 1970s struggled to explain the mildly reformist tendencies within the power elite during the Progressive Era and the New Deal. But suddenly a new problem emerged in the 1980s: explaining the conservative policy changes that produced tax cuts for the rich and cuts in income and social benefits for at least the bottom 40 percent of the income ladder. This unexpected turn of events provided new opportunities for journalists and political scientists to try out new ideas, but great difficulties for structural Marxists and state autonomy theorists, who are not used to capitalists so blatantly taking charge of the state and trying to shrink parts of it.

At first glance many liberal commentators divined a right-wing takeover by a counterestablishment. This counterestablishment was said to be based in cleverly marketed ideas and large amounts of money from Sunbelt parvenues who feel snubbed by the eastern establishment. In a typical statement of this kind of view, Sidney Blumenthal claims that these counterestablishmentarians are economic egotists who lack "both the patrician heritage of noblesse oblige and the managerial instinct for conformity" (1986:56), a characterization that both idealizes the eastern rich, who are as money-grubbing as anyone else under a thin veneer, and underestimates the Sunbelt rich, who are as likely to be from old money as the easterners and to go to eastern prep schools or Ivy League colleges as they are to go to schools (usually private) in their home region.

Moreover, these cowboys from the Southwest and West supposedly set up a series of think tanks, such as the Heritage Foundation, that soon had a major influence on policy, pushing aside the old-line policy organizations like the Brookings Institution. They then financed their man Ronald Reagan into the presidency, where he ruled with the help of his nouveau-rich California kitchen cabinet and right-wing ideologues.

But this superficially plausible theory turned out to have major problems. It became clear, for example, that traditional think tanks such as the Brookings Institution had changed to a more conservative tune in 1975 and 1976, long before the right-wingers had a chance to pressure them (Peschek, 1987:134–35, 170–75). One of the newly conservative experts from Brookings, Charles

Schultze, chaired the CEA under Carter. Problems also were created for the cowboy capitalist theory by the fact that the CED began its right turn in the mid-1970s as well, producing conservative documents that anticipated most of the Reagan program (Dye, 1984:250–51). Four top CED leaders later testified before Congress for Reagan's tax-reduction program. Then, too, a member of the CED's anti-inflation subcommittee, Donald Reagan, became Reagan's secretary of treasury even though he was president of Merrill Lynch on Wall Street (CED, 1979). A member of the CED's Research Advisory Board, Martin Feldstein, became chair of Reagan's CEA at one point, even though he was from Harvard University and the old-line National Bureau of Economic Research (CED, 1980).

Nor did the people who were central to the Reagan campaign fit the cowboy theory, for too many of them were from major industries in all parts of the country (Ferguson and Rogers, 1981). Most important of all, the selection of the internationalist George Bush for vice-president—eastern preppie, Yalie, Texas oil man, member of both the Council on Foreign Relations and the Trilateral Commission—was a clear signal that Reagan did not intend to battle centrist business leaders in the way Barry Goldwater did in 1964 by picking a right-wing running mate and triggering a massive defection to Johnson. Early studies of Reagan appointees also belied the Blumenthal-type theory (Sklar and Lawrence, 1981; Brownstein and Easton, 1982), and a later systematic study of virtually everyone involved in the rise of the New Right think tanks said to shape Reagan's thinking showed that business leaders from all over the country, many of them connected to centrist policy-planning organizations as well, were the major supporters (Jenkins and Shumate, 1985). Even the kitchen cabinet in Los Angeles turned out to include wealthy people from the eastern part of the upper class—e.g., Alfred Bloomingdale of New York's Bloomingdale's Department Stores, William French Smith of an old New England family and Harvard, and Justin Dart, who went to prep school in Pennsylvania, married the boss's daughter at Walgreen Drugs on the way to the top at Rexall Drugs, and only later moved to California.

Rather clearly, then, what is needed is a theory that explains why the sophisticated conservatives decided to join the practical conservatives in a more right-wing stance. Two plausible possibilities are offered by *Washington Post* journalist Thomas Edsall (1984) and political scientist David Vogel (1989), whose work will be the primary object of my critical attention in this chapter, along with a few comments on Ferguson and Rogers's (1986) right-turn theory outlined in the previous chapter. Both Edsall and Vogel see a good part of the answer in the fact that an aroused business community finally got itself together in the middle 1970s. It learned how to lobby and use think tanks after being pushed around and actually defeated on numerous occasions in the late 1960s and early 1970s by antibusiness liberals and Democrats. There are also differences in their viewpoints, however, that are crucial.

For Edsall, the resurgence of big business was as much political as economic.

Politics and economics are "irrevocably linked," and changes in the political arena can have as much effect on economic policies as economic changes have on politics (1984:35). Edsall's rejection of a strictly economic explanation can be seen in the brief explanation he gives for the liberalism of the 1960s: "Just as the shift to the left in public policy in the early 1960s resulted from fundamental alterations in the balance of power—ranging from rapid postwar economic growth, to the cohesiveness of the liberal-labor coalition, to the political vitality of the civil rights movement—the shift to the right over the past decade has resulted from complex, systematic alterations in the terms of the political and economic debate and in the power of those participating in the debate" (1984:15).

Edsall believes that the rise of conservatism was made possible by problems within the Democratic party, which up until then "loosely functioned as the representative of those on the bottom half of the economic spectrum" (1984:24). He sees the dissolution of the party as due to a number of factors, including the decline in organized labor and in voting turnout by low-income people, but the heart of the matter is that young liberal elites shaped by events in the 1960s gained a disproportionate share of party power through open primaries and other procedural reforms. These liberal elites of the upper middle class do not have the same sympathy as the machine leaders did for the symbolic and substantive issues of concern to the voting base of the party. They tend to pick safe issues and cater to the middle class, but all they end up doing is alienating old-style Democrats. The fact that the labor movement has been more or less hostile to the civil rights, environmental, and women's movements also helped to destroy the cohesiveness of the party.

However, the problems of the Democratic party are not the whole story. At the same time as that party was sinking, the Republican party was transformed and unified because the revitalized business community and the New Right decided they shared enough in common to work together harmoniously. The economic problems of the 1970s and the dissension among the Democrats gave the reorganized Republicans the opening they needed.

Things are much more simple and straightforward in Vogel's view. For Vogel, changes in the public's "perception" of the long-term health of the economy explain the "fluctuating fortunes" of business (1989:8, 228, 290). When the economy is strong, as it was from 1961 through 1973, the strength of business actually declines because people are more willing to see it taxed and regulated. When the economy is weak or suffering from high inflation, as it was during most of the years between 1974 and 1982, in good part for the reasons suggested by Ferguson and Rogers (1986), then the power of business increases because people side with it against consumer activists, environmentalists, and government regulators. Vogel (1989:8, 11) expressly denies that these perceptions are related to the business cycle.

Although there is at least a little something that can be said for all of these arguments by Edsall and Vogel, I do not think any of them go to the heart of the matter. However, most of my criticism will be directed at Vogel's theory because it incorrectly sees business as highly disorganized in the 1960s, vastly exaggerates any "defeats" suffered by business, and leaves out class conflict, the conservative coalition, and the New Right. Before demonstrating these points in detail, I will offer a rival theory that will be used as the comparison point in my critique of the inadequacies of Edsall and Vogel.


## Disruption and Power

Given the power structure of the Democratic party, the veto power of the conservative coalition in Congress, and the overall power of the internationalist segment of the capitalist class, the primary task is not to explain the return of conservatism. Instead, the real problem is to explain how a basically conservative, business-dominated country without strong unions or a social democratic party could generate some liberal legislation and wage increases between 1965 and 1974 in the first place.

The arguments and evidence I have presented in previous chapters suggest that there usually are very narrow limits to what can be accomplished by poor people, minorities, trade unionists, and liberals through elections and the legislative process. The costs of running for office are enormous for average people in terms of time and money, and the impediments to change built into the legislative process make it very hard to sustain a pressure-group coalition or legislative social movement that does not have a great amount of money and patience.

But if average people have very little power through voting or lobbying, at least when things are quiet, they do have power when they disrupt the system, when labor markets are tight, or when the country is at war. Only in such circumstances, I would argue, do the leaders from any segment of the ruling class pay any attention to the social problems that are everywhere apparent through social statistics, sensational newspaper accounts, or encounters with people suffering from homelessness, discrimination, or poverty. This is not a theory that will be welcomed by *Washington Post* liberals like Edsall, nor by business school professors like Vogel, who think of political power primarily in terms of voting, letter writing, campaign finance, and lobbying. But it is the only one that can explain why liberals, labor, and minorities, despite their great numbers, never win much against the conservative coalition unless there is a fear of disruption and violence loose in the land due to the actions of strikers, civil rights demonstrators, angry rioters in northern ghettos, or students demonstrating against wars.

There are many different factors that can trigger social protest, but they share in common a loosening or breaking of the institutional framework that usually keeps most people involved in everyday routines. Sometimes the failure is economic, as in a depression, dislodging people from their jobs and making them more amenable to joining social movements. At other times an old power struc-ture is in the process of change or decline, or previously oppressed people have been able to alter gradually their life circumstances, as was the case shortly before the disruptive phase of the civil rights movement began with sit-ins in 1960. Whatever the cause, however, I am asserting that social disruption, whether violent or nonviolent, is an essential factor in any successful challenge to the power structure in the United States (cf. Flacks, 1988).

Essential, but not sufficient. Mainstream theorists will rush forward to assert that disruption is not enough for other than short-term or symbolic victories, and it is true that the turmoil must lead to increased voter turnout or changes in voting patterns, or else there have to be enough liberals who are already inside the government to bring about legislative remedies. All of these factors played a role in breaching conservative bulwarks in 1934 and 1964, years when social unrest brought large numbers of liberals into office.

I am not asserting that this formula for social change holds for all times and all places. For example, the pattern may be different in countries where most work-ers are organized into unions, have their own political party, and are able to develop alliances with farmers. In the United States, however, the two-party system and the conservative coalition make social change through normal pol-icies almost impossible. The system is structured in such a way that militant social movements and other forms of disruption are the only ways for most people to have any effect (cf. Lipset, 1963).

The highly original work of Frances Piven and Richard Cloward (1971) on the expansion and contraction of welfare rolls and relief work is one powerful piece of evidence for this type of theory. They show that throughout the history of capitalism there has been no government response to growing unemployment until there is disruption or fear of disruption; then the government support is taken away as soon as the turmoil subsides. They also show (1971:Chapter 3) that a fear of disruption clearly motivated the temporary work programs of the New Deal, which were quickly closed down when the danger of disruption passed and then stigmatized as worthless and morally corrupting even though their accomplishments were in fact very great with a minimum of featherbed-ding. Quantitative studies of relief spending at the national level for 1947 to 1977 support Piven and Cloward's claims (Isaac and Kelly, 1981; Schrau and Turbett, 1983; Hicks and Swank, 1983; Swank and Hicks, 1984). In addition, quan-titative studies linking ghetto riots to urban expenditures on social problems also show that disruption increased government responsiveness (Welch, 1975; Friedland, 1982). More generally, the effectiveness of disruption in American social protest is demonstrated in the work by William Gamson (1975), and in studies summarized by Alford and Friedland (1975).

The correlation between disruption and amelioration is not perfect. There are "mediating" factors that can muffle the effect of disruption or continue the reforms for some time after the protests have subsided. However, what these studies show is that mere "need" is not enough to gain a response. Nor is routine party involvement or lobbying adequate. Beneath the benign surface and smooth words that encase American politics, there is a power structure, and power structures are not moved by kindness or arguments.

It is this general argument that explains any liberal gains that were made in the late 1960s and early 1970s. More specifically, these gains were triggered by the unexpected, noneconomic social disruptions that started with the civil rights movement and then spread to northern university campuses, northern ghettos, other minorities, antiwar activists, consumer activists, and many others. Economic conditions do not explain the civil rights struggles, ghetto uprisings, or antiwar protests; instead, these protests, rooted in the loosening or weakening of power structures, made possible whatever victories were won in Congress by liberals, environmentalists, and consumer activists.

Vogel comes close to this explanation in discussing the rise of the consumer movement. He rightly notes that its leaders drew their inspiration from the civil rights movement, and that many of them had participated in it (1989:100). However, he does not emphasize that the civil rights movement and stirrings in the northern ghettos also created the social climate in which the consumer leaders operated. Nor does he stress that the civil rights movement, combined with a fear of Goldwater's views on social security and states rights, was the basis for the election of a liberal Congress in 1964 that made it possible for consumer legislation to gain a hearing. Edsall's earlier-quoted comment on the "political vitality" of the civil rights movement as one factor in the rise of liberalism in the 1960s also approaches the point I am making, but it doesn't go far enough unless it is a euphemism for social disruption.

But social disruption is not the sole explanation for the liberal gains of the late 1960s and early 1970s. Tight labor markets caused by economic growth and the Vietnam War generated the kind of direct conflict between capital and labor over economic issues that Marxists emphasize. Capital and its power elite were restrained in this battle because of their overarching desire to maintain "hard hat" and union support for a war that was being challenged as illegitimate by students, liberals, and, finally, American soldiers on the battlefields. Civil rights leaders also began to speak against the war, most notably the Student Non-Violent Coordinating Committee and Martin Luther King, greatly upsetting some of their supporters within the power elite. The power elite's need for patriotic support of the war between 1967 and 1971, so pervasive, taken for granted, and palpable at the time, barely surfaces in the explanatory apparatus of the theorists I am challenging. It is as if the war has been forgotten. The arguments over tax increases and business-related legislation in the late 1960s apparently happened in a vacuum surrounded by an expanding economy.

Just as social disruption made liberal reforms possible, so too did the decline in disruption make the return of conservatism possible (cf. Jenkins and Shumate, 1985). There were many reasons for this decline, including debilitating conflicts within some of the movements and between the movements. Repression and harassment by the government also played a role at a certain point. However, the main reason the social movements declined is that their victories made it possible for the protesters to resume their everyday lives (Flacks, 1988). Civil rights victories meant that large numbers of African-Americans and other minorities could enter college, take part in the normal routines of the society, and obtain middle-class jobs, particularly with governmental agencies. The end of the draft and then the winding down of the war meant that young adult males could go about their business again without fear of facing injury or death in Southeast Asia. Antiwar liberals could heave a sigh of relief and turn to more routinized causes. The women who fought for expanded rights went to law school, medical school, and business school in far greater numbers than at any time in the past. Only African-Americans in the ghettos fell far short of their goals, but even some of them received something for a short time, as noted earlier in this section.

But the point is this: The decline in disruption made it possible for conservatives to take the offensive again and for the conservative coalition to assert itself in Congress on a wide range of issues. The conservative rewriting of history also got underway. Liberal programs supported by foundations and the government were mere "experiments" that were created because (1) professors wanted to try out their ideas, and (2) there was plenty of money floating around. The fear was gone, so now the lies could begin.

The return of conservatism was facilitated by the concurrent rise of a New Right that was a reaction to the civil rights and social freedoms that had been won by minorities, women, gays, and liberals. Affirmative action and abortion came to be the symbols of all that is wrong with the United States for a militant minority of devout Catholics and fundamentalist Protestants (e.g., Luker, 1984; Vidich, 1987). Their highly visible activities caused problems for some of the social movements, such as women and gays, who were taken aback or demoralized by the attacks on them. The efforts of the New Right also facilitated the process by which average southern whites left the Democratic party, now portrayed by the New Right as antireligious, antifamily, and antiwhite (cf. Himmelstein, 1989).

The role of the New Right has been vastly exaggerated by the New Right and by theorists of postindustrial society, as Jerome Himmelstein and James McCrae (1984) demonstrate. Fundamentalists did not make the difference in the 1980 election (Johnson and Taney, 1982; Himmelstein and McCrae, 1984). However, I agree with Arthur Vidich (1987) that such people had a big part in shaping the new political climate of the 1970s and 1980s. Then, too, the 5–6 percent of the population who identify closely with evangelical movements did have an 83 percent turnout rate in 1980 and favored Reagan 86–14, providing about 10 percent of his total vote (Brudney and Copeland, 1984). Furthermore, it is possible that they made a difference in some elections below the presidential level in the 1970s as activists who helped energize the Republican party and its supporters (Himmelstein, 1989). This social dynamism of the New Right is missed by Ferguson and Rogers (1986:Chapter 1) when they use the stability of public opinion on most issues over the past 15 years to argue that the general public did not play a role in the right turn.

In this context, helped along by the return of patriotic fervor in reaction to the Iranian hostage crisis, the sophisticated conservatives within the power elite could joint the conservative coalition in a "new class war" to undercut the improved social wage that had been won while the power elite was on the defensive (Piven and Cloward, 1982/85). The decline in the social wage, along with high interest rates, an oil glut, and frontal attacks on unions whose patriotism was no longer needed, made it possible to control inflation and individual wages after nearly 14 years of failure on one or the other. Unemployment rose to its highest levels since the 1930s, and the number of people on the streets reached crisis proportions, but nothing was done for those in need because there was no large-scale spontaneous or organized disruption. Even the few social protests that occurred had become routinized and expected, causing no serious problems for the police and courts.

In the remainder of this chapter I will attempt to demonstrate the superiority of this theory over rival interpretations in a number of ways. First I will show that the corporate community was fully ready and mobilized during the 1960s, contrary to Edsall and Vogel, thereby eliminating one of the alternative explanations. Then I will discuss the alleged "defeats" of business that are chronicled by Edsall and Vogel, showing how minor most of them were, if they can be called defeats at all, and how social disruption and tight labor markets provide a better explanation for what happened than optimism about the economy and pressure from consumer groups. Finally, I will demonstrate that the same old conservative coalition was at the heart of the counterattack that is still stomping on all workers in the United States, thereby increasing class hatred and despair.

## Was Business Disorganized?

Edsall and Vogel set up their arguments by claiming that the business community was not very coordinated and active before 1970. Edsall says that the business community became "politicized" in the 1970s, gaining influence it hadn't enjoyed since the 1920s (1984:107). It "refined its ability to act as a class" (1984:128). Moreover, it did this against "devastating odds" because it had been discredited by its involvement in Watergate and faced a "reform-minded Democratic party" that was ascendant in Congress and friendly to the consumer and environmental movements (1984:107).

Vogel's discussion of the ineffectiveness of business prior to the 1970s is much like Edsall's (1984) and Blumenthal's (1986) before him. Indeed, he even recycles many of the same statements in the business press from business leaders, lobbyists, and congressional aides. First there is the quote from John Harper of Alcoa, a trustee of the CED and the Business Council since the 1960s, but nonetheless claiming that business was not very involved or effective before he and his buddies started the Business Roundtable:

> We were not involved. What we were doing wasn't working. All the polls showed business was in disfavor. . . . We were getting short shrift from Congress. I thought we were powerless in spite of all the stories of how we could manipulate everything (Blumenthal, 1986:77; Vogel, 1989:194).

Then there is the interview with Bryce Harlow, the ultimate insider who came to Washington with Eisenhower and became a lobbyist for Proctor and Gamble. Speaking of the months before the Congress elected in 1974 went into action, he recalled that: "The danger had suddenly escalated. We had to prevent business from being rolled up and put in the trash can by that Congress" (Edsall, 1984:113–14; Vogel, 1989:194). And to demonstrate the new coordination among business groups, someone who knows nothing about the history of lobbying is quoted by Vogel as follows in celebration of the defeat of legislation for a Consumer Protection Agency early in 1978:

> For the first time in history you had 'The coalition': National Association of Manufacturers, Grocery Manufacturers of America, the U.S. Chamber of Commerce, National Federation of Independent Business, all together, and thousands of people underneath them, in a highly structured, organized way, taking positions, moving, dividing up the Hill, and lobbying. Tremendous power was brought to bear (Vogel, 1989:161).

There are several alleged differences between the bad old days and the 1970s. First, Vogel (1989:76) claims that business organization prior to the 1970s was focused at the trade association level. Moreover, the trade associations used to stick pretty much to their own knitting (1989:200, 291). Only in the 1970s did they create a broad-based alliance that finally made business effective (1989:238). Both Edsall and Vogel talk about the "revitalization" (Edsall, 1984:123; Vogel, 1989:199) of the U.S. Chamber of Commerce; they note its role as a coordinator of lobbying efforts, its dissemination of information on the voting records of members of Congress, and its close connections with the grassroots. Much is made of the creation of the Business Roundtable in 1973, with its direct lobbying of Congress through chief executive officers (Edsall, 1984:121; Vogel, 1989:198 ff.).

Quite a bit is made out of the increased funding for old think tanks, such as the National Bureau of Economic Research, the Hoover Institution, and the American Enterprise Institute, and the creation of new ones, such as the Heritage Foundation. The coordination among newly legalized business PACs is given a big play, along with the claim that more business money was being funneled into the electoral arena. This is said to be important because the individuals who make donations, who are overwhelmingly business people according to all studies, "may or may not be interested in the welfare of business" according to Vogel (1989:210). The coordination provided by the PACs is ironic because liberal legislation supposedly created it: "Thus, ironically, the restrictions placed on the amount that any one PAC could contribute helped encourage the business community to coordinate its campaign spending—something that individual businessmen had only infrequently attempted to do prior to the legalization of PACs" (1989:208). Finally, grassroots lobbying is seen as something business only began to utilize in a serious way in the 1970s (Edsall, 1984:110–11; Vogel, 1989:203–6).

Given the tremendous amount of evidence that has been published on the coordination of the corporate community throughout the twentieth century, much of which has been presented or cited in previous chapters, the claim that business wasn't mobilized in the 1960s is remarkable. What seems like disunity is in fact something else: disagreement with the special pleadings of a specific industry, such as the automobile industry on pollution control and mileage standards, or disagreements among different segments of the capitalist class, as shown in the previous chapters. But neither Edsall nor Vogel thinks in terms of class segments, let alone classes. There is only business, divided into big and small. There is no awareness of distinct interests for international companies either.

So, it will be useful to run briefly through the organization of business from top to bottom and add to the earlier evidence. At the peak levels, for the purpose of general discussions, there was of course first of all the Business Council, whose activities have been chronicled for the years 1933 to 1974 through the archival and interview research of Kim McQuaid (1976, 1979, 1982). Most of its members are from the big international companies, but there is always a minority from the nationalist segment. The Business Council alone shows business is organized, but our research demonstrates it is also at the center of a very large social-business-policy network (Domhoff, 1974:a,b:102–9; 1975; Bonacich and Domhoff, 1981; Salzman and Domhoff, 1983). Then there is the CED, active since the 1940s, potent on the policy issues discussed in Chapters 7 and 8, and chronicled in proper historical detail for its influence in the 1950s and 1960s by Robert Collins (1981). And obviously the Council on Foreign Relations, which may not count as a business organization by the narrow definitions of Edsall and Vogel. There is also a great amount of network research showing that the CED and the Council on Foreign Relations connect to major foundations, think tanks, university institutes, and other business groups through common trustee and money flows (e.g., Domhoff, 1967; Dye, 1976; Salzman and Domhoff, 1983; Useem, 1984), and numerous case studies demonstrating the influence of this larger network (e.g., Eakins, 1966; Shoup and Minter, 1977; Peschek, 1987). It might be argued that the people in these networks are ineffective, lazy, stupid, or a million other things, but it is hard for me to see how anybody can claim that they aren't organized, coordinated, and mobilized.

Edsall and Vogel make the Business Roundtable sound like a new organization, but it was in fact the Business Council adding a new function. Rather than
turn the Business Council into an organization to hassle Congress, thereby
jeopardizing its status as a lofty policy organization that met regularly with
leaders within the executive branch, the members created a separate organization
when they decided they needed to push harder on Congress. Fully two-thirds of
the members of the Business Roundtable were members of the Business Council
in the mid-1970s; 12 of the 35 founders were trustees of the CED and another 4
were directors of the NAM. Irving Shapiro, the chair of du Pont Corporation for
much of the 1970s, explained the difference between the Business Council and
Business Roundtable as follows in an interview with Richard L. Zweigenhaft in
February, 1981:

> The Roundtable is only for chief executive officers. Once I'm through with that I am out.
> There's a counterpart to the Roundtable that you may not be familiar with, and that's the
> Business Council, and that you stay involved with. It is not an advocacy organization. It
> simply deals with public issues. The Roundtable was created to have an advocacy organiza-
> tion. It wasn't created by the Business Council, but by the same people. I am a member of the
> Council and will stay with that. People who are retired stay with it the rest of their lives if they
> choose to (Domhoff, 1983a:135).

It used to be thought that the NAM and the Chamber of Commerce were
highly organized and in close touch with each other, but now Edsall and Vogel
say that they weren't very coordinated until the 1970s. We are told that they had
to be rejuvenated and whipped into playing shape. But such a claim is standard
fare over the years. There were stories about a "new" NAM in *Fortune* after
World War II (Editors, 1948), and in the *Wall Street Journal* in the 1960s (Prial,
1966). Ferguson and Rogers (1986:62) date the "revival" of NAM and the
Chamber of Commerce to the Johnson years as part of a buildup to oppose an
anticipated "labor offensive" on the Taft-Hartley Act that, of course, failed. For
a long time the NAM was regarded as "the kiss of death" rather than an
influential lobbying organization, but Richard Gable (1953) suggests it was
highly organized and successful on the Taft-Harley Act. As for the chamber,
Donald Hall (1969:222) wrote in his book on lobbying in the 1950s and 1960s
that "several recent Chamber successes, notably passage of the Landrum-Griffin
Act, have helped to restore the Chamber's image as a politically powerful
group." He then goes on to give examples of other victories for the Chamber
(1969:237–39).

The idea that trade associations seldom worked with each other in the past will
come as a surprise to those familiar with Hall's *Cooperative Lobbying* (1969), a
book that does not appear in Edsall or Vogel's bibliography. Hall shows that the
leaders of several business organizations, along with representatives from the
American Medical Association, the National Cotton Council, and the American
Farm Bureau Federation, met each year from 1951 on for a long weekend to

coordinate lobbying strategy for the upcoming legislative session (1969:191–96). My correspondence with some of those who took part in these meetings revealed that they lasted until 1972, just about the time when Edsall and Vogel think that business was starting to become organized. They have mistaken re-organization and the ability to adapt organizationally for lack of organization. Then, too, Robert Ross (1967) used interviews and testimony before the House to conclude that lobbying groups were very stable in their policy proposals and alliances over a 16-year period in the 1950s and 1960s.

The involvement of the American Bar Association in the business lobbying complex was spelled out in great detail in research by Albert Melone (1972, 1977); it worked in tandem with the NAM and the Chamber, except on matters of judicial procedure, where it upheld the integrity of the court system instead of going along with the special-interest pleading of the business groups. The similarities of the positions taken by all business groups also are demonstrated in Melone's work.

One of the best books ever written on how lobbying works in Washington (McCune, 1956) shows the detailed coordination between business and farm lobbyists. Conservative business leaders are trustees of most of the farm groups and provide them with financial support. The American Farm Bureau Federation is the largest and most visible group in this well-coordinated complex, but there are many other organizations around it that play specialized parts. It is hard to read McCune, who was first a farm reporter and then an official of the Department of Agriculture during the Truman administration, without becoming convinced that the lobbying complex that parallels the conservative coalition was organized and active during the 1940s and 1950s.

The incorporation of "small business" into this lobbying network is vastly overrated by both Edsall and Vogel because of their uncritical attitude toward an organization inaccurately named the National Federation of Independent Business (Edsall, 1984:125–26; Vogel, 1989:161, 199). The federation began as a very lucrative private business in which the owner sold memberships to small business owners and then used their fees in a lobbying effort for his conservative preferences. Now the organization is nonprofit but controlled by a board. Because it is a private organization, there are no elections of officers or group discussions. The federation of course pays very handsome commissions to its sales staff for signing up new members.

Edsall and Vogel are impressed by the fact that the federation can tell members of Congress where federation "members" in each Congressional district stand on a given piece of legislation, but these "surveys" have been the trademark of the company since its founding. There is no likelihood that these surveys represent anything but the most conservative views among the millions of small business owners, for the few studies on small business and politics defy all the usual stereotypes by showing a wide range of opinion from liberal to conservative (Hamilton, 1975:Chapter 2). What the federation has done is to provide a service for big business and conservatives while paying its top officers huge salaries, and members of Congress understand this fact (Zeigler, 1961; Hamilton, 1975:Chapter 7). It is a conservative business, not a "representative" of "small business."

Both Edsall (1984:134–35) and Vogel (1989:155) point to a successful lobbying campaign against legislation permitting union picketing at all entrances to a construction site as evidence for the claim that business began to work together more effectively in the 1970s. Vogel (1989:160–63) also stresses that the rejection of a Consumer Protection Agency a few months later through the same lobbying techniques marked the decline of the consumer movement. The lobbying victories were seen as critical ones because President Carter was in favor of both bills and the Democrats controlled Congress. Without quite realizing it, Vogel himself provides the explanation for why business seemed ineffective when such legislation passed both Houses earlier in the 1970s, only to be abandoned because of the threat of a veto. Business didn't need to be "organized" on this issue because it knew President Gerald Ford would veto the legislation (1989:195).

Similarly, Vogel doesn't quite grasp that Congress could vote for such legislation in the past because it, too, knew that the president would veto it. Only with a Democrat in the White House was it necessary for the conservative coalition to swing into action once again. Those who think this attributes too much cunning to members of Congress have failed to read Bauer et al. (1963) and forgotten the three basic rules of politics: be able to count votes, alienate as few people as possible, and make some votes that throw your critics off stride. The voting patterns on the two issues in question make my point. In a House of Representatives that Vogel (1989:149) stresses had changed very little in party composition between 1974 and 1976, 63 of 89 (71 percent) southern Democrats voted with all 31 southern Republicans and 94 other Republicans to provide 188 of the 218 negative votes needed to defeat the Consumer Protection Agency. The same thing happened on common site picketing: 65 of the 85 southern Democrats who voted (76 percent) joined all 30 southern Republicans who voted and 99 other Republicans to provide 196 of the 217 negative votes on that legislation (Congressional Quarterly, 1977:79–83; 1978:37–44). So the question is the same as it had been for the previous 40 years: When does the conservative coalition flex its muscles? And the answer is: When there are enough Republicans to make it work, when the interests of businesspeople are threatened, and when there is no social disruption to keep moderates and fencesitters from going along with the conservatives.

Think tanks, as a part of the policy networks of the two corporate segments, were a very old story by the 1970s. The National Bureau of Economic Research, for example, was founded in the 1920s and has had a major role ever since that is fully chronicled by Eakins (1966). Since Edsall (1984:216) says it is "perhaps the most directly influential" of the think tanks, he seems to have provided evidence against his own thesis that think-tank power is recent. However, there were two new producers of conservative ideas in the 1970s, the American Enterprise Institute and the Heritage Foundation. The American Enterprise Institute (AEI) was new in the sense that it received a very large infusion of corporate money along about 1970–71 to pump new life into what had been a minor offshoot of the Chamber of Commerce since its founding in 1944 and slight growth in the 1960s. When former Nixon appointees, retired Harvard economists, and former President Gerald Ford became fellows or in-residence-scholars in the 1970s, it received a big boost in stature, and everybody began focusing on it as a key to the rise of conservatism. But the AEI was a symptom, not a cause, and it came along a little too late to be of great moment in the alleged turnaround.

As for the Heritage Foundation, it actually is new. When ultraconservatives Joseph Coors and Richard Mellon Scaife (the latter of fourth-generation eastern wealth) gave three or four policy intellectuals several hundred thousand dollars in 1974, it was up and running, soon to be the recipient of even more money from major ultraright foundations and the employer of dozens of eager young conservative thinkers. But a new think tank on the extreme right is hardly evidence that business used to be disorganized, especially when it is added that moderate think tanks like the Brookings Institution had been in place alongside the more conservative NBER and Hoover Institution for decades.

Vogel and Edsall both see PACs as bringing coordination and unity to the business community, but there is no evidence to show that businesspeople were less coordinated in their political donations in the 1960s than they were in the 1970s. Improved record keeping and the existence of PACs merely give that impression to those who do not know the literature on campaign finance. Vogel himself (1989:208) notes that the Business-Industry PAC (BIPAC) was formed as early as 1963, and it was giving advice on donations to all business groups from that time on. But it was not only BIPAC that coordinated donations. Individuals did so, too, just as they do today more than Vogel seems to realize. This point is demonstrated in detail in Herbert E. Alexander's (1958) interview and questionnaire study of 30 major Democratic and Republican fund-raisers in New York City in the 1950s. Most of these people were businessmen and attorneys who had been raising funds for their respective parties for many years. They tended to belong to more organizations than a control group of contributors and to have leadership roles in those organizations (Alexander, 1958:74–76). They were seen by the contributors as people who represented the interests of all large donors. Thus, it is clear that the fund-raisers tended to be leaders within the corporate community.

Nor is there any reason to believe that the business community gave more money to politicians after 1970 if inflation and the increasing costs of media advertising are factored into the equation. Alexander puts it most succinctly when he says there is no way to know for sure given the incompleteness of earlier records (personal communication, July 20, 1989). But that is not a reason to make wild speculations about increasing coordination and donations just because

PACs came along as an artifact of the law. Money, once called the mother's milk of politics by Jesse Unruh, is also like water—it will find its level, it will seep through somehow, it is everywhere.

Everything we know tells us that campaign finance records from before 1970 understate business donations. When the records filed by the two parties with the clerk of the House in 1936 were compared with direct reports by donors obtained by a Senate investigating committee, it was found that the party records were extremely inadequate (Overacker, 1937). William Benton, chairman of Encyclopedia Brittanica in the 1960s, told the Citizens Research Foundation that the 1968 records understated his contribution by a magnitude of four, recording him for $12,500 instead of the $50,000 he actually gave (Domhoff, 1972:155). Harry Ashmore told me in an interview in 1970 that an Arkansas oil man who supported Stevenson in the 1950s gave far more to Stevenson than the records show, which he knew because he was the go-between on a considerable amount of the money.

In short, when it comes to campaign finance, Edsall and Vogel have committed the standard fallacy of all public pundits who talk about new developments. They don't bother to ascertain whether or not anything is really different from the past, which is usually no problem because most people weren't around, or don't remember, or mix things up in their memories. Were people more narcissistic in the 1970s than earlier? Are we more anxious in the twentieth century than in the past? Are businessmen giving more money in the 1970s than the 1960s? The positive answers usually given to these questions are doubtful at best, but they make the advocates into original thinkers because they allegedly have spotted new trends that the rest of us have missed. The new always sells better than the old, except for the Bible, and there is nothing new about that.

Perhaps it is at the grass roots that something has changed. But there were massive letter-writing campaigns in the 1930s against New Deal measures, and the grass roots were stimulated as well as they possibly could have been against the Wagner Act. The idea that any of these strategies are new also is contradicted by the activities of the textile industry during the battles over trade policy that were discussed in Chapter 8 (Bauer et al., 1963:62) and by the material in Hall (1969). Newspaper and magazine articles from the 1960s spoke in the same hushed tones as Vogel and Edsall do about how much material the business community was putting into the hands of ordinary folks. There were frequent boasts about how many people could be activated to write or petition Congress on a moment's notice.

Of what, then, does the alleged revitalization of business organization in the 1970s consist? More companies had public affairs offices in Washington. Public affairs people had more status in their corporations. More trade associations moved their offices to Washington. Chief executive offices increased their direct political contacts with government officials, especially through the vaunted Business Roundtable. More money was spent on institutional ads, whose effects are unknown. Everybody acquired a computer so they could talk to everyone else quickly and punch out mailgrams to targeted audiences at the "grass roots" (Vogel, 1989:Chapter 8).

This is not exactly a revolution. It is a mild evolution at best. Edsall and Vogel have been taken in by Bryce Harlow, John Harper, and other business lobbyists.

But the clincher point against the idea that business was disorganized—one that I missed—is made by Jerome Himmelstein (1989) in his excellent book on the rise of the Right from the late 1950s to 1980s: if the business community was so chaotic, how in the world was it able to mobilize so quickly in the 1970s? Whence did this strength come if not from prior organization? Theorists such as Edsall and Vogel can't have it both ways, a previously impotent business community and a suddenly mobilized one:

> The pluralist image of big business thus remains only partly convincing because it cannot explain where business suddenly found the capacity to mobilize. The idea that big business was disorganized and powerless until the mid-70s may be superficially appealing, but it makes the political mobilization seem all the more implausible (1989:155).

But being organized is one thing and winning is another. What did business lose, if anything, during the late 1960s and early 1970s?

## What Did Business Lose?

Edsall does not go into detail on the alleged losses by business because his greatest concern is with the rise of business power between 1973–74 and 1983, when he thinks it reached a point that had not been attained since the days of Calvin Coolidge. Thus, he merely lists the following as a series of defeats for business just as it was facing a new Congress in 1974 that included 49 new Democrats in the House and five in the Senate:

> Before these Democratic gains, and despite the presence of a Republican in the White House, Congress by 1974 had already enacted into law the Environmental Protection Agency (1970), the Occupational Safety and Health Administration (1970), the Consumer Product Safety Commission (1972), the National Traffic Safety Commission (1970), the Mine Safety and Health Administration (1973), increased food stamp funding (1970), a 20 percent Social Security increase (1974), Supplemental Security Income (1972), and the Employee Retirement Income Security Act (Edsall, 1984:113).

Since Vogel is concerned to explain both the decline in business power and its subsequent rise, he spends much more time on the alleged losses, which include Edsall's list and more. Indeed, Vogel calls every piece of regulatory and tax legislation between 1966 and 1972 a defeat for business:

> During the second half of the 1960s, the political defeats experienced by business were confined to individual industries. But from 1969 through 1972, virtually the entire American

business community experienced a series of political setbacks without parallel in the postwar period. In the space of only four years, Congress enacted a significant tax-reform bill, four major environmental laws, an occupational safety and health act, and a series of additional consumer-protection statutes. The government also created a number of important new regulatory agencies, including the Environmental Protection Agency (EPA), the Occupational Safety and Health Administration (OSHA), and the Consumer Product Safety Commission (CPSC), investing them with broad powers over a wide range of business decisions (1989:59).

In saying all this Vogel's main focus is on the public interest movement, and especially the consumer and environmental movements. It is his belief (1989:293) that the public interest movement is the "central countervailing force to the power and values of business."

Most of the defeats discussed by Vogel hardly look like defeats when he gets down to presenting specific cases. After telling about numerous consumer protection bills that passed between 1965 and 1968, he points out that none of them had much teeth, and furthermore, it turns out that business did not oppose a single one of these bills with the exception of automobile industry opposition to the National Traffic and Motor Vehicle Safety Act. Vogel himself admits the effects of these acts were "rather modest," but nonetheless calls them defeats because "the significant increase in the volume of regulatory legislation between 1966 and 1969 indicated that the relative political influence of business had begun to erode" (1989:53).

Vogel then turns to the more significant legislation of the late 1960s, such as the enabling act for the Environmental Protection Agency. Although it was one of the agencies conservative businesspeople complained about the most in the 1970s, the Environmental Protection Agency was supported at the outset by big business according to Vogel (1989:66–69). Some businesspeople welcomed a national environmental protection agency because they did not want to contend with varying regulations, and sometimes tougher regulations, in individual states. Others saw it as a welcome distraction from the criticism business was receiving over the Vietnam War; these companies were among the many sponsors of Earth Day in 1970 (1989:69).

Moreover, the environmental movement that allegedly defeated business was not uniformly antibusiness. The origins of the conservationist movement can be found in upper-class Republicans of earlier eras, and some of their organizations were still going strong in the 1960s. While Friends of the Earth and the Environmental Defense Fund were new liberal organizations, the Conservation Foundation, the Nature Conservancy, the National Wildlife Federation, the National Audubon Society, and other environmental groups were directed and financed by the same people who run businesses and take part in policy-discussion groups. These people played the central role in creating the EPA, and as Vogel (1989:104) states in a later context, 83 public interest organizations studied in 1977 received over half of their funds from foundations, with the Ford Foundation playing the key role for several environmental organizations.

It is not until Vogel's account comes to the origins of the Occupational Health and Safety Act of 1970 that there is even a whiff of broad-based opposition within the business community. When the Johnson administration first suggested such legislation in 1968, both the NAM and the Chamber opposed it (Vogel, 1989:84). Remarkably, given Vogel's claims about the power of antibusiness forces in Congress by 1968, the bill did not make it to the floor of either house. Moreover, as Vogel admits, "the business community was divided" (1989:84). In other words, although he does not say it this way because he does not think in terms of classes or class segments, the sophisticated conservatives of the internationalist segment supported such legislation in principle. They even had a private policy-planning network in place on the safety issue that could play a role in shaping an agency and in creating safety standards (Berman, 1978; Noble, 1986).

When the Nixon administration introduced its own legislation on the issue, the entire business community decided to support it. The NAM and the chamber reversed their objections of the previous year. The battle was not over, however. The unions and the environmentalists, in a rare coalitional action, insisted that the agency be in the Department of Labor, not independent as in the Republican bill. This environmental–labor coalition also wanted higher standards and tougher enforcement procedures. After almost two years of jockeying back and forth, a compromise was reached: the agency would be in the Department of Labor, but a separate three-person commission would enforce the regulations. As for the standards, they were essentially the ones developed over the years by private organizations sponsored by large corporations (Berman, 1978). Neither side was enthusiastic about the final bill because it didn't get all that it wanted, but neither opposed the bill, and it passed easily in both houses.

Most people might be at least a little hesitant about calling this chain of events a "defeat" for business, but Vogel does just that: "Nonetheless, on balance, the OSH Act constituted a political defeat for the business community, even though its provisions did not affect all firms equally" (1989:86–87). A compromise favored by business at a time when labor support was needed for the Vietnam War is not a victory, but a defeat. Vogel has created a straw man in which power and dominance mean total control on each and every issue in each and every year.

Whatever the standard of judgment, the Occupational Safety and Health Act is the last significant legislative loss for business in the Vogel chronicle. Later ones concern temporary strengthening of the Federal Trade Commission and higher standards on pollutants, but none has the breadth of the Environmental Protection Agency or the Occupational Safety and Health Administration, and one of the toxin bills was supported by the chemical manufacturers in its final version (Vogel, 1989:135). Legislationwise, the worst was over for business in 1970.

However, there were other problems for business in the 1970s that Vogel sees as defeats, and some of them actually were. For example, public-interest law firms challenged development projects in the courts, causing delays and even cancellations of projects (Vogel, 1989:106–10). I think these are significant issues that show the power structure was on the defensive in the early 1970s. Business also suffered many embarrassments in the 1970s due to accidents, scandals, oil leaks, and chemical spills. For example, a disastrous oil leak led to a ban on further offshore drilling along the coast of an expensive retirement villa, Santa Barbara, where even the rich joined Get Out Oil to protect the beautiful environment (Molotch, 1970). But the oil companies pushed the Alaska pipeline through Congress in 1973 despite the environmentalists. Further, many businessmen were exposed for making illegal campaign contributions to Nixon and illegal overseas bribes to foreign governments. The public image of business fell to an all-time low, but there were no legislative losses. Congress couldn't even agree to legislation to prohibit bribes of foreign government officials by American corporations (Vogel, 1989:114, 122).

Then the oil industry came under attack again in 1974 after the massive OPEC price hike, which produced huge windfall profits for the oil companies. The Federal Trade Commission filed an antitrust suit against the big companies, but nothing came of it. Two bills to break up the oil giants came before Congress, but nothing came of them either. However, the Ford administration refused to remove price controls on oil, and Congress abolished the oil depletion allowance for the major companies.

The "losses" and "defeats" alleged by Edsall and Vogel for business in the legislative arena now can be put into perspective. They show a small loss of power when under great pressure from African-American and antiwar demonstrators. But these were not serious losses; they were nicks, and the surprise is that they were so minor in a time of great turmoil. Businesspeople always scream and yell far beyond the actual threat to their power and privileges. Partly this is tactic, as Grant McConnell (1966:294) pointed out, but partly this is genuine hysteria rooted in the volatility of capitalism (you never know when it will crash) and a fear of populist strains in American ideology. Vogel (1978) did fine work years ago when he made these points in explaining "why businessmen mistrust their state," but by 1989 he didn't even think it was "their" state.

However, people did fight off threats to their everyday lives that were created by new industries and new industrial products. They battled the nuclear industry to a standstill because they feared its radioactive fuels and wastes might kill them. They said nyet to sonic booms, some kinds of pesticides, oil spills, and toxins in the workplace, although oil spills still go on in places that couldn't ban offshore drilling or tanker landings, and there are still plenty of toxins around. These are indeed victories, but there is something perversely antibusiness about calling a ban on a pesticide or a toxin a defeat for business as a whole. It seems unlikely to me that most members of the business community were prepared to poison their own everyday living space for a few products in the gigantic oil–chemical complex.

As for the social movements that provided the backdrop for these challenges to business, I already have agreed that they won more freedom for a wider range of people, and more room for alternative lifestyles. However, this does not mean that the "power elite" or even "business" was "defeated" or that these movements gained any social power. Personal freedom increased, but the distribution of power did not become more equal. Put another way, African-Americans won civil rights and people in general are now more free to "do their own thing" as individuals, but individual freedoms do not challenge the overall power structure. People won, but the power structure did not lose.

Still, the power elite did take some beatings in the capital–labor struggle, and it is now time for a closer look at why that struggle heated up in the late 1960s and early 1970s. Surprisingly, Vogel (1989:201) has given little attention to the most important defeats that big corporations suffered between 1968 and 1974. Labor gained a bigger piece of the pie in the form of wages, and people in general, including retirees, benefited from an improved social wage in the form of increases in pensions, food stamps, unemployment compensation, and public housing assistance, among many programs (Himmelstein, 19889:134). Here were the issues of real concern to "business," and here is where Reagan laid the ax to "big government" when he came into office.

## The Rise of Capital-Labor Conflict

In the midst of all the ferment created by the civil rights, feminist, and antiwar movements, the issue of capital–labor conflict suddenly came to center stage for the first time in many years. This does not mean that corporations had come to approve of unions in the 1950s and early 1960s, but it does mean they were willing to live with them when profits were on an upswing or their patriotism was needed.

From 1961 to 1968, one or both of those factors was operating. The economy had enjoyed sustained growth without inflation and profits were soaring. Even more, perhaps, labor unions were strongly supportive of an aggressive, anticommunist foreign policy. On many issues some of the most prominent union leaders outside the United Auto Workers, such as George Meany, were to the right of any American leaders except the most militaristic Republicans. At a time when students and liberals were demanding that the United States get out of Vietnam and attacking corporations for their involvement in "imperialism," a word that disappeared in favor of the more benign "multinationalism" in the 1970s, the organized labor movement was foursquare behind the war.

Nixon especially appreciated this support for the war from labor. He publicly thanked "hard hats" and contrasted their patriotism with the un-American actions of the antiwar protesters. Moreover, at a time when most people still thought of themselves as Democrats, he knew that he was going to need votes from blue-collar workers to win again in 1972. It is these factors that explain the restraint Nixon and big business showed toward labor in the late 1960s and early 1970s. It was a restraint that Nixon continued even after corporations asked him through the Business Council in 1970 to abandon it (McQuaid, 1982:267). But Nixon did not agree to "zap" labor with his wage and price freeze until a year later, when the Vietnamization of the war had slowed down the antiwar movement.

As noted earlier, the resurgence of the class war between capital and labor was triggered by the tight labor markets created by the tax-cut boom of the mid 1960s and the war-spending boom of the late 1960s. Wages finally went up, as they always do in this kind of situation, and it is here that we can see the actual basis for any gain in power by labor in the late 1960s: the power elite was dealing with a tight labor market and a war at the same time.

The problems created by the wage increases won through labor's improved bargaining position were exacerbated by the inflation caused by Johnson's inability to obtain a large tax increase from Congress without cutting welfare spending. The Keynesian economists of the day clearly warned that there was a danger of runaway inflation if taxes were not raised or domestic spending reduced, but Johnson could do neither. He faced resistance from congressional conservatives if he tried to raise taxes and possible disruption by liberals and minorities if he tried to cut benefit programs. Indeed, he knew that the conservatives would not let him raise taxes because they hoped to force him to make such cuts (McQuaid, 1982:242–54). The surcharge that was enacted was too little and too late in the face of even greater war spending than had been anticipated.

The result was serious inflation, but organized labor not only kept even, it gained in the process through settlements that went beyond inflation. Very importantly, it often gained contracts that provided automatic cost of living increases that were tied to the Consumer Price Index. This arrangement gave a major push to wages because the index used at the time was very sensitive to oil prices and mortgages rates. As Edsall explains:

> The CPI is heavily weighted toward oil and mortgage interest rates, which in the eyes of many economists made it a flawed price index in the 1970s, giving labor a 6 to 8 percentage point wage hike above settlements consonant with actual increases in the cost of living. The result was, just at a time of increased overseas competition, an inadvertent CPI-pegged wage hike that functioned to push U.S. wage rates up, in international terms, to noncompetitive levels, levels that were, in the view of at least management, not sustainable (1984:157).

Construction unions were among those that did well in this situation. The price of new office buildings and factories for large corporations went up dramatically, and the reaction by big business was the first return shot by capital in the new class war. United States Steel, joined by several other large corporations, created an organization known as the Construction Users Anti-Inflation Roundtable. Its purpose was to help the many small firms in the construction industry resist further wage hikes. It encouraged members to use nonunion firms when possible, worked to coordinate construction firms, and aided unionized firms in starting nonunion subsidiaries (Burck, 1979). This organization eventually became the Business Roundtable, which figures so heavily in Edsall's and Vogel's accounts of how business mobilized in the 1970s.

From that point on the battle was fully joined across the board. The corporations began to resist unionization as the 1970s rolled on. They hired antiunion consulting firms to organize campaigns against any attempts at unionization (Chernow, 1981). They fired workers who tried to create unions; even though such an action was illegal, employees had decided it was worth paying the fine and back wages when the case finally was decided if unions could be defeated in that way. They moved to decertify unions that already had been established. Edsall (1984:151ff.) provides a summary of the many prongs of this counterattack.

Organized labor was not in a good position to fight back when the battle heated up in the 1970s. Its gradual decline within blue-collar sectors, masked in part by a growth in teacher, service-worker, and governmental unions, was accelerated by the economic problems of the decade. It also was in bad shape politically because of its hostility to the civil rights, antiwar, feminist, and environmental movements, which meant that it was in effect estranged from minorities and upper-middle-class liberals. The liberal–labor coalition that had been the only counterweight in the political arena to the conservative coalition was split asunder, and once again Edsall (1984:160) is right on the money. Labor had to face its class enemies alone, and it lost.

The tightening of labor markets coincided with and intensified the movement of American manufacturing facilities overseas (Bennett and Bluestone, 1988). This had two direct effects: a rise in unemployment and a further weakening of industrial unions. With labor on the defensive due to the globalization of the economy, another basis for counterpressure and insurgency had been removed. This point is fully understood by Edsall (1984:143), and it is in this context that the claims by Ferguson and Rogers (1986) about the effects of internationalization can be taken out of their economistic framework and incorporated into a class-conflict theory. Internationalization did help make a right turn possible, but by weakening organized labor inside and outside the Democratic party, not by moving Democratic fat cats over to the Republicans.

Vogel has a weak grasp of all this because he expressly denies that the fluctuating fortunes of business and labor are tied to the business cycle. Nor does he give much weight to the war in explaining the reactions to organized labor by corporations and the Nixon administration. He talks about the tax hike in 1969 as a defeat for business when it was an attempt by Nixon and his business advisers to control inflation, fight a war, and deal with ghetto uprisings all at the same time.

Indeed, the CED (1968:10–12) expressly recommended this tax increase, so it can hardly be seen as defeated.

Vogel's failure to see that his perceptual theory of business power is but a pale, pale reflection of the grim reality of the business cycle is rendered surprising because he once coauthored a book with Leonard Silk (Silk/Vogel, 1976) that made this point by recounting discussions among business leaders at the Conference Board in 1974. The assembled business leaders, as we might expect by now, were extremely annoyed by events of the previous few years. They thought that people were not showing the proper respect for business. They said that students and environmentalists were ruining the country. The system was becoming overloaded due to the selfish demands by too many special interests among the ordinary citizenry. Everyone was becoming uppity.

The business leaders had a solution for all this, and it was called depression and unemployment. They said things like "This recession will bring about the healthy respect for economic values that the depression did," and "It would be better if the recession were allowed to weaken more than it will, so that we would have a sense of sobriety." One person said it all, or almost all, when it comes to a power analysis in terms of the business cycle:

> People need to recognize that a job is the most important thing they can have. We should use this recession to get the public to better understand how our economic system works (Silk and Vogel, 1976:89).

Some of the business leaders went further, right in front of Silk and Vogel, wondering whether or not democracy might have to be abandoned so that business could get down to business again. However, Silk and Vogel hurry to reassure us that the American business community couldn't possibly become fascistic because it was so antigovernment. Nastily conservative and antilabor, yes, but not much more:

> Even with their elitist, anti-populist, and even anti-democratic bias, however, few American businessmen can fairly be regarded as "fascist," if by that term one means a believer in a political system in which there is a combination of private ownership and a powerful, dictatorial government that imposes major restrictions on economic, political, social and religious freedoms. Basically, the anti-governmental mind set of the great majority of American businessmen has immunized them against the virus of fascism (1976:197).

Vogel's theory of perceptions aside, then, the situation was as follows when business took the offensive in the mid-1970s. The war finally had ended, however badly, and it was no longer necessary to appeal to blue-collar patriotism as a counterweight to antiwar liberals. The student left had self-destructed and then been repressed by the government, and there had been no student demonstrations of any moment since the Cambodian invasion of 1970. The civil rights movement had been over for years, and the African-Americans in the ghettos hadn't burned down a business district since 1968. Feminist leaders were going to graduate school or working through channels, and the unions were in decline for a number of reasons. It is in this context of restored domestic tranquility and rising unemployment, reinforced by attacks from the New Right, that the real basis for the counterattack can be found.

Much was made of the heroics of the Reagan budget and the tax cuts in 1981. Business lobbyists nearly broke their arms patting themselves on the back, inventing a new past in which their only problem was lack of organization and a failure to take the offensive (Vogel, 1989:246). Reagan had his picture taken talking on the telephone to congressmen, and he became the great persuader. This is mostly nonsense. With labor flat on its back due to the movement of U.S. companies overseas, Reagan's destruction of the air traffic controller's unions, competition from foreign multinations, and now a recession induced by the Federal Reserve Board to boot; with minorities, students, and women back into their daily routines; and with the middle-class baby boomers overemphasized by Vogel supporting business out of fear of inflation, these victories were not quite the big deal they are made out to be. There also was lots of talk about the supposed defections by the Democrats in the House who made these victories possible, but this was old news. Most of the defectors were the same southern Democrats who always support conservative legislation when it comes to labor and welfare issues. Now called "Boll Weevils," 47 of the 63 (75%) Democratic defectors on the budget resolution were southerners, far more than the 27 Democrats that were needed for a Republican victory. Meanwhile, 35 southern Democrats provided the winning margin on the tax cut (*Congressional Quarterly*, 1981a, 1981b, 1981c).

There had been one change. Given the influx of Republicans into the House in the 1980 election, including an increase from 31 to 41 from the once-solid South, there was no longer any need for the conservatives to have a majority of southern Democrats in order to carry the day. A majority (59) of the 79 southern Democrats who voted did support Reagan on the budget resolution, but only 35 of the 77 (45%) who voted on the tax bill were on Reagan's side. However, the replacement of conservative southern Democrats by even more conservative southern Republicans only affected the long-standing definition of the conservative coalition as "a majority of southern Democrats voting with a majority of Republicans," not the actual power of the class segments that stand behind that coalition.

Many liberals claimed in 1981 that the northern Democrats had lost their nerve or sold out in the face of the Reagan onslaught, but such an accusation does not take the power of conservative Democrats seriously. True, some northern Democrats were afraid they might be swept out of office in the 1982 elections if the tide kept running in Reagan's direction. However, it made no sense for them to stick their necks out when they knew that the 14-person Conservative Democratic

Caucus in the Senate gave the Republicans enough votes to overcome a filibuster and that the 47-member Conservative Democratic Forum in the House could supply Reagan with many more than the 27 Democratic defectors he needed to win. Significantly, 11 of the 14 conservative Democrats in the Senate were from the South, joined by the two Democrats from Nebraska and one from Arizona. And 43 of the 47 members of the Conservative Democratic Forum in the House were southerners, joined by one representative each from Arizona, Maryland, Nevada, and New York.

The successful ultraright media attacks in the 1980 elections on the moderate to liberal Democratic senators from Idaho, Wisconsin, South Dakota, Iowa, and Indiana therefore played a crucial role by providing enough Republicans to make it impossible for a liberal–labor coalition to exercise any veto power. It thus became possible for the center-right coalition to undercut organized labor and workers in general by eliminating or reducing the kind of programs that benefited poor and low-income workers, whether young or old, black or white. I think Piven and Cloward (1982/85) are exactly right that the result was a new class war that had the goal of undermining the social wage provided by the welfare state in order to weaken the bargaining power of individual workers and destroy unions. The main disagreement I had with them at the time they wrote was in their prediction that a coalition of women, environmentalists, minorities, and the elderly based in a "new moral economy" would organize to reverse these cuts (Domhoff, 1983b). On this point time has proven me right for a change, although Piven and Cloward put the best possible face on things in a new final chapter for the 1985 edition by saying that the cuts could have been a lot worse.

To his credit, Edsall also understands that there was at least an element of class war in the conservative program, although he does not give it the theoretical centrality that it deserves:

> Perhaps one of the most substantial achievements of the policy changes in the Reagan administration has been to consistently weaken the governmental base of support provided organized labor in its dealing with management—through sharp reductions in unemployment insurance, through the complete elimination of the public service job program, through the weakening of the Occupational Safety and Health Administration, and through appointments of persons hostile to organized labor both to the National Labor Relations Board and to the Department of Labor (Edsall, 1984:228–29).

Vogel almost backs into this type of analysis, providing support for it without drawing any implications. He does so by presenting the results of a survey of business executives in the spring of 1982 concerning their attitudes toward the recession. Despite the huge number of small-business bankruptcies, the loss of manufacturing jobs to foreign countries, and high unemployment due to the Volcker–Reagan monetary policies, "a majority of the 800 executives at large and medium-sized companies" said that the recession was good for the country (Vogel, 1989:256). They believed this, Vogel reports, because of the recession's beneficial effects on labor costs. So there it is once again—business understands the uses of the downside of the business cycle, and it approves of government creating or reinforcing those downsides, just as it did when its leaders spoke frankly in the presence of Vogel and Silk in 1974.

The conservatism of the Reagan years, then, represented what business had been waiting to do for a long time, but couldn't because of social activism and the Vietnam War. Now all was quiet and labor was on its knees, so business retaliated with a vengeance, even though that meant destroying needed infrastructure, creating a homeless underclass, and crushing many small businesses. Meanwhile, Vogel is writing that the fluctuating fortunes of business are not tied to the business cycle.

Although the state did nothing to help workers in the 1980s, Reagan continued to use it to support, regulate, and subsidize business. Increases in the interest rate through the actions of the Federal Reserve Board were used to control inflation by throwing people out of work. The use of this form of "fine tuning" had been made possible, of course, by reducing the ability of organized labor to protest. Then too, increased defense spending defended the empire and pumped up the economy. Some of the right-wing ideologues wanted to cut the Export-Import Bank down to size, but the big corporations put a stop to that. Others wanted to deregulate more businesses, but by 1983 the business press was pointing out that many businesses knew they needed regulation (Lublin, 1983; Crock, 1984). Secretary of Interior James Watt wanted to sell more government oil leases and remove all environmental regulations on the use of government land, but corporate officials called for his removal (Cheshire, 1983; Pasztor, 1983; Shabecoff, 1985; Shabecoff, 1989). Agribusiness had a couple of bad years, but massive government "assistance" took care of that problem. In other words, the state and the ruling class remained intimately intertwined in the Reagan years, contrary to any claim that the administration was "antistate" in anything but rhetoric and programs that aided labor (*pace* Himmelstein, 1989:160–161).

In conclusion, two of the most respectable theories meant to explain the return of conservatism have been examined and found wanting. It was not "perceptions" in the middle class, elitist liberals in the Democratic party, or the "revitalization" of business organizations like the Chamber of Commerce that led to the right turn. Instead, it was the decline of disruption and the weakening of the labor movement. The need is for a materialist theory of power, not a perceptual or electoral one. Classes and class conflict, along with protest and social disruption, have to be taken seriously to understand power in America.

# ENVOI

As the 1990s began, after ten long years of Reagan and Bush, the same old power elite was in the saddle as never before. The southern and nationalist segments of the capitalist class had melded into one, and the conflicts between the internationalists and nationalists were relatively minor. The usual tensions still could develop between local growth machines and national corporations, but even here there were new sources of cohesion as corporations went into the real estate business and components of local growth machines became national and international in scope (Friedland, 1982; Logan and Molotch, 1987:Chapter 7).

The Soviets had sued for peace in the Cold War, admitting that their bureaucratic economy was no match for Western capitalism, but the ever-expansionist American leadership decided to press its advantage by working for complete victory in Afghanistan, Angola, and Nicaragua. This aggressiveness on the part of the Bush administration was covered over by a seeming inability to make a decision. All this was done in the name of freedom, of course, but only mild sanctions were imposed when young democrats in China were brutally suppressed by a communist government allied with the United States.

Domestically, the unions and most liberal social movements were on the defensive, if not completely dead. People were either into their routines or too beaten down to fight back. It was the 1950s all over again, or so the Bush administration tried to pretend as it prattled on demagogically about the flag, school prayer, and drugs, while trying to turn back the clock on abortion and affirmative action.

The wealth and income distributions were as skewed as they had been in over 50 years. Business leaders made 38 times as much as school teachers and 41 times as much as blue-collar workers in 1962, but by 1988 they were making 72 times as much as the school teachers and 93 times as much as the blue-collar workers (*Business Week,* 1989:146). There was little or no sympathy for the many people living on the streets and in the alleyways. Only 20 percent of the youngsters who started first grade in the 1960s graduated from a four-year college, and the number of African-American males entering college actually declined from 1976 to 1986. Racial clashes were on the increase, and violence within low-income minority communities was on the upswing as well. Maybe it wasn't the 1950s after all—maybe it was the 1920s.

Meanwhile, a third-generation rich Texan with degrees from a New Jersey prep school and Princeton was in charge at the State Department, representing those allegedly uncouth Sunbelt capitalists, and a third-generation Wall Street banker with degrees from a New England prep school and Yale was looking after things at the Treasury. A superficial multimillionaire from Indiana with only a Robert Redford look to recommend him was being groomed as the heir-apparent, but he didn't seem able to get his lines straight. The Democrats were still hemorrhaging in the South and the traditional fat cats of the North were sitting on their wallets while they waited for acceptable presidential candidates to emerge.

Still, there were rays of hope for those who would like to see more equality, opportunity, and freedom for everyone. The end of the Cold War meant that the old bogeyman of the "red menace" no longer could be used to scare people into quiet acceptance because of their patriotism. Now that there were no credible outside enemies, it became possible for more people to turn their attention to new ways to solve problems at home. And if the end of the Cold War means a decline in the military budget, which is an outside possibility that could be a rallying point for egalitarians, then it is likely that new government programs will have to be developed to keep the economy humming along. Keynesianism may be discredited in theory among conservative ideologues, but in practice everyone knows that government spending is essential to the American economy. The only question is whether that spending will be directed to social needs or to space exploration, agricultural subsidies, and similar boondoggles for the wealthy and powerful.

The destruction of the union movement also created room for new thinking and organization, for there are no longer privileged workers who can look out for their own interests. Union power made some industrial workers into high-wage labor, but now everyone without a management position or professional degree is in the same low-wage boat. It is therefore likely that future actions by ordinary American workers will not be aimed at specific companies or industries, but at legislation to improve health care, job safety, child care, and minimum wages for everyone. This possibility was a dead end in the past because of the southern elite's hold on the Democratic party and Congress, but the changes of the past 20 years in civil rights and the southern economy make such a strategy feasible.

On balance, given the power of American elites and the problems of organizing large numbers of people, the prospects for greater fairness and equality did not look very good as the 1990s began. There will be no natural evolution to a better future for everyone, only a natural evolution to the rich getting richer and the poor getting poorer, for that is how capitalism works without intervention by a countervailing political party and the state. But the power elite described in this book is precisely in the business of making sure that such intervention does not happen.

However, the prospects for social change didn't look very good at the end of the 1920s or the 1950s either. No one foresaw the New Deal, and no one expected a massive civil rights movement. If history teaches us anything, it is that no one can predict the future.

# BIBLIOGRAPHY

Adams, Frederick C. 1976. *Economic Diplomacy: The Export-Import Bank and American Foreign Policy, 1934–1939*. Columbia: University of Missouri Press.

Adams, Gordon. 1981. *The Politics of Defense Contracting*. New Brunswick, NJ: Transaction.

Adams, Graham Jr. 1966. *The Age of Industrial Violence, 1910–1915*. New York: Columbia University Press.

Alba, Richard. 1973. A Graph-Theoretic Definition of a Sociometric Clique. *Journal of Mathematical Sociology* 3:113–126.

Albion, Robert G. 1939. *The Rise of New York Port, 1815–1860*. New York: C. Scribner's Sons.

Alexander, Herbert. 1958. The Role of the Volunteer Political Fund Raiser: A Case Study in New York in 1952. Ph.D. diss. Yale University, New Haven, CT.

Alexander, Herbert. 1971. *Financing The Election, 1968*. Lexington, MA: Heath Lexington Books.

Alexander, Herbert. 1976. *Financing Politics*. Washington: Congressional Quarterly Press.

Alexander, Herbert. 1983. *Financing The Election, 1980*. Lexington, MA: Heath Lexington Books.

Alexander, Herbert. 1987. *Financing The Election, 1984*. Lexington, MA: Heath Lexington Books.

Alford, Robert. 1975. "Paradigms of Relations Between State and Society." In *Stress and Contradiction in Modern Capitalism,* edited by Leon N. Lindberg et al. Boston: Lexington Books.

Alford, Robert and Roger Friedland. 1975. "Political Participation and Public Policy." *Annual Review of Sociology* 1:429–479.

Alford, Robert and Roger Friedland. 1985. *Powers of Theory*. Cambridge: Cambridge University Press.

Alford, Robert and Eugene Lee. 1968. "Voting Turnout in American Cities." *American Political Science Review* 62:796–813.

Allen, George E. 1950. *Presidents Who Have Known Me*. New York: Simon & Schuster.

Allen, Michael P. 1987. *The Founding Fortunes: A New Anatomy of the Super-rich Families in America*. New York: Truman Talley.

Allen, Michael P. and Philip Broyles. 1989. "Class Hegemony and Political Finance." *American Sociological Review* 54:275–287.

Alpert, Irvine and Ann Markusen. 1980. "Think Tanks and Capitalist Policy." In *Power Structure Research*, edited by G. William Domhoff. Beverly Hills, CA: Sage Publications.

Althusser, Louis. 1971. *Lenin and Philosophy, and Other Essays*. London: New Left Books.

Altmeyer, Arthur. 1968. *The Formative Years of Social Security*. Madison: University of Wisconsin Press.

Arluck, Mary S. 1974. *Guide to the Microfilm Edition of the Papers of the American Association for Labor Legislation, 1905–1943*. Ithaca, NY: Labor Management Documentation Center, Cornell University.

Armstrong, Barbara N. 1932. *Insuring the Essentials: Minimum Wage, Plus Social Insurance—A Living Wage Problem*. New York: Macmillan.

Auerbach, Jerold S. 1966. *Labor and Liberty: The LaFollette Committee and the New Deal*. Indianapolis, IN: Bobbs Merrill.

Auerbach, Jerold S. 1976. *Unequal Justice: Lawyers and Social Change in America*. New York: Oxford University Press.

Bailey, Stephen. 1950. *Congress Makes a Law: The Story Behind the Employment Act of 1964*. New York: Columbia University Press.

Balbus, Isaac. 1971. "Ruling Elite Theory vs. Marxist Class Analysis." *Monthly Review* 23:40–41.

Baltzell, E. Digby. 1958. *Philadelphia Gentlemen: The Making of a National Upper Class*. New York: Free Press.

Baltzell, E. Digby. 1964. *The Protestant Establishment*. New York: Random House.

Banning, Lance, ed. 1989. *After the Constitution: Party Conflict in the New Republic*. Belmont, CA: Wadsworth.

Bauer, Raymond, Ithiel De Sola Pool, and Lewis Dexter. 1963. *American Business and Public Policy*. Chicago: Aldine-Atherton. Paperback edition with new preface, 1972.

Bay Area Kapitalistate Group. 1975. "Book Review: The Fiscal Crisis of the State." *Kapitalistate* 3:149–158.

Beard, Charles. 1934. *The Idea of National Interest*. New York: Macmillan.

Benjamin, Jessica. 1988. *The Bonds of Love* New York: Random House.

Bennett, Harrison and Barry Bluestone. 1988. *The Great U-Turn*. New York: Basic Books.

Benson, Lee. 1961. *The Concept of Jacksonian Democracy*. Princeton, NJ: Princeton University Press.

Berkowitz, Edward and Kim McQuaid. 1980. *Creating the Welfare State*. New York: Praeger.

Berman, Daniel M. 1978. *Death on the Job: Occupational Health and Safety Struggles in the United States*. New York: Monthly Review.

Berman, Larry. 1982. *Planning a Tragedy*. New York: Norton.

Bernstein, Irving. 1950. *The New Deal Collective Bargaining Policy*. Berkeley: University of California Press.

Bernstein, Irving. 1960. *The Lean Years*. Boston: Houghton Mifflin.

Bernstein, Irving. 1970. *The Turbulent Years*. Boston: Houghton Mifflin.

Biddle, Francis. 1962. *In Brief Authority*. New York: Doubleday.

Black, Earl and Merle Black. 1987. *Politics and Society in the South*. Cambridge, MA: Harvard University Press.

Block, Fred. 1977a. "The Ruling Class Does Not Rule." *Socialist Revolution* 33:6–28.

Block, Fred. 1977b. "Beyond Corporate Liberalism." *Social Problems* 24:352–361.

Block, Fred. 1977c. *The Origins of International Economic Disorder*. Berkeley: University of California Press.

Block, Fred. 1987. *Revising State Theory*. Philadelphia: Temple University Press.

Blum, John. 1959. *From the Morgenthau Diaries: Years of Crisis, 1928–1938*. Boston: Houghton Mifflin.

Blum, John. 1967. *From the Morgenthau Diaries: Years of War, 1941–1945*. Boston: Houghton Mifflin.

Blum, John. 1970. *Roosevelt and Morgenthau*. Boston: Houghton Mifflin.

Blum, Robert M. 1982. *Drawing the Line*. New York: Norton.

Blumenthal, Sidney. 1986. *The Rise of the Counter-Establishment*. New York: Random House.

Bonacich, Phillip. 1972. "Technique for Analyzing Overlapping Memberships." In *Sociological Methodology*, edited by Herbert L. Costner. San Francisco: Jossey-Bass.

Bonacich, Phillip. 1982. "The Common Structure Graph: Common Structural Features of a Set of Graphs." *Mathematical Social Sciences* 2:275–288.

Bonacich, Phillip. 1987. "Power and Centrality: A Family of Measures." *American Journal of Sociology* 92:1170–1182.

Bonacich, Phillip and G. William Domhoff. 1981. "Latent Classes and Group Membership." *Social Networks* 3:175–196.

Bonnett, Clarence E. 1921. *Employer Associations in the United States*. New York: Macmillan.

Breiger, Ronald. 1974. "The Duality of Persons and Groups." *Social Forces* 53:181–190.

Brents, Barbara. 1984. "Capitalism, Corporate Liberalism and Social Policy: The Origins of the Social Security Act of 1935." *Mid-American Review of Sociology* 9:23–40.

Brents, Barbara. 1989. "Class Power and the Control of Knowledge: Policy Reform Groups and the Social Security Act." Paper presented to the meeting of the American Sociological Association, San Francisco.

Brinkley, Alan. 1984. "The New Deal and Southern Politics." In *The New Deal and the South*, edited by James C. Cobb and Michael V. Namorato. Jackson: University of Mississippi Press.

Brody, David. 1980. *Workers in Industrial America*. New York: Oxford University Press.

Brown, J. Douglas. 1972. *An American Philosophy of Social Security*. Princeton, NJ: Princeton University Press.

Brown, Richard. 1966. "The Missouri Crisis, Slavery, and the Politics of Jacksonionism." In *After the Constitution*, edited by Lance Banning. Belmont, CA: Wadsworth.

Brownstein, Ronald and Nina Easton. 1982. *Reagan's Ruling Class: Portraits of the President's 100 Officials*. Washington, DC: Presidential Accountability Group.

Brudney, Jeffrey and Gary Copeland. 1984. "Evangelicals as a Political Force: Reagan and the 1980 Religious Vote." *Social Science Quarterly* 65(4):1072–1079.

Burch, Philip. 1973. "The NAM as an Interest Group." *Politics and Society* 4:100–105.

Burch, Philip. 1980/1981. *Elites in American History*. Three volumes. New York: Holmes and Meier.

Burck, Gilbert. 1979. "A Time of Reckoning for the Building Unions." *Fortune* (June):82–95.

Business Week. 1989. "Bring CEO Pay Back Down to Earth." *Business Week* (May 1):146.

Callow, Alexander. 1966. *The Tweed Ring*. New York: Oxford University Press.

Carosso, Vincent. 1970. *Investment Banking in America*. Cambridge, MA: Harvard University Press.

Casebeer, Kenneth. 1987. "Holder of the Pen: An Interview with Leon Keyserling on Drafting the Wagner Act." *University of Miami Law Review* 42:285–363.

Chambers, William N. 1964. *The Democrats, 1789–1964*. Princeton, NJ: Van Nostrand.

Chernow, Ron. 1981. "Gray Flannel Goons: The Latest in Union Busting." *Working Papers,* (Jan–Feb):19–25.

Cheshire, Herbert. 1983. "Secretary Watt Will Go—But Later." *Business Week* (October 10):131.

Chodorow, Nancy. 1978. *The Reproduction of Mothering* Berkeley: University of California Press.

Claessen, Henri J. M. and Peter Skalnik, eds. 1978. *The Early State*. New York: Moulton.

Clausen, Aage. 1973. *How Congressmen Decide*. New York: St. Martin's.

Cohen, Ronald and Elman R. Service, eds. 1978. *Origins of the State*. Philadelphia: Institute for the Study of Human Issues.

Cohen, Stephen S. 1977. *Modern Capitalist Planning: The French Model*. Berkeley: University of California Press.

Cohen, Steven M. 1989. *The Dimensions of American Jewish Liberalism*. New York: The American Jewish Committee.

Collins, Robert M. 1981. *The Business Response to Keynes, 1929–1964*. New York: Columbia University Press.

Committee for Economic Development. 1953. *Britain's Economic Problem and Its Meaning for America*. New York: CED.

Committee for Economic Development. 1954. *United States Tariff Policy*. New York: CED.

Committee for Economic Development. 1959. *The European Common Market and Its Meaning to the United States*. New York: CED.

Committee for Economic Development. 1960. *National Objectives and the Balance of Payments*. New York: CED.

Committee for Economic Development. 1962. *A New Trade Policy for the United States*. New York: CED.

Committee for Economic Development. 1968. *The National Economy and the Vietnam War*. New York: CED.

Committee for Economic Development. 1979. *Redefining Government's Role in the Market System*. New York: CED.

Committee for Economic Development. 1980. *Fighting Inflation and Rebuilding a Sound Economy*. New York: CED.

Commons, John R. 1934. *Myself*. New York: Macmillan.

Congressional Quarterly. 1977. House Rejects Labor-Backed Picketing Bill. CQ House Votes 79–83:578–579.

Congressional Quarterly. 1978. *Carter Dealt Major Defeat on Consumer Bill.* CQ House Votes 37–44:374–375.

Congressional Quarterly. 1981a. *Reagan Economic Plan Nears Enactment.* CQ House Votes 161–167:1412–1413.

Congressional Quarterly. 1981b. *Conservative Southerners Are Enjoying Their Wooing as Key to Tax Bill Success:* 1023–1026.

Congressional Quarterly. 1981c. *House Provides President Victory on the 1982 Budget.* CQ House Votes 29–31:832–833.

Cortner, Richard. 1964. *The Wagner Act Cases.* Knoxville: University of Tennessee Press.

Council on Foreign Relations. *Studies of American Interests in the War and the Peace.* "Geographical Distribution of United States Foreign Trade: A Study in National Interests," E-B15, June 28, 1940; "The War and United States Foreign Policy: Needs of Future United States Foreign Policy," E-B19, October 19, 1940; "American Far Eastern Policy," E-B26, January 15, 1941; "Economic War Aims: General Considerations," E-B32, April 17, 1941; "Economic War Aims: Main Lines of Approach," E-B36, June 22, 1941; "Basic American Interests," P-B23, July 10, 1941;

"Methods of Economic Collaboration: The Role of the Grand Area in American Economic Policy," E-B34, July 24, 1941; "Digests of Discussion," E-A20, September 20, 1941; "International Collaboration to Secure the Coordination of Stabilization Policies and to Stimulate Investment," E-B44, November 28, 1941; "Tentative Draft of a Joint Economic Declaration by the Governments of the United States and the United Kingdom," E-B45, January 3, 1942; "Digests of Discussion," E-A25, Part II, January 24, 1942; "Digests of Discussion," T-A25, May 20, 1942; "Digests of Discussion," E-A24, March 6, 1943; "International Adjustment of Exchange Rates," E-B64, April 6, 1943; "Regionalism in Southeast Asia," T-B67, September 14, 1943.

Crock, Stan. 1984. "A Slowdown in Deregulation Doesn't Bother Business." *Business Wekk* (June 11):45.

Dahl, Robert A. 1958. "A Critique of the Ruling Elite Model." *American Political Science Review* 52:463–469.

Dahl, Robert A. 1960. "Book Review: Top Leadership, U.S.A." *The Journal of Politics* 22:148–151.

Dahl, Robert A. 1961. *Who Governs?* New Haven, CT: Yale University Press.

Danforth, Brian J. 1974. "The Influence of Socio-Economic Factors Upon Political Behavior: A Quantitative Look at New York City Merchants, 1828–1844." Ph.D. diss., New York University.

Daniel, Pete. 1984. "The New Deal, Southern Agriculture, and Economic Change." In *The New Deal and the South,* edited by James C. Cobb and Michael V. Namorato. Jackson: University of Mississippi Press.

David, Paul T., Malcolm Moos, and Ralph M. Goldman. 1954. *Presidential Nominating Politics in 1952.* Baltimore, MD: Johns Hopkins University Press.

Davidson, Chandler and George Korbel. 1981. At-Large Elections and Minority-Group Representation: A Re-Examination of Historical and Contemporary Evidence." *Journal of Politics* 43:982–1005.

Davis, Norman. Collected Papers. Library of Congress, Washington, D.C.

Dempsey, Joseph R. 1961. *The Operation of the Right-to-Work Laws*. Milwaukee, MN: Marquette University Press.

Diebold, William. 1941. *New Directions in Our Trade Policy*. New York: Council on Foreign Relations.

DiTomaso, Nancy. 1980. "Organizational Analysis and Power Structure Research." In *Power Structure Research*, edited by G. William Domhoff. Beverly Hills, CA: Sage Publications.

Divine, Robert. 1967. *Second Chance*. New York: Atheneum.

Dobson, Alan P. 1986. *U.S. Wartime Aid to Britain, 1940–1946*. London: Croom Helm.

Domhoff, G. William. 1967. *Who Rules America?* Englewood Cliffs, NJ: Prentice-Hall.

Domhoff, G. William. 1969a. "Historical Materialism, Cultural Determinism, and the Origin of the Ruling Classes." *The Psychoanalytic Review* 56:271–287.

Domhoff, G. William. 1969b. "How the Power Elite Makes Foreign Policy." In *Corporations and the Cold War*, edited by David Horowitz. New York: Monthly Review.

Domhoff, G. William. 1970a. "But Why Did They Sit on the King's Right in the First Place?" *Psychoanalytic Review* 56:586–596.

Domhoff, G. William. 1970b. "Two Luthers: The Traditional and the Heretical in Freudian Psychology." *Psychoanalytic Review* 57:5–17.

Domhoff, G. William. 1970c. *The Higher Circles*. New York: Random House.

Domhoff, G. William. 1972. *Fat Cats and Democrats*. Englewood Cliffs, NJ: Prentice-Hall.

Domhoff, G. William. 1974a. "State and Ruling Class in Corporate America." *Insurgent Sociologist* 4:3–16.

Domhoff, G. William. 1974b. *The Bohemian Grove and Other Retreats*. New York: Harper and Row.

Domhoff, G. William. 1975. "Social Clubs, Policy-Planning Groups, and Corporations: A Network Study of Ruling-Class Cohesiveness." *Insurgent Sociologist* 5:173–184.

Domhoff, G. William. 1976. "I Am Not An Instrumentalist." *Kapitalistate* 4–5:221–224.

Domhoff, G. William. 1978. *Who Really Rules: New Haven and Community Power Re-Examined*. New Brunswick, NJ: Transaction Books.

Domhoff, G. William. 1979. *The Powers That Be*. New York: Random House.

Domhoff, G. William. 1980. "Introduction." In *Power Structure Research*, edited by G. William Domhoff. Beverly Hills, CA: Sage Publications.

Domhoff, G. William. 1981. "Provincial in Paris: Finding the French Council on Foreign Relations." *Social Policy* (March/April):5–13.

Domhoff, G. William. 1983a. *Who Rules America Now?* Englewood Cliffs, NJ: Prentice-Hall.

Domhoff, G. William. 1983b. "Review: The New Class War." *Social Policy* (Winter):53–59.

Domhoff, G. William. 1986/87. "Corporate Liberal Theory and the Social Security Act." *Politics and Society* 15:297–330.

Domhoff, G. William. 1986a. "The Power Elite and the Growth Machine: A Challenge to Pluralists and Marxists Alike." In *Community Power*, edited by Robert J. Waste. Beverly Hills, CA: Sage Publications.

Domhoff, G. William. 1986b. State Autonomy and the Privileged Position of Business:

An Empirical Attack on a Theoretical Fantasy." *Journal of Political and Military Sociology* 14:149–162.

Domhoff, G. William. 1986c. "On Welfare Capitalism and the Social Security Act of 1935." *American Sociological Review* 51:445–446.

Domhoff, G. William. 1987a. "The Wagner Act and Theories of the State." *Political Power and Social Theory* 6:159–185.

Domhoff, G. William. 1987b. "Where Do Government Experts Come From?" In *Power Elites and Organizations,* edited by G. William Domhoff and Thomas R. Dye. Beverly Hills, CA: Sage Publications.

Domhoff, G. William. 1988. "Big Money in American Politics." *Theory and Society* 17:589–596.

Domhoff, G. William and Hoyt B. Ballard, eds. 1968. *C. Wright Mills and The Power Elite.* Boston: Beacon.

Donovan, John C. 1974. *The Cold Warriors: A Policy-Making Elite.* Lexington, MA: Heath Lexington Books.

Dorsett, Lyle W. 1968. *The Pendergast Machine.* New York: Oxford University Press.

Dorsett, Lyle W. 1977. *Franklin D. Roosevelt and the City Bosses.* Port Washington, NY: Kennikat.

Dubofsky, Melvin and Warren Van Tine. 1977. *John L. Lewis.* New York: Quadrangle.

Dye, Thomas R. 1976. *Who's Running America?* Englewood Cliffs, NJ: Prentice-Hall.

Dye, Thomas R. 1984. *Who's Running America? The Reagan Years.* Englewood Cliffs, NJ: Prentice-Hall.

Eakins, David. 1966. "The Development of Corporate Liberal Policy Research in the United States, 1885–1965." Ph.D. diss. University of Wisconsin, Madison.

Eakins, David. 1969. "Business Planners and America's Postwar Expansion." In *Corporations and the Cold War,* edited by David Horowitz. New York: Monthly Review.

Eakins, David. 1972. "Policy-Planning for the Establishment." In *The New Leviathan,* edited by Ronald Radosh and Murray Rothbard. New York: Dutton.

Eckes, Alfred E. 1975. *A Search for Solvency.* Austin: University of Texas Press.

Editors, 1948. "Renovation in NAM." *Fortune* 38(1):72–75, 166–169.

Editors of Studies on the Left. 1962. "The Ultra-Right and Cold War Liberalism." *Studies on the Left* 3:3–8.

Edsall, Thomas. 1984. *The New Politics of Inequality.* New York: Norton.

Ely, Richard. 1938. *Ground under Our Feet.* New York: Macmillan.

Erie, Stephen. 1988. *Rainbow's End.* Berkeley: University of California Press.

Feigenbaum, Harvey. 1985. *The Politics of Public Enterprise: Oil and the French State.* Princeton, NJ: Princeton University Press.

Fenno, Richard. 1978. *Home Style.* Boston: Little, Brown.

Ferguson, Thomas. 1984. "From Normalcy to New Deal." *International Organizations* 38:41–94.

Ferguson, Thomas and Joel Rogers. 1981. *The Hidden Election.* New York: Pantheon.

Ferguson, Thomas and Joel Rogers. 1986. *Right Turn.* New York: Hill and Wang.

Fifield, Russell. 1963. *Southeast Asia in United States Policy.* New York: Praeger.

Finegold, Kenneth and Theda Skocpol. 1984. "State, Party, and Industry: From Business Recovery to the Wagner Act in America's New Deal." In *Statemaking and Social*

*Movements,* edited by Charles Bright and Susan Harding. Ann Arbor: University of Michigan Press.

Flacks, Richard. 1988. *Making History.* New York: Columbia University Press.

Foner, Philip Sheldon. 1941. *Business and Slavery: The New York Merchants and the Irrepressible Conflict.* Chapel Hill, NC: University of North Carolina Press.

Fraser, Steve. 1984. From the 'New Unionism' to the New Deal." *Labor History* 25:422–423.

Fraser, Steve. 1989. "The Labor Question." In *The Rise and Fall of the New Deal Order, 1930–1980,* edited by Steve Fraser and Gary Gerstle. Princeton, NJ: Princeton University Press.

Freidel, Frank. 1984. "The New Deal and the South." In *The New Deal and the South,* edited by James C. Cobb and Michael V. Namorato. Jackson: University of Mississippi Press.

Freitag, Peter. 1975. "The Cabinet and Big Business." *Social Problems* 23:137–152.

Freud, Sigmund. 1913. "Totem and Taboo." In *The Standard Edition of the Complete Psychological Works of Sigmund Freud,* edited by James Strachey. London: Hogarth.

Freud, Sigmund. 1921. "Group Psychology and the Analysis of the Ego." In *The Standard Edition of the Complete Psychological Works of Sigmund Freud,* edited by James Strachey. London: Hogarth.

Freud, Sigmund. 1927. "The Future of an Illusion." In *The Standard Edition of the Complete Psychological Works of Sigmund Freud,* edited by James Strachey. London: Hogarth.

Freud, Sigmund. 1930. "Civilization and Its Discontents." In *The Standard Edition of the Complete Psychological Works of Sigmund Freud,* edited by James Strachey. London: Hogarth.

Frieden, Jeff. 1988. "Sectoral Conflict and U.S. Foreign Economic Policy, 1914–1940." In *The State and American Foreign Economic Policy,* edited by G. John Ikenberry, David A. Lake and Michael Mastanduno. Ithaca, NJ: Cornell University Press.

Friedland, Roger. 1982. *Power and Crisis in the City.* London: Macmillan.

Friedlander, Peter. 1987. "The Origins of the Welfare State: The Keynesian Elite and the Second New Deal." Manuscript. Wayne State University, Detroit, MI.

Fuchs, Lawrence H. 1956. *The Political Behavior of American Jews.* New York: Free Press.

Gable, Richard. 1953. "The NAM: Influential Lobby or Kiss of Death?" *Journal of Politics* 15:254–273.

Gaddis, John. 1972. *The United States and the Origin of the Cold War, 1941–1947.* New York: Columbia University Press.

Gaddis, John. 1983. "The Emerging Post-Revisionist Synthesis on the Origins of the Cold War." *Diplomatic History* 7:171–190.

Gaddis, John. 1987. *The Long Peace.* New York: Oxford University Press.

Gailbraith, John K. 1971. *Economies, Peace and Laughter.* Boston: Houghton Mifflin.

Gamson, William A. 1975. *The Strategy of Social Protest.* Homewood, IL: Dorsey.

Gardner, Lloyd. 1964. *Economic Aspects of New Deal Diplomacy.* Madison: University of Wisconsin Press.

Gardner, Richard N. 1956. *Sterling-Dollar Diplomacy.* New York: McGraw Hill.

Gelb, Leslie and Richard Betts. 1979. *The Irony of Vietnam: The System Worked*. Washington: Brookings Institution.

Genovese, Eugene D. 1965. *The Political Economy of Slavery*. New York: Pantheon.

Gitelman, H. M. 1984a. "The Rockefeller Network in Industrial Relations." Paper presented to meeting of the Social Science History Association, New York.

Gitelman, H. M. 1984b. "Being of Two Minds: American Employers Confront the Labor Problem, 1915–1919." *Labor History* 25:189–216.

Gitelman, H. M. 1988. *Legacy of the Ludlow Massacre*. Philadelphia: University of Pennsylvania Press.

Gold, David, Clarence Lo, and Erik Wright. 1975. "Recent Developments in Marxist Theories of the Capitalist State." *Monthly Review* 27:29–43.

Goldfield, Michael. 1987. *The Decline of Organized Labor in the United States*. Chicago: University of Chicago Press.

Goldfield, Michael. 1989. "Worker Insurgency, Radical Organization, and New Deal Labor Legislation." *American Political Science Review* 83:1257–1282.

Goldman, Ralph M. 1966. *The Democratic Party in American Politics*. New York: Macmillan.

Goldmark, Josephine. 1953. *The Impatient Crusader*. Urbana: University of Illinois Press.

Goodall, Leonard E. 1968. *The American Metropolis*. New York: Merrill.

Goodman, Paul. 1964. *The Democratic-Republicans of Massachusetts*. Cambridge, MA: Harvard University Press.

Goulden, Joseph L. 1971. *The Super Lawyers*. New York: Weybright and Talley.

Graebner, William. 1980. *A History of Retirement: The Meaning and Function of an American Institution*. New Haven, CT: Yale University Press.

Graebner, William. 1982. "From Pensions to Social Security: Social Insurance and the Rise of Dependency." In *The Quest for Security*, edited by John N. Schact. Iowa City: Center for the Study of the Recent History of the United States.

Granovetter, Mark. 1973. "The Strength of Weak Ties." *American Journal of Sociology* 78:1360–1380.

Grantham, Dewey W., Jr. 1963. *The Democratic South*. Athens: University of Georgia Press.

Green, Marguerite. 1956. *The National Civic Federation and the American Federation of Labor, 1900–1925*. Washington: Catholic University of America Press.

Gregor, Thomas. 1985. *Anxious Pleasures* Chicago: University of Chicago Press.

Greider, William. 1987. *Secrets of the Temple*. New York: Simon & Schuster.

Gross, Bertram. 1953. *The Legislative Struggle: A Study in Social Combat*. New York: McGraw-Hill.

Gross, James A. 1974. *The Making of the National Labor Relations Board*. Albany: State University of New York Press.

Gross, James A. 1981. *The Reshaping of the National Labor Relations Board*. Albany: State University of New York Press.

Guttsman, W. L. 1963. *The British Political Elite*. New York: Basic Books.

Haggard, Stephan. 1988. "The Institutional Foundations of Hegemony: Explaining the Reciprocal Trade Agreements Act of 1934." In *The State and American Foreign*

*Economic Policy,* edited by G. John Ikenberry, David A. Lake and Michael Mastanduno. Ithaca, NY: Cornell University Press.

Hall, Donald. 1969. *Cooperative Lobbying.* Tucson: University of Arizona Press.

Haller, Mark H. 1962. "The Rise of the Jackson Party in Maryland, 1820–1829." *Journal of Southern History* 28:307–326.

Hamilton, Richard. 1972. *Class and Politics in the United States.* New York: Wiley.

Hamilton, Richard. 1975. *Restraining Myths.* New York: Wiley.

Hamilton, Richard. 1990. *The Bourgeois Epoch.* Unpublished book manuscript. Department of Sociology, Ohio State University.

Hammond, Bray. 1957. *Banks and Politics in America.* Princeton, NJ: Princeton University Press.

Hansen, Alvin. Collected Papers. Harvard University Library, Cambridge, MA.

Hansen, Alvin. 1965. *The Dollar and the International Monetary System.* New York: McGraw-Hill.

Hargrove, E. and S. Morley. 1984. *The President and the Council of Economic Advisers: Interviews with CEA Chairman.* Boulder, CO: Westview.

Harris, Howell. 1985. "The Snares of Liberalism? Politicians, Bureaucrats, and the Shaping of Federal Labour Relations Policy in the United States, ca. 1915–1947." In *Shop Floor Bargaining and the State,* edited by Steven Tolliday and Jonathan Zeitlin. New York: Cambridge University Press.

Harrod, Roy F. 1951. *The Life of John Maynard Keynes.* New York: Harcourt Brace.

Hawley, Ellis. 1966. *The New Deal and the Problem of Monopoly.* Princeton, NJ: Princeton University Press.

Hawley, Ellis. 1975. "The New Deal and Business." In *The New Deal: The National Level,* edited by John Braeman et al. Columbus: Ohio State University Press.

Hayes, Samuel A. 1971. *The Beginnings of American Aid to Southeast Asia.* Lexington, MA: Heath.

Hays, Samuel P. 1964. "The Politics of Reform in Municipal Government in the Progressive Era." *Pacific Northwest Review* 55:157–169.

Heilbroner, Robert. 1980. *Marxism: For and Against.* New York: Norton.

Heilbroner, Robert. 1988. "Economies without Power." *New York Review* (March 3):23–25.

Hess, Gary R. 1987. *The United States' Emergence as a Southeast Asian Power, 1940–1950.* New York: Columbia University Press.

Hewitt, Christopher. 1977. "The Effect of Political Democracy and Economic Democracy on Equality in Industrial Societies." *American Sociological Review* 42:450–464.

Hicks, Alexander and Duane H. Swank. 1983. "Civil Disorder, Relief Mobilization and AFDC Caseloads: A Reexamination of the Piven and Cloward Thesis." *American Journal of Political Science* 27:695–716.

Higley, John and Michael Burton. 1989. "The Elite Variable in Democratic Transitions and Breakdowns." *American Sociological Review* 54:17–32.

Higley, John and Gwen Moore. 1981. "Elite Integration in the U.S. and Australia." *American Political Science Review* 75:581–597.

Himmelfarb, Harold, Michael Loar, and Susan Mott. 1983. "Sampling by Ethnic Surnames: The Case of American Jews." *Public Opinion Quarterly* 47:247–260.

Himmelstein, Jerome. 1989. *To the Right*. Berkeley: University of California Press.

Himmelstein, Jerome and James McRae. 1984. "Social Conservatism, New Republicans, and the 1980 Election." *Public Opinion Quarterly* 48:592–605.

Hinchey, Mary H. 1965. "The Frustrations of the New Deal Revival." Ph.D. diss. University of Missouri, Columbia.

Hirsch, Glenn. 1975. "Only You Can Prevent Ideological Hegemony: The Advertising Council and Its Place in the American Power Structure." *Insurgent Sociologist* 5:64–82.

Hollingsworth, J. Rogers. 1963. *The Whirligig of Politics*. Chicago: University of Chicago Press.

Horowitz, Irving L. 1963. "The Unfinished Writings of C. Wright Mills: The Last Phase." *Studies on the Left* 3:2–23.

Huff, Darrell. 1954. *How to Lie with Statistics*. New York: Norton.

Hull, Cordell. 1948. *The Memoirs of Cordell Hull*. New York: Macmillan.

Hunter, Floyd. 1953. *Community Power Structure*. Chapel Hill: University of North Carolina Press.

Hunter, Floyd. 1959. *Top Leadership, USA*. Chapel Hill: University of North Carolina Press.

Huntington, Samuel P. 1977. "A Policy Adviser's Response on Vietnam." *Washington Post* (February 1):A-17.

Huthmacher, J. Joseph. 1968. *Senator Robert F. Wagner and the Rise of Urban Liberalism*. New York: Atheneum.

Irons, Peter. 1982. *The New Deal Lawyers*. Princeton, NJ: Princeton University Press.

Isaac, Larry and William Kelly. 1981. "Racial Insurgency, the State and Welfare Expansion: Local National Level Evidence from Post-War United States." *American Journal of Sociology* 86:1348–1386.

Isaacs, Stephen D. 1974. *Jews and American Politics*. Garden City, NY: Doubleday.

Jenkins, J. Craig and Barbara Brents. 1989. "Social Protest, Hegemonic Competition, and Social Reform." *American Sociological Review* 54:891–909.

Jenkins, J. Craig and Teri Shumate. 1985. "Cowboy Capitalists and the Rise of the 'New Right': An Analysis of Contributors to Conservative Policy Formation Organizations." *Social Problems* 33:130–145.

Jensen, Gordon. 1956. "The National Civic Federation: American Business in Our Age of Social Change and Social Reform, 1900–1910." Ph.D. diss. Princeton University, Princeton, NJ.

Johnson, Mark. 1978. "The Consensus Seekers: How the Power Elite Shape National Policy." Master's thesis. University of California, Santa Barbara.

Johnson, Stephen and Joseph Taney. 1982. "The Christian Right and the 1980 Presidential Election." *Journal for the Scientific Study of Religion* 21(2):123–131.

Jones, Byrd L. 1972. "The Role of Keynesians in Wartime Policy and Postwar Planning, 1940–1946." Papers and proceedings of the 84th annual meeting of the American Economic Association, New Orleans, 1971. *American Economic Review* 62:125–133.

Kadushin, Charles. 1968. "Power, Influence and Social Circles: A New Methodology for Studying Opinion Makers." *American Sociological Review* 33:685–699.

Kanter, Rosabeth. 1977. *Men and Women of the Corporation*. New York: Basic Books.

Kattenburg, Paul M. 1980. *The Vietnam Trauma in American Foreign Policy, 1945–1975.* New Brunswick, NJ: Transaction.

Katz, Irving. 1968. *August Belmont: A Political Biography.* New York: Columbia University Press.

Key, V. O., Jr. 1949. *Southern Politics in State and Nation.* New York: Knopf.

Keyserling, Leon. 1960. "The Wagner Act: Its Origin and Current Significance." *George Washington Law Review* 29:199–233.

King, John K. 1956. *Southeast Asia in Perspective.* New York: Macmillan.

Klare, Karl. 1978. "Judicial Deradicalization of the Wagner Act and the Origins of Modern Legal Consciousness, 1937–1941." *Minnesota Law Review* 62:265–339.

Klehr, Harvey. 1984. *The Heyday of American Communism.* New York: Basic Books.

Kolko, Gabriel. 1964. *The Triumph of Conservatism.* New York: Free Press.

Kolko, Gabriel. 1965. *Railroads and Regulation.* Cambridge, MA: Harvard University Press.

Kolko, Gabriel. 1980. "Intelligence and the Myth of Capitalist Rationality in the United States." *Science and Society* 44:130–154.

Krasner, Stephen. 1977. "United States Commercial and Monetary Policy." *International Organization* 31:51–87.

Krasner, Stephen. 1978. *Defending the National Interest.* Princeton, NJ: Princeton University Press.

LaBarre, Weston. 1954. *The Human Animal.* Chicago: University of Chicago Press.

LaBarre, Weston. 1970. *The Ghost Dance.* New York: Dell Publishing.

Lamis, Alexander P. 1984. *The Two Party South.* New York: Oxford University Press.

Langer, William L. and S. Everett Gleason. 1953. *The Undeclared War, 1940–1941.* New York: Harper and Row.

Lash, Joseph P. 1988. *Dealers and Dreamers.* New York: Doubleday.

Laslett, John. 1970. *Labor and the Left.* New York: Basic Books.

Lazarsfield, Paul. 1966. "Concept Formation and Measurement." In *Concepts, Theory, and Explanation in the Behavioral Sciences,* edited by Gordon DiRenzo. New York: Random House.

Lazerwitz, Bernard. 1986. "Some Comments on the Use of Distinctive Jewish Names in Surveys." *Contemporary Jewry* 7:85–91.

Lehmann, Ingrid. 1975. "Corporate Capitalism and the Liberal State." *Kapitalistate* 3:159–166.

Leuchtenberg, William. 1963. *Franklin D. Roosevelt and The New Deal.* New York: Harper and Row.

Levine, Rhonda F. 1988. *Class Struggle and the New Deal.* Lawrence: University of Kansas Press.

Lindblom, Charles. 1977. *Politics and Markets.* New York: Basic Books.

Lipset, Seymour. 1963. *The First New Nation.* New York: Basic Books.

Lipset, Seymour and Earl Raab. 1984. "The American Jews, the 1984 Elections, and Beyond." *Tocqueville Review* 6:401–419.

Lo, Clarence. 1982. "Theories of the State and Business Opposition to Increases in Military Spending." *Social Problems* 29:424–438.

Logan, John and Harvey Molotch. 1987. *Urban Fortunes.* Berkeley: University of California Press.

Loth, David. 1958. *Swope of G.E.* New York: Simon & Schuster.

Lublin, Joann. 1983. "Federal Deregulation Runs into a Backlash, Even from Business." *Wall Street Journal* (December 14):1.

Lubove, Roy C. 1968. *The Struggle for Social Security, 1900–1935.* Cambridge, MA: Harvard University Press.

Luker, Kristin. 1984. *Abortion and the Politics of Motherhood.* Berkeley: University of California Press.

Lundberg, Ferdinand. 1937. *America's Sixty Families.* New York: Vanguard.

Lyon, Richard M. 1952. "The American Association for Labor Legislation and the Fight for Workmen's Compensation, 1906–1942." Master's thesis. Cornell University, Ithaca, NY.

Magruder, Calvert. 1937. "A Half Century of Legal Influence upon the Development of Collective Bargaining." *Harvard Law Review* 50:1071–1117.

Malinowski, Bronislaw. 1922. *Argonauts of the Western Pacific.* New York: Dutton.

Mandelbaum, Seymour. 1965. *Boss Tweed's New York.* New York: Wiley.

Manley, John F. 1973. "The Conservative Coalition in Congress." *American Behavioral Scientist* 17:223–247.

Mann, Michael. 1975. The Ideology of Intellectuals and Other People in the Development of Capitalism." In *Stress and Contradiction in Modern Capitalism,* edited by Leon Lindberg et al. Lexington, MA: Lexington Books.

Mann, Michael. 1977. "States, Ancient and Modern." *Archives of European Sociology* 18:226–298.

Mann, Michael. 1980. "State and Society, 1130–1815: An Analysis of English State Finances." *Political Power and Social Theory* 1:165–208.

Mann, Michael. 1984. The Autonomous Power of the State: Its Origins, Mechanisms and Results. *Archives of European Sociology* 25:185–213.

Mann, Michael. 1986. *The Sources of Social Power.* New York: Cambridge University Press.

Marger, Martin M. 1981. *Elites and Masses.* Belmont, CA: Wadsworth.

Margolin, Sally O. 1976. "Who Rules? Who Governs? Who Cares?" Master's paper. Arizona State University, Tempe.

Mariolis, Peter. 1975. "Interlocking Directorates and Control of Corporations." *Social Sciences Quarterly* 56:425–439.

Maslow, Abraham. 1954. *Motivation and Personality.* New York: Harper and Row.

Matthews, Donald. 1954. *The Social Background of Political Decision-Makers.* New York: Doubleday.

Mayhew, David R. 1966. *Party Loyalty Among Congressmen.* Cambridge, MA: Harvard University Press.

McConnell, Grant. 1958. "Major Economic Groups and National Policy." *American Roundtable Digest Report, People's Capitalism, Part III, October 22, 1958.*

McConnell, Grant. 1966. *Private Power and American Democracy.* New York: Knopf.

McCormick, Richard P. 1964. *The Second Party System.* Chapel Hill: University of North Carolina Press.

McCune, Wesley. 1956. *Who's Behind Our Farm Policy?* New York: Praeger.

McLellan, David S. and Charles E. Woodhouse. 1960. "The Business Elite and Foreign Policy." *Western Political Quarterly* 13:172–90.

McLellan, David S. and Charles E. Woodhouse. 1966. "American Business Leaders and Foreign Policy: A Study in Perspectives." *American Journal of Economics and Sociology* 25:267–180.

McNall, Scott. 1977. "Does Anybody Rule America? A Critique of Elite Theory and Method." Paper presented at the annual meeting of the American Sociological Association, Chicago, Sept. 5–9.

McQuaid, Kim. 1976. "The Business Advisory Council in the Department of Commerce, 1933–1961." *Research in Economic History* 1:171–197.

McQuaid, Kim. 1979. "The Frustration of Corporate Revival in the Early New Deal." *Historian* 41:682–704.

McQuaid, Kim. 1982. *Big Business and Presidential Power from FDR to Reagan*. New York: Morrow.

Melone, Albert. 1972. "Lawyers and the Republic: The American Bar Association and Public Policy." Ph.D. diss. University of Iowa, Ames.

Melone, Albert. 1977. *Lawyers, Public Policy and Interest Group Politics*. Washington: University Press of America.

Mencken, H. L. 1924. *Prejudices: Fourth Series*. New York: Knopf.

Merrill, Horace. 1953. *Bourbon Democracy of the Middle West, 1865–1896*. Baton Rouge: Louisiana State University Press.

Miliband, Ralph. 1969. *The State in Capitalist Society*. New York: Basic Books.

Miller, Norman C. 1970. "The Machine Democrats." *Washington Monthly* (June):70–73.

Mills, C. Wright. 1948. *The New Men of Power*. New York: Harcourt Brace.

Mills, C. Wright. 1956. *The Power Elite*. New York: Oxford University Press.

Mills, C. Wright. 1959. *The Sociological Imagination*. New York: Oxford University Press.

Mills, C. Wright. 1962. *The Marxists*. New York: Dell.

Mills, C. Wright. 1968. "Comment on Criticism." In *C. Wright Mills and the Power Elite*, edited by G. William Domhoff and Hoyt B. Ballard. Boston: Beacon.

Mink, Gwendolyn R. 1986. *Old Labor and New Immigrants in American Political Development, 1870–1925*. Ithaca, NY: Cornell University Press.

Mintz, Beth. 1975. "The President's Cabinet, 1897–1972." *Insurgent Sociologist* 5:131–148.

Mintz, Beth and Michael Schwartz. 1981a. "The Structure of Intercorporate Unity in American Business." *Social Problems* 29:87–103.

Mintz, Beth and Michael Schwartz. 1981b. "Interlocking Directorates and Interest Group Formation." *American Sociological Review* 46:857–869.

Mintz, Beth and Michael Schwartz. 1983. "Financial Interest Groups and Interlocking Directorates." *Social Science History* 7:183–204.

Mintz, Beth and Michael Schwartz. 1985. *The Power Structure of American Business*. Chicago: University of Chicago Press.

Mizruchi, Mark. 1982. *The Structure of the American Corporate Network, 1904–1974*. Beverly Hills, CA: Sage Publications.

Moley, Raymond. 1949. *27 Masters of Politics*. New York: Funk and Wagnalls.

Mollenkopf, John. 1975a. "Theories of the State and Power Structure Research." *Insurgent Sociologist* 5:245–264.

Mollenkopf, John. 1975b. "The Post-War Politics of Urban Development." *Politics and Society* 5:247–295.

Molotch, Harvey. 1970. "Oil in Santa Barbara and Power in America." *Sociological Inquiry* 40:131–144.

Molotch, Harvey. 1976. "The City as a Growth Machine." *American Journal of Sociology* 82:309–330.

Molotch, Harvey. 1979. "Capital and Neighborhood in the United States." *Urban Affairs Quarterly* 14:289–312.

Moore, Gwen. 1979. "The Structure of a National Elite Network." *American Sociological Review* 44:673–692.

Moore, Stanley. 1957. *A Critique of Capitalist Democracy.* New York: Monthly Review.

Morgenstern, Oskar. 1963. *On the Accuracy of Economic Observations.* Princeton, NJ: Princeton University Press.

Morgenthau, Henry. Morgenthau Diaries. Franklin D. Roosevelt Library, Hyde Park, New York.

Mulherin, James P. 1979. "The Sociology of Work and Organizations: Historical Context and Pattern of Development." Ph.D. diss. University of California, Berkeley.

Murrin, John. 1980. "The Great Inversion, or Court versus Country." In *After The Constitution,* edited by Lance Banning. Belmont, CA: Wadsworth.

Mushkat, Jerome. 1971. *Tammany.* Syracuse, NY: Syracuse University Press.

Mushkat, Jerome. 1981. *The Reconstruction of the New York Democracy, 1861–1874.* Rutherford, NJ: Associated University Press.

Nelson, Daniel. 1969. *Unemployment Insurance: The American Experience, 1915–1935.* Madison: University of Wisconsin Press.

*New York Times.* 1934. "General Motors Earns $1.51 a Common Share in Half Year." (July 26):27.

*New York Times.* 1935a. "General Motors Plans Expansion to Cost $50,000,000." (August 12):1.

*New York Times.* 1935b. "Business Advisors Uphold the President." (May 3):1.

*New York Times.* 1935c. "Three Members Quit the Roper Council." (June 27):5.

*New York Times.* 1935d. "Say Lund Has Quit as Roper Adviser." (June 29):2.

*New York Times.* 1935e. "Quits Roper Council." (July 4):29.

*New York Times.* 1935f. "Ecker Questions Federal Financing." (February 3):29.

*New York Times.* 1935g. "W. Aldrich Quits Business Council." (August 8):11.

*New York Times.* 1958. "Pressure Groups Called Integral." (July 12):48.

*New York Times.* 1988. "Portrait of the Electorate." (November 10):A16.

Noble, Charles. 1986. *Liberalism at Work.* Philadelphia: Temple University Press.

Nordlinger, Eric. 1981. *On the Autonomy of the Democratic State.* Cambridge, MA: Harvard University Press.

Notter, Harley. 1949. *Postwar Foreign Policy Preparation, 1939–1945.* Washington: USGPO.

O'Connell, Charles. 1988. "Talcott Parsons and The German Summer of 1948." Paper presented to the meeting of the American Sociological Association, Atlanta, GA.

O'Connell, Charles. 1989. "Social Structure and Science: Soviet Studies at Harvard." Ph.D. diss. University of California, Los Angeles.

O'Connor, James. 1973. *The Fiscal Crisis of the State.* New York: St. Martin's.

O'Connor, James. 1984. *Accumulation Crisis*. London: Basil and Blackwell.

Offe, Claus. 1974. "Structural Problems of the Capitalist State." In *German Political Studies,* edited by Klaus von Beyme. Beverly Hills, CA: Sage Publications.

Oliver, Robert W. 1971. "Early Plans for a World Bank." *Princeton Studies in International Finance* 29. Princeton, NJ: Princeton University.

Oliver, Robert W. 1975. *International Economic Co-operation and the World Bank*. London: Macmillan.

Overacker, Louise. 1932. *Money in Elections*. New York: Macmillan.

Overacker, Louise. 1933. "Campaign Funds in a Depression Year." *American Political Science Review* 27:769–783.

Overacker, Louise. 1937. "Campaign Funds in the Presidential Election of 1936." *American Political Science Review* 31:473–498.

Overacker, Louise. 1941. "Campaign Finance in the Presidential Election of 1940." *American Political Science Review* 35:701–727.

Overacker, Louise. 1945. "Presidential Campaign Funds, 1944." *American Political Science Review* 39:899–925.

Pastor, Robert A. 1980. *Congress and the Politics of U.S. Foreign Economic Policy*. Berkeley: University of California Press.

Pasztor, Andy. 1983. "Watt Tries to Project New, Moderate Image But Encounters Growing Number of Critics." *Wall Street Journal* (August 3):25.

Paterson, Thomas G. 1973. *Soviet-American Confrontation*. Baltimore, MD: John Hopkins University Press.

Patterson, James T. 1967. *Congressional Conservatism and the New Deal*. Lexington: University of Kentucky Press.

Patterson, Orlando. 1987. "The Unholy Trinity: Freedom, Slavery, and the American Constitution." *Social Research* 54:543–577.

Pearson, Drew and Jack Anderson. 1968. *The Case Against Congress*. New York: Simon & Schuster.

Penrose, Ernest F. 1953. *Economic Planning for the Peace*. Princeton, NJ: Princeton University Press.

*Pentagon Papers*. 1971. Edited by Senator Mike Gravel. Boston: Beacon Press.

Peschek, Joseph. 1987. *Policy-Planning Organizations*. Philadelphia: Temple University Press.

Pessen, Edward. 1984. *The Log Cabin Myth*. New Haven, CT: Yale University Press.

Pierce, Lloyd F. 1953. "The Activities of the American Association for Labor Legislation in Behalf of Social Security and Protective Labor Legislation." Ph.D. diss. University of Wisconsin, Madison.

Piven, Frances and Richard Cloward. 1971. *Regulating the Poor*. New York: Pantheon.

Piven, Frances and Richard Cloward. 1977. *Poor People's Movements*. New York: Random House.

Piven, Frances and Richard Cloward. 1982/1985. *The New Class War*. New York: Random House.

Plotke, David. 1989. "The Wagner Act, Again: Politics and Labor, 1935–37." In *Studies in American Political Development,* edited by Karen Orren and Stephen Skowronek. New Haven, CT: Yale University Press.

Polsby, Nelson. 1963. *Community Power and Political Theory*. New Haven, CT: Yale University Press.

Polsby, Nelson. 1980. *Community Power and Political Theory*. 2nd ed. New Haven, CT: Yale University Press.

Polsby, Nelson. 1984. *Political Innovation in America*. New Haven, CT: Yale University Press.

Potter, David M. 1972. *The South and the Concurrent Majority*. Baton Rouge: Louisiana State University Press.

Poulantzas, Nicos. 1969. "The Problem of the Capitalist State." *New Left Review* 58:67–78.

Poulantzas, Nicos. 1973. *Political Power and Social Classes*. London: New Left Books.

Preeg, Ernest. 1970. *Traders and Diplomats: An Analysis of the Kennedy Round of Negotiations under the General Agreement on Tariffs and Trades*. Washington: Brookings Institution.

Prewitt, Kenneth and Alan Stone. 1973. *The Ruling Elites*. New York: Harper and Row.

Prial, Frank J. 1966. "A New NAM? Business Group Edges from Far Right, Pushes Its Own Social Plans." *Wall Street Journal* (May 31):1.

Quadagno, Jill S. 1984. "Welfare Capitalism and the Social Security Act of 1935." *American Sociological Review* 49:632–647.

Quadagno, Jill S. 1988. *The Transformation of Old Age Security*. Chicago: University of Chicago Press.

Radosh, Ronald. 1966. "The Corporate Ideology of American Labor Leaders from Gompers to Hillman." *Studies on the Left* 6:66–88.

Radosh, Ronald. 1967. "The Development of the Corporate Ideology of Organized Labor, 1914–1933." Ph.D. diss. University of Wisconsin, Madison.

Radosh, Ronald. 1972. "The Myth of the New Deal." In *The New Leviathan*, edited by Ronald Radosh and Murray N. Rothbard. New York: Dutton.

Ramirez, Bruno. 1978. *When Workers Fight*. Westport, CT: Greenwood.

Randall, Stephen J. 1980. "Raw Materials and United States Foreign Policy." *Reviews in American History* 8:413–418.

Randall, Stephen J. 1985. *United States Foreign Oil Policy, 1919–1948*. Kingston, Ontario, Canada: McGill-Queen's University Press.

Reagan, Michael. 1963. *The Managed Economy*. New York: Oxford University Press.

Rees, David. 1973. *Harry Dexter White: A Study in Paradox*. New York: Coward, McCannand Geoghegan.

Reider, Jonathan. 1989. "The Rise of the Silent Majority." In *The Rise and Fall of the New Deal Order, 1930–1980*, edited by Steve Fraser and Gary Gerstle. Princeton, NJ: Princeton University Press.

Rockefeller Brothers Fund. 1959. *Prospect for America*. New York: Doubleday.

Roheim, Geza. 1943. *The Origin and Function of Culture*. New York: Nervous and Mental Disease Monographs.

Roheim, Geza. 1945. *War, Crime and Covenant*. Monticello, NY: Medical Journal Press.

Roheim, Geza. 1950. *Psychoanalysis and Anthropology*. New York: International Universities Press.

Roosevelt, Franklin D. Roosevelt Papers. Franklin D. Roosevelt Library, Hyde Park, New York.

Rose, Arnold M. 1967. *The Power Structure*. New York: Oxford University Press.

Rosenau, James N. 1961. *Public Opinion and Foreign Policy*. New York: Random House.

Ross, Robert L. 1967. "Dimensions and Patterns of Relating among Interest Groups at the Congressional Level of Government." Ph.D. diss. Michigan State University, East Lansing.

Rumbarger, John J. 1989. *Profits, Power and Prohibition*. Albany: State University Press of New York.

Russell, Bertrand. 1938. *Power: A New Social Analysis*. London: Allen and Unwin.

Salzman, Harold and G. William Domhoff. 1980. "The Corporate Community and Government: Do They Interlock?" In *Power Structure Research*, edited by G. William Domhoff. Beverly Hills, CA: Sage Publications.

Salzman, Harold and G. William Domhoff. 1983. "Nonprofit Organizations and the Corporate Community." *Social Science History* 7:205–215.

Schaller, Michael. 1985. *The American Occupation of Japan*. New York: Oxford University Press.

Scheinberg, Stephen J. 1966. "The Development of Corporation Labor Policy, 1900–1940." Ph.D. diss. University of Wisconsin, Madison.

Scheisl, Martin J. 1977. *The Politics of Efficiency*. Berkeley: University of California Press.

Schlesinger, Arthur M., Jr. 1959. *The Coming of the New Deal*. Boston: Houghton Mifflin.

Schlesinger, Arthur M., Jr. 1960. *The Politics of Upheaval*. Boston: Houghton Mifflin.

Schlesinger, Arthur M., Jr. 1965. *A Thousand Days*. Boston: Houghton Mifflin.

Schrau, Sanford F. and J. Patrick Turbett. 1983. "Civil Disorder and the Welfare Explosion: A Two-Step Process." *American Sociological Review* 48:408–414.

Schriftgiesser, Karl. 1942. *The Amazing Roosevelt Family*. New York: Funk.

Schriftgiesser, Karl. 1960. *Business Comes of Age*. New York: Harper and Row.

Schriftgiesser, Karl. 1967. *Business and Public Policy*. Englewood Cliffs, NJ: Prentice-Hall.

Schriftgiesser, Karl. 1974. *The Commission on Money and Credit: An Adventure in Policy-Making*. Englewood Cliffs, NJ: Prentice-Hall..

Schurmann, Franz. 1974. *The Logic of World Power*. New York: Pantheon.

Shabecoff, Philip. 1985. "Hodel Plans to Reduce Scope of Offshore Leasing Program." *New York Times* (March 12):11.

Shabecoff, Philip. 1989. "Reagan and Environment: To Many, A Stalemate." *New York Times* (January 2):1.

Shelley, Mack C., II. 1983. *The Permanent Majority*. Tuscaloosa: The University of Alabama Press.

Sherman, Arnold K. and Aliza Kolker. 1987. *The Social Bases of Politics*. Belmont, CA: Wadsworth.

Shoup, Laurence. 1974. "Shaping the National Interest: The Council on Foreign Relations, the Department of State, and the Origins of the Postwar World." Ph.D. diss. Evanston, IL: Northwestern University.

Shoup, Laurence. 1975. "Shaping the Postwar World: The Council on Foreign Relations and United States War Aims." *Insurgent Sociologist* 5:9–52.

Shoup, Laurence. 1977. "The Council on Foreign Relations and American Policy in Southeast Asia, 1940–1973." *Insurgent Sociologist* 7:19–30.

Shoup, Laurence and William Minter. 1977. *Imperial Brain Trust*. New York: Monthly Review.

Silk, Leonard and David Vogel. 1976. *Ethics and Profits.* New York: Simon & Schuster.

Silva, Edward. 1978. "Before Radical Rejection: A Comment on Block's 'Beyond Corporate Liberalism.' " *Social Problems* 25:345–349.

Silva, Edward and Sheila Slaughter. 1984. *Serving Power: The Making of the Academic Social Science Expert.* Westport, CT: Greenwood.

Sinclair, Barbara. 1982. *Congressional Realignment, 1925–1978.* Austin: University of Texas Press.

Sinclair, Barbara. 1985. "Agenda, Policy, and Alignment Change from Coolidge to Reagan." In *Congress Reconsidered,* edited by Lawrence Dodd and Bruce Oppenheimer. Washington: Congressional Quarterly.

Sipe, Daniel. 1981. "A Moment of the State." Ph.D. diss. Philadelphia, PA: University of Pennsylvania.

Sklar, Holly and Robert Lawrence. 1981. *Who's Who in the Reagan Administration.* Boston: South End.

Skocpol, Theda. 1979. *States and Social Revolution.* New York: Cambridge University Press.

Skocpol, Theda. 1980. "Political Responses to Capitalist Crisis: Neo-Marxist Theories of the State and the Case of the New Deal." *Politics and Society* 10:155–202.

Skocpol, Theda. 1985. "Introduction." In *Bringing the State Back In,* edited by Peter Evans, Dietrich Rueschemeyer, and Theda Skocpol. New York: Cambridge University Press.

Skocpol, Theda. 1986/87. "A Brief Reply." *Politics and Society* 3:331–332.

Skocpol, Theda and Edwin Amenta. 1985. "Did the Capitalists Shape Social Security?" *American Sociological Review* 50:572–575.

Skocpol, Theda and John Ikenberry. 1982. "The Political Formation of the American Welfare State in Historical and Comparative Perspective." Paper presented at the meeting of the American Sociological Association, San Francisco.

Skocpol, Theda and John Ikenberry. 1983. "The Political Formation of the American Welfare State in Historical and Comparative Perspective." In *Comparative Social Research,* edited by Richard F. Tomasson. Greenwich, CT: JAI.

Skowronek, Stephen. 1982. *Building a New American State.* Cambridge: Cambridge University Press.

Smith, Robert F. 1974. "Businessmen, Bureaucrats, Historians, and the Shaping of United States Foreign Policy." *Reviews in American History* 2:575–581.

Snowiss, Leo M. 1966. "Congressional Recruitment and Representation." *American Political Science Review* 60:627–639.

Sonquist, John and Thomas Koenig. 1975. "Interlocking Directorates in the Top U.S. Corporations." *Insurgent Sociologist* 5:196–229.

Soule, George. 1935. "Sidney Hillman Turns Architect." *The Nation* 140:383–384.

Stanley, David, Dean Mann, and James Doig. 1967. *Men Who Govern.* Washington: Brookings Institution.

Stave, Bruce M. 1970. *The New Deal and the Last Hurrah.* Pittsburgh: University of Pittsburgh Press.

Stein, Herbert. 1969. *The Fiscal Revolution in America.* Chicago: University of Chicago Press.

Stepan-Norris, Judith and Maurice Zeitlin. 1989. "Who Gets the Bird? or, How the

Communists Won Power and Trust in America's Unions: The Relative Autonomy of Intraclass Political Struggles." *American Sociological Review* 54:503–523.

Stephens, John. 1980. *The Transition from Capitalism to Socialism.* Atlantic Highlands, NJ: Humanities Press.

Stern, Daniel. 1985. *The Interpersonal World of the Infant.* New York: Basic Books.

Stewart, Frank M. 1950. *A Half Century of Municipal Reform.* Berkeley: University of California Press.

Stone, Alan. 1984. "Capitalism, Case Studies, and Public Policy: Trade Expansion Legislation Re-examined." In *The Political Economy,* edited by Thomas Ferguson and Joel Rogers. Armonk, NY: Sharpe.

Stone, Clarence. 1976. *Neighborhood and Discontent.* Chapel Hill: University of North Carolina Press.

Stone, Clarence. 1989. *Regime Politics.* Lawrence: University of Kansas Press.

Supple, Barry. 1957. "A Business Elite: German-Jewish Financiers in Nineteenth-Century New York." *Business History Review* 31:143–178.

Swank, Duane and Alexander Hicks. 1984. "Militancy, Need and Relief: The Piven and Cloward. AFDC Caseload Thesis Revisited." *Research in Social Movements, Conflict and Change* 6:1–29.

Teeple, Gary. 1984. *Marx's Critique of Politics, 1842–1847.* Toronto: University of Toronto Press.

Tolchin, Martin and Susan Tolchin. 1971. *To the Victor. . . .* New York: Random House.

Tomlins, Christopher. 1985. *The State and the Unions.* New York: Cambridge University Press.

U.S. Senate, 76th Congress. 1939. *Violations of Free Speech and Rights of Labor, Part 45, The Special Conference Committee.* Washington: USGPO.

U.S. Senate, Subcommittee on Employment and Manpower. 1965. *History of Employment and Manpower Policy in the United States. Parts III and IV. Looking Ahead to the Postwar Economy and the Concept of Full Employment in Congress.* Washington, DC: USGPO.

Useem, Michael. 1984. *The Inner Circle.* New York: Oxford University Press.

Van Dormael, Armand. 1978. *Bretton Woods: Birth of a Monetary System.* London: Macmillan.

Vidich, Arthur J. 1987. "Religion, Economics, and Class in American Politics." *International Journal of Politics, Culture and Society* 1(1):4–22.

Viner, Jacob. Collected Papers. Princeton University, Princeton, NJ.

Viner, Jacob. 1942. "Objectives of Post-War International Economic Reconstruction." In *American Economic Objectives,* edited by William McKee. New Wilmington, PA: Economic and Business Foundation.

*Vital Speeches.* 1934–35: Volume 1. New York: City News Publishing Co.

Vittoz, Stanley. 1987. *New Deal Labor Policy and the American Industrial Economy.* Chapel Hill: University of North Carolina Press.

Vogel, David. 1978. "Why Businessmen Mistrust Their State." *British Journal of Political Science* 8:45–78.

Vogel, David. 1989. *Fluctuating Fortunes.* New York: Basic Books.

Wagner, Robert F. Unpublished Papers. Special Collections, Georgetown University Library. Washington, D.C.

Walton, John. 1976. "Community Power and the Retreat from Politics: Full Circle after Twenty Years?" *Social Problems* 23:292–303.

Webber, Michael. 1990. "The Material Bases of the Democratic Party: Class and Campaign Finance in the 1930s." Ph.D. diss. University of California, Santa Cruz.

Weinstein, James. 1962. "Organized Business and the Commission and Manager Movements." *Journal of Southern History* 28:166–182.

Weinstein, James. 1963. "Socialism's Hidden Heritage: Scholarship Reinforces Political Mythology." *Studies on the Left* 3:88–108.

Weinstein, James. 1965. "Gompers and the New Liberalism, 1900–1909." *Studies on the Left* 5:94–105.

Weinstein, James. 1967. *The Decline of Socialism in America, 1912–1925*. New York: Monthly Review.

Weinstein, James. 1968. *The Corporate Ideal in the Liberal State, 1900–1918*. Boston: Beacon.

Weinstein, James. 1975. *Ambiguous Legacy: The Left in American Politics*. New York: Franklin Watts.

Weinstein, James and David Eakins. 1970. *For a New America: Essays in History and Politics from "Studies on the Left," 1959–1967*. New York: Random House.

Welch, Susan. 1975. "The Impact of Urban Riots on Urban Expenditures." *American Journal of Political Science* 19:741–760.

Williams, John H. 1943. "Currency Stabilization: The Keynes and White Plans." *Foreign Affairs* 21:645–658.

Williams, John H. 1944. "Currency Stabilization: American and British Attitudes." *Foreign Affairs* 22:233–247.

Williams, William A. 1961. *The Contours of American History*. Cleveland: World.

Wilson, Edward O. 1975. *Sociobiology: The New Synthesis*. Cambridge, MA: Harvard University Press.

Wilson, Theodore A. 1969. *The First Summit*. Boston: Houghton Mifflin.

Wise, T. A. 1957. "The Bustling House of Lehman." *Fortune* (December):157–160, 185–192.

Wise, T. A. 1963. "Wherever You Look, There's Loeb Rhoades." *Fortune* (April):128–131, 145–157.

Wise, T. A. 1968. "Lazard: In Trinity There Is Strength." *Fortune* (August):100–103, 156–165.

Witte, Edwin E. 1963. *The Development of the Social Security Act*. Madison: University of Wisconsin Press.

Wolfinger, Raymond. 1974. *The Politics of Progress*. Englewood Cliffs, NJ: Prentice-Hall.

Wright, Gavin. 1986. *Old South, New South*. New York: Basic Books.

Wrong, Dennis. 1979. *Power: Its Forms, Bases and Uses*. New York: Harper and Row.

Yellowitz, Irwin. 1965. *Labor and the Progressive Movement in New York State, 1897–1916*. Ithaca, NY: Cornell University Press.

Young, Alfred F. 1967. *The Democratic Republicans of New York*. Chapel Hill: University of North Carolina Press.

Zalaznick, Sheldon. 1969. "The Small World of Washington Lawyers." *Fortune* (Sept.):120–125.

Zeiger, Robert H. 1968. "From Hostility to Moderation: Railroad Labor Policy in the 1920s." *Labor History* 9:23–38.

Zeiger, Robert H. 1986. *American Workers, American Unions, 1920–1985*. Baltimore, MD: Johns Hopkins University Press.

Zeigler, Harmon. 1961. *The Politics of Small Business*. Washington: Public Affairs Press.

Zeitlin, Maurice. 1980. "On Classes, Class Conflict, and the State." In *Classes, Class Conflict, and the State*, edited by Maurice Zeitlin. Cambridge, MA: Winthrop Publishers.

Zeitlin, Maurice. 1984. *The Civil Wars in Chile*. Princeton, NJ: Princeton University Press.

Zeitlin, Maurice and Richard Ratcliff. 1988. *Landlords and Capitalists: The Dominant Class of Chile*. Princeton, NJ: Princeton University Press.

Zweigenhaft, Richard. 1975. "Who Represents America?" *Insurgent Sociologist* 5:119–130.

Zweigenhaft, Richard and G. William Domhoff. 1982. *Jews in the Protestant Establishment*. New York: Praeger.

Zweigenhaft, Richard and G. William Domhoff. 1991. *Blacks in the White Establishment? A Study of Race and Class in America*. New Haven, CT: Yale University Press.

# INDEX